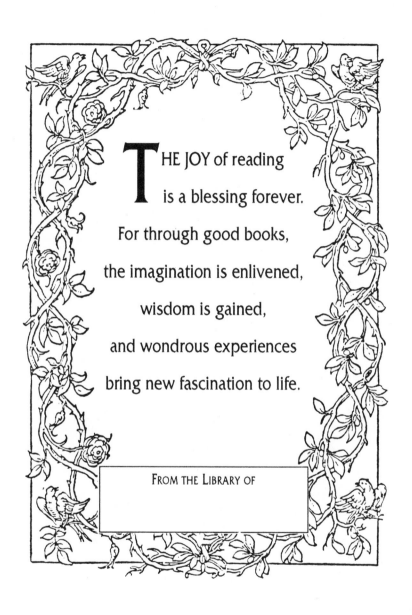

THE JOY of reading
is a blessing forever.
For through good books,
the imagination is enlivened,
wisdom is gained,
and wondrous experiences
bring new fascination to life.

FROM THE LIBRARY OF

PHILIP YANCEY

WHERE IS GOD WHEN IT HURTS?

TWO BESTSELLERS IN ONE VOLUME

DISAPPOINTMENT WITH GOD

ZondervanPublishingHouse

Grand Rapids, Michigan

A Division of HarperCollinsPublishers

Where Is God When It Hurts & Disappointment with God
Copyright © 1996 by Philip D. Yancey

Where Is God When It Hurts?
Copyright © 1990, 1977 by Philip Yancey

Disappointment with God
Copyright © 1988 by Philip Yancey

Requests for information should be addressed to:

ZondervanPublishingHouse
Grand Rapids, Michigan 49530

ISBN: 0-310-21176-X

Library of Congress Cataloging-in-Publication Data

Yancey, Philip.

Where is God when it hurts?: / Philip Yancey.
    p.   cm.
Includes bibliographical references.
ISBN: 0-310-35411-0
1. Suffering—Religious aspects—Christianity.   I. Title.
BT732.7.Y36 1990
248.8'6—dc20   90-34624

Disappointment with God: / Philip Yancey
    p.   cm.
ISBN: 0-310-51781-8
1. God—knowableness. 2. Theodicy. 3. Faith. I. Title.
BT102.Y36 1988
231.7   88-20848
                                           CIP

This edition printed on acid-free paper and meets the American National Standards Institute Z39.48 standard.

Printed in the United States of America

96 97 98 99 00 01 02 03 /❖ DH/ 10 9 8 7 6 5 4 3 2 1

Where Is God When It Hurts?

To DR. PAUL BRAND, who
unselfishly shared with me
a lifetime of medical and
spiritual wisdom

Contents

Preface

There's a cardinal rule in book publishing that applies equally to brain surgery and auto mechanics: "If it ain't broke, don't fix it." Since people are still buying the original *Where Is God When It Hurts,* I may be breaking that rule by attempting a major revision.

I wrote *Where Is God When It Hurts* back in the mid-1970s, when I was in my mid-twenties. In the years that have passed since then, I have never ceased thinking about the subject. Like a dog on a fresh spoor I keep circling around the problem of pain, searching for clues. In that time I have also heard from hundreds of readers, many of whom wrote wrenching letters describing their own odysseys with pain. For these reasons I felt it necessary to go back to a work I had completed long ago and bring it up to date.

Many biblical scholars date the book of Job as the oldest in the Bible, and it amazes me that the questions Job voiced so eloquently have not faded away. They have grown even louder and shriller over the centuries. A recent novel, *The Only Problem,* gets its title from a phrase in a conversation about how a good God can allow suffering. "It's the only problem, in fact, worth discussing," concludes the main character.

Another thing amazes me. Books on the problem of pain divide neatly into two groupings. The older ones, by people like Aquinas, Bunyan, Donne, Luther, Calvin, and Augustine, ungrudgingly accept pain and suffering as God's useful agents. These authors do not question God's actions. They merely try to "justify the ways of God to man." The authors wrote with confidence, as if the sheer force of their reasoning could calm emotional responses to suffering.

Modern books on pain make a sharp contrast. Their authors assume that the amount of evil and suffering in the world cannot be matched with the traditional view of a good and loving God. God is thus bumped from a "friend of the court" position to the box reserved for the defendant. "How can you possibly justify yourself, God?" these angry moderns seem to say. Many of them adjust their notion of God, either by redefining his love or by questioning his power to control evil.

When you read the two categories of books side by side, the change in tone is quite striking. It's as if we in modern times think we have a corner on the suffering market. Do we forget that Luther and Calvin lived in a world without ether and penicillin, when life expectancy averaged thirty years, and that Bunyan and Donne wrote their greatest works, respectively, in a jail and a plague quarantine room? Ironically, the modern authors—who live in princely comfort, toil in climate-controlled offices, and hoard elixirs in their medicine cabinets—are the ones smoldering with rage.

After reading several shelffuls of such books I asked myself, "Does the world really need another book on the problem of pain?" As I spent time among suffering people, however, I had to conclude yes. I learned that many books on pain seem oddly irrelevant to suffering people. For them the problem of pain is not a theoretical problem, a theology game of lining up all the appropriate syllogisms. It is a problem of relationship. Many suffering people want to love God, but cannot see past their tears. They feel hurt and betrayed. Sadly, the church often responds with more confusion than comfort.

Fifteen years ago, at an age when I had no right to tackle the daunting problem of pain, I wrote *Where Is God When It Hurts* for those people. Partly because I have heard from so many of them, I have now revised and expanded that book. In a sense, this new edition represents a dialogue with my readers, the next step in my own pilgrimage.

I have especially expanded the section "How Can We Cope with Pain?" because I believe God has given the church a mandate of representing his love to a suffering world. We usually think of the problem of pain as a question we ask of God, but it is also a question he asks of us. How do we respond to hurting people?

In this revision, I have drawn from several of my articles published in *Christianity Today* as well as the booklet *Helping the Hurting,* published by Multnomah Press. I am grateful to them for permission to incorporate that material.

Think too
  of all who suffer
    as if
      you
        shared their pain.

Hebrews 13:3 (J. B. PHILLIPS)

Meanwhile, where is God? This is one of the most disquieting symptoms. When you are happy, so happy that you have no sense of needing Him, if you turn to Him then with praise, you will be welcomed with open arms. But go to Him when your need is desperate, when all other help is vain and what do you find? A door slammed in your face, and a sound of bolting and double bolting on the inside. After that, silence. You may as well turn away.
                                              C. S. Lewis
                                          A Grief Observed

1

A Problem
That Won't Go Away

I feel helpless around people in great pain. Helpless, and also guilty. I stand beside them, watching facial features contort and listening to the sighs and moans, deeply aware of the huge gulf between us. I cannot penetrate their suffering, I can only watch. Whatever I attempt to say seems weak and stiff, as if I'd memorized the lines for a school play.

One day I received a frantic plea for help from my close friends John and Claudia Claxton. Newlyweds in their early twenties, they were just beginning life together in the Midwest. I had watched in amazement as the experience of romantic love utterly transformed John Claxton. Two years of engagement to Claudia had melted his cynicism and softened his hard edges. He became an optimist, and now his letters to me were usually bubbly with enthusiasm about his young marriage.

But one letter from John alarmed me as soon as I opened it. Errors and scratches marred his usually neat handwriting. He explained, "Excuse my writing . . . I guess it shows how I'm fumbling for words. I don't know what to say." The Claxtons'

15

young marriage had run into a roadblock far bigger than both of them. Claudia had been diagnosed with Hodgkin's disease, cancer of the lymph glands, and was given only a fifty percent chance to live.

Within a week surgeons had cut her from armpit to belly, removing every visible trace of the disease. She was left stunned and weak, lying in a hospital bed.

At the time, ironically, John was working as a chaplain's assistant in a local hospital. His compassion for other patients dipped dangerously. "In some ways," he told me, "I could understand better what other patients were undergoing. But I didn't care any more. I only cared about Claudia. I wanted to yell at them, 'Stop that sniveling, you idiots! You think you've got problems—my wife may be dying right now!'"

Though both John and Claudia were strong Christians, an unexpected anger against God surged up—anger against a beloved partner who had betrayed them. "God, why us?" they cried. "Have you teasingly doled out one happy year of marriage to set us up for this?"

Cobalt treatments took their toll on Claudia's body. Beauty fled her almost overnight. She felt and looked weary, her skin darkened, her hair fell out. Her throat was raw, and she regurgitated nearly everything she ate. Doctors had to suspend treatment for a time when her swollen throat could no longer make swallowing motions.

When the radiation treatments resumed, she was periodically laid out flat on a table, naked. She could do nothing but lie still and listen to the whir and click of the machinery as it bombarded her with invisible particles, each dose aging her body by months. As she lay in that chill steel room, Claudia would think about God and about her suffering.

Claudia's Visitors

Claudia had hoped that Christian visitors would comfort her by bringing some perspective on what she was going through. But their voices proved confusing, not consoling.

A deacon from her church solemnly advised her to reflect on what God was trying to teach her. "Surely something in your life must displease God," he said. "Somewhere, you must have stepped out of his will. These things don't just *happen*. God uses circumstances to warn us, and to punish us. What is he telling you?"

A few days later Claudia was surprised to see a woman from church whom she barely knew. Evidently, this plump, scatterbrained widow had adopted the role of professional cheerleader to the sick. She brought flowers, sang hymns, and stayed long enough to read some happy psalms about brooks running and mountains clapping their hands. Whenever Claudia tried to talk about her illness or prognosis, the woman quickly changed the subject, trying to combat the suffering with cheer and goodwill. But she only visited once, and after a while the flowers faded, the hymns seemed dissonant, and Claudia was left to face a new day of pain.

Another woman dropped by, a faithful follower of television faith healers. Exuding confidence, she assured Claudia that healing was her only escape. When Claudia told her about the deacon's advice, this woman nearly exploded. "Sickness is never God's will!" she exclaimed. "Haven't you read the Bible? The Devil stalks us like a roaring lion, but God will deliver you if you can muster up enough faith to believe you'll be healed. Remember, Claudia, faith can move mountains, and that includes Hodgkin's disease. Simply name your promise, in faith, and then claim the victory."

The next few mornings, as Claudia lay in the sterile cobalt treatment room, she tried to "muster up" faith. She wondered if she even understood the procedure. She did not question God's supernatural power, but how to go about convincing God of her sincerity? Faith wasn't like a muscle that could be enlarged through rehabilitation exercises. It was slippery, intangible, impossible to grasp. The whole notion of mustering up faith seemed awfully exhausting, and she could never decide what it really meant.

Perhaps the most "spiritual" woman in Claudia's church brought along some books about praising God for everything that happens. "Claudia, you need to come to the place where you can say, 'God, I *love* you for making me suffer like this. It is your will, and you know what's best for me. And I praise you for loving me enough to allow me to experience this. In all things, including this, I give thanks.'"

As Claudia pondered the words, her mind filled with rather grotesque images of God. She envisioned a figure in the shape of a troll, big as the universe, who took delight in squeezing helpless humans between his fingernails, pulverizing them with his fists, dashing them against sharp stones. The figure would torture these humans until they cried out, "God, I love you for doing this to me!" The idea repulsed Claudia, and she decided she could not worship or love such a God.

Yet another visitor, Claudia's pastor, made her feel she was on a select mission. He said, "Claudia, you have been appointed to suffer for Christ, and he will reward you. God chose you because of your great strength and integrity, just as he chose Job, and he is using you as an example to others. Their faith may increase because of your response. You should feel privileged, not bitter. What we see as adversity, God sees as opportunity." He told her to think of herself as a track star, and to view adversity as the series of hurdles she would need to leap over on the way to the victory circle.

Sometimes the notion of being a privileged martyr appealed to Claudia, in a self-pitying sort of way. Other times, when the pain crescendoed, when she vomited up food, when her facial features aged, Claudia would call out, "God, why me? There are millions of Christians stronger and more honorable than I—couldn't you choose one of them instead?" She didn't feel like a track star at all, and she wondered why God would deliberately place hurdles in the path of someone he loved.

I, too, visited Claudia, and found her desperately confused by all these contradictory words. She repeated for me the advice given her by well-meaning Christians, and I listened to her bewildered response. Which of these lessons was she supposed to be learning? How could she have more faith? Who should she listen to? In the midst of much confusion, Claudia had one certainty: her happy world with John was disintegrating. Above all, she didn't want that to end.

I had little advice for Claudia that day. In fact, I came away with even more questions. Why was she lying in a hospital bed while I stood beside her, healthy? Something inside me recoiled as I heard her repeat the clichéd comments from her visitors. Is Christianity supposed to make a sufferer feel even worse?

At the time I visited Claudia, I was working for *Campus Life* magazine while also moonlighting as a free-lance journalist. In a short span I wrote six "Drama in Real Life" stories for *Reader's Digest*. I interviewed a young Canadian couple who had been mauled by a grizzly bear. Although both survived, the young man lost one eye, and no amount of plastic surgery could hide the scars across his face. In another city, two young adults told me the story of a childhood camping trip taken with their father up Mount Rainier. Caught in a blizzard, they frantically dug a snow cave. Their father, lying protectively across the face of the cave, froze to death overnight.

All these people repeated their own versions of the cacophony of voices from Christian "comforters." One amputee told me, "My religious friends were the most depressing, irritating part of the entire experience." That pattern disturbed me greatly. Something was wrong. A faith founded on the Great Physician should bring peace, not confusion, at a time of crisis.

Why do people have to suffer so? What does the Bible really say? Because of the questions that arose from my contacts with Claudia* and others like her, I began a quest that culminated in this book. I have looked for a message we Christians can give to people who are suffering. At the same time, I've hunted for a message that can strengthen my own faith when I suffer. Where is God when it hurts? Is he trying to tell us something through our pain?

A Personal Approach

After an extensive tour of the United States, the well-known German pastor and theologian Helmut Thielicke was asked what he had observed as the greatest deficiency among American Christians. He replied, "They have an inadequate view of suffering." I have come to agree with him.

That deficiency stands out as a huge blemish to the non-Christian world. I've asked college students what they have against Christianity, and most of them echo variations on the theme of suffering: "I can't believe in a God who would allow Auschwitz and Cambodia"; "My teenage sister died of leukemia despite all the Christians' prayers"; "One-third of the world went to bed hungry last night—how can you reconcile that with Christian love?"

No other human experience provokes such an urgent response. No one sits in smoky coffeehouses late into the night

---

*Claudia's dilemma was eventually resolved when the cobalt treatments effectively destroyed the cancer cells. She's had no recurrence of the disease.

debating the cosmic implications of the sense of smell or taste. *Smell! Why this strange sensation? What did God intend? Why was scent apportioned so capriciously, lavished on roses but not on oxygen? And why must humankind get by with one-eighth the sensory ability of the dog?* Oddly, I hear no one debating "the problem of pleasure"; why do we take for granted sensations of pleasure but react so violently against pain?

As I did library research on the problem of pain, I discovered that many great philosophers, otherwise sympathetic to Christian principles and ethics, have stumbled over this problem of pain and suffering, ultimately rejecting Christianity because of it. C. E. M. Joad wrote, "What, then, are the arguments which for me have told so strongly against the religious view of the universe? . . . First, there was the difficulty presented by the facts of pain and evil."[1] Other philosophers, such as Bertrand Russell and Voltaire, share Joad's complaint.

The messy problem of pain and suffering keeps popping up despite erudite attempts to explain it away. The great British writer C. S. Lewis offered perhaps the most articulate treatment of the subject in this century with *The Problem of Pain,* written at the height of his intellectual powers. But years later, after his own wife died of bone cancer, Lewis wrote another book, *A Grief Observed,* which he published under a pseudonym. It covers the same topic, but in a very different way. As the quote at the beginning of this chapter reveals, Lewis's confidence had been shattered, his emotions stretched to the breaking point— stretched beyond the breaking point. "You never know how much you really believe anything until its truth or falsehood becomes a matter of life and death to you," he said.

As in Hercules's battle against the Hydra, all our attempts to chop through agnostic arguments are met with writhing new examples of suffering. Novelist Peter De Vries has called the problem of pain "the question mark turned like a fishhook in the human heart." And too often the Christian defense sounds like a red-faced, foot-shuffling, lowered-head apology.

"The problem of pain" represents a profound riddle, and the philosophers' approach to the subject sometimes takes the form of abstract reasoning, such as you might find in a textbook on pure mathematics. I will not attempt to address philosophers with this book; others with far more training have done that. Rather, I have tried to keep before me the scene of my friend

Claudia Claxton lying on a hospital bed. Most of our problems with pain are not exercises in mental gymnastics. They are problems like Claudia's: the loss of youth, an ulcerous throat, the prospect of a new marriage gouged by death, the paralyzing fear of the unknown. Claudia heard much conflicting advice about these problems from fellow Christians. What can we believe with confidence?

To prepare for this book, I talked to Christians who suffer at a level far worse than most of us will ever experience. For some of them, pain nearly defines life. It is the first sensation to greet them in the morning and the last they feel before drifting off to sleep, if they are lucky enough to fall asleep despite it. Ironically, I also spent time among people with leprosy, who feel no pain physiologically but desperately wish they could. With such people as my guides, I have entered the world of the sufferer to find out what difference it makes to be a Christian there.

First, I will examine pain biologically—through the microscope, you might say—to see what role it plays in life. Then, stepping back, I will look at our planet as a whole, asking what God is up to. Is suffering God's one great goof? And, finally, I will ask what response we can give when suffering strikes, and how we can also reach out to others.

Perhaps the next time I'm sick, when the flu hits and I toss in bed, fighting off waves of nausea, perhaps then my conclusions about pain will offer no solace. But as a Christian trying to fathom what God is up to in this world, I have learned a great deal. And as I've come to better understand the suffering of this world, my attitude toward God has changed dramatically.

Part 1

Why Is There Such a Thing as Pain?

The symptoms and the illness are not the same thing. The illness exists long before the symptoms. Rather than being the illness, the symptoms are the beginning of its cures. The fact that they are unwanted makes them all the more a phenomenon of grace—a gift of God, a message from the unconscious, if you will, to initiate self-examination and repair.

M. Scott Peck
The Road Less Traveled

2

The Gift Nobody Wants

I am sitting in Chicago's ornate Orchestra Hall. I have exulted in the works by Beethoven and Mozart, but the long, complex concerto by Prokofiev is another matter. As energy-giving blood is shunted away from my brain down toward my stomach to help digest the Sunday brunch, I find it increasingly difficult to stay awake.

The concert hall is warm and stuffy. Gradually the sounds from various instruments begin to meld together into one muted tone. My eyelids sag. Catching myself, I glance around and see scores of well-dressed concertgoers who have already succumbed. And so I rest my chin on my right hand and prop my elbow on the wooden armrest. The music fades. . . .

THUNK!! My limbs are splayed out in all directions. People in surrounding seats are glaring at me, their necks craned in my direction. My overcoat is on the floor. Startled and embarrassed, I retrieve the overcoat, straighten in my seat, and try again to attend to the music. Blood is now pounding in my head.

What happened? Even as I was drifting into dreamland, my body was loyally working to protect me. Though my conscious brain had already shut down, my reflex system had not. When my head nodded forward, two small sacs in my inner ear, filled

25

with fluid and lined with ultrasensitive hairs, detected an alarming shift in my equilibrium. Just at the last moment, as my head was about to crash downward to the armrest, the inner ear sounded an all-points-alert. Suddenly my arms jerked out, my head shot upward, and my whole torso twitched in a spasm. The dramatic act, an embarrassment to me, was merely my body's emergency effort to prevent injury. And all these complex maneuvers took place while I was drifting off to sleep.

The mechanism of pain in the human body operates much like the warning system I experienced in Orchestra Hall. Pain sensors loudly alert my body to danger—*It hurts!*—and force me to concentrate on the problem area.

Sometimes the reaction occurs at an involuntary level. For example, when I go to the doctor for a checkup and he taps my knee with a rubber hammer, my leg straightens violently. Why? The doctor's tap gives the knee the impression that it is bending: his hammer hits the same nerves that would be affected if my knee suddenly buckled while walking. My body rushes to compensate, lest I stumble and experience a greater pain. The reaction is too spontaneous and lightning-quick to allow the brain time to reason that I'm seated on a table, not standing, and no actual danger of falling exists.

Marks of a Designer

Yet despite the obvious protective value of these millions of warning sensors, the pain network is easily the most unappreciated bodily system. It attracts mostly abuse and bad feelings. I have never read a poem extolling the virtues of pain, nor seen a statue erected in its honor, nor heard a hymn dedicated to it. Pain is usually defined as "unpleasantness."

Christians, who believe in a loving Creator, don't really know how to interpret pain. If pinned against the wall at a dark, secret moment, many Christians would confess that pain was God's one mistake. Really, he should have worked a little harder to devise a better way for us to cope with danger. I used to feel that way exactly.

Now, however, I am convinced that pain gets a bad press. Perhaps we should see poems, statues, and hymns to pain. Why has my attitude changed? Because up close, under a microscope, the pain network is seen in an entirely different light. My discussion of pain, then, must begin with a look at the human body. Why do I need pain? When I hurt, what is my body telling me?

I begin here, with the closeup view, because that perspective is the one most often overlooked by people fumbling with the question "Where is God when it hurts?" I have read scores of philosophical and theological books on "the problem of pain," but at best these give token acknowledgment to the fact that pain may serve some useful biological purpose. The pain network deserves far more than token acknowledgment. It bears the mark of creative genius.

Consider a single organ from the human body: the skin, a flexible-yet-tough organ that stretches over the body's frame as an advance guard against the dangers of the outside world. Millions of pain sensors dot the surface of the skin, scattered not randomly, but in precise accord with the body's specific needs. Actually, the body does not seem to have any dedicated "pain cells," for the sensation of pain ties in with an elaborate network of sensors that also report information about pressure, touch, heat, and cold.

Scientists blindfold their research subjects (usually hapless medical students) and measure their skin sensitivity. For example, how much pressure must be applied before a blindfolded person becomes aware of an object touching his skin? The scale, called the *absolute threshold of touch*, is measured in grams (per square millimeter of skin surface), and this is what researchers have discovered:

Tip of tongue	sensitive to 2 grams of pressure
Fingers	sensitive to 3 grams of pressure
Back of hand	sensitive to 12 grams of pressure
Back of forearm	sensitive to 33 grams of pressure
Sole of foot	sensitive to 250 grams of pressure

Thus the skin, a single organ, displays a very wide range of sensitivity to pressure. We use our tongues for such intricate acts as forming words and picking food particles from between our teeth. We use our fingers for playing the guitar, writing with a felt-tip pen, and the caresses of love. These areas of the skin require a fine-tuned sensitivity.[1]

But less critical areas hardly need such sensitivity: we

would tire very quickly indeed if our brains had to listen to such dainty pressure reports from the foot, which faces a daily rigor of stomping, squeezing, and supporting weight. Thus, while fingers and tongue can detect a feather touch, other parts of the body need a good sound slap before they report unusual activity to the brain.

These measurements of threshold barely scratch the surface of the marvels of the pain network. For example, sensitivity to pressure varies depending on context. I can distinguish a letter that weighs 1¼ ounces from one that weighs 1½ ounces just by holding it in my hand. But if I'm holding a ten-pound package, I could not discern that difference; I would need a change of at least three ounces before noticing.

Another test assesses the *absolute threshold of pain*. In this test, the scientist measures how much pressure must be applied to a very sharp needle before the subject begins to experience pain.

Cornea	0.2 grams	produces painful sensation
Forearm	20 grams	produces painful sensation
Back of hand	100 grams	produces painful sensation
Sole of foot	200 grams	produces painful sensation
Fingertip	300 grams	produces painful sensation

Note how these figures contrast with the thresholds of pressure.[2] The fingertip, for example, shows an astounding difference: it can detect a mere 3 grams of pressure, but not until that pressure exceeds 300 grams will I feel pain there! Why? Think about the fingers' activities. The concert violinist must sense an amazing range of pressures to produce perfect sound and volume. A skilled baker, swishing his hands through batches of dough, can notice as little as a two percent variance in the "stickiness" or consistency. Cloth feelers in textile industries compare the qualities of cloth by touch. The fingertips must be incredibly sensitive to the slightest differences in touch.

But sensitivity to touch is not enough. The fingertips must also be *tough* in order to withstand rigorous activity. Feel the calloused, scaly hand of a carpenter or a professional tennis player. Life would be miserable indeed if the fingertip fired a message of pain to the brain each time a person squeezed a tennis racket or pounded a hammer. So the design of the body includes a fingertip extraordinarily sensitive to pressure, but relatively insensitive to pain. Hands and fingertips serve us well as the most used parts of our bodies.*

The cornea of the eye, however, lives a different existence. Due to its transparency—essential, to admit light rays—it has a limited blood supply and is thus very fragile. A small wound could cause blindness, and any intrusion in the eye, a wood splinter or a speck of dirt, represents a serious threat. Therefore the cornea's pain sensors have an electronic hot line to the brain.

I have seen a World Series baseball game delayed for the simple reason that the pitcher got a stray eyelash in his eye. The infielders and umpires gathered around while he looked in a mirror and fished it out. He could not possibly continue pitching until he removed the source of the pain. Such an eyelash lying on his nose, arm, or any other part of the body would go unnoticed.

Colic, Kidney Stones, and Ice Cream Headaches

Inside, the body presents even more evidence of the pain network's intelligent design. Pinpricks and heat burns, the scientists' favored techniques for measuring pain on the skin surface, prove useless on internal organs, which simply don't respond to those stimuli. Why should they? Since the body has designated the skin to sort through alarms from cuts and burns and pressures, internal organs can get along without such elaborate warning systems.

Slip past the skin's defenses with the aid of a local anesthetic, and you could burn the stomach with a match, insert

*We have exactly as many pain sensors as we need. Scientists measure another phenomenon of the nervous system called the *two-point threshold*. They press two stiff bristles against the skin of a blindfolded person to determine how close together they must be brought before that person feels one pinprick rather than two. In other words, it demonstrates how close together the individual pain sensors are. On the leg, I can no longer distinguish two pinpricks when the pins are brought in to a distance of 68 mm. But I can distinguish two pinpricks on the back of the hand at a distance of 32 mm, and on the fingertip at only 2 mm. The tip of the tongue, however, has sensors every 1 mm. This explains the common phenomenon I feel when food is caught between my teeth. With my tongue I can search it out and quickly determine in what crevice the food is caught. But with the fingertip, the food is harder to locate. Spaces between the teeth "feel smaller" with the finger than with the tongue.[3]

a needle through the lung, cut the brain with a knife, crush the kidney in a vise, or bore through bone, all without causing the patient any discomfort. Such internal pain signals would be redundant—the skin and skeleton already protect internal organs from such dangers.

Instead, the body's sheltered organs possess unique sets of pain receptors specific to the dangers they face. If a doctor inserts a balloon inside my stomach and fills it with air to distend my stomach slightly, urgent messages of pain would shoot to my brain—the pain of colic, or gas. The stomach's pain network is custom-designed to protect it from specific dangers. Likewise, the kidney sends out excruciating signals of pain when a BB-sized kidney stone is present. Linings of the joints, which are insensitive to a needle or knife, are very sensitive to certain chemicals.[4]

On rare occasions, an internal organ must inform the brain of an emergency that its pain sensors are not equipped to handle. How can it alert the brain to the damage it senses? In this event, the organ uses the remarkable phenomenon of *referred pain,* recruiting nearby pain sensors to sound the alarm. For example, heart attack victims may notice a burning or constricting feeling in the neck, chest, jaw, or left arm. Skin cells there, though perfectly healthy, obligingly send off alarm messages to the brain as if *they* were damaged, when in fact the problem lies with their neighbor the heart. In this way the skin "loans" its pain sensors to the heart as a relay warning station.

Anyone who has eaten homemade ice cream too fast on a hot summer day may experience a related phenomenon. Suddenly a headache strikes, just behind the eyes. Quite obviously, ice cream is not entering the forehead. Rather, the stomach's vagus nerve is sending out strong signals of cold to the brain; at the junction with the trigeminal nerve from the face, forehead, and jaw, pain jumps across from one nerve to the other and the chill in the stomach is felt as pain in the head.

The mystery of referred pain can make for some challenging medical diagnoses. Spleen injuries are sometimes felt in the tip of the left shoulder. A damaged appendix may borrow pain sensors in a variety of places, on either side of the abdomen. A neck injury may cause pain in the arm. Each of these demonstrates how the body's backup systems cooperate to warn of possible injury.

Medical libraries contain massive volumes filled with amazing facts about the operation of the body's pain network, and I have mentioned a mere sampling. Such facts as these—the exact distribution of needed pain cells, the customized pressure/pain thresholds, and the backup system of referred pain—convince me that, whatever it is, the pain network is not an accident.

Pain is not an afterthought, or God's great goof. Rather, it reveals a marvelous design that serves our bodies well. Pain is as essential to a normal life, it could be argued, as eyesight or even good circulation. Without pain, as we shall see, our lives would be fraught with danger, and devoid of many basic pleasures.

But Must It Hurt?

My appreciation for the engineering aspects of the pain network traces back to the beginning of my friendship with Dr. Paul Brand. I came across his name in 1975, when I was first researching the topic of pain. Already I had read many books on the subject. But one day my wife, who was rummaging through a closet at a medical supply house, came across a pamphlet with the unusual title, "The Gift of Pain." Its author was Dr. Brand. A short time later, we met together on the grounds of the leprosarium in Carville, Louisiana, and since then we have collaborated on two books (*Fearfully and Wonderfully Made* and *In His Image*).

Dr. Brand has received widespread recognition for his medical work, including awards from the Albert Lasker Foundation, the U.S. Public Health Service, and also from Queen Elizabeth II, who made him Commander of the British Empire. Yet, oddly, he got most of his recognition as a crusader on behalf of pain. Without hesitation Dr. Brand declares, "Thank God for inventing pain! I don't think he could have done a better job. It's beautiful." As one of the world's foremost experts on leprosy, a disease of the nervous system, he is well-qualified to make such a judgment.

Once, in fact, Dr. Brand received a several-million-dollar grant for the express purpose of designing an artificial pain system. He knew that people with diseases like leprosy and diabetes were in grave danger of losing fingers, toes, and even entire limbs simply because their warning system of pain had been silenced. They were literally destroying themselves una-wares. Perhaps he could design a simple substitute that would alert them to the worst dangers.

In this project Dr. Brand had to think like the Creator, anticipating the needs of the body. For assistance, he signed on three professors of electronic engineering, a bioengineer, and several research biochemists. The team decided to concentrate on fingertips, the part of the body most often used and therefore most vulnerable to abuse. They developed a kind of artificial nerve, a pressure-sensitive transducer that could be worn on the finger like a glove. When subjected to pressure, the electronic nerve triggered an electric current which in turn set off a warning signal.

Dr. Brand and his assistants confronted daunting technical problems. The more they studied nerves, the more complex their task appeared. At what level of pressure should the sensor sound a warning? How could a mechanical sensor distinguish between the acceptable pressure of, say, gripping a railing and the unacceptable pressure of gripping a thornbush? How could it be adjusted to allow for rigorous activities like playing tennis?

Brand also recognized that nerve cells change their percep-tion of pain to meet the body's needs. Due to the pressure of inflammation, an infected finger may become ten times more sensitive to pain. That's why a finger swollen from a hangnail feels awkward and in the way: your body is telling you to give it time to heal. Nerve cells "turn up the volume," amplifying bumps and scrapes that would normally go unreported. In no way could these well-funded scientists duplicate that feat with current technology.

The artificial sensors cost about $450 each, and it took many of them to protect a single hand or foot, but each new design would deteriorate from metal fatigue or corrosion after a few hundred uses. Each month Dr. Brand and his colleagues gained more appreciation for the remarkable engineering of the body's pain network, which includes several hundred million sensors that function maintenance-free throughout a healthy person's life.

At first Dr. Brand sought a way to make his artificial pain system work without actually hurting the patient. He had read the complaints of various philosophers against the created world. Why hadn't God designed a nervous system that protects us, but without the unpleasant aspects of pain? Here was his chance to improve on the original design with a protective system that did not hurt.

First his team tried sending an audible signal through a hearing aid, a signal that would hum when tissues were receiving normal pressures and buzz loudly when they were actually in danger. But the signal proved too easy to ignore. If a patient with a damaged hand was turning a screwdriver too hard, and the loud warning signal went off, he would simply override it and turn the screwdriver anyway. This happened not once, but many times. People who did not feel pain could not be persuaded to trust the artificial sensors.

Brand's team next tried blinking lights, but soon eliminated them for the same reason. Finally they had to resort to electric shock, taping electrodes to a still-sensitive portion of the body, such as the armpit. People had to be *forced* to respond; being alerted to the danger was not enough. The stimulus had to be unpleasant, just as pain is unpleasant.

"We also found out that the signal had to be out of the patient's reach," Brand says. "For even intelligent people, if they wished to do something which they were afraid would activate the shock, would switch off the signal, do what they had in mind to do, and then switch it on again when there was no danger of receiving an unpleasant signal. I remember thinking how wise God had been in putting pain out of reach."

After five years of work, thousands of man-hours, and several million dollars, Brand and his associates abandoned the entire project. A warning system suitable for just one hand was exorbitantly expensive, subject to frequent mechanical breakdown, and hopelessly inadequate to interpret the profusion of sensations. A system sometimes called "God's great mistake" was far too complex for even the most sophisticated technology to mimic.

That is why Paul Brand says with utter sincerity, "Thank God for pain!" By definition, pain is unpleasant, enough so to force us to withdraw our fingers from a stove. Yet that very quality saves us from destruction. Unless the warning signal demands response, we might not heed it.

Listen to Your Pain

The typical American response to pain is to take an aspirin at the slightest ache and silence the pain. That approach only deals with the symptom of the problem. We dare not shut off the warning system without first listening to the warning.

A tragic example of someone not heeding the warning occurred in an NBA basketball game in which a star player, Bob Gross, wanted to play despite a badly injured ankle. Knowing that Gross was needed for the important game, the team doctor injected Marcaine, a strong painkiller, into three different places of his foot. Gross did start the game, but after a few minutes, as he was battling for a rebound, a loud *snap!* could be heard throughout the arena. Gross, oblivious, ran up and down the court two times, then crumpled to the floor. Although he felt no pain, a bone had broken in his ankle. By overriding pain's warning system with the anesthetic, the doctor caused permanent damage to Gross's foot and ended his basketball career.

Pain is not God's great goof. The sensation of pain is a gift—the gift that nobody wants. More than anything, pain should be viewed as a communication network. Just as the warning system of my equilibrium saved me in the embarrassing episode at Orchestra Hall, a remarkable network of pain sensors stands guard duty with the singular purpose of keeping me from injury.

I do not say that all pain is good. Sometimes it flares up and makes life miserable. For someone with crippling arthritis or terminal cancer, pain dominates so much that any relief, especially a painless world, would seem like heaven itself. But for the majority of us, the pain network performs daily protective service. It is effectively designed for surviving life on this sometimes hostile planet.

In Dr. Brand's words, "The one legitimate complaint you can make against pain is that it cannot be switched off. It can rage out of control, as with a terminal cancer patient, even though its warning has been heard and there is no more that can be done to treat the cause of pain. But as a physician I'm sure that less than one percent of pain is in this category that we might call out of control. Ninety-nine per cent of all the pains that people suffer are short-term pains: correctable situations that call for medication, rest, or a change in a person's lifestyle."

Admittedly, the surprising idea of the "gift of pain" does not answer many of the problems connected with suffering. But it is a beginning point of a realistic perspective on pain and suffering. Too often the emotional trauma of intense pain blinds us to its inherent value.

When I break an arm and swallow bottles of aspirin to dull the ache, gratitude for pain is not the first thought that comes to mind. Yet at that very moment, pain is alerting my body to the danger, mobilizing anti-infection defenses around the wound, and forcing me to refrain from activities that might further compound the injury. Pain demands the attention that is crucial to my recovery.

He jests at scars who never felt a wound.
William Shakespeare
Romeo and Juliet

3

Painless Hell

Almost by definition, if we have pain we don't want it. Why would Dr. Brand and his associates spend so much time and energy trying to create pain even as most other medical professionals were working diligently to silence it?

I had learned many facts about the design of the pain network. I had even come to see it as a "gift." But knowledge alone was not enough to overcome my instinctive resistance to pain. I had strong doubts until I spent a week in Louisiana with Dr. Brand, the crusader for pain.

Dr. Brand came to appreciate pain by living among people with leprosy. It was he who discovered that leprosy patients suffer for the simple reason that they have a defective pain system.

The word leprosy conjures up exaggerated images: stubby fingers, ulcerous wounds, missing legs, distorted facial features. Literature and movies such as *Ben Hur* and *Papillon* (frequently inaccurate) have conditioned us to view leprosy as an unbearably cruel affliction. It is the oldest recorded disease, and one of the most feared. For centuries leprosy victims had to call out "Unclean! Unclean!" whenever someone approached.

Leprosy is indeed cruel, but not in the manner of most

diseases. Primarily, it works like an anesthetic, attacking the pain cells of hands, feet, nose, ears, and eyes to produce numbness. Not so bad, really, one might think. Most diseases are feared because of their pain; what makes a painless disease so horrible?

Yet leprosy's numbing quality is precisely the reason for the fabled destruction of tissue. For thousands of years people thought the disease itself caused the ulcers on hands and feet and face that so often led to infection and ultimately loss of limbs. Dr. Brand's pioneering research in India established that in virtually all cases leprosy only numbs the extremities. Tissue damage results solely because the warning system of pain has fallen silent.

How does the damage occur? Dr. Brand asked himself that question thousands of times as he treated the infected hands of Indian villagers. It seemed a losing battle. He would heal wounds and bind them up, only to have the patients come back several months later with far worse damage. Like other leprosy workers, he assumed the disease worked like a fungus, destroying tissue indiscriminately.

But Brand soon learned to question his patients carefully about any activities that might have contributed to the injury. He once watched horrified as a person with leprosy reached directly into a charcoal fire to retrieve a potato someone had dropped. Brand knew he would soon be treating sores on that patient's hand—sores caused by burns from the fire, not by leprosy. The villager, insensitive to pain, had unwittingly exposed his hand to terrible abuse.

Brand started following around the patients at the leprosarium in India. How else might they be damaging themselves? He saw one man hard at work in the garden, oblivious to blood running down his hand; Brand examined the shovel and found a nail protruding just at the spot his hand had been gripping. Other leprosy patients would reach over and extinguish a burning wick with their bare hands, or walk barefoot across broken glass. Watching them, Brand began formulating his radical theory that leprosy was chiefly anesthetic, and only indirectly a destroyer. He would need much more evidence, however, to overturn centuries of medical tradition.

One day, in the midst of this time of field research, Dr. Brand went to fetch some supplies from a little storeroom behind the hospital. He tried to open the door, but a rusty padlock would not yield. Just at that moment, one of his youngest patients strolled by—an undersized, malnourished ten-year-old. Brand liked the boy for his pleasant, cooperative spirit.

"Oh, sahib doctor, let me try," the boy said, and reached for the key. With a quick jerk of his hand he turned the key in the lock. Brand was dumbfounded. How could this weak youngster, half his size, exert such force?

His eyes caught a telltale clue. Was that a drop of blood on the floor? Upon examining the boy's index finger, Brand discovered the act of turning the key had gashed it open to the bone; skin, fat, and joint were all exposed. Yet the boy was completely unaware of it! To him, the sensation of cutting his finger to the bone was no different from that of picking up a stone or turning a coin in his pocket.

After that incident, Brand redoubled his efforts to test his theory about leprosy being a secondary, not primary cause of injury. He began measuring the fingers of his patients each day, and tried to account for every blister, ulcer, and cut. He learned that his patients were living in great danger because of their painlessness.

Foot injuries were easy to explain. If an ankle turned, tearing tendon and muscle, the leprosy patient would simply adjust and walk with a crooked gait. No warning system of pain announced the need to rest the ankle or seek treatment, and the injury would then lead to permanent damage. The most puzzling injuries, though, occurred at night. How could pieces of fingers and toes disappear while the patients were sleeping? Brand found the unsettling answer: rats were coming into the open-air wards and nibbling on unsuspecting patients. Feeling no pain, the patients would sleep on, and not until the next morning would they notice the injury and report it to Dr. Brand. That discovery led to a firm rule: every patient released from the hospital had to take along a cat, for nocturnal protection.

Listening to Dr. Brand tell these horror stories, I could easily understand why he could say with absolute conviction, "Thank God for pain!" For him, pain represents God's great gift, one Brand desperately desires to share with fifteen million victims of leprosy.

After twenty years in India, Dr. Brand moved to the

Hansen's disease* research center and hospital in Carville, Louisiana. There, under the auspices of the U.S. Public Health Service, he could continue his research and potentially help many more patients worldwide.

I first met Dr. Brand at the Carville hospital, a visit that changed forever the way I think about pain. Because of the stigma of leprosy, the hospital is remote and difficult to reach. It was built in the 1890s on the swampy site of a plantation by the banks of the Mississippi. (Land was purchased under the pretense of starting an ostrich farm so that neighbors would not suspect the buyers' true intent.)

The leprosy center stretches out over 337 acres and includes a nine-hole golf course and a stocked lake in addition to modern medical facilities. Barbed wire around Carville has come down, and visitors are now welcome. Tours are conducted three times daily.

A pleasant environment, buildings designed for wheelchair patients, the best medical care, free treatment with the latest drugs—on the surface life in this shaded plantation setting seems almost enviable. The disease is under control now, and most cases can be arrested in early stages. But, as I quickly learned, one horrible aspect of leprosy remains: the loss of pain sensation.

Visit to Carville

I am visiting a patient clinic at Carville. Two physical therapists, a nurse, and Dr. Brand are seated in chairs arranged in a semicircle around a TV monitor. Together they will examine three patients with health problems.

The first enters, a middle-aged Hawaiian man named Lou (not his real name). I notice that Lou has more visible deformities than most patients here. He came to Carville with an advanced case of leprosy. His eyebrows and eyelashes are gone, which gives his face a naked, unbalanced appearance. Because his eyelids are paralyzed, tears tend to overflow and he seems to be perpetually crying.

Dr. Brand has already told me that Lou is virtually blind. Blind from lack of pain: tiny pain cells on the surface of his eye stopped signaling the irritation and discomfort that call for

*The medical name for leprosy.

blinking, and as his dulled eyelids blinked less frequently Lou's eyes gradually dried up. Preventing blindness is a real challenge at Carville. A few patients destroyed their eyes by the simple act of washing their faces, their hands not sensitive enough to warn of scalding water.

In addition to blindness, Lou suffers from many other side-effects of leprosy. His feet are smooth stumps, without toes—all ten toes were lost due to inadvertent injury and infection. His hands are lined with deep cracks and thickened scars. But Lou's main problem, the reason he has come to the clinic, is more psychological than physical.

Lou feels a door has been shut between him and the rest of the world. He can't see people. Having lost so much sensation, he cannot feel a handshake or any other form of human touch. His last remaining unaffected sense is hearing, and that is the source of his fear. A new experimental drug is causing some loss of hearing.

His voice trembling, Lou tells the group how much he loves the Autoharp. He can strum the Hawaiian melodies of his childhood and dream of younger days. A devout Christian, he sings as a form of praise to God, and sometimes volunteers to play hymns for his church. In order to play, Lou must tape the pick onto the one patch of his thumb that still has some sensation. With that sensitive spot, he can detect enough variation in pressure to know how to strum the chords correctly.

But Lou's thumb is not sensitive enough to recognize dangerous pressures. Hours of practicing the Autoharp have left calluses on the thumb, and now an ulcer has broken out. He has been afraid to come to the clinic until now. "Can you find some way for me to continue playing without damaging my hand?" he asks in a thick accent, almost pleading.

The committee of doctors and physical therapists view Lou's hand on the TV monitor. They are using thermography, a process by which a machine detects differing temperature bands and projects them visually as bright colors. Weather satellites use the same technology.

On the thermogram Lou's hand appears as a psychedelic pattern of chartreuse, yellow, scarlet, and all shades in between. The coolest portions show up green or blue. Bright red is a danger sign that indicates an infection: blood has rushed to the site, raising the temperature. Yellow shows extreme danger. It's easy to see the single most useful spot on Lou's thumb, for constant use has inflamed the area, and it now stands out as a yellow pinpoint of heat.

Thermography has revolutionized treatment at Carville because for the first time it offers a warning system for painless persons. Unfortunately, unlike the pain network, this technology detects danger *after* the period of stress, not during it. A person with a healthy pain system would have sought treatment long before. His or her thumb would throb all day long, loudly demanding attention and rest. But Lou has no such advantage. He never knows when he is further damaging the tiny spot of infection in his thumb.

The committee designs a glove to fit Lou's hand, one that will relieve some of the pressure of the Autoharp pick. Dr. Brand delivers a stern lecture about the need for Lou to give his thumb a rest, to wear the glove at all times, and to report in every few days. But after Lou leaves, the physical therapist expresses pessimism. "Lou hates gloves. They call attention to his hands, and undoubtedly he'll lose some control over the pick. Probably he'll try it for a day, then throw it away."

Already Lou is withdrawing from people, cutting off contact as his senses of sight, hearing, and touch gradually fade. Now his last great love, his self-expression through music, is also threatened. He may return to the clinic in a few weeks with a further infection that has caused permanent damage to his thumb. He may even lose the thumb. But at Carville treatment is voluntary. Without his own pain network to force him to act, Lou has the risky option of ignoring the thermogram's warning.

A Mop and a Shoe

Another patient, Hector, enters the room. Although his face shows none of the deformities of Lou's, still I must catch myself from gasping when I see it. By now I have grown accustomed to seeing colors projected on a thermogram monitor, but not on a man's face. Hector has blue skin! Dr. Brand, noticing my reaction, whispers to me that Hector has shown resistance to the sulfone drugs most commonly used for treatment, and the team has been experimenting with a new drug that happens to be a blue dye. Hector has gladly forfeited normal flesh tones in hopes of halting the spread of leprosy in his body.

Hector, a most cooperative patient, answers all the committee's questions thoughtfully, speaking in a deep Texas drawl. No, he's had no problems since the last checkup. Hector's thermogram, however, disagrees, revealing a vivid red danger spot in the webbing between his right thumb and forefinger. A callus has hidden any external signs of infection, but underneath an infection is festering.

Quizzing him like a police investigation team, Dr. Brand and the others ask Hector to trace his day's activities. How does he shave? Put on his shoes? Does he have a job? Does he play golf? Shoot pool? At some point in his day, Hector has been grasping something too firmly between his thumb and forefinger. Unless they can find the faulty activity and get him to stop, his hand will deteriorate further.

At last, in the course of the grilling, Hector identifies the problem. After each day's mild work as a canteen cashier, he helps with the cleanup, mopping the floor to erase any spilled soft drinks or candy. That back-and-forth motion, coupled with Hector's inability to sense how firmly he is squeezing the mop handle, has damaged tissue inside his thumb. The mystery is solved.

Hector thanks the group profusely. A physical therapist makes a note to ask the canteen supervisor to substitute some other activity for Hector.

One more patient comes in—Jose. In contrast to most people at Carville, Jose is wearing the latest in fashion. His pants have a sharp crease, and his all-cotton shirt is neatly tapered to fit. His shoes are nothing like the dull, black orthopedic shoes I have seen on most patients. They have a contemporary, narrow-toe design and are polished to a high brown gloss.

Jose's shoes are, in fact, the problem. He dresses meticulously because of his full-time job as a furniture salesman back in California. Carville therapists have tried to persuade Jose to wear less stylish, and safer, shoes, but he has always refused. His job and image are more important to him than the condition of his feet.

When Jose removes his shoes and socks, his feet show the worst injury I have seen. I cannot find the slightest nub where his toes should be. After years of infection, his body has absorbed the bone tissue, and Jose now walks on rounded stumps, like an amputee. With no toes to cushion the impact when his heel lifts upward, he is systematically wearing down even the stumps. Thermography graphically illustrates the ongoing problem. Dr. Brand calls Jose's attention to bright yellow patches marking the extent of infection.

Normally, a person would automatically limp, or change walking styles, to break in a new pair of shoes, and if the feet hurt too badly, out would come a more comfortable pair. But Jose can't feel the danger signs. Members of the committee take turns trying to impress on Jose the gravity of the problem, but he is politely unyielding. He will not wear Carville-made shoes. To him, they look like training shoes for cripples, and they'd tip off his customers that something is wrong. His facial features and hands are almost normal; he won't let his feet betray him.

Finally, Dr. Brand calls in the shoemaker and asks him to make some minor adjustments on Jose's shoes that may partially relieve the pressure.

At the end of the clinic, after the last patient has left, Dr. Brand turns to me and says, "Pain—it's often seen as the great inhibitor, keeping us from happiness. But I see it as a giver of freedom. Look at these men. Lou: we're desperately searching for a way to allow him the simple freedom of playing an Autoharp. Hector: he can't even mop a floor without harming himself. Jose: he can't dress nicely and walk normally. For that, he would need the gift of pain."

A Deadly Indifference

Leprosy is not the only affliction that muffles the protective warnings of pain. The research at Carville has also been applied to other medical conditions of insensitivity. In advanced cases, diabetics lose pain sensations and face exactly the same dangers. Many have lost fingers, toes, and entire limbs as a result of preventable injuries. Alcoholics and drug addicts can likewise deaden their sensitivity: each winter alcoholics die of exposure, their bodies numb to the biting cold.

A few people, however, are born with a defective pain network, and some of these too have sought treatment at Carville. Victims of the rare condition known informally as "congenital indifference to pain" have a warning system of sorts, but, like Dr. Brand's flashing lights and audible signals, theirs does not *hurt*. To them, running fingers over a hot stove gives the same sensation as running fingers over an asphalt driveway. They feel both as neutral sensations.

Congenital indifference to pain poses unique problems of child-rearing. One family told of a horrifying incident that occurred when their infant daughter grew four teeth. The mother, hearing the baby daughter laughing and cooing in the next room, went in expecting to find some new game the child had discovered. She screamed. Her daughter had bitten off the tip of her finger and was playing in the blood, making patterns with the drips.

How do you explain the danger of matches, knives, and razor blades to such children? How do you punish them? The little girl, seeing the effect of her "game" on her mother, started using it mischievously. Whenever her mother forbade her to do something, the girl would put her finger in her mouth and begin to bite it. By the time she reached sixteen, she had chewed off all her fingers.

About a hundred cases of this strange affliction have been reported on in medical literature. One seven-year-old picked at her nose until her nostrils became ulcerated. An eight-year-old English girl, in a fit of anger, pulled out all but nine of her teeth and poked both eyes out of their sockets. Afflicted children can impress their friends with bizarre feats like pushing a straight pin through their fingers.

But insensitivity to pain dooms such people to lives of constant peril. They can sprain a wrist or ankle without knowing it, or bite through their tongues while chewing gum. Joints deteriorate because they fail to shift weight while sleeping or standing. One afflicted woman lost her life because she could not feel a simple headache, the warning symptom of a serious illness.[1]

These people can undergo surgery without anesthesia, but how do they know when surgery is required? Whereas a healthy person would feel symptoms in advance of a heart attack or appendicitis, they feel nothing. Where most people would respond immediately, spurred on by pain, the congenitally insensitive must consciously attend to the faintest clues and ponder the appropriate response. *A tickling sensation in the abdomen . . . does that mean my appendix has burst?*

Medical textbooks had done much to convince me of pain's value before I visited Carville. Already I was beginning to see that, even in Claudia Claxton's case, pain was not the root problem—the disease was. Pain was merely her body's loyal way of informing her that cancer cells and cobalt rays were harming her. Apart from these warnings she might have died, unaware of the disease's presence.

The week at Carville left me with indelible memories. Whenever I am tempted to curse God for pain, I remember Lou: his eyes running, his face scarred, oblivious to human touch, longing for a way to retain his music, his last love in life. Pain allows us, the fortunate ones at least, to lead free and active lives. If you ever doubt that, visit a leprosarium and observe for yourself a world without pain.

Pain is not an unpleasantness to be avoided at all costs. In a thousand ways large and small, pain serves us each day, making possible normal life on this planet. If we are healthy, pain cells alert us when to go to the bathroom, when to change shoes, when to loosen the grip on a mop handle or rake, when to blink. Without pain, we would lead lives of paranoia, defenseless against unfelt dangers. The only safe environment for a painless person is to stay in bed all day ... but even that produces bedsores.

How singular is the thing called pleasure and how curiously related to pain, which might be thought to be the opposite of it . . . yet he who pursues either is generally compelled to take the other; their bodies are two but they are joined by the same head.

Socrates

4

Agony and Ecstasy

When confronted with the facts, most of us will admit that pain—some pain, at least—serves a good and useful purpose. Apart from the warning system it provides, hidden dangers would shadow our everyday existence. Even more neglected, however, is the intimate connection that links pain and pleasure. The two sensations work together so closely they sometimes become almost indistinguishable.

Pain is an essential component of our most satisfying experiences. Does that sound odd? It may, for modern culture barrages us with opposite messages. We are told that pain is the antithesis of pleasure. If you feel a slight headache, dull it immediately with the newest extra-strength pain reliever. If your nose drips more than a drop, by all means reach for the latest sinus decongestant spray. At the slightest cramp of constipation, visit a drugstore and select from the dazzling display of candies, liquids, pills, and enemas.

I think back to Thielicke's criticism of Americans' "inadequate view of suffering." Little wonder. We moderns have cut ourselves off from the stream of human history, which has always accepted pain as an integral part of life. Until very recently, any balanced view of life had to account for pain as a normal, routine occurrence. Now it looms as the great intruder.

Let me quickly add that I buy shrink-wrapped, bloodless hunks of meat in grocery stores, work in an air-conditioned office, and wear shoes to protect my feet from Chicago sidewalks. But in doing so I realize that abundant luxuries and conveniences such as these give me a perspective on the world and on pain that was not shared by any other century and is still unrealized by two-thirds of the world. I, along with most Americans, tend to see pain as a sensation that can and should be mastered by technology. That distorted viewpoint helps foster the notion that pain and pleasure are diametrically opposed: our lifestyles murmur it to us every day.

Nobel Prize winner George Wald reflected on this fact: "Just realize, I am 69 and have never seen a person die. I have never even been in the same house while a person died. How about birth? An obstetrician invited me to see my first birth only last year. Just think, these are the greatest events of life and they have been taken out of our experience. We somehow hope to live full emotional lives when we have carefully expunged the sources of the deepest human emotions. When you have no experience of pain, it is rather hard to experience joy."

Buzzed Brains

In some ways the human brain resembles an electronic amplifier, coordinating input from a bewildering array of sources. Instead of phono turntables, VCR machines, compact disc players, and tape decks, we have such input sources as touch, vision, hearing, taste, and smell. In a healthy body, pain is just one of many input sources assigned to report on the state of the extremities.

When a sense organ begins to degenerate, the brain automatically turns up the volume control. Sometimes a person with leprosy will not notice a loss of touch sensation until it fades completely; his brain has compensated by increasing the volume of the slight impulses until the sensors die and give off no more impulses.

Modern culture saddens me because, while it seeks to turn down the volume on pain, it constantly turns up the volume from all other sources. We have ears: they are bombarded with decibels until the subtle tones are lost forever. Listen to music from any other century, twelfth, sixteenth, even nineteenth, and compare it to what most people listen to today. We have eyes: the world assaults them with neon lights and phosphorescent colors until a sunset or butterfly pales in comparison. Imagine what a glimpse of a tiger swallowtail butterfly did for the senses in a village of medieval Europe—compared to the same butterfly in downtown Las Vegas today. We have noses: chemical droplets come printed like ink on magazine pages so that we need only scratch and sniff. Take away the spray cans from our closets indoors and the pollution particles from the air outdoors, and most of us would have no idea how the natural world is supposed to smell.

We use the word "stoned" for people so blitzed with sensations, often chemically induced, that they are dulled almost senseless. I prefer the word "buzzed," following the brain/amplifier analogy. In such a high-tech environment, it is easy for the young, especially, to mistake vicarious pleasure for true fulfillment—life as video game. They don't see pleasure as something to reach out for and actively attain after struggle. Pleasure is something done to you; merely strap yourself in the amusement-park ride.

The drug problems in the U.S. demonstrate this pattern: by heightening powers of perception, chemical stimulants open up a new world to a generation that has never learned to appreciate fully the world we have. It is not enough to walk alongside a swamp and listen to the frogs and crickets, to watch the turtles plop like bloated submarines into the water, to seek out the faint scent of wildflowers. It is not enough, even, to visit the outer reaches of wilderness, where nature is far from subtle. Instead, too often we experience all these things vicariously, slumped in front of a flickering television with its beams of Trinitron color and low-frequency radiation, receiving sensory stimulation through our eyes alone. We have been to Everest and back, we think, when in fact some of us have never climbed the Appalachians.

Substituting vicarious and artificial sensations for natural ones takes a toll on the human body. Like muscles, our senses can atrophy. French scientists have proved this in experiments with darkened isolation chambers in which volunteers float in tepid water. In the absence of outside stimuli, the senses have nothing to report, and begin to fail. Soon the subjects become restless and disoriented, and before long begin to hallucinate. High altitude jet pilots and military sentinels in isolated outposts have experienced similar hallucinations. When deprived of sensory reports from the body, the brain appears to manufacture its own.

On the other hand, through regular use our sensory faculties can develop even more responsiveness. Nerve endings actually "improve" with use. Some scientists theorize that fingertips develop their incredible sensitivity due to our constant reliance on them from infancy onwards. Similarly, you can increase skin sensitivity by brushing your own arm daily with a nylon brush. Eventually the skin surface there will detect a much wider range of pleasure and pain sensations.

Going barefoot also helps to vary skin sensation, especially if you walk on the sand of a beach or on grass. The subtle variations in a lawn's shape and texture feed the brain with needed sensory input, which is vital for the brain's healthy development.

For this reason Dr. Brand, half in jest but half seriously, suggests that babies should be raised on coarse coconut matting rather than on down comforters and blankets. Surrounding babies with softness and neutral sensations stifles their nerve-growth and limits their range of interpreting the world. Brand also confesses his wife discouraged him from stringing barbed wire around his children's playpens. Cruel? It would merely train a child to accept a world where certain things (like sharp objects and hot stoves) are off-limits and painful. The more you coddle children, he says, the more you condition them to an insulated, sensation-starved life.

Dr. Brand tries to follow this principle throughout his life, even as he approaches the last decades of his life. "At one time, I thought of pain as the opposite of happiness. I would have illustrated life by drawing a graph with a peak at each end and a trough in the middle. The peak at the left would represent the experience of pain or acute unhappiness. The peak at the right would represent pure happiness or ecstasy. In between is quiet, normal living. My goal, I thought, was to face firmly toward happiness and away from pain. But now I see things differently. If I drew such a graph today, it would have a single, central peak with a surrounding plain. The peak would be Life with a capital

L, the point at which pain and pleasure meet. The surrounding plain would be sleep or apathy or death."

Pain and Pleasure

Nature, ever economical, uses the same nerve sensors and pathways that convey messages of pain to carry also messages of pleasure. At the cellular level, the sensation of a mosquito-bite itch (unpleasant) and that of a tickle (pleasant) are virtually identical, the difference being that tickling involves the motion of something acting upon you—a feather pulled across skin, a finger wiggled on a sensitive area. The same nerve sensors are involved, firing off identical responses to the brain, but we interpret one action as pleasant and one as unpleasant.

The body contains no dedicated "pleasure" sensors. Sensors in your fingers that report to your brain information about heat, or the extent of a mild electric shock, or the degree of coarseness of a rough surface, are the same sensors that convey to you the feel of velvet or satin. Indeed, even the sensors that produce feelings of sexual pleasure are the same ones that carry messages of alarm. Dissection of the erogenous zones yields an abundance of touch and pressure cells (which explains why those areas are so sensitive to pain), but no cells devoted to pleasure. Nature is never so lavish.

Some pains—the sharp prick of a fingernail to stop the itching of a mosquito bite, or the twang of a sore muscle being stretched after a hard day's work—are perceived as more pleasant than unpleasant. After skiing all day in the mountains, I want the hottest Jacuzzi available. I wait a few minutes, then gingerly lower a hand or leg into the water. Ouch! A stinging shot of pain. I withdraw, then try again. Up to my ankles now, and the pain is far less. I gradually lower my body into the water. The same water that a moment before caused me pain now feels wonderful. My sore muscles feel better than they have felt all day. (Liniments like Ben Gay work on the same principle: they slightly irritate the skin, which causes something akin to a "burning" sensation. Blood rushes to the site, bringing relief to overtaxed muscles.)

This close association between pain and pleasure holds true not just on the cellular level, but in many experiences that involve the whole body working together. Often the most intense pleasure comes after prolonged struggle.

I once went on a stress camping trip, designed after the Outward Bound program, in the north woods of Wisconsin. Such programs offer an instant cure for anyone who feels isolated from the natural world, or from pain. Getting awakened at 4:00 A.M., scrambling up a bare rock wall with no gloves, running a marathon race after ten days in the woods, invading the world headquarters of black flies and "no-see-ums"—such delights await the soft city slicker. I have never felt more tired at the end of a day as I forced weary muscles into a sleeping bag still damp from last night's dew. Even so, I have never gotten less sleep, thanks mainly to the nocturnal "no-see-ums," smaller than any mosquito net opening and fiercer than any killer bee.

Yet what I now remember most about that week is how it affected my senses. They seemed to come alive. When I breathed in, I could "taste" the air—and in an entirely different way than I taste the air around my Chicago home. I noticed things with my eyes and ears that I would normally overlook.

Once, after an afternoon of hiking in the dust and heat, while loaded down with seventy-pound packs, we paused for a brief rest stop. One of the group followed a honeybee to a small patch of wild strawberries growing nearby. No self-respecting grocery store would ever have accepted these strawberries. They were small and scrawny, and coated with dust. We didn't care; they were food, and perhaps contained some moisture. I picked a handful, popped them into my mouth, and was immediately overwhelmed by the incredible flavor of sweet, luscious strawberry juice. These desiccated little berries were the best I had ever eaten! I spent my rest time picking more and stuffing them into plastic bags for an afternoon snack.

At first I thought we had stumbled upon a new species, the discovery of which would revolutionize the fruit-growing industry. Gradually I figured out that the taste had to do with *my* physical condition, not the strawberries'. The process of using my body and connecting with all my senses had freed up a whole new level of pleasure awareness. The extraordinary, delicious taste of those strawberries would never have been mine if I had not first felt the heat and toil of hiking all day, as well as the pangs of hunger that sharpened my senses.

Athletes know well this strange brotherhood. Watch an

Olympic weight lifter. He approaches the steel bar with its bulging wheels of weight. He takes deep breaths, grimaces, flexes his muscles. Reaching down, he gives a few preparatory tugs to limber up. Then he squats, sucks in air, tenses his body in one mighty reflex, and begins to hoist. Oh, the pain in a weight lifter's face. Each millisecond it takes him to jerk the weight to his shoulders and raise it over his head etches lines of agony on his face. His muscles scream for relief.

If he succeeds, he drops the bar with a tremendous *thong* on the floor and jumps in the air, his hands clasped above his head. In a millisecond, absolute ecstasy replaces absolute agony. One would not have existed without the other. Ask the weight lifter what he thought of the pain—and he will stare at you, bewildered. He has already forgotten, for it has been swallowed up in pleasure.

Lin Yutang describes an ancient Chinese philosophy in his book *My Country and My People:* "To be dry and thirsty in a hot and dusty land—and to feel great drops of rain on my bare skin—ah, is this not happiness! To have an itch in the private part of my body—and finally to escape from my friends and to a hiding place where I can scratch—ah, is this not happiness!" In Yutang's long list of happiness experiences, virtually every one combines pain with pleasure.

Augustine's *Confessions* contains a remarkably similar passage. "What is it, therefore," he begins, "that goes on within the soul, since it takes greater delight if things that it loves are found or restored to it than if it had always possessed them?" Augustine proceeds to mention a victorious general who experiences the greatest satisfaction when the danger is greatest, a seafarer who exults in calm seas after a violent storm, and a sick man who upon recovery walks with a joy he had never known before his illness.

"Everywhere a greater joy is preceded by a greater suffering," Augustine concludes.[1] Like other church fathers, he understood that depriving some senses, such as through fasting, heightened others. Spiritual experience is nourished best in the wilderness.

When I am old, I hope I do not spend my days between sterile sheets, hooked up to a respirator in a germ-free environment, protected from the hazards of the world outside. I hope I'm on a tennis court, straining my heart with a septuagenarian overhead smash. Or perhaps on a final hike, huffing and puffing along a trail to Lower Yosemite Falls for one more feel of the spray against my wrinkled cheek. In short, I hope I do not so insulate myself from pain that I no longer feel pleasure.

Befriending Enemies

Athletes and artists alike learn that a long period of struggle and effort precedes nearly all worthwhile human accomplishments. It required years of toil and misery for Michelangelo to create the Sistine Chapel frescoes that have since given pleasure to so many others. And anyone who has built cabinets in a kitchen or tended a vegetable garden knows the same truth in a more mundane way: the pleasure, coming after the pain, absorbs it. Jesus used childbirth as an analogy: nine months of waiting and preparation, intense labor, then the ecstasy of birth (John 16:21).

I once interviewed Robin Graham, the youngest person ever to sail around the world alone. (His story was told in the book and movie *Dove*.) Robin set sail as an immature sixteen-year-old, not so much seeking his future as delaying it. In the course of the long voyage, he was smashed broadside by a violent ocean storm, had his mast snapped in two by a rogue wave, and barely missed annihilation by a waterspout. He went through such despair in the Doldrums, a windless, currentless portion of the ocean near the Equator, that he emptied a can of kerosene in his boat, struck a match, and jumped overboard. (A sudden gust of wind soon caused him to change his mind and he jumped back in to extinguish the blaze and continue the voyage.)

After five years, Robin sailed into the Los Angeles harbor to be greeted by boats, banners, crowds, reporters, honking cars, and blasts from steam whistles. The joy of that moment was on a different level from any other experience he had known. He could never have felt those emotions returning from a pleasure outing off the coast of California. The agony of his round-the-world trip had made possible the exultation of his triumphant return. He left a sixteen-year-old kid and returned a twenty-one-year-old man.

Impressed by the sense of health that self-accomplishment could bring, Robin immediately bought a farm plot in Kalispell,

Montana, and built a cabin from hand-cut logs. Publishers and movie agents tried to entice him with round-the-country publicity trips, talk show engagements, and fat expense accounts, but Robin declined them all.

We moderns, in our comfort-controlled environments, have a tendency to blame our unhappiness on pain, which we identify as the great enemy. If we could somehow excise pain from life, ah, then we would be happy. But, as experiences like Robin's show, life does not yield to such easy partitioning. Pain is a part of the seamless fabric of sensations, and often a necessary prelude to pleasure and fulfillment. The key to happiness lies not so much in avoiding pain at all costs as in understanding its role as a protective warning system and harnessing it to work on your behalf, not against you.

I have learned that this same principle applies not only to pain, but to other "enemies" as well. When I encounter an apparent enemy, I ask myself, *Can I find even in this a reason for gratitude?* To my surprise, the answer is almost always yes.

What about fear, for example—Why be grateful for fear? I know the physiology behind fear, the way in which the body uses minute quantities of adrenaline to speed heart rate, increase skin friction, heighten reaction time and supply added strength—all this in a millisecond of fear. I try to imagine a sport like downhill skiing without the protective response of fear that keeps me from being even more foolhardy. Fear, like pain, serves as a warning system, only with the added benefit of functioning in advance of harm.

Someone asked the Swiss physician and author Paul Tournier how he helped his patients get rid of their fears. He replied, "I don't. Everything that's worthwhile in life is scary. Choosing a school, choosing a career, getting married, having kids—all those things are scary. If it is not fearful, it is not worthwhile."

Consider another apparent enemy: guilt, a universal human response that many people want to purge from their lives. But try to envision a world without guilt, a society with no curbs on behavior. The U.S. court system defines sanity as the ability to discern between good and evil, and a world with no guilt would tilt toward insanity.

Guilt is a pain message to the conscience, informing it that something is wrong and should be dealt with. Two steps are necessary. First, the person must locate the cause of the guilt, just as a person must locate the cause of his or her pain. Much of modern counseling deals with this process of weeding out reasons for false guilt. But a further step must follow, a pathway out of the guilt.

The *perceived* function of guilt, like pain, is an impulse to get rid of the unpleasant sensation. Underlying that, however, is the more significant purpose of dealing with the root cause. In the long run, it won't help you to try to purge authentic guilt feelings unless you first let them guide you toward forgiveness and reconciliation. Guilt by itself doesn't lead you anywhere, just as pain does not: both are directional, symptoms of a condition that requires your urgent attention.

Or, I think of a world without another pain, the pain of loneliness. Would friendship and even love exist apart from our inbuilt sense of need, the prod that keeps us all from being hermits? Do we not need the power of loneliness to pry us away from isolation and push us toward others?

I do not mean to gloss over or discount the very real suffering in this world. Nevertheless, when something bad happens and we feel we have no control over the tragedy itself, we still have some control over our own responses. We can lash out in bitterness and anger against the unfairness of life that has deprived us of pleasure and joy. Or, we can look for good in unexpected sources, even our apparent enemies.

I heard recently about a poll of senior citizens in London. To the question, "What was the happiest period of your life?" sixty percent answered, "The Blitz." Every night squadrons of fat Luftwaffe bombers would dump tons of explosives on the city, pounding a proud civilization to rubble—and now the victims recall that time with nostalgia! In those dark, fearful days, they learned to huddle together and strive toward a common goal. They learned such qualities as courage, and sharing, and hope.

When something bad happens—a disagreement with my wife, a painful misunderstanding with a friend, an ache of guilt over some responsibility I have let slide—I try to view that occurrence as I would view a physical pain. I accept it as a signal alerting me to attend to a matter that needs change. I strive to be grateful, not for the pain itself, but for the opportunity to respond, to form good out of what looks bad.

Surprised by Happiness

Jesus captured succinctly the paradoxical nature of life in his one statement most repeated in the Gospels: "Whoever finds his life will lose it, and whoever loses his life for my sake will find it." Such a statement goes against the search for "self-fulfillment" in advanced psychology—which turns out to be not advanced enough. Christianity offers the further insight that true fulfillment comes, not through ego satisfaction, but through service to others. And that brings me to the last illustration of the pain/pleasure principle: the Christian concept of service.

In my career as a journalist, I have interviewed diverse people. Looking back, I can roughly divide them into two types: stars and servants. The stars include NFL football greats, movie actors, music performers, famous authors, TV personalities, and the like. These are the people who dominate our magazines and our television programs. We fawn over them, poring over the minutiae of their lives: the clothes they wear, the food they eat, the aerobic routines they follow, the people they love, the toothpaste they use.

Yet I must tell you that, in my limited experience, these "idols" are as miserable a group of people as I have ever met. Most have troubled or broken marriages. Nearly all are hopelessly dependent on psychotherapy. In a heavy irony, these larger-than-life heroes seem tormented by incurable self-doubt.

I have also spent time with servants. People like Dr. Paul Brand, who worked for twenty years among the poorest of the poor, leprosy patients in rural India. Or health workers who left high-paying jobs to serve with Mendenhall Ministries in a backwater town of Mississippi. Or relief workers in Somalia, Sudan, Ethiopia, Bangladesh, or other such repositories of world-class human suffering. Or the Ph.D.'s scattered throughout jungles of South America translating the Bible into obscure languages.

I was prepared to honor and admire these servants, to hold them up as inspiring examples. I was not, however, prepared to envy them. But as I now reflect on the two groups side by side, stars and servants, the servants clearly emerge as the favored ones, the graced ones. They work for low pay, long hours, and no applause, "wasting" their talents and skills among the poor and uneducated. But somehow in the process of losing their lives they have found them. They have received the "peace that is not of this world."

When I think of the great churches I have visited, what comes to mind is not an image of a cathedral in Europe. These are mere museums now. Instead, I think of the chapel at Carville, of an inner-city church in Newark with crumbling plaster and a leaky roof, of a mission church in Santiago, Chile, made of concrete block and corrugated iron. In these places, set amidst human misery, I have seen Christian love abound.

The leprosarium in Carville, Louisiana, offers a wonderful example of this principle in action. A government agency bought the property and promised to develop it, but could find no one to clear the roads, repair the plantation's slave cabins, or drain the swamps. The stigma of leprosy kept everyone away.

Finally an order of nuns, the Sisters of Charity, moved to Carville to nurse the leprosy patients. Getting up two hours before daybreak, wearing starched white uniforms in bayou heat, these nuns lived under a more disciplined rule than any Marine boot camp. But they alone proved willing to do the work. They dug ditches, laid foundations for buildings, and made Carville livable, all the while glorifying God and bringing joy to the patients. They learned perhaps the deepest level of pain/pleasure association in life, that of sacrificial service.

If I spend my life searching for happiness through drugs, comfort, and luxury, it will elude me. "Happiness recedes from those who pursue her." Happiness will come upon me unexpectedly as a by-product, a surprising bonus for something I have invested myself in. And, most likely, that investment will include pain. It is hard to imagine pleasure without it.

Part 2

Is Pain a Message from God?

5

The Groaning Planet

Consider earth, our home. Let your eyes savor the brilliant hues and delicate shadings of a summer sunset. Tunnel your toes into wet sand, stand still, and feel the dependable foam and spray of an ocean tide. Visit a butterfly garden and study the abstract designs: 10,000 variations, more imaginative than those of any abstract painter, all compressed into tiny swatches of flying fabric. Belief in a loving Creator is easy among these good things.

Yet the sun that lavishes dusk with color can also bake African soil into a dry, cracked glaze, dooming millions. The rhythmic, pounding surf can, if fomented by a storm, crash in as a twenty-foot wall of death, obliterating coastal villages. And the harmless swatches of color fluttering among wildflowers survive on average two weeks before succumbing to the grim ferocity of nature's food chain. Nature is our fallen sister, not our mother. And earth, though God's showplace, is a good creation that has been bent.

Witness the human species. The fatherland of Bach, Beethoven, Luther, and Goethe also gave us Hitler, Eichmann, and Goering. A nation weaned on the Bill of Rights also brought us slavery and the Civil War. As a species and as individuals, in every one of us wisdom, creativity, and compassion vie with deceit, pride, and selfishness.

And so it is with pain. Up close, pain may seem a trusted, worthy friend. From the myopic perspective of, say, a bioengineer, the pain network surely appears as one of creation's finest works. The nervous system, bearing the stamp of genius, merits admiration and awe, like an exquisite Rembrandt painting.

Yet most often pain comes to our attention not through a microscope eyepiece, but through unwelcome tokens of personal misery. If you relate each warning signal to a specific cause, the pain network may seem rational and well-designed. But if you step back and view all humanity—a writhing, starving, bleeding, cancerous progression of billions of people marching toward death—there, a problem arises.

The "problem of pain" encompasses far more than the loyal responses of nerve cells. What about the side effects of pain as it grinds down the soul toward despair and hopelessness? Why the caprice of some lives dominated by arthritis, cancer, or birth defects, while others escape unafflicted for seven decades? The poet William Blake summed up human existence this way:

> My mother groaned, my father wept,
> into the dangerous world I leapt . . .

Philosophers love sweeping discussions of the sum total of human suffering, as if all human pain could be extruded into one great cauldron and presented to God: "Here is the pain and suffering of Planet Earth. How do you account for all this misery?" But as Ivan Karamazov pointed out in Dostoyevksi's great novel, pain comes to one person at a time, and the undeserved suffering of a single human being—a child beating its breast with its fist—raises the problem just as acutely.

Pain may have been intended as an efficiently protective warning system, but something about this planet has gone haywire and pain now rages out of control. We need another word for the problem: perhaps *pain* to signify the body's protective network and *suffering* to signify the human misery. After all, a leprosy patient feels no pain, but much suffering.

Though some people stay mercifully free of acute physical

pain, everyone has a form of suffering that will not go away: a personality flaw, a broken relationship, an unhealed childhood memory, a suffocating guilt. To understand suffering we must step away from the microscope, with its array of nerve cells obediently responding to stimuli, and look full in the face of agonized human beings. The question "Where is God when it hurts?" becomes "Where is God when it won't stop hurting?" How can God allow such intense, unfair pain?

Best Possible World?

For centuries philosophers have debated the question "Is earth the best of all possible worlds?" The debate follows from the presumption that an all-knowing, all-powerful, all-loving God naturally would have created a wonderful domain for his creatures. But look around at some of the features of our planet—the AIDS virus and Down's syndrome, spina bifida and poliomyelitis, scorpions and tsetse flies, earthquakes and typhoons. Couldn't God have done a better job? As Voltaire put it sarcastically in *Candide,* "If this is the best of all possible worlds, then what are the others like?"

In former times, Christian theologians such as Augustine and Thomas Aquinas argued that God had indeed created the best of all possible worlds. Nowadays, after the twentieth century's display of natural and man-made horrors, only the bravest of thinkers would make such an assertion.

I certainly would not attempt to build a case that earth represents the best of all possible worlds. But one reason I have spent so much time on the biology of pain is that I believe modern philosophers may fail to appreciate the difficulties involved in the act of creation. They presume all God has to do is wave a magic wand to eliminate most hazards of life on earth.

In order to make their point convincingly, critics of this planet need to describe a superior universe, with a complete system of natural laws that would result in significantly less human suffering. Imagine a few possibilities. Why not simply do away with bacteria? That would be a disaster: 24,000 different species of bacteria have been identified, only a few score of which cause illness. Eliminate bacteria and we would never be able to digest food. Typhoons? Bangladesh and India have learned painfully that the earth's climatic system depends upon such major disturbances; in years that typhoons stay away, rains stay away as well.

Creation involves a selection from alternatives. If I break my leg skiing I might wish for stronger bones. Perhaps bone could have been made stronger (though scientists have not been able to find a stronger, suitable substance for implanting), but then my legs would be thicker and heavier, probably making me too bulky and inert to ski at all. If my fingers were thicker and more durable, many human activities—such as playing the piano—would be impossible. A creator had to make those difficult choices between strength and mobility and weight and volume.

Dr. Paul Brand had a taste of such difficult choices when he was trying to design a simple pain sensor to protect the hands of his leprosy patients. This is what he learned:

> The more I delve into natural laws—the atom, the universe, the solid elements, molecules, the sun, and even more, the interplay of all the mechanisms required to sustain life—I am astounded. The whole creation could collapse like a deck of cards if just one of those factors were removed. Some people really believe that all the design and precision in nature came about by chance, that if millions of molecules bombard each other long enough a nerve cell and sensory ending at exactly the right threshold will be bound to turn up. To those people I merely suggest that they try to make one, as I did, and see what chance is up against.
>
> I have spent most of my life in the field of hand surgery. I could fill a good-size room with books that explain various techniques for repairing damaged hands. But I have never seen one procedure—not one—that suggests a way to improve a healthy hand. The design is incredible, and pain is, of course, a part of that design. Ninety-nine out of 100 hands are perfectly normal. But the statistics are exactly reversed for those people insensitive to pain: 99 percent of them have some sort of malformation or dysfunction, simply because their pain network has not been working properly.

Much of the suffering on our planet has come about because of two principles that God built into creation: a physical world that runs according to consistent natural laws, and human freedom.

By committing himself to those two principles, both good principles in themselves, God allowed for the possibility of their abuse. For example, water proves useful to us and all creation because of its "softness," its liquid state, and its specific gravity. Yet those very properties open up its rather disagreeable capacity to drown us—or the even more alarming possibility that we might drown someone else.

Take another example, from wood. It bears the fruit of trees, supports leaves to provide shade, and shelters birds and squirrels. Even when taken from the tree, wood is valuable. We use it as fuel to warm ourselves, and as construction material to build houses and furniture. The essential properties of wood—hardness, unpliability, flammability—make possible these useful functions.

But as soon as you plant a tree with those properties in a world peopled by free human beings, you introduce the possibility of abuse. A free man may pick up a chunk of wood and take advantage of its firmness by bashing the head of another man. God could, I suppose, reach down each time and transform the properties of wood into those of sponge, so that the club would bounce off lightly. But that is not what he is about in the world. He has set into motion fixed laws that can be perverted to evil by our misguided freedom.

(God may have had something like this argument in mind in his address at the end of Job. After listening to Job's complaints, thirty-five chapters' worth, he finally makes a personal appearance, blasting Job off his feet with magnificent descriptions of the created world. God points with pride to a few of the most remarkable features of creation, then gives Job a chance to suggest improvements. Would he care to propose how to run the world differently? You might say that God and Job compare résumés—guess who wins?)

Is God somehow responsible for the suffering of this world? In this indirect way, yes. But giving a child a pair of ice skates, knowing that he may fall, is a very different matter from knocking him down on the ice.

In a world that runs according to fixed laws and is populated by free human beings, the protective pain network, a wonderful gift, is likewise subject to abuse. Could God have done it another way? Could he have maintained some of the benefits of the pain network without the disadvantages? There is some question as to whether any warning system that excludes the element of suffering would work effectively. As Dr. Brand's experiments and the experience of painless people show, it is not enough for us to be alerted when pain is present. It must *hurt,* so as to demand action.

One can argue forever about whether God could have designed our world differently. A cut-off switch for pain? Tropical storms but not hurricanes? One less virus, or three less bacteria? None of us knows the answer to those questions, or even to the prior question of how a specific virus entered the world. (Was it a direct creative activity of God? A consequence of the Fall? An act of Satan? A genetic mutation?) But such speculation is mooted by God's own straightforward answer to the question, "Does earth represent the best of all possible worlds?" And that answer is an unqualified *NO!*

The Wild Animal

The Bible traces the entrance of suffering and evil into the world to the grand but terrible quality of human freedom. What makes us different from porpoises, muskrats, and grizzly bears? Alone, *homo sapiens* have been released from the unbreakable pattern of instinctual behavior. We have true, self-determining choice.

As a result of our freedom, human beings introduced something new to the planet—a rebellion against the original design. We have only slight hints of the way earth was meant to be, but we do know that humanity has broken out of the mold. "We talk of wild animals," says G. K. Chesterton, "but man is the only wild animal. It is man that has broken out. All other animals are tame animals; following the rugged respectability of the tribe or type."[1]

Man is wild because he alone, on this speck of molten rock called earth, stands up, shakes his fist, and says to God, "I do what I want to do because I want to do it." As a result, a huge gulf separates us, and this planet, from God. Most remarkably, God allows us the freedom to do what we want, defying all the rules of the universe (at least for a time). Chesterton again: "In making the world, He set it free. God had written, not so much a poem but rather a play; a play He had planned as perfect, but which had necessarily been left to human actors and stage-managers, who have since made a great mess of it."[2]

Theologians use the term "the Fall" to summarize the massive disruption of creation caused by the initial rebellion when evil first entered the world. The shorthand account in Genesis 3 gives a bare sketch of the consequences of that rebellion, but enough to indicate that all of creation, not just the human species, was disrupted. As Milton said in *Paradise Lost,* "Earth felt the wound, and Nature from her seat / Sighing through all her works gave signs of woe, / That all was lost."

The apostle Paul expressed it this way: "The creation waits in eager expectation for the sons of God to be revealed. For the creation was subjected to frustration, not by its own choice, but by the will of the one who subjected it. . . . We know that the whole creation has been groaning as in the pains of childbirth right up to the present time" (Romans 8:19–20, 22).

Somehow, pain and suffering multiplied on earth as a consequence of the abuse of human freedom. When man and woman chose against God, their free world was forever spoiled. As Paul sees it, since the Fall the planet and all its inhabitants have been emitting a constant stream of low-frequency distress signals. We now live on a "groaning" planet.

Thus, any discussion of the unfairness of suffering must begin with the fact that God is not pleased with the condition of the planet either. The story of the Bible, from Genesis to Revelation, is the story of God's plan to restore his creation to its original state of perfection. The Bible begins and ends with the same scene: Paradise, a river, the luminous glory of God, and the Tree of Life. All of human history takes place somewhere between the first part of Genesis and the last part of Revelation, and everything in between comprises the struggle to regain what was lost.

To judge God solely by the present world would be a tragic mistake. At one time, it may have been "the best of all possible worlds," but surely it is not now. The Bible communicates no message with more certainty than God's *displeasure* with the state of creation and the state of humanity.

Imagine this scenario: vandals break into a museum displaying works from Picasso's Blue Period. Motivated by sheer destructiveness, they splash red paint all over the paintings and slash them with knives. It would be the height of unfairness to display these works—a mere sampling of Picasso's creative genius, and spoiled at that—as representative of the artist. The same applies to God's creation. God has already hung a "Condemned" sign above the earth, and has promised judgment and restoration. That this world spoiled by evil and suffering still exists at all is an example of God's mercy, not his cruelty.

The Megaphone

What can God use to get our attention? What will convince human beings, we who started the rebellion, that creation is not running the way God intended?

C. S. Lewis introduced the phrase "pain, the megaphone of God." "God whispers to us in our pleasures, speaks in our conscience, but shouts in our pains," he said; "it is His megaphone to rouse a deaf world."[3] The word *megaphone* is apropos, because by its nature pain shouts. When I stub my toe or twist an ankle, pain loudly announces to my brain that something is wrong. Similarly, the existence of suffering on this earth is, I believe, a scream to all of us that something is wrong. It halts us in our tracks and forces us to consider other values.

The animal fable *Watership Down* tells of a colony of wild rabbits uprooted from their homes by a construction project. As they wander, they come across a new breed of rabbits huge and beautiful, with sleek, shiny hair and perfect claws and teeth. How do you live so well? the wild rabbits ask. Don't you forage for food? The tame rabbits explain that food is provided for them, in the form of carrots and apples and corn and kale. Life is grand and wonderful.

After a few days, however, the wild rabbits notice that one of the fattest and sleekest of the tame rabbits has disappeared. Oh, that happens occasionally, the tame rabbits explain. But we don't let it interfere with our lives. There's too much good to enjoy. Eventually, the wild rabbits find that the land is studded with traps, and death "hangs like a mist" over their heads. The tame rabbits, in exchange for their plush, comfortable lives, had willingly closed their eyes to one fact: the imminent danger of death.

Watership Down is a fable with a moral point. Like the fat, sleek rabbits, we could—some people do—believe that the sole purpose of life is to be comfortable. Gorge yourself, build a nice home, enjoy good food, have sex, live the good life. That's all there is. But the presence of suffering vastly complicates that lifestyle—unless we choose to wear blinders, like the tame rabbits.

It's hard to believe the world is here just so I can party, when a third of its people go to bed starving each night. It's hard to believe the purpose of life is to feel good, when I see teenagers smashed on the freeway. If I try to escape toward hedonism, suffering and death lurk nearby, haunting me, reminding me of how hollow life would be if this world were all I'd ever know.

Sometimes murmuring, sometimes shouting, suffering is a "rumor of transcendence" that the entire human condition is out of whack. Something is wrong with a life of war and violence and human tragedy. He who wants to be satisfied with this world, who wants to believe the only purpose of life is enjoyment, must go around with cotton in his ears, for the megaphone of pain is a loud one.

Three centuries ago the French mathematician Blaise Pascal worried about some of his friends who seemed to him to be avoiding the most important issues of life. Here is how he characterized them, almost in a parody:

> I know not who put me into the world, nor what the world is, nor what I myself am. I am in terrible ignorance of everything. . . . All I know is that I must soon die, but what I know least is this very death which I cannot escape.
>
> As I know not whence I come, so I know not whither I go. I know only that, in leaving this world, I fall forever either into annihilation or into the hands of an angry God, without knowing to which of these two states I shall be for ever assigned. Such is my state, full of weakness and uncertainty. And from all this I conclude that I ought to spend all the days of my life without caring to inquire into what must happen to me. Perhaps I might find some solution to my doubts, but I will not take the trouble, nor take a step to seek it.

Pascal shook his head in perplexity over people who concern themselves with trifles or even with important matters, all the while ignoring the most important matter of all. "It is an incomprehensible enchantment, and a supernatural slumber," he said.[4]

Some other religions try to deny all pain, or to rise above it. Christianity starts, rather, with the assertion that suffering exists, and exists as proof of our fallen state. One may dismiss the Christian explanation for the origin of suffering—that it was *introduced* into the world as a consequence of man's aborted freedom—as being unsatisfactory. But at least the concept of a great-but-fallen world matches what we know of reality. It fits the dual nature of this world, and of us.

We are like the survivors of a wreck, like Crusoe cast ashore with relics from another land. It is this aspect of Christianity that made Chesterton say, "The modern philosopher had told me again and again that I was in the right place, and I had still felt depressed even in acquiescence. But I had heard that I was in the wrong place, and my soul sang for joy, like a bird in spring." Optimists had told him the world was the best of all possible worlds, but he could never accept it. Christianity made more sense to him because it freely admitted that he was marooned on a mutinous planet.

"The important matter was this," Chesterton concluded, "that it entirely reversed the reason for optimism. And the instant the reversal was made it felt like the abrupt ease when a bone is put back in the socket. I had often called myself an optimist, to avoid the too evident blasphemy of pessimism. But all the optimism of the age had been false and disheartening for this reason, that it had always been trying to prove that we fit in to the world. The Christian optimism is based on the fact that we do *not* fit in to the world."[5]

The megaphone of pain sometimes, of course, produces the opposite effect: I can turn against God for allowing such misery. On the other hand, pain can, as it did with Chesterton, drive me to God. I can believe God when he says this world is not all there is, and take the chance that he is making a perfect place for those who follow him on pain-racked earth.

It is hard to be a creature. We think we are big enough to run our own world without such messy matters as pain and suffering to remind us of our dependence. We think we are wise enough to make our own decisions about morality, to live rightly without the megaphone of pain blaring in our ears. We are wrong, as the Garden of Eden story proves. Man and woman, in a world without suffering, chose against God.

And so we who have come after Adam and Eve have a choice. We can trust God. Or we can blame him, not ourselves, for the world.

Hearing the Echoes

If you doubt the megaphone value of suffering, I recommend that you visit the intensive care ward of a hospital. There you'll find all sorts of people pacing the lobby: a mixture of rich, poor, beautiful, plain, black, white, smart, dull, spiritual, atheistic, white collar, blue collar. But the intensive-care ward is the one place in the world where none of those divisions make a speck of difference.

In an intensive care ward, all visitors are united by a single, awful thread: concern over a dying relative or friend. Economic differences, even religious differences, fade away. You'll see no sparks of racial tension there. Sometimes strangers will console one another or cry together quietly and unashamedly. All are facing life at its most essential. Many call for a pastor or priest for the first time ever. Only the megaphone of suffering is strong enough to bring these people to their knees to ponder ultimate questions of life and death and meaning. As Helmut Thielicke has wryly observed, there is a hospital chaplaincy but no cocktail-party chaplaincy.

That, I believe, is the megaphone value of suffering. This planet emits a constant "groaning," a cry for redemption and restoration, but very often we ignore the message until suffering or death forces us to attend. I do not say that God permits suffering *because of* its megaphone value. (Nor do I believe it carries a specific message—"You're suffering as a consequence of this action"—as the next chapter will make clear.) But the megaphone of pain does announce a general message of distress to all humanity.

John Donne, a seventeenth-century poet, found himself listening to the megaphone of pain. An angry father-in-law got him fired from his job and blackballed from a career in law. Donne turned in desperation to the church, taking orders as an Anglican priest. But the year after he took his first parish job, his wife Anne died, leaving him seven children. And a few years later, in 1623, spots appeared on Donne's own body. He was diagnosed with the bubonic plague.

The illness dragged on, sapping his strength almost to the point of death. (Donne's illness turned out to be a form of typhus, not the plague.) In the midst of this illness, Donne wrote a series of devotions on suffering which rank among the most poignant meditations ever written on the subject. He composed the book in bed, without benefit of notes, convinced he was dying.

In *Devotions,* John Donne calls God to task. As he looks back on life, it doesn't make sense. After spending a lifetime in confused wandering, he has finally reached a place where he can be of some service to God, and now, at that precise moment, he is struck by a deadly illness. Nothing appears on the horizon but fever, pain, and death. What to make of it?

What is the meaning of disease? John Donne's book suggests the possibility of an answer. The first stirrings came to him through the open window of his bedroom, in the form of church bells tolling out a doleful declaration of death. For an instant Donne wondered if his friends, knowing his condition to be more grave than they had disclosed, had ordered the bell to be rung for his own death. But he quickly realized that the bells were marking a neighbor's death from the plague.

Donne wrote Meditation XVII on the meaning of the church bells, one of the most celebrated passages in English literature ("No man is an island. . . . Never send to know for whom the bell tolls; it tolls for thee"). He realized that although the bells had been sounded in honor of another's death, they served as a stark reminder of what every human being spends a lifetime trying to forget: We will all die.

> When one man dies, one chapter is not torn out of the book, but translated into a better language; and every chapter must be so translated; God employs several translators; some pieces are translated by age, some by sickness, some by war, some by justice; but God's hand is in every translation, and his hand shall bind up all our scattered leaves again for that library where every book shall lie open to one another. . . . So this bell calls us all; but

how much more me, who am brought so near the door by this sickness.[6]

Three centuries before C. S. Lewis, Donne used a different phrase than "pain, the megaphone of God" to express the same concept: the singular ability of pain to break through normal defenses and everyday routines. "I need thy thunder, O my God; thy music will not serve thee," he said.[7] The tolling of the bell became, for him, an advance echo of his own death. For the dead man, it was a period, the end of a life; for Donne, clinging to life, it was a penetrating question mark. Was he ready to meet God?

The tolling of that bell worked a curious twist in Donne's progression of thought. The megaphone, or thunder, of pain caused Donne to reexamine his life, and what he saw was like a revelation. "I am the man that has seen affliction," he had once told his congregation, in a self-pitying mood. But it now seemed clear that the periods of sharpest suffering had been the very occasions of spiritual growth. Trials had purged sin and developed character; poverty had taught him dependence on God and cleansed him of greed; failure and public disgrace had helped cure worldly ambition. A clear pattern emerged: pain could be transformed, even redeemed.

Donne's mental review next led him to reflect on present circumstances. Could even *this* pain be redeemed? Illness prevented him from many good works, of course, but his physical weakness surely did not curb all spiritual growth. He had much time for prayer: the bell had reminded him of his less fortunate neighbor, and the many others suffering in London. He could learn humility, and trust, and gratitude, and faith. Donne made a kind of game of it: he envisioned his soul growing strong, rising from the bed, and walking about the room even as his body lay flat.

In short, Donne realized that his life, even in his bedridden state, was not meaningless. He directed his energy toward spiritual disciplines: prayer, confession of sins, keeping a journal (which became *Devotions*). He got his mind off himself and onto others.

Devotions records a seismic shift in Donne's attitude toward pain. He began with prayers that the pain be removed; he ends with prayers that the pain be redeemed, that he be "catechized by affliction." Such redemption might take the form of miracu-lous cure—he still hoped so—but even if it did not, God could take a molten ingot and through the refiner's fire of suffering make of it pure gold.

I can read my affliction as a correction, or as a mercy, and I confess I know not how to read it. How should I understand this illness? I cannot conclude, though death conclude me. If it is a correction indeed, let me translate it and read it as a mercy; for though it may appear to be a correction, I can have no greater proof of your mercy than to die in thee and by that death to be united to him who died for me.

John Donne
Devotions

6

What Is God Trying to Tell Us?

A *Time* magazine report from Yuba City, California:

§   Flanked by weeping relatives, a Spanish-American couple sat in the shimmering heat of Sutter Cemetery, holding hands and staring dully at the bronze coffin that held the remains of their 17-year-old son Bobby. Six of Bobby's classmates placed their white carnation boutonnieres on the coffin. Bobby's young niece threw herself on the coffin and sobbed brokenly. Several in the large crowd also cried. Bobby's father silently shook his head a couple of times as though he had been struck, then moved woodenly with his wife toward the green limousine at the head of the long cortege.

      In the same cemetery Mrs. Harry Rosebrough watched dry-eyed as her son was buried. He had died on his 16th birthday. Pamela Engstrom, wearing a blue-and-white gingham dress—a gift from her mother—had died the day after her 18th birthday. The victims also included twins Carlene and Sharlene Engle, 18, who loved to sing songs composed by their mother, "Wake and Smile in the

75

§   Sunshine" and "Take Pride in America." After the funeral, Sharlene's dusty Ford station wagon was parked across the street from her home. A FOR SALE sign was in the window.

So it was as 15,000 citizens mourned their dead. A bus bearing 53 members of the local high school choir and chaperon Christina Estabrook had ripped through 72 feet of guardrail as it turned onto an exit ramp. The bus plunged 21½ feet to the ground. It landed on its top, wheels still spinning and roof crushed down to the seats.

Blood dripped on scattered sheets of choir music. "I heard someone scream 'Oh my God' from the front of the bus," sobbed Kim Kenyon, a 16-year-old junior whose girl friend was killed in the seat beside him. Added Perry Martin, 18, the choir's chief tenor: "Everything was a tangle of weeping and moaning and of scattered arms and legs." The final toll: 29 dead and 25 injured.

The boys and girls had gone through junior high school together. They had all performed together in *Fiddler on the Roof* earlier this year. Only three weeks from graduation, many of them had gone to their prom on the previous Saturday. Now their friends dazedly shuffled through Yuba City High School, pausing disconsolately from time to time at the principal's window to read the daily notice that listed the condition of the injured. Said Karen Hess, 18, president of the student body: "This is the first time that most of us have ever had close friends die."[1]

Why Yuba City?

Why not Salina, Kansas . . . or Clarkston, Georgia . . . or Ridgewood, New Jersey?

Why the high-school choir? Why not the band, or the debate team, or the football team?

It was a normal, everyday traffic accident—more fatalities than most, perhaps, but nothing like the devastation of a California earthquake, a flood in Pakistan, or a ferry boat accident in Manila. Nevertheless, an ordinary tragedy like the Yuba City bus wreck brings questions snarling to the surface.

Why did those twenty-nine kids deserve a grisly mass highway death? Was God trying to tell them something? Or was he sending a warning to their parents and friends? If you were a teenager in Yuba City High School, you couldn't avoid those questions. And if you survived the bus accident as a passenger, the rest of your life you would wonder why you had lived when so many friends died.

Does God reach down, slightly twist the wheels of school buses, and watch them career through guardrails? Does he draw a red pencil line through a map of Indiana to plot the exact path of a tornado? *There, hit that house, kill that six-year-old, but skip over this next house.* Does God program the earth like a video game, constantly experimenting with tidal waves, seismic temblors, and hurricanes? Is that how he rewards and punishes us, his helpless victims?

Posing the questions so brazenly may sound sacrilegious. But they've long haunted me, and in various forms have been tossed at me like spears by agnostic friends. Wondering about God is an almost universal part of the experience of suffering. I have a book on my shelf, *Theories of Illness,* that surveys 139 tribal groups from around the world; all but four of them perceive illness as a sign of God's (or the gods') disapproval.

Pain has value in protecting physical bodies—almost everyone grants that. Suffering has some moral value in exposing our needful state as mortal creatures on a Groaning Planet; most Christians, at least, take that further step, accepting that God speaks to the human race in general through the megaphone of pain. But pain never comes to us *in general.* It comes in specific: in a synaptic firestorm of nerves and spinal cord, or in an emotional cloud of sorrow and grief.

I once watched a television interview with a famous Hollywood actress whose lover had drowned in a harbor near Los Angeles. The police investigation revealed he had rolled off a yacht in a drunken stupor. The actress looked at the camera, her beautiful features contorted by grief, and asked, bizarrely, "How could a loving God let this happen?"

That actress probably had not thought about God for months, or years. But suddenly, faced with suffering, she lashed out in anger against God. For her and for nearly everyone, doubt follows pain quickly and surely, like a reflex action. Suffering calls our most basic beliefs about God into question. When it strikes, I cannot help wondering: what is God trying to tell me by this strep throat? By my friend's death? Does he have a specific message for me?

At a banquet, a guest at my table referred to a recent earthquake in South America. "Did you know that a much lower percentage of Christians than non-Christians died in the earthquake?" he asked with utter sincerity. I wondered about the Christians who did not survive—what had they done to deserve being cast in with the vulnerable pagans? And I wondered about the hint of smugness in his remark—like the old Colosseum scores: Christians 4, Gladiators 3.

I also thought about occasional tragedies that seem to target Christians: the Armenian massacres, a bus accident involving a church choir, a flash flood that ravaged a Campus Crusade campground in Estes Park, Colorado, a dam break at Toccoa Falls Bible College. Faith in God offers no insurance against tragedy.

Nor does it offer insurance against feelings of doubt and betrayal. If anything, being a Christian complicates the issue. If you believe in a world of pure chance, what difference does it make whether a bus from Yuba City or one from Salina crashes? But if you believe in a world ruled by a powerful God who loves you tenderly, then it makes an awful difference.

What the Bible Says

Much of the mental turmoil about pain and suffering hinges, I think, on the important issue of *cause*. If God is truly in charge, somehow connected to all the world's suffering, why is he so capricious, unfair? Is he the cosmic Sadist who delights in watching us squirm, who stamps out human beings like cigarette butts?

If you scour the Bible for an answer to the question, "Who did it?" you will come away with mixed answers. To illustrate this, I have sometimes handed out Bibles to individuals within a group, asking them to read a passage and comment on what answer it gives to the *cause* question.

Genesis 38:7. Quite clearly, God is portrayed as the direct cause of Er's suffering. He "was wicked in the Lord's sight; so the Lord put him to death."

Luke 13:10–16. Satan, or at least "a spirit" was the direct cause of this woman's infirmity, a condition that had crippled her for eighteen years. The apostle Paul also called his affliction, the thorn in his flesh, "a messenger of Satan."

Job 2:4–7. Job offers a combination of the two causes: Satan inflicts the pain, but only after obtaining God's permission.

Proverbs 26:27. This verse, typical of Proverbs, stresses the natural consequences of a person's actions: follow an evil pattern and you will one day suffer because of it.

As I explained in the first chapter, this book came about because of my friendship with Claudia Claxton and my concern over the muddled advice she received from fellow Christians. In view of these Bible passages, is there any wonder people have such confused words of advice? I could list dozens of passages that offer various explanations for the cause of specific suffering, but I have yet to find in the Bible any grand unifying theory of causation.

The Old Testament, in particular, presents many situations—the ten plagues on Egypt, for example—in which God supernaturally intervened in human history in order to punish evil. I have studied each of these instances in detail, and though I cannot propose a grand unifying theory, I can offer two overall observations.

(1) Many Old Testament passages warn against painful consequences that will follow specific actions. The German biblical scholar Klaus Kloch persuasively shows that Psalms, Proverbs, and most other Old Testament books present this notion of "wrong choices lead to painful consequences."[2] Proverbs is full of such advice: "Laziness brings on deep sleep, and the shiftless man goes hungry" (19:15). As those authors saw it, God set up human beings and human society to operate according to fixed principles. Honesty, truthfulness, and compassion yield good results; cheating, lying, and greed yield just the opposite.

(2) Some Old Testament passages show God causing human suffering as punishment for wrong behavior. The prophetic books bristle with dire warnings of judgment to come. But look closer. Their predictions of doom usually follow a long, explicit forewarning. Amos, Jeremiah, Isaiah, Habakkuk, Hosea, and

Ezekiel all spell out impressive lists of sin and wickedness that will provoke the punishment.

In almost every case, the prophets also hold out the hope that God will restrain himself if Israel repents and turns back to God. If she continues in rebellion, she will be crushed. Thus the judgment clearly comes from God, but is in no way capricious or unjust. Old Testament punishment was consistent with God's "covenant," or contract, with Israel, and came after much warning.

I agree that the Old Testament is replete with reward/punishment type of thinking, and presents life in terms of this principle: "Do good, get rewarded; do bad, get punished." However, I do not believe the principle applies in precisely the same way today. In the book *Disappointment with God,* I argue that the "rules" governing God's contract relationship with the Israelites expressed a unique relationship that we cannot, nor should we expect to, emulate.

Consider the principles from the Old Testament in light of the kinds of questions people raise today. "Why me?" we ask almost instinctively when tragedy hits. Claudia Claxton asked that question, as did the grieving friends and relatives in Yuba City, and even the actress who lost her lover. *Two thousand cars were driving in the rain on the expressway—why did mine skid into a bridge? Lift lines were crowded with skiers all day—why was I the one to break a leg and ruin my vacation? A rare type of cancer strikes only one in a hundred people—why did my father have to be among the victims?*

Suffering people torment themselves with such questions, and the biblical examples offer some guidance. As to the first overall observation, that certain actions may lead to painful consequences, that principle applies in full force today. A person who skis beyond a boundary, toward avalanche country and ungroomed slopes, puts her life in peril. A person who speeds on rain-slick highways courts the danger of hydroplaning. A person who eats all fried foods and Twinkies exposes his body to certain health risks.

The book of Proverbs goes further than these simple examples, making clear that our actions have a moral dimension that will affect our health and comfort on earth. Our modern versions—smoking, promiscuous sex, doing drugs, abusing the environment, gluttony—all have direct and painful consequences. Scientists recognize the connections and advertise them widely. The principles, built into creation, apply to Christians and non-Christians alike. Actuarial tables demonstrate this fact beyond dispute: Utah, home of health-conscious Mormons, has one of the lowest rates of heart disease while its neighbor Nevada, home of loose living, has one of the highest.

What of the second principle, that God sometimes intervenes directly, to punish people for wrong behavior? I have been astonished at how commonly and unthinkingly Christians apply that principle today. They visit the hospital room bearing gifts of guilt ("You must have done something to deserve this") and accusation ("You must not be praying hard enough").

But there is a huge difference between the suffering most of us encounter—a skiing injury, a rare form of cancer, the bus accident—and the suffering-as-punishment described in the Old Testament. There, punishment follows repeated warnings against specific behavior. To be effective, in fact, punishment *requires* a clear tie to behavior. Think of a parent who punishes a young child. It would do little good for that parent to sneak up at odd times during a day and whack the child with no explanation. Such tactics would produce a neurotic, not an obedient, child.

The people of Israel knew why they were being punished; the prophets had warned them in excruciating detail. The Pharaoh of Egypt knew exactly why the ten plagues were unleashed against his land: God had predicted them, told him why, and described what change of heart could forestall them. Biblical examples of suffering-as-punishment, then, tend to fit a pattern. The pain comes after much warning, and no one sits around afterward asking, "Why?" They know very well why they are suffering.

Does that pattern resemble what happens to most of us today? Do we get a direct revelation from God warning us of a coming catastrophe? Does personal suffering come packaged with a clear explanation from God? If not, I must question whether the pains most of us feel—cancer, a traffic mishap—are indeed punishments from God. If suffering does come as punishment, we are getting confusing messages indeed, for the occurrence of disease and pain seems random, unrelated to any pattern of virtue or vice.

Frankly, I believe that unless God distinctly reveals otherwise, we would do better to look to other biblical models. And the Bible contains some stories of people who suffered but definitely were not being punished by God.

What Jesus Says

Christians believe that with the coming of Jesus, God fully entered human history. He was no longer "out there," sometimes dipping into history to change things. Now he resided in the body of a human being on earth, making himself subject to the physical laws and limitations of this planet. Therefore, the best clue we have into how God feels about human pain is to look at Jesus' response.

Jesus never gave a poor or suffering person a speech about "accepting your lot in life," or "taking the medicine that God has given you." He seemed unusually sensitive to the groans of suffering people, and set about remedying them. And he used his supernatural powers to heal, never to punish.

Miracles of healing were great crowd pleasers, of course, but even so Jesus refused to make them the centerpiece of his ministry. More than anything, he used physical healings as "signs" of some deeper truth. At times Jesus seemed almost reluctant to intervene, telling his followers he performed the signs only because they had need of them. Often he hushed up the spreading rumors about his miracles. On certain occasions Jesus deliberately elected not to intervene in the natural order of things, for example, by not calling on angels to deliver him from his most painful hour.

Was Jesus saying to us that it is not good for God to intervene in our world on a day-to-day basis? The important thing, the kingdom of heaven—isn't that a kingdom of the spirit to be worked out inside hearts and minds, not by an external, spectacular display of God's power? At the least, Jesus declined to make radical changes in the natural laws governing the planet. Rather than, say, rewiring the nervous system to make some design improvement, he himself took on the pain network with all its undesirable features. And when he faced suffering personally, he reacted much as we do: with fear and dread.

How did Jesus deal with the question "Who is responsible for suffering?" The clearest insight into that question appears in Luke 13. Again, just as in the Old Testament, there are several answers. For example, in verse 16 Jesus declares that Satan caused the pain of a woman bound in disease for eighteen years. And at the end of the chapter, Jesus grieves over the future of Jerusalem: like the Old Testament prophets, he could see that her actions of stubborn rebellion would bring about much suffering.

But early on in that same chapter, Jesus is asked about two "current events" that had evidently prompted much local discussion. One was an act of political oppression, in which Roman soldiers slaughtered members of a religious minority; the other, a construction accident that killed eighteen people. As I study the Bible, I can find no other situation more parallel to the kinds of suffering that bother most of us. Those first-century Jews were asking about their equivalents to the Yuba City bus accident, or the collapse of a stadium roof.

Jesus' response is at once enigmatic and brilliant. He does not fully answer the question most on their mind, the question of cause. Jesus never explains, "Here's why those two tragedies occurred." But he makes one thing clear: they did not occur as a result of specific wrongdoing: "Do you think that these Galileans were worse sinners than all the other Galileans because they suffered this way? I tell you, no! . . . Or those eighteen who died when the tower in Siloam fell on them—do you think they were more guilty than all the others living in Jerusalem? I tell you, no!"

No grieving relative need stand around wondering what brought about the calamity; Jesus makes plain that the victims had done nothing unusual to deserve their fates. They were the same as other persons. He doesn't say so, but perhaps the tower simply fell because it was built poorly. I believe Jesus would have replied similarly to the Yuba City tragedy: "Do you think they were worse sinners than other teenagers?" Perhaps the bus crashed because of driver error or mechanical failure.

But Jesus does not stop there. He uses both tragedies to point to eternal truths relevant to everyone ("Unless you repent, you too will all perish") and follows with a parable about God's restraining mercy. He implies that we "bystanders" of catastrophe have as much to learn from the event as do the victims. A tragedy should alert us to make ourselves ready in case we are the next victim of a falling tower, or an act of political terrorism.

Catastrophe thus joins together victim and bystander in a call to repentance, by abruptly reminding us of the brevity of life.

Is God the Cause?

I once attended a funeral service for a teenage girl killed in a car accident. Her mother wailed, "The Lord took her home. He must have had some purpose. . . . Thank you, Lord." I have been with sick Christian people who agonize over the question, "What is God trying to teach me?" Or, they may plead, "How can I find enough faith to get rid of this illness? How can I get God to rescue me?"

Maybe such people have it all wrong. Maybe God *isn't trying to tell us anything specific* each time we hurt. Pain and suffering are part and parcel of our planet, and Christians are not exempt. Half the time we know why we get sick: too little exercise, a poor diet, contact with a germ. Do we really expect God to go around protecting us whenever we encounter something dangerous?

As I understand it, the approach Jesus takes corresponds exactly to what I have suggested about "pain, the megaphone of God." Suffering offers a *general* message of warning to all humanity that something is wrong with this planet, and that we need radical outside intervention ("Unless you repent. . . ."). But you cannot argue backward and link someone's *specific* pain to a direct act of God.

Another, similar story from the Gospels may clarify this approach even further. In John 9, Jesus refutes the traditional explanation of suffering. His followers point to a man born blind. Clucking with pity, they ask, "Who sinned, this man or his parents?" In other words, why did he deserve blindness? Jesus answers bluntly, "Neither this man nor his parents sinned, but this happened so that the work of God might be displayed in his life."

The disciples wanted to look backward, to find out "Why?" Jesus redirected their attention. Consistently, he points forward, answering a different question: "To what end?" And that, I believe, offers a neat summary of the Bible's approach to the problem of pain. To backward-looking questions of cause, to the "Why?" questions, it gives no definitive answer. But it does hold out hope for the future, that even suffering can be transformed or "redeemed." A human tragedy, like blindness, can be used to display God's work.

Sometimes, as with the man born blind, the work of God is manifest through dramatic miracle. Sometimes it is not. But in every case, suffering offers an opportunity for us to display God's work.

It was only when I lay there on rotting prison straw that I sensed within myself the first stirrings of good. Gradually, it was disclosed to me that the line separating good and evil passes not through states, nor between classes, nor between political parties either—but right through every human heart—and through all human hearts ... I nourished my soul there, and I say without hesitation: Bless you, prison, for having been in my life.

Alexander Solzhenitsyn
The Gulag Archipelago

7

Why Are We Here?

The Bible may seem to give mixed signals on the question of cause. But its most exhaustive treatment of the topic of suffering has an unmistakable message. It appears in the book of Job, smack in the middle of the Old Testament.

One of the oldest stories in the Bible, Job nevertheless reads like the most modern, for it faces head-on the problem of pain that so bedevils our century. In recent times, such authors as Robert Frost, Archibald MacLeish, and Muriel Spark have all tried their hands at retelling the story of Job.

Job, the most upright, spiritual man of his day, loves God with all his heart. Indeed, God handpicks him to demonstrate to Satan how faithful some humans can be. If anyone does not deserve suffering for his actions, it is Job.

But what happens? Incredibly, a series of wretched calamities descend upon Job, any one of which would suffice to crush most people. Raiders, fire, bandits, and a great wind ravage his ranch and destroy all his possessions. Of Job's large family only his wife survives, and she is scant comfort. Then, in a second phase of trials, Job breaks out in ulcerous boils.

Thus in a matter of hours all the terrors of hell are poured out on poor Job, utterly reversing his fortune and his health. He scratches his sores and moans. The pain he can somehow put up with. What bothers him more is the sense of betrayal. Until now he has always believed in a loving, fair God. But the facts simply don't add up. He asks anguished questions, the same questions asked by nearly everyone in great pain. *Why me? What did I do wrong? What is God trying to tell me?*

In that setting, Job and his friends discuss the mystery of suffering. The friends, devout and reverent men, fill the air with erudition. Boiled down, their arguments are virtually identical. *Job, God is trying to tell you something. No one suffers without cause. Common sense and all reason tell us that a just God will treat people fairly. Those who obey and remain faithful, he rewards. Those who sin, he punishes. Therefore, confess your sin, and God will relieve your misery.*

Job's wife suggests one more alternative: Curse God and die. Job, however, can't accept that choice either. Although what has happened to him does not correspond to justice, he simply can't bring himself to deny God. Where is the answer for Job? In desperation, he even toys with the notion of God as a Sadist who "mocks the despair of the innocent" (9:23).

In the face of his friends' verbal assaults Job wavers, contradicts himself, and sometimes even agrees with them. But as he reflects on life, he also recognizes other signs of unfairness. Thieves grow fat and prosper, while some holy men live in poverty and pain. Evidently, evil and good are not always punished and rewarded in this life.

Job's own uncontrolled outbursts contrast with the calm reason of his friends. But as he mulls over his particular case, he concludes they are wrong. Against all evidence, he holds on to two seemingly contradictory beliefs: he, Job, does not deserve his tragedy, but still God deserves his loyalty. Job holds firm in the face of such jabs as "Are you more righteous than God?"

Perhaps the most unsettling aspect of the book is that the arguments of Job's friends sound suspiciously like those offered by Christians today. One must search hard for a defense of suffering, in this book or any other, that does not appear somewhere in their speeches. And yet, in a wonderful ironic twist at the end of the book, God dismisses all their high-sounding theories with a scowl. "I am angry with you and your two friends," God said to one, "because you have not spoken of me what is right, as my servant Job has" (42:7).

Thus even in the Old Testament, where suffering is so frequently identified with God's punishment, Job's example shines brightly. The book of Job should nail a coffin lid over the idea that every time we suffer it's because God is punishing us or trying to tell us something. Although the Bible supports the general principle that "a man reaps what he sows" even in this life (see Psalms 1:3; 37:25), the book of Job proves that other people have no right to apply that general principle to a particular person. Nobody deserved suffering less than Job, and yet few have suffered more.

A Perfectly Fair World

On the surface, the book of Job centers around the problem of suffering, the same problem I have been discussing in this book. Underneath, a different issue is at stake: the doctrine of human freedom. Job had to endure undeserved suffering in order to demonstrate that God is ultimately interested in freely given love.

It is a hard truth, one at which great minds have stumbled. C. G. Jung, for example, went to strange lengths to account for God's behavior in the book of Job. He taught that God decided on the Incarnation and Jesus' death as a guilt response to the way he had treated Job. God entered the world in Jesus so that he could grow in moral consciousness.[1]

Jung may be underestimating the premium God places on freely given love. The trials of Job stemmed from a debate in heaven over the question, "Are human beings truly free?" In the first two chapters of Job, Satan reveals himself as the first great behaviorist. He claimed that faith is merely a product of environment and circumstances. Job was *conditioned* to love God. Take away the positive rewards, Satan challenged, and watch Job's faith crumble. Poor Job, oblivious, was selected for the cosmic contest to determine this crucial matter of human freedom.

The contest posed between Satan and God was no trivial exercise. Satan's accusation that Job loved God only because "you have put a hedge around him," stands as an attack on God's character. It implies that God is not worthy of love in himself; faithful people like Job follow him only because they are "bribed" to do so. Job's response when all the props of faith were removed would prove or disprove Satan's challenge.

To understand this issue of human freedom, it helps me to imagine a world in which everyone truly does get what he or she deserves. What would a world of perfect fairness look like?

In a perfectly fair world, morality would operate according to fixed laws, just like the laws of nature. Punishment for wrongdoing would work like physical pain. If you touch a flame, you are "punished" instantly with a pain warning; a fair world would punish sin just that swiftly and surely. Extend your hand to shoplift, and you'd get an electrical shock. Likewise, a fair world would reward good behavior: Fill out an IRS form honestly, and you'd earn a pleasure sensation, like a trained seal given a fish.

That imaginary world has a certain appeal. It would be just and consistent, and everyone would clearly know what God expected. Fairness would reign. There is, however, one huge problem with such a tidy world: it's not at all what God wants to accomplish on earth. He wants from us love, freely given love, and we dare not underestimate the premium God places on that love. Freely given love is so important to God that he allows our planet to be a cancer of evil in his universe—for a time.

If this world ran according to fixed, perfectly fair rules, there would be no true freedom. We would act rightly because of our own immediate gain, and selfish motives would taint every act of goodness. We would love God because of a programmed, inborn hunger, not because of a deliberate choice in the face of attractive alternatives. It would be a B. F. Skinner, automaton world of action/response, action/response. In contrast, the Christian virtues described in the Bible develop when we choose God and his ways in spite of temptation or impulses to do otherwise.

Throughout the Bible, an analogy that illustrates the relationship between God and his people keeps surfacing. God, the husband, is pictured as wooing the bride to himself. He wants her love. If the world were constructed so that every sin earned a punishment and every good deed a reward, the parallel would not hold. The closest analogue to that relationship would be a kept woman, who is pampered and bribed and locked away in a room so that the lover can be sure of her faithfulness. God does not "keep" his people. He loves us, gives himself to us, and eagerly awaits our free response.

God wants us to choose to love him freely, even when that choice involves pain, because we are committed to him, not to our own good feelings and rewards. He wants us to cleave to him, as Job did, even when we have every reason to deny him hotly. That, I believe, is the central message of Job. Satan had taunted God with the accusation that humans are not truly free. Was Job being faithful simply because God had allowed him a prosperous life? Job's fiery trials proved the answer beyond doubt. Job clung to God's justice when he was the best example in history of God's apparent injustice. He did not seek the Giver because of his gifts; when all gifts were removed he still sought the Giver.

Vale of Soul-Making

If a world of perfect fairness would not produce what God wants from us, our freely given love, neither would it produce what God wants *for* us. In the first few chapters I used the example of leprosy to demonstrate that pain is valuable, even essential, for life on this planet. In a related way, suffering can become a valuable instrument in accomplishing God's goals for human beings.

I have said that the megaphone of pain makes it difficult to accept that we have been placed on this "groaning" planet to pursue hedonistic pleasure. But if our happiness is not God's goal, what, then, does God intend for this world? Why bother with us at all?

To help understand, think of an illustration from a human family. A father determined to exclude all pain from his beloved daughter's life would never allow her to take a step. She might fall down! Instead, he picks her up and carries her wherever she goes or pushes her in a carriage. Over time such a pampered child will become an invalid, unable to take a step, totally dependent on her father.

Such a father, no matter how loving, would end up failing in his most important task: to nurture an independent person into adulthood. It would be far better *for the daughter herself* if her father stands back and lets her walk, even if it means allowing her to stumble. Apply the analogy directly to Job who, by standing on his own in the midst of suffering, without the benefit of soothing answers, gained powerful new strength. As Rabbi Abraham Heschel has said, "Faith like Job's cannot be shaken because it is the result of having been shaken."

C. S. Lewis expands on this idea in *The Problem of Pain,* where he says in part:

> We want not so much a father in heaven as a grandfather in heaven—whose plan for the universe was such that it might be said at the end of each day, "A good time was had by all."
>
> I should very much like to live in a universe which was governed on such lines, but since it is abundantly clear that I don't, and since I have reason to believe nevertheless that God is love, I conclude that my conception of love needs correction. . . .
>
> Over a sketch made idly to amuse a child, an artist may not take much trouble: he may be content to let it go even though it is not exactly as he meant it to be. But over the great picture of his life—the work which he loves, though in a different fashion, as intensely as a man loves a woman or a mother a child—he will take endless trouble—and would, doubtless, thereby give endless trouble to the picture if it were sentient. One can imagine a sentient picture, after being rubbed and scraped and re-commenced for the tenth time, wishing that it were only a thumb-nail sketch whose making was over in a minute. In the same way, it is natural for us to wish that God had designed for us a less glorious and less arduous destiny; but then we are wishing not for more love but for less.[2]

Once again, these issues trace back to the most basic questions of human existence. Why are we here? The presence of suffering puzzles or even enrages those people who assume that human beings are fully formed creatures who need a suitable home. In the Christian view, though, as Professor John Hick has summarized it in the book *Philosophy of Religion,* God is dealing with incomplete creatures. The environment of earth should therefore primarily nurture the process of "soul-making."

We have already seen some advantages of a world of fixed laws and human freedom, even though humans can abuse the freedom and harm one another. John Hick explores another alternative, envisioning a Utopian world designed to protect us from all pain and evil, and concludes that a world free of mistakes would actually abort God's purpose for us.

§   Suppose, contrary to fact, that this world were a paradise from which all possibility of pain and suffering were excluded. The consequences would be very far-reaching. For example, no one could ever injure anyone else: the murderer's knife would turn to paper or his bullets to thin air; the bank safe, robbed of a million dollars, would miraculously become filled with another million dollars (without this device, on however large a scale, proving inflationary); fraud, deceit, conspiracy, and treason would somehow always leave the fabric of society undamaged. Again, no one would ever be injured by accident: the mountain-climber, steeple-jack, or playing child falling from a height would float unharmed to the ground; the reckless driver would never meet with disaster. There would be no need to work; there would be no call to be concerned for others in time of need or danger, for in such a world there could be no real needs or dangers.

To make possible this continual series of individual adjustments, nature would have to work "special providences" instead of running according to general laws which men must learn to respect on penalty of pain and death. The laws of nature would have to be extremely flexible: sometimes an object would be hard and solid, sometimes soft. . . .

One can at least begin to imagine such a world. It is evident that our present ethical concepts would have no meaning in it. If, for example, the notion of harming someone is an essential element in the concept of wrong action, in our hedonistic paradise there could be no wrong actions—nor any right actions in distinction from wrong. Courage and fortitude would have no point in an environment in which there is, by definition, no danger or difficulty. Generosity, kindness, the *agape* aspect of love, prudence, unselfishness, and all other ethical notions which presuppose life in a stable environment, could not even be formed. Consequently, such a world, however well it might promote pleasure, would be very ill adapted for the

§   development of the moral qualities of human personality. In relation to this purpose it would be the worst of all possible worlds.

It would seem, then, that an environment intended to make possible the growth in free beings of the finest characteristics of personal life, must have a good deal in common with our present world. It must operate according to general and dependable laws; and it must involve real dangers, difficulties, problems, obstacles, and possibilities of pain, failure, sorrow, frustration, and defeat. If it did not contain the particular trials and perils which—subtracting man's own very considerable contribution—our world contains it would have to contain others instead.

To realize this is . . . to understand that this world, with all its "heartaches and the thousand natural shocks that flesh is heir to," an environment so manifestly not designed for the maximization of human pleasure and the minimization of human pain, may be rather well adapted to the quite different purpose of "soul-making."[3]

In some ways it would be easier for God to step in, to have faith for us, to help us in extraordinary ways. But he has instead chosen to stand before us, arms extended, while he asks *us* to walk, to participate in our own soul-making. That process always involves struggle, and often involves suffering.

To What End?

The notion of earth as a "vale of soul-making" (the poet John Keats's phrase) sheds light on some of the most difficult passages in the Bible. Although the Bible remains vague on the cause of specific sufferings, it does give many examples, as in this verse from Amos, of God using pain for a purpose: "'I gave you empty stomachs in every city and lack of bread in every town, yet you have not returned to me,' declares the Lord" (Amos 4:6). On almost every page the Hebrew prophets warned Israelites that they would face calamity if they continued to flout God's laws.

Most of us operate on a different scale of values than God. We would rank life as the greatest value (and thus murder as the greatest crime). "Life, liberty, and the pursuit of happiness" is how the founding fathers of the United States defined the highest values a government should strive to protect. But clearly God operates from a different perspective. He indeed values human life, so much so that he declared it "sacred," meaning he alone, and no human being, has the right to take life. But in Noah's day, for example, God did not hesitate to exercise that right; numerous times in the Old Testament he took human life in order to halt the spread of evil.

Similarly, many Bible passages show that some things are more awful to God than the pain of his children. Consider the sufferings of Job, or Jeremiah, or Hosea. God did not even exempt himself from suffering: consider the awesome pain involved in himself becoming a man and dying on a cross. Do these show God's lack of compassion? Or do they, rather, demonstrate that some things are more important to God than a suffering-free life for even his most loyal followers?

As I have said, the Bible consistently changes the questions we bring to the problem of pain. It rarely, or ambiguously, answers the backward-looking question "Why?" Instead, it raises the very different, forward-looking question, "To what end?" We are not put on earth merely to satisfy our desires, to pursue life, liberty, and happiness. We are here to be changed, to be made more like God in order to prepare us for a lifetime with him. And that process may be served by the mysterious pattern of all creation: pleasure sometimes emerges against a background of pain, evil may be transformed into good, and suffering may produce something of value.

Is God speaking to us through our sufferings? It is dangerous and perhaps even unscriptural to torture ourselves by looking for his message in a specific throb of pain, a specific instance of suffering. The message may simply be that we live in a world with fixed laws, like everyone else. But from the larger view, from the view of all history, yes, God speaks to us through suffering—or perhaps in spite of suffering. The symphony he is composing includes minor chords, dissonance, and tiresome fugal passages. But those of us who follow his conducting through early movements will, with renewed strength, someday burst into song.

Two Great Errors

Discussions about the problem of pain tend to drift toward the abstract and philosophical. Phrases like "the best of all possible worlds," "the advantages of human freedom," and "vale of soul-making" creep in, and these can deflect attention away from the actual problems of people in pain. Yet I have felt it necessary to explore some of these issues because I believe they have a direct and practical effect on our response to suffering.

In fact, I believe Christians walk a mental tightrope and are in constant danger of falling in one of two directions. On this subject, errors in thinking can have tragic results.

The first error comes when we attribute all suffering to God, seeing it as his punishment for human mistakes; the second error does just the opposite, assuming that life with God will never include suffering.

I have already mentioned one unfortunate consequence of the first error. I have interviewed many Christians with life-threatening illnesses, and every one without exception has told me how damaging it can be to have a visitor plant the thought, "You must have done something to deserve this punishment." At the very moment when they most need hope and strength to battle the illness, they get instead a frosty dose of guilt and self-doubt. I'm glad the author of Job took such care to record the rambling conversations of Job's friends: that book serves as a permanent reminder to me that I have no right to stand beside a suffering person and pronounce, "This is the will of God," no matter how I cloak that sentiment in pious phrases.

The error of attributing all suffering to God's punishment has far-reaching consequences, as the history of the church has grievously shown. During the late Middle Ages, women were burned at the stake for the heretical act of taking pain-relieving medicines for childbirth. "In sorrow shalt thou bring forth children," priests admonished as they condemned the women to death.[4] And after Edward Jenner had perfected the smallpox vaccine he faced his strongest opposition from clergy, who opposed any interference with the will of God. Even today some religious sects reject modern medical treatment.

Secular writers have seized on this weakness. In his novel *The Plague*, Albert Camus portrays a Catholic priest, Father Paneloux, torn by a dilemma. Should he devote his energy to fighting the plague or to teaching his parishioners to accept it as from God? He grapples with this issue in a sermon: "Paneloux assured those present that it was not easy to say what he was about to say—since it was God's will, we, too, should will it. Thus and thus only the Christian could face the problem squarely.... The sufferings of children were our bread of affliction, but without this bread our souls would die of spiritual hunger." Father Paneloux preaches this, but cannot quite believe it: later in the novel he abandons his faith after watching a small child die horribly of the plague.[5]

If the Bible were not so pronounced in denying that all suffering results from specific sins, if it did not paint Job's predicament in such sweeping terms, if it did not show the Son of God spending his days on earth healing diseases and not inflicting them, then the dilemma that Camus posed would be unresolvable. For, if we accept that suffering comes from God as a lesson to us (as, for example Islam does), the next logical step would be a resigned fatalism. Polio, AIDS, malaria, bubonic plague, cancer, yellow fever—why should a person fight any of these if they are God's agents sent to teach us a lesson?

When the Black Death hit England in the seventeenth century, some street prophets delighted in pronouncing the plague a judgment from God. But other believers, among them doctors and clergy, chose to stay in London to fight the disease. One sacrificial rector gathered the 350 villagers of Eyam around him and got them to agree to a self-imposed quarantine as a health measure to keep the plague among them from spreading to surrounding villages. In all, 259 villagers died, but in the process they ministered to each other in their illness and prevented further contamination.

In his *Journal of the Plague Year,* Daniel Defoe contrasted the Christians' response with the Mohammedans'. When plague struck the Middle East, the religious fatalists there did not alter their behavior in the least, but continued going out in public at will. A much higher percentage among them died than among the Londoners who took precautions.[6]

In modern times, some Christians still lean dangerously toward a fatalism that more befits Islam or Hinduism than Christianity. Several years ago researchers studied why Southerners in the U.S. tended to suffer a higher frequency of tornado-related deaths than Midwesterners. After taking into account such factors as differences in building materials, the researchers concluded that some Southerners, being more religious, had developed a fatalistic attitude toward disaster: "If it hits, it hits, and there's nothing I can do to stop it." In contrast, Midwesterners were more likely to listen to weather reports, secure loose equipment, and take shelter.[7]

If the researchers' conclusions are accurate, I take that trend as a dangerous perversion of Christian dogma. Southerners should listen to the weather service and take precautions. Father Paneloux should have been on the front lines, arms linked with doctors, battling the plague. Jesus himself spent his life on earth fighting disease and despair. Not once did he hint at fatalism or a resigned acceptance of suffering.

We the inhabitants of this "groaning" planet have the right, even the obligation, to fight against human suffering. Anyone who thinks otherwise should reread the parable of the Good Samaritan in Luke 10, and the parable of the sheep and the goats in Matthew 25.

Health and Wealth Theology

In recent times, some parts of the church have tilted in a very different direction, toward the second great error. They teach that life with God will never include suffering. Such a "health and wealth theology" could only spring up in times of affluence, in a society well-stocked with pain-relieving aids.

Christians in Iran, say, or Cambodia could hardly come up with such a smiley-face theology. As one East European Christian observed, "You Western Christians often seem to consider material prosperity to be the only sign of God's blessing. On the other hand, you often seem to perceive poverty, discomfort, and suffering as signs of God's disfavor. In some ways we in the East understand suffering from the opposite perspective. We believe that suffering may be a sign of God's favor and trust in the Christians to whom the trial is permitted to come."[8]

Nowadays we reserve our shiniest merit badges for those who have been miraculously healed, featuring them in magazine articles and television specials, holding out the unreserved promise that healing is available to everyone if only they would claim it.

In no way do I mean to discount the wonderfulness of physical healing. But obviously miracles do not offer a permanent solution for the problem of suffering because the eventual mortality rate is exactly the same for Christians and non-Christians alike—100 percent. We all have eyes subject to the need for corrective lenses, bones subject to breaking, and soft tissue subject to destruction from auto accidents and terrorist bombs. Christians get cancer too; they fully share the sorrow of this world.

The modern emphasis on miraculous healing has the frequent side effect of causing unhealed ones to feel as though God has passed them by. Recently I watched a televised call-in healing program. The biggest applause came when a caller reported his leg had been healed just one week before he was scheduled for amputation. The audience yelled, and the emcee burbled, "This is the best miracle we've had tonight!" I couldn't help wondering how many amputees were watching, forlornly wondering where their faith had failed.

Unlike many television evangelists, the apostle Paul seemed to expect from the Christian life not health and wealth, but a measure of suffering. He told Timothy, "In fact, everyone who wants to live a godly life in Christ Jesus will be persecuted" (2 Timothy 3:12). A sick person is not unspiritual. And Christian faith does not magically equip us with a germ-free, hermetically sealed space suit to protect against the dangers of earth. That would insulate us from complete identification with the world—a luxury God did not allow his own Son.

To hold out the inducement that becoming a Christian will guarantee you health and prosperity—why, that is the very argument advanced by Satan in the book of Job, and decisively refuted.

To restore balance to this issue, we would do well to relearn the lessons about faith taught in the Bible's greatest chapter on the subject, Hebrews 11. The author compiles a list of faithful persons through the centuries. Most of the saints listed in the first part of the chapter received miraculous deliverance: Isaac, Joseph, Moses, Rahab, Gideon, David. But the latter part of the chapter mentions others who were tortured and chained, stoned, and sawed in two.

Hebrews 11 gives vivid details about the second group: they went about in sheepskins and goatskins, were destitute, wandered in deserts and mountains, and lived in holes in the ground. The chapter offers the blunt assessment, "These were all commended for their faith, yet none of them received what had been promised." It adds, though, God's own appraisal of these sojourners on earth who placed their hopes in a better, heavenly country: "Therefore God is not ashamed to be called their God, for he has prepared a city for them."

I thought about this list of "God's favorites" recently as I read through *Fear No Evil*, the last book written by David Watson, a well-known English preacher and writer. Struck down with colon cancer at the height of his career, Watson rallied his Christian friends around him and began a desperate journey of faith. He had gained prominence in the charismatic movement, and Watson and most of his friends were convinced that God would solve the cancer through a miraculous healing.

Over time, as Watson grew sicker and weaker, he had to reach for another kind of faith, the kind cultivated by the saints mentioned in the latter part of Hebrews 11. He needed the faith that sustained Job, barely, in his darkest days, and his book tells how he attained that faith.

David Watson wrote the last words of his book in January, and died in February. Many people received his book with a touch of disappointment; they had hoped rather for an account of supernatural healing. But J. I. Packer, who wrote the foreword after Watson's death, saw it as recovering an ancient tradition of Christian books on the "art of dying." Until recently, a good death was seen as a godly man's crowning achievement, the climax of his good life.

Packer gives this assessment:

> The fact that David, right to his last page, hopes for supernatural healing that never comes is not important. In the providence of God, who does not always show his servants the true point of the books he stirs them to write, the theme of *Fear No Evil* is the conquest of death—not by looking away from it, nor by being shielded from it, but by facing it squarely and going down into it knowing that for a believer it is the vestibule of glory.
>
> David's theology led him to believe, right to the end, that God wanted to heal his body. Mine leads me rather to say that God evidently wanted David home, and healed his whole person by taking him to glory in the way that he will one day heal us all. Health and life, I would say, in the full and final sense of those words, are not what we die *out of,* but what we die *into.*[9]

Some say that to the gods we are like flies that boys idly swat on a summer day. Others say that not a feather from a sparrow falls to the ground without the will of the Heavenly Father.

Thornton Wilder
The Bridge of San Luis Rey

8

Arms Too Short to Box with God

You are lying in a hospital bed, kept alive artificially by tubes of plastic spilling from your arm and nose. A killer tornado has destroyed everything you own. All you've worked for—your house, car, savings account—has disappeared forever. Your family decimated, you have no visitors except some rather cranky neighbors. You are barely hanging on to life.

You move through the usual stages of grief, your prayers and questions tinged with bitterness. *If only God would visit me personally and give some answers,* you say to yourself. *I want to believe him, but how can I? What has happened contradicts everything I know about a loving God. If I could just see him once and hear him explain why I must go through this hard time, then I could endure.*

One person in very similar straits to these got his wish. Job, the prototype of innocent suffering, received a personal visit from God himself, who answered him out of a whirlwind. God's reply to Job comprises one of his longest single speeches in the Bible, and because it appears at the end of the Bible's most complete treatise on suffering it merits a close-up look. Perhaps God has already recorded what he would say directly to us.

First, recall the setting. What could God say to Job? He might have laid a gentle hand on Job's head and told him how much he would grow in personhood through the time of trial. He might have expressed a little pride in Job, who had just won for him a decisive victory: "Job, I know you've had unfair treatment, but you came through. You don't know what this means to me and even to the universe." God might have delivered a lecture on the necessity of preserving human freedom, or on the tragic results of the Fall. (He might even have enlightened Job on the value of pain, explaining how much worse his life would be with leprosy!)

A few kind phrases, a smile of compassion, a brief explanation of what went on—any of these would have helped Job. God did nothing of the kind. To the contrary, he turned the tables on Job, rushing in aggressively,

> *Who is this that darkens my counsel*
> *with words without knowledge?*
> *Brace yourself like a man;*
> *I will question you,*
> *and you shall answer me. (38:2–3)*

From there, God proceeded to sweep Job off his feet with a series of questions—not answers—that virtually ignore thirty-five chapters' worth of debates on the problem of pain.

A Nature Lesson

Much has been made about God's magnificent speech in Job 38–41. In a passage that could be addressed to the Sierra Club or Audubon Society, God took Job on a verbal tour of all the wonders of nature. I, too, marvel at the splendid imagery, but along with my marvel comes a nagging sense of bewilderment. Why this speech, at this moment?

Readers who quote admiringly from God's speech, or needlepoint its beautiful poetry into slogans for wall plaques, may have lost sight of the context in which Job heard those majestic words: he was homeless, friendless, naked, ulcerous, in despair. What a time for a nature-appreciation course! Why did

God sidestep the very questions that had been tormenting poor Job?

Before a thoroughly dejected audience, God sang out with peals of divine glee. He called to mind:

sunrise. "Have you ever given orders to the morning, or shown the dawn its place . . . ?"

rain and snow. "Have you entered the storehouses of the snow or seen the storehouses of the hail? . . . From whose womb comes the ice? . . . Who can tip over the water jars of the heavens when the dust becomes hard and the clods of earth stick together?"

thunderstorms. "Who cuts a channel for the torrents of rain, and a path for the thunderstorm? . . . Do you send the lightning bolts on their way? Do they report to you, 'Here we are'?"

lions. "Do you hunt the prey for the lioness and satisfy the hunger of the lions when they crouch in their dens or lie in wait in a thicket?"

mountain goats. "Do you know when the mountain goats give birth? Do you watch when the doe bears her fawn?"

wild donkeys. "Who let the wild donkey go free? Who untied his ropes? I gave him the wasteland as his home, the salt flats as his habitat. He laughs at the commotion in the town; he does not hear a driver's shout."

the ostrich. "The wings of the ostrich flap joyfully, but they cannot compare with the pinions and feathers of the stork. . . . God did not endow her with wisdom or give her a share of good sense. Yet when she spreads her feathers to run, she laughs at horse and rider."

the horse. "Do you give the horse his strength or clothe his neck with a flowing mane? Do you make him leap like a locust, striking terror with his proud snorting?"

birds of prey. "Does the hawk take flight by your wisdom and spread his wings toward the south? Does the eagle soar at your command and build his nest on high?" (from Job 38– 39)

Stalking lionesses, soaring eagles, streaks of lightning, crocodiles, wild oxen—God summoned up these and other images for Job with the satisfaction and delight of a proud artist. After each description, he either stated or implied, "Job, are you powerful enough to duplicate these feats? Are you wise enough to run the world? . . . Do you have an arm like God's, and can your voice thunder like his?" God even employed sarcasm in 38:21: "Surely you know, for you were already born! You have lived so many years!"

God's words hit Job with devastating power, prompting an overwhelmed, repentant surrender. "I know that you can do all things; no plan of yours can be thwarted. . . . Surely I spoke of things I did not understand, things too wonderful for me to know" (42:2–3).

Did God answer Job's questions about suffering and unfairness? Not really. He seemed deliberately to avoid a logical, point-by-point explanation. (I find it ironic that so many people have written books attempting to defend God's reputation as it regards this messy problem of pain when God himself saw no need for self-defense.) Why, then, the combative tone? What did God want from Job?

God wanted, simply, an admission of trust. The message looming behind the splendid poetry reduces down to this: *Until you know a little more about running the physical universe, Job, don't tell me how to run the moral universe.*

If we, like Job, are so ignorant about the wonders of the world we live in, a world we can see and touch, who are we to sit in judgment of God's moral government of the universe? Until we are wise enough to orchestrate a blizzard—or even manufacture a single perfect snowflake—we have no grounds to sue God. Let him who is about to accuse God consider the greatness of the God accused.

A God wise enough to rule the universe is wise enough to watch over his child Job, regardless of how things seem in the bleakest moments. A God wise enough to create me and the world I live in is wise enough to watch out for me.

A Best-seller's Oversight

God's speech at the end of Job is one of the central reasons I cannot agree with the conclusions of a well-written popular book on the problem of pain, *When Bad Things Happen to Good People*. Rabbi Harold Kushner wrote it after watching his son battle the cruel disease progeria, which bizarrely speeds up the aging process so that the young boy grew bald, wrinkled, and weak, then finally died.

In the book, which became a surprise best-seller, Kushner explains that he learned to accept God's love but question God's power. He came to believe that God is good, and hates to see us suffer, but simply is not powerful enough to straighten out the problems of this world—problems such as children with progeria. Suffering exists on this planet because "even God has a hard time keeping chaos in check," and God is "a God of justice and not of power."[1] In other words, God is as outraged by the suffering on this planet as anyone, but his hands are tied.

Kushner's book became a best-seller because people found it comforting. The rabbi had voiced for them what they had wanted to believe all along: that God desires to help, but cannot. When we call on him to solve our problems, we are simply expecting too much of God. Kushner's ideas sound like something we may want to be true. But are they true?

If Kushner has discovered hidden truths about God, why didn't God reveal these same truths in his speech to Job? That biblical book could conveniently be subtitled "When the Worst Things Happened to One of the Best People." The final climactic scene offered God a perfect platform from which to discuss his lack of power, if that indeed was the problem. Surely Job would have welcomed these words from God: "Job, I'm sorry about what's happening. I hope you realize I had nothing to do with the way things have turned out. I wish I could help, Job, but I really can't."

Instead, Job 38–41 contains as impressive a description of God's power as you'll find anywhere in the Bible. God never once apologized to Job for his lack of power; rather his verbal fugues about ostriches, wild oxen, snowstorms, and constellations all served to underscore it.

If God is less-than-powerful, why did he choose the worst possible situation, when his power was most called into question, to boast about his power? Elie Wiesel might have had the most perceptive comment on the God portrayed by Rabbi Kushner: If that's who God is, I think he ought to resign and let someone more competent take his place.

Response, Not Cause

Although God's speech resolved Job's questions, it may not resolve ours. (Looking back, we may have trouble understanding why Job felt so satisfied with a seemingly evasive answer, but, then, we didn't hear God speak out of a whirlwind either.) In the end, it was God's presence that filled the void. But what lessons apply to the rest of us, those of us who did not have the privilege of hearing God's speech in person?

In my view the book of Job reinforces the pattern followed by Jesus in Luke 13 and John 9. Suffering involves two main issues: (1) *cause*—Why am I suffering? Who did it?—and (2) *response*. By instinct, most of us want to figure out the cause of our pain before we decide how to respond. But God does not allow Job that option. He deflects attention from the issue of cause to the issue of Job's response.

It's as if God has walled off two areas of responsibility. He fully accepts responsibility for running the universe, with all its attendant problems. To someone like Job, who focuses on those problems, God has one word of advice: "Stop your whining. You have no idea what you're talking about." Or, as Frederick Buechner puts it, "God doesn't explain. He explodes. He asks Job who he thinks he is anyway. He says that to try to explain the kind of things Job wants explained would be like trying to explain Einstein to a little-neck clam. . . . God doesn't reveal his grand design. He reveals himself."[2]

As for Job, he had only one thing to worry about: his response. God never explained the origin of Job's suffering, but rather moved the focus to the future. Once the tragedy has happened—*now what* will you do? Casting about for blame would get him nowhere; he needed to exercise responsibility in his response, the one area he, and not God, had control over.

This biblical pattern is so consistent that I must conclude the important issue facing Christians who suffer is not "Is God responsible?" but "How should I react now that this terrible thing has happened?" For that very reason, I will shift my main focus in this book away from the theoretical questions about suffering. Instead, I will direct attention to personal examples of actual people who respond to pain.

In the Bible, at least, the problem of pain is less a philosophical riddle than a test of human response and faithfulness. As Florida pastor Stephen Brown expressed it, in a statement not to be taken too literally, every time a non-Christian gets cancer, God allows a Christian to get cancer as well, so the world can see the difference.

What difference? What response is best? The Bible replies often, with an unwavering but disturbing answer:

> Consider it pure *joy*, my brothers, whenever you face trials of many kinds, because you know that the testing of your faith develops perseverance. Perseverance must finish its work so that you may be mature and complete, not lacking anything. (James 1:2–4)
>
> Dear friends, do not be surprised at the painful trial you are suffering, as though something strange were happening to you. But *rejoice* that you participate in the sufferings of Christ, so that you may be overjoyed when his glory is revealed. (1 Peter 4:12–13)
>
> In this you greatly *rejoice*, though now for a little while you may have had to suffer grief in all kinds of trials. (1 Peter 1:6–7)

One of the best expressions of the Bible's ideal attitude toward suffering emerges from a rift between Paul and the Christians in Corinth. In a fit of pique, Paul had sent a strongly worded letter. Reflecting on it later, he writes, "I am no longer sorry that I sent that letter to you, though I was very sorry for a time, realizing how painful it would be to you. But it hurt you only for a little while. Now I am glad I sent it, not because it hurt you, but because the pain turned you to God. It was a good kind of sorrow you felt, the kind of sorrow God wants his people to have. . . ." (2 Corinthians 7:8–9 LB).

"Pain turned you to God"—Paul's succinct phrase serves as an accurate summary of the role of suffering. It underscores the Bible's emphasis on response, not cause. It also fits the lesson that Jesus applied from the two tragedies in his day (Luke 13): "Don't you realize that you also will perish unless you leave your evil ways and *turn to God*?"

Something Produced

"Rejoice!" "Be glad!" How do these suggestions differ from the insensitive hospital visitor who brings a smile and a

"Look on the bright side!" pep talk? Read further in each biblical passage, for every such admonition leads to a discussion of productive results. Suffering *produces* something. It has value; it changes us.

By using words like "Rejoice!" the apostles were not advocating a spirit of grin-and-bear-it or act-tough-like-nothing-happened. No trace of those attitudes can be found in Christ's response to suffering, or in Paul's. If those attitudes were desirable, self-sufficiency would be the goal, not childlike trust in God.

Nor is there any masochistic hint of enjoying pain. "Rejoicing in suffering" does not mean Christians should act happy about tragedy and pain when they feel like crying. Rather, the Bible aims the spotlight on the end result, the productive use God can make of suffering in our lives. To achieve that result, however, he first needs our commitment of trust, and the process of giving him that commitment can be described as rejoicing.

Romans 5:3–5 breaks down the process into stages: "We also rejoice in our sufferings, because we know that suffering produces perseverance; perseverance, character; and character, hope. And hope does not disappoint us, because God has poured out his love into our hearts by the Holy Spirit, whom he has given us." Quite simply, a quality like perseverance will *only* develop in the midst of trying circumstances. Think about it: a person who always gets what he or she wants has no chance to learn perseverance, or patience. Suffering can be one of the tools to help fashion those good qualities.

Seen in this light, the apostles' command to "Rejoice!" makes sense. James does not say, "Rejoice *in the trials* you are facing," but rather "Count it pure joy when you face trials. . . ." The difference in wording is significant. One celebrates the fact of pain; the other celebrates the opportunity for growth introduced by pain. We rejoice not in the fact that we are suffering, but in our confidence that the pain can be transformed. The value lies not in the pain itself, but in what we can make of it. The pain need not be meaningless, and therefore we rejoice in the object of our faith, a God who can effect that transformation.

A few chapters after his step-by-step analysis in Romans 5, Paul makes a grand, sweeping statement, "And we know that in

all things God works for the good of those who love him. . . ."
That statement is sometimes twisted and made to imply that
"Only good things will happen to those who love God." Paul
meant just the opposite. The remainder of chapter 8 defines
what kind of "things" he had in mind: trouble, hardship,
persecution, famine, nakedness, danger, sword—all pages from
Paul's autobiography. Yet, as the apostle's life well illustrates,
God used even those things to advance his will in and through
Paul. It would be more accurate to say that God was working *in
Paul* through harsh circumstances than to say he was at work in
the circumstances themselves.

Does God introduce suffering into our lives so that these
good results will come about? Remember the pattern established
at the end of Job. Questions about cause lie within God's
domain; we cannot expect to understand those answers. We
have no right to speculate, "Some relatives came to Christ at the
funeral—that must be why God took him home." Instead,
response is our assignment. Paul and other New Testament
authors insist that if we respond with trust God will, without
doubt, work in us for good. As Job himself said so presciently,
". . . those who suffer he delivers in their suffering; he speaks to
them in their affliction" (36:15).

The notion of suffering as productive brings a new
dimension to our experience of pain. Human beings undergo
goal-directed suffering quite willingly, as athletes and pregnant
women can attest. According to the Bible, a proper Christian
response to suffering gives similar hope to the person on the
hospital bed. As we rely on God, and trust his Spirit to mold us
in his image, true hope takes shape within us, "a hope that does
not disappoint." We can literally become better persons because
of suffering. Pain, however meaningless it may seem at the time,
can be transformed.

Where is God when it hurts? He is in *us*—not in the things
that hurt—helping to transform bad into good. We can safely
say that God can bring good out of evil; we cannot say that God
brings about the evil in hopes of producing good.

Mary's Journey

Once Dr. Paul Brand and I were discussing individual
Christians who had undergone great suffering. After he had

related several personal stories, I asked whether the pain had turned those people toward God or away from God. He thought at length, and concluded that there was no common response. Some grew closer to God, some drifted bitterly away. The main difference seemed to lie in their focus of attention. Those obsessed with questions about cause ("What did I do to deserve this? What is God trying to tell me? Am I being punished?") often turned against God. In contrast, the triumphant sufferers took individual responsibility for their own responses and trusted God despite the discomfort.

Then Dr. Brand told me about one of his most famous patients, Mary Verghese.*

Mary was not a leprosy patient. Rather, she worked as a medical resident at Brand's leprosy hospital in India. One day she went on a picnic outing in a station wagon driven by a young student out to demonstrate his bravery. After following a poky school bus for several miles the driver, thoroughly exasperated, jerked the car into the passing lane and floored the accelerator. When he saw another car coming head-on, he instinctively stomped on the brake pedal—but hit the gas instead. The station wagon veered over a bridge and tumbled down a steep embankment.

Mary Verghese, promising young physician, lay motionless at the bottom of the bank. Her face was slit in a deep gash from cheekbone to chin. Her lower limbs dangled uselessly, like two sticks of wood.

Mary's next few months were almost unbearable. As summer temperatures reached 110 degrees outside, Mary lay in her sweltering hospital room, in traction, wrapped in a perspex jacket and plastic brace. She faced agonizing hours of therapy. Each week nurses would test her for sensation, and each week she would fail, never feeling the pinpricks on her legs.

After observing her downward spiral of despair, Dr. Brand stopped by her room for a visit. "Mary," he began, "I think it's time to begin thinking of your professional future as a doctor." At first she thought he was joking, but he went on to suggest that she might bring to other patients unique qualities of sympathy and understanding. She pondered his suggestion a

*Mary's story is told in *Take My Hands* by Dorothy Clarke Wilson.

long time, doubting whether she would ever recover sufficient use of her limbs to function as a doctor.

Gradually, Mary began to work with the leprosy patients. The hospital staff noticed that patients' self-pity, hopelessness, and sullenness seemed to fade when Mary Verghese was around. Leprosy patients whispered among themselves about the wheelchair doctor (the first in India) who was more disabled than they were, whose face, like theirs, bore scars. Before long Mary Verghese began assisting at surgery—tedious, exhausting work for her in a sitting position.

One day Dr. Brand met Mary rolling her wheelchair between buildings of the hospital and asked how she was doing. "At first the threads seemed so tangled and broken," she replied, "but I'm beginning to think life may have a pattern after all."

Mary's recovery was to involve many excruciating hours of therapy, as well as major surgery on her spine. She remained incontinent for life and fought constantly against pressure sores. But she now had a glimmer of hope. She began to understand that the disability was not a punishment sent by God to entrap her in a life of misery. Rather, it could be transformed into her greatest asset as a doctor. In her wheelchair, with her crooked smile, she had immediate rapport with disabled patients.

Eventually Mary learned to walk with braces. She worked under scholarship in New York's Institute of Physical Medicine and Rehabilitation, and ultimately headed up a new department at the Physiotherapy School in Vellore, India.

Mary stands as an outstanding example of a person who got nowhere asking *why* a tragedy happened. But as she turned toward God and asked *to what end,* she learned to trust him to weave a new design for her life. In doing so, Mary Verghese has probably achieved far more than she would have had the accident not occurred.

Mary Verghese offers a great contrast to people I know who have turned away from God because of their suffering. They talk about their illness, often hypochondriacally, as if it's the only part of their lives. They give full vent to the self-pity that smolders beneath the surface in each of us.

The suffering person faces choices. She can recoil in anger and despair against God. Or she can accept the trial as an opportunity for joy. I do not mean to imply that God loves one type of sufferer and rejects the other, or even that one is more "spiritual" than the other. I believe God understands those people who kick and struggle and scream as well as those who learn that suffering can be a means of grace, of transformation. (Remember, God had far more sympathy for Job's honest ravings than for his friends' pieties.)

God does not need our good responses for himself, to satisfy some jealous parental hunger. He directs attention from cause to response for our sakes, not his. Indeed, the path of joyful acceptance is self-healing: an attitude of joy and gratitude will reduce stress, calm nerves, allay fears, help mobilize bodily defenses.

Would it really help us to know exactly why God permits a specific instance of suffering? Such awareness may engender even more bitterness. But it does help our actual condition when we turn to him in trust. It can break down self-sufficiency and create in us a profound new level of faith in God. It can transform our suffering into qualities of lasting, even eternal, value.

> I ask you neither for health nor for sickness, for life nor for death; but that you may dispose of my health and my sickness, my life and my death, for your glory. . . . You alone know what is expedient for me; you are the sovereign master; do with me according to your will. Give to me, or take away from me, only conform my will to yours. I know but one thing, Lord, that it is good to follow you, and bad to offend you. Apart from that, I know not what is good or bad in anything. I know not which is most profitable to me, health or sickness, wealth or poverty, nor anything else in the world. That discernment is beyond the power of men or angels, and is hidden among the secrets of your Providence, which I adore, but do not seek to fathom.
> —a prayer by Blaise Pascal[3]

Part 3

How People Respond to Suffering

Pain that cannot forget
falls drop by drop
upon the heart
until in our despair
there comes wisdom
through the awful grace of God.

Aeschylus

9

After the Fall

Notions about the productive value of suffering and the crucial role of a person's response may sound fine in theory, but few people concern themselves with theoretical suffering. The important question is, Do these principles work out in actual life situations?

To learn more, I visited two Christians who fight daily battles against pain, physical and psychological, that sometimes rages out of control. Both were cut down in the prime of life; in many ways their identities ever since have been defined by the misfortune they met. Yet the two, Brian Sternberg and Joni Eareckson Tada, have given contrasting human responses. Their experience with suffering has been so all-consuming that each deserves a full chapter.

On July 2, 1963, Brian Sternberg fell ten feet, and that one-second fall completely altered his life, as well as that of his family. In high school Brian had devoted himself to the uncommon sport of pole-vaulting. He liked the experience of fashioning a single graceful event from many different parts— the mad dash down the runway, the jarring thrust of the pole plant, the leap of recoiled strength like a cougar's, the feet-first propulsion, the slight hesitation of weightlessness at the top of the bar, the quick, scary descent like a high dive into air cushions.

For Brian it was not enough to excel at vaulting technique. Knowing the slight edge some extra refinement could give his body, he took up gymnastics as well. A ballet of strength, gymnastics is perhaps sport's highest claim to art. Nearly every day after high school classes Brian would head to the gym to practice his vault approaches, leaps, and falls on the trampoline. He learned to twist and loop and turn flips high in the air, exulting in the sheer pleasure of his bodily mastery. Vaulting required rigorous control and discipline; gymnastics set him free.

As a freshman at the University of Washington, Brian established a national collegiate freshman mark of 15'8". The following year track magazines ranked him the number-one pole-vaulter in the world. The year was 1963. John Kennedy was president, and beating the Russians a national pastime. It looked as if the U.S. had a winner in Brian Sternberg, and world attention focused on the nineteen-year-old.

In 1963 Brian made sports headlines nearly every week. Undefeated in outdoor competition, he set an American record in indoor competition. Then he set his first world mark with a vault of 16'5". In quick succession Brian racked up new records of 16'7" and 16'8", capturing both the NCAA and AAU titles. Other elite vaulters reached a plateau; Brian kept climbing.

Those were happy days for the Sternbergs. They all knew the glory was fleeting, for track stars fade quickly. But it was fun for the whole family to pile into the car and drive to see Brian single-handedly pack out a field house and bring the crowd wildly to its feet.

Everything changed on July 2, three weeks after Brian's last world record. Now, several decades later, Brian Sternberg still competes, but in a far more lonely and desperate contest. There have been no more vaults.

The Accident

The ordeal began when he grabbed his sweater and yelled, "I'm going to limber up at the pavilion, Mom." He drove across the river to the University of Washington and began a gymnastics warm-up. The U.S. track team was preparing for a tour to the Soviet Union, and Brian's workouts were now indispensable. This is how Brian described what happened next:

§   If there is ever a frightening moment in trampolining, it is just as you leave the trampoline bed, on your way up. At that moment, even the most experienced gymnast sometimes gets a sensation of panic, for no good reason, that does not disappear until he is down safe on the bed again. It hit me as I took off. I got lost in midair and thought I was going to land on my hands and feet, as I had done several times before when the panic came. Instead I landed on my head.

I heard a crack in my neck, then everything was gone. My arms and legs were bounding around in front of my eyes, but I couldn't feel them moving. Even before the bouncing stopped, I was yelling, "I'm paralyzed," in as loud a voice as I could, which was pretty weak because I had practically no lung power. The paralysis was affecting my breathing.

There was nothing I could do. I couldn't move. It scared me at first, but then, for some reason, the panic disappeared. I told the people looking down at me, "Don't move me, especially don't move my neck." At one point, when I started losing my power to breathe and could feel myself passing out, I remember telling a buddy about mouth-to-mouth resuscitation: "Do everything, but don't tilt my head back."

Real anguish hit me a couple of times while we waited for the doctor. It was not physical pain: I just broke from the thought of what had happened to me. But at the time I was thinking only about the near future. I had not begun to think about the possibility of never walking again.[1]

Doctors know little about the spinal-cord system, because they can't easily study it without damaging the patient. For the first forty-eight hours they did not know whether Brian would survive. When he did, they could only guess at what range of movement might be restored to him.

For the next eight weeks Brian lay strapped onto a Foster

frame, a steel-and-canvas device nicknamed "the canvas sandwich." Hinged at both ends, it allowed a nurse to flip Brian upside down every few hours, in order to prevent bedsores and other complications.

Once out of the Foster frame, he could move his head, although for a long time he wouldn't, because of the terrible memory of that snapping sound in his neck. He could also contract a few shoulder muscles. Superb shoulder development had always marked him as a vaulter; now those muscles too began to atrophy. To slow the deterioration, technicians would attach electrodes to his muscles and, by sending voltage through them, cause them to contract. Brain found it very strange to watch his own muscles twitch while he felt nothing.

For a while he had no pain. The sensations from his nervous system, in fact, offered no proof that he had legs or arms or a torso. He felt suspended, as if floating around the room. He couldn't even feel the mattress under him.

Lying in bed, a "head" and nothing more, Brian began to experience tactile hallucinations. He developed an imaginary pair of legs and arms that he could command at will. He would concentrate hard on, say, "basketball," and somehow his subconscious would bring to his nerve center the exact memory of a basketball. The sensation felt exactly as if he was holding one between his hands. The games were fun at first, giving him hope that one day his tactile perceptions would reconnect to reality.

But before long the games began to turn against him. The basketball would stick to his imaginary fingers, and he couldn't let go. Or instead of a basketball, he'd feel a razor blade. Its sharp edges would slide across his hands, with an excruciating effect—imaginary, of course, but quite real to Brian's pain network. For a time he could not escape the illusion of having a metal nut screwed tightly to each fingertip.

At night came the nightmares: leering, haunted nightmares of himself stomping all over the walls and ceiling of his room, like a fly. Others had little shape or plot, just a formless, disembodied sense of terror. And always after the nightmares came the morning; that was far worse, because he could not awake from the nightmare of reality.

Fits of emotional depression, even more severe than the hallucinations, would overtake him without warning. He could see his athlete's body shriveling, adapting to inactivity. For hours Brian would look at the same walls and with the same desperate mental lunges try to make his muscles obey the brain's commands. And every time he worked hard and failed, he'd dig himself deeper into an emotional pit. He would cry out to the doctors, "I've had it. I don't know what I'm going to do. Nothing's happening; I can't stand lying tied up like this. I'm exhausted. I've tried to move for too long, and I just can't. . . ."[2] The tears and sobs would choke away his speeches.

When the depression hit in waves, like nausea, Brian had a few sources of comfort to cling to. His girlfriend and his family stood by him, and he heard from thousands of sympathizers, as far away as Japan and Finland. For an hour or so each day his parents would read the letters and cards aloud, until the emotions got too thick and they couldn't continue. One seventy-nine-year-old man wrote, "My body's not good, but my spinal cord is fine. I wish I could give it to you."

Support also poured in from the world athletic community. The Soviet Union struck an unprecedented special medal to honor Brian. Football's Kansas City Chiefs played a benefit game to help allay his medical expenses.

After a few weeks, however, nothing seemed to help the depression. Doctors could give little hope—no one with Brian's injury had ever walked again. What pulled him out of that pit was a phone hookup with delegates at a Fellowship of Christian Athletes conference in Ashland, Oregon. For more than an hour Brian spoke to the athletes and talked with coaches and sports people. In return the Christian athletes, expressing their faith in Brian's recovery, sparked his own search for faith.

Three months after the accident is when Brian dates his awakening as a Christian. He realized that apart from a miracle he would never walk again. No amount of straining could budge his limbs. Dead nerve fiber in his spinal cord would have to be remade, and medicine could not do that. Yet he also recognized that faith in God was not a transaction: "You heal me, God, and I'll believe." He had to believe because God was worthy of his faith. Brian took that risk.

He then began a prayer that has not ended. Scores, hundreds, thousands of times he's presented to God the same request. Everything about his life reminds him that the prayer has not been answered. He's prayed with bitterness, with pleading, with desperation, with fervent longing. Others too have prayed—churches, college students, small clusters of athletes. Always the same prayer, never the answer Brian desires and believes in.

Less than a year after the accident, Brian told a reporter from *Look* magazine, "Having faith is a necessary step toward one of two things. Being healed is one of them. Peace of mind, if healing doesn't come, is the other. Either one will suffice." But Brian has a different view now. To him there's only one option—complete healing.

Brian's World

In order to meet Brian, I had to fly to Seattle, leave a message, and wait until he felt well enough to see a visitor. The pain, he says, "oscillates from ridiculously high to excruciating."

What could anneal a faith to survive years of suffering and unanswered prayers? Over time, some who first sought physical healing for Brian have changed their prayers. But not the Sternbergs. Are they superhuman or merely stubborn? I wondered as I drove to their Seattle home the first time. Others had warned me: "It's strange—they just won't accept Brian's condition."

The Sternberg home perches on a ridge above Seattle Pacific University. It overlooks a steep street which cars slide down helplessly in severe rain or ice storms. The street was dry, and I made it up okay. Mrs. Helen Sternberg, Brian's trim, blonde mother, met me at the door. On the roof a friend of Brian's was adjusting a rotating radio antenna. Inside the house, the view of Seattle was spectacular through full-length windows. I watched the street and water traffic for twenty minutes while an orderly prepared Brian.

What strikes a visitor first is how totally Brian must depend on other people. If left alone for forty-eight hours, he would die. Orderlies from high schools and Seattle Pacific bathe him, give him medication, feed him, hold glasses of water for him. Brian has always resisted this dependence, but what choice does he have? His body lies exactly where the last orderly placed it.

Brian's head is of normal size, but the rest of his body has shrunk due to muscle atrophy. He has learned to control his shoulder muscles so that he can make some motions with his full arm. He can hit switches, turn knobs (with difficulty), and even type with the use of a special contraption that restrains all but one finger.

Brian's room, no larger than an average bedroom, fences in his life. He has no ten-speed bike or skis or ice skates in a garage. With his eyes he pointed out for me the various objects around him. An Adidas sports blanket hangs above his bed, a memento of the 1964 Tokyo Olympics Brian never attended. On one wall is a letter from John F. Kennedy, dated August 15, 1963. "I want you to know that you have been much in our thoughts during these past weeks and that we hope for continued improvement in the days ahead." The letter was read at the pro football benefit game, and Brian cried when he heard those words.

He showed the greatest enthusiasm, though, when demonstrating a complex assortment of ham radio equipment surrounding his bed. He has developed a consuming interest in amateur radio as a way of forming connections to the outside world.

Brian talked slowly and carefully about a variety of subjects. He loves to talk electronics. And he loves to tell stories of his role as area representative for the Fellowship of Christian Athletes. Speaking from his wheelchair, he has often addressed athletes in gyms, classrooms, and locker rooms.

I found it hard to leave Brian's room. Although much of what he said fascinated me, he seemed to lack the sense of balance and proportion that governs conversation. After a couple of hours, as I edged toward the door, he began talking louder, more urgently. He asked me to do certain favors for him. Long after I told him I must be going, he kept bringing up new topics of conversation.

When I finally broke away, an orderly explained that Brian often acted this way around visitors. Maybe it had something to do with the paralysis, he suggested. Unable to control his own body, Brian was subconsciously seeking control of others.

The Miracle That Won't Come

One fact did become clear in my visit with Brian: now more than ever, he refuses to accept his condition. He has one hope and one prayer—for total healing. He tells that to every visitor. Medically, he needs a miracle; time has done little, and his chances of natural recovery have steadily diminished.

The worst part is the pain. Brian lives with a constant state of bodily revolt. Originating from deep within, the pain spreads throughout his entire body, like the pain machine in Orwell's *1984* that tapped right into the central nervous system. Taken at a single jolt, the pain is enough to knock a strong man howling across the floor. To Brian, it's an unceasing daily routine.

Brian's family has shared the long pain and frustration close up. In the living room his parents told me of their struggle. Outside, lights of the city blinked as thousands of commuters snaked along the city's streets and bridges. That view, combined with the fire blazing in the fireplace, made the setting seem idyllic. Mrs. Sternberg leaned forward to speak of Brian's dilemma.

During the first six months after the accident, the Sternbergs were flooded with genuine expressions of hope and support. Many Christians believed Brian would recover. It must be God's will, they said, for such a young, talented athlete to walk again. Brian met with famous Christians known for their healing ministry. At one point, leaders from seven different denominations gathered in his room to pray and anoint him with oil. Everyone felt stirred, everyone believed, but nothing changed.

For comfort and guidance the Sternbergs turned to the Bible. They had talked to pastors and theologians, and had read shelffuls of books on why God allows suffering. As they read the Bible, they became even more convinced Brian would be healed.

"What we found," Mrs. Sternberg told me, "was that God loves. No, it's more than that. God *is* love. All around us people were telling us to accept this tragedy as what God must want for us. But the Jesus we saw in the Bible came to bring healing. Where there was hurt, he touched and made well. He never cursed anyone or brought affliction.

"Jesus was God's language to man. What God is, Jesus lived. Has God's language changed? Does our son's condition contradict what God revealed as himself? I never read about Jesus saying to a blind man, 'Sorry, buddy, I wish I could help, but God is trying to teach you something, so get used to it.' When Jesus saw a blind man, he healed. And he taught us to pray for God's will to 'be done on earth as it is in heaven.'

"To put it bluntly, I don't think God is very pleased with Brian's condition. The Bible holds up God's will as a full, abundant life. It represents wholeness and health—not the withered body Brian's trapped in. We must not use 'God's will' as a pious period to every question mark. We can't stop searching and grow fatalistic, saying, 'I know God's will has been done.'"

She paused. The words were strong, and they were emerging against a background of pain few others have felt. Other Christians, like Mary Verghese, have found comfort in first accepting their condition. The Sternbergs aren't satisfied with acceptance.

She pressed her hands together and continued, "In this life, we don't know full answers to all questions. We take a lot on faith. My husband and I and Brian cling most strongly to God's love. If something—like the accident—doesn't tally with God's love, we look elsewhere. We know it's not from him. Where there is dis-ease between me and God, between me and myself, or between me and a fellow-man, this is disease, and it calls for healing.

"I don't know why Brian's not on his feet yet. I believe God is all-powerful, but I also believe he limits himself. Evil is strong. And I think it is greatly to Satan's advantage to incapacitate us. Anything to keep us from wholeness. He'll exploit our weakness, like a boxer jabbing again and again at a sore jaw or bloody eye. He doesn't quit."

As she talked of the battle between good and evil, my mind shifted to the life of Christ on earth, and attacks directed against him: a slaughter of babies, temptations, betrayal, and finally death. Yet God transformed seeming defeat, even the unimaginable death of his own Son, into victory. In smaller, more subtle ways he has used Brian Sternberg's tragedy, too. Yet, will he crash through with a resounding reversal, overpowering their family tragedy with a physical healing as he had overpowered death with a resurrection? The Sternbergs were staking everything on this hope.

Mrs. Sternberg continued, "No one in Brian's condition has ever walked. No one. Yet we still have faith. I have no idea when God will heal Brian. Conceivably, this particular battle will not be won here on earth. Some people you pray for are healed and some aren't, in this world. But that matter of timing doesn't change God's desire for our wholeness in body, mind, and spirit. We won't give up. We're like doctors searching for a cure; we won't stop investigating. We think it pleases God for us to persevere."

It was late, and our conversation had to end. Before I left the Sternberg home, though, I asked to see Brian's sports mementos. We went into a separate room crowded with trophies, plaques, and certificates. One named him the outstanding athlete of the continent for 1963.

A photo on one wall caught my eye. It showed Brian breaking his last world record at Compton, California. He was sailing against the sky, almost horizontally, with shoulders thrust back and arms outstretched, his hips barely clearing the bar. Every muscle in his body was rippling and tense. The action was frozen by electronic flash, and in a way it's been frozen ever since.

I felt a wash of sorrow—the body of the person I had met and held a conversation with was a pitiful shell of this superb body. Brian has grown, of course, emotionally, spiritually. But he has shrunk, too. Pain crushes. I couldn't get the two images out of my mind as I stepped out of the warmth into a chilly Seattle wind. The Brian of the photo. And Brian today—a twisted, helpless body on the bed where it will lie tomorrow, the next day . . . who knows how long?

Could I believe if that were me? Would I rationalize the suffering, or learn to accept it, or rebel against it? Would my faith in healing survive years, decades? Were the Sternbergs right in gambling everything on a miracle that has not come despite thousands of prayers? Were they unfairly dictating terms to God? Should they "praise the Lord anyhow" as some would suggest?

I had no answers. What stood out mainly was the fierce, fighting quality of their faith. As I drove away, I felt no pity for the Sternbergs. Pity implies weakness, and I had met great strength. Strength that would endure, even if the specifics never fell into line. "A spinal cord injury occurs in this country every thirty minutes," Mrs. Sternberg had told me. "Half a million people are in wheelchairs. So many of them have given up. We feel we can't. We intend to keep on hoping."

A Second Visit

I first visited the Sternbergs in 1972, still in the first decade after Brian's accident. The persistence of their faith impressed me then, and I wondered what I would find when I visited them again in 1987, fifteen years later. Brian was now a middle-aged man. The physical healing he had longed for, and longs for still, has not come. He has now spent more years paralyzed than with movement.

Seattle was in the full bloom of summer, and as I drove up the steep hill to their house, I found the entire family sitting in lawn chairs outdoors. Brian's parents had aged gracefully, and looked little different. Brian, however, had gained the paunch of middle age and his hair was liberally streaked with gray.

Over coffee, the Sternbergs brought me up to date. They had seen some slight physical improvement over the years. The line of paralysis on Brian's chest had crept down several inches, allowing his arms more range of motion. The pain was much more controlled. And sensation had returned to most of his body: although he could not move his legs, at least he was aware of them now. As a result, most of the tactile hallucinations had ceased.

The Sternbergs took pains to point out all the good things that had happened. "One real miracle," said Mr. Sternberg, "is that neither Helen nor I have gotten sick. In almost twenty-five years of caring for Brian, we've managed to keep our health."

For several years the Sternbergs prayed for a healing ministry that would encompass their broadened definition of disease. Finally one came into being: a monthly, Sunday-night prayer service in a Seattle church. People with hurts and needs are invited to come forward and spend a few silent minutes with the pastor, while all the rest direct their prayers to the one person's needs. The shared experience pulled the church together remarkably, and the practice spread far beyond Seattle.

In 1976 Brian nearly died. Pneumonia attacked his fragile lungs, and in the hospital he developed a staph infection. He lay in a coma for two weeks and suffered two cardiac arrests. Doctors installed a pacemaker, but he lingered near death for more than two months. He lost his voice for a long time, and lost some short-term memory.

This time, the prayers for healing were answered. Brian eventually regained all his faculties except what he had lost through the spinal cord injury. Something else seemed clear to me, as we sat around and talked: Brian's personality had changed as well. He was more mellow, and serene, and showed none of the symptoms of personality imbalance that had stood out before.

Gently, I asked the Sternbergs if their belief about physical healing had changed over the years. They said no. "Some people like to point to the good that has come about and interpret that as the reason for Brian's accident. We don't think so. We believe in a loving God, and we still believe God wants Brian whole. Our timing may be off. It looks less and less likely that Brian will have a whole body in this life. You know, in the book of Daniel there's a story about an angel dispatched to answer Daniel's prayer. It takes him three weeks to reach Daniel—but when he arrives he assures Daniel that God heard the prayer the moment he prayed it."

As we talked, watching the afternoon sun slip behind the hills, I couldn't help comparing my two visits. It occurred to me as I listened to the Sternbergs that a slow, gradual miracle had been taking place, one they might have overlooked. An accident traumatic enough to crack most families apart had instead brought theirs together. They had resisted the easier path of consigning Brian to a nursing home or rehab hospital. For more than two decades they had been pouring selfless love into their son, and it seemed evident to me, as I watched Brian now, that their love had borne fruit. Against their will the Sternbergs, all of them, had come to terms with suffering.

An analogy used by Paul Tournier came to mind as I started the jerky, braking descent of their street. He said the Christian life resembles a trapeze act. You can swing on the bar, exercising and building muscles all you want. But if you want to improve and excel, you have to take risks. You have to let go, knowing that nothing is beneath you, and reach out for the next trapeze bar.

Brian would have liked that analogy, I thought. A long time ago the Sternbergs together let go of the props and announced to the world they would believe God, despite . . . anything. Brian sees that as his personal calling. Not as many spectators are standing around watching now, but the Sternbergs still believe. I drove away, inspired again by their tenacious belief.

He can be revealed only to the child; perfectly, to the pure child only.
All the discipline of the world is to make men children, that God may
be revealed to them.

George MacDonald
Life Essential

10

On My Feet Dancing

Not long after my first visit with Brian Sternberg, I traveled to
Baltimore, Maryland, to interview a remarkable teenager named
Joni Eareckson. Of course, Joni has by now become a familiar
name because of her work as a painter, author, and popular
Christian speaker. But when I met her nothing had yet been
published, and I had heard only bits and pieces of her story.

Joni's story had close parallels to Brian's: both were teenage
athletes cut down in their prime and forced to adjust to life as
quadriplegics. On the way to the interview, I anticipated a mood
similar to what I had found at the Sternbergs, that of an uneasy
struggle mixed with tough, undying faith. But when I arrived at
Joni's house, the breadth of a continent removed from Brian's, I
found a quite different atmosphere.

I reached Joni Eareckson's home by following one of the
tranquil creeks west of Baltimore. In sharp curves and S-turns
the road slithered around abrupt, lumpish hills. A stand of
hardwood forest lined both sides of the roadway until the road
climbed to the crest of the highest hill, where suddenly a
sweeping panoramic landscape came into view. Joni's house was
on that hill. It was a cottage made of large boulders and hand-
hewn timber, painstakingly fitted together by Joni's father.

The full-length glass walls of Joni's art studio jutted out over the hill. A brown stallion was grazing in the valley, swishing his tail at flies. A Great Dane romped across the lawn. Many artists aspire to work in such a rustic setting, but Joni's professional life was different from most others. She can only go into her studio if someone pushes her, and she draws with a pen or brush held between her teeth.

As a teenager Joni used to ride her stallion through forest trails at breakneck speed, splash in the creek with the Great Dane, and slap basketballs against a backboard beside the cottage. Sometimes she would even join a fox hunt through the property.

But now her daily exercise consists of far subtler movements. With the aid of a biceps-and-shoulder brace she can move her arm enough to turn the pages of a book. And the act of drawing requires a long succession of meticulous, labored head nods. Slowly, a recognizable scene takes form.

A two-second mistake completely changed Joni's life, but her buoyant optimism was not one of the things it changed. When I was introduced to her, I was mostly struck by the aliveness of her facial expression, and the brightness of her eyes. Her spirit was so effervescent that she faintly brought to mind all those "Think positive—love yourself!" courses taught by former Miss Americas. In contrast to most of them, however, Joni's spirit was formed by tragedy.

A Fateful Dive

§   The summer of 1967 was unusually hot and humid. July was stifling. In the morning I practiced with the horses, working up a sweat that only a dip in the Chesapeake Bay could cool. My sister Kathy and I rode to the beach and dove into the murky water.

I was never content to swim laps in a pool or splash around in the shallow part of the bay. I preferred free swimming, in the open water. A raft floating fifty or sixty yards offshore made a perfect goal, and Kathy and I raced to it. We were both athletic, and sometimes reckless.

When I reached the raft, I climbed on it and quickly dove off the side, almost without thinking. I first felt the familiar drag of the water, and then a stunning jolt—my

§ head had crashed into a rock on the bottom. My limbs splayed out. I felt a loud buzzing, like an electric shock accompanied by intense vibration. Yet there was no pain.

I couldn't move! My face pressed hard into the grinding sand on the bottom, but I couldn't pull away. My brain was directing my muscles to make swimming motions, but none of them responded. I held my breath, prayed, and waited, suspended facedown in the water.

After maybe a minute I heard Kathy calling me—a faint, muffled voice above the water surface. Her voice came closer and clearer, and then I saw her shadow right above me. "Did you dive in here? It's so shallow," I heard her say through the water.

Kathy bent down, tried to lift me, then stumbled. *Oh, God. How much longer,* I thought. Everything was going black.

Just as I was about to faint, my head broke through the surface and I choked in a great gulp of air. I tried to hold on to Kathy, but again my muscles would not respond. She draped me over her shoulders and began paddling to shore.

Feeling certain that my hands and legs were tied together around my chest, I noticed with a sudden shock of terror that instead they were dangling motionless across Kathy's back. *I had lost touch with my body.*

An ambulance rushed Joni from the solitude of the bay into a whirl of activity at Baltimore's City Hospital. She lay in a small room blocked off by privacy curtains. One nurse asked about her medical history. Another clipped off her brand-new swimming suit, leaving her feeling exposed and helpless. A doctor with a long metal pin kept asking "Do you feel this?" as he pressed it against her feet, her calves, her fingers, and her arms. Concentrating on the stimuli with all her might, Joni could honestly answer "Yes" only when he tested her shoulders.

After a hurried consultation of doctors, one named Dr. Sherrill chopped off Joni's flowing blonde hair with electric clippers, and a nurse shaved her head. As she began fading from consciousness, she thought she heard the high whine of an electric drill. Her last memory was of someone holding her head while the doctor drilled two neat holes, one on either side of her skull.

The Mirror

When Joni awoke, she found herself strapped into a Stryker frame (similar to Brian Sternberg's Foster frame). Metal tongs, inserted into the holes in her skull, were attached to a spring-like device that pulled her head away from her body. Her face poked through a small opening in the canvas sheet to which she was strapped. Every few hours a nurse would flip the frame. All day she alternated views: the floor, the ceiling.

Despite her lack of mobility and the depressing atmosphere of the intensive care unit, Joni survived the first few weeks in good spirits. The pain was slight, and doctors held out hope that some of the nerves might repair themselves. In those early days her room was crowded with visitors and flowers and gifts. Her sisters would spread out *Seventeen* magazines on the floor for her to read facedown.

After four weeks, once Joni had passed the critical stage, Dr. Sherrill performed a fusion procedure on her spine. Joni was jubilant, hoping that the surgery would solve her problems and put her on her feet again. The surgery was indeed successful, but that same day Dr. Sherrill leveled with her. "Joni," he said, "I'm sorry, but the injury is permanent. Fusion surgery did not change that. You'll never walk again, and your arms will have limited use."

For the first time since the accident, that harsh fact sank in. She had expected a few more months' treatment, then rehabilitation, then recovery. Suddenly she saw that her whole life would change. No more sports cars, horse shows, lacrosse matches. Maybe no more dates. Ever.

"I was devastated," she recalls. "My life had been so full. I was involved in as many school activities as I could squeeze in. And suddenly I found myself all alone, just a bare, immobile body between two sheets. My hobbies and possessions were meaningless to me. Those beautiful horses in the barn which I used to trick-ride, standing on their shoulders—I would never ride them again. I couldn't even feed myself. I could sleep and breathe; everything else someone did for me."

Strapped to the canvas facing downward, Joni watched

hot, salty tears fall from her face and drip designs on the floor. Her nose ran, and she had to call for a nurse. She even needed help to cry.

Joni's spirits fell to greater depths a few days later, when two friends from school visited her for the first time. Their image of Joni was of a vivacious, energetic athlete, and nothing had prepared them for the transformation. When they came to Joni's bedside, their mouths dropped. "Oh, my God," whispered one of the girls. They stood for a few seconds in awkward silence, then ran outside. Joni could hear one girl vomiting and one girl sobbing outside her hospital door. She wondered what could be so horrible to cause such a reaction.

A few days later, she found out. Joni asked a visitor named Jackie to bring her a mirror. When Jackie stalled, Joni insisted. Apprehensive, Jackie obeyed, finding a mirror and holding it before her nervously. Joni took one look in the glass and screamed, "Oh, God, how can you do this to me!"

The person in the mirror had eyes that were bloodshot and sunken into dark cavities far back into her skull. Her skin color had faded to a dull yellow, and teeth were black from medication. Her head was still shaved, with metal clamps on either side. And her weight had shrunk from 125 to 80 pounds.

Joni sobbed uncontrollably. Finally she wailed, "Oh, Jackie, I need your help. Please do one thing for me. I can't face it any longer."

"What's that, Joni? I'll do anything for you."

"Help me die. Bring me some pills, or a razor blade even. I can't live inside a grotesque body like this. Help me die, Jackie."

Jackie could not bring herself to obey that request, regardless of Joni's condition. So Joni learned another cruel fact: she was too helpless even to die on her own.

Fullness

Millions of people have gotten acquainted with Joni since that awful day in City Hospital. She speaks at conferences around the world, appears on national television programs, records a daily radio broadcast, has acted out the role of her life in a Worldwide Pictures movie, and has been the subject of articles in numerous magazines like *People* and *Saturday Evening Post*. In addition to her life story, *Joni*, she has written numerous books and made best-selling recordings of her singing. Her artwork graces a line of cards, posters, and stationery.

Almost everyone who meets Joni Eareckson Tada today (she also got married along the way) comes away feeling happier, more hopeful. She is miles away from the shriveled, pitiable girl in the mirror. How has she done it?

"Once during those depressing days in the hospital, when my day consisted of pancake flips to ease the bedsores, a visitor tried to cheer me up," Joni remembers. "He quoted a Bible verse to me, a promise which Jesus left his followers: 'I have come to give you life in all its fullness.'

"I was so bitter and cynical then, the thought struck me as almost mockery. Life in all its fullness? If I struggled the rest of my life, the most I could foresee would be some pitiful, inferior half-life. No more tennis, no making love, or marriage, no real contribution to the world.

"But over the years, my outlook has changed. I awake every day grateful for what God has given me. Somehow—and it took me three years even to believe it might be possible—God has proven to me that I, too, can have a fullness of life."

Joni's first lesson was to overcome the barrier facing any disabled person by accepting her condition and its limitations. It was futile to waste energy moaning about her awful physical state. Wishing would not change the face in the mirror. She had to accept herself as a quadriplegic and search for new ways of coping.

The process was painful. When her boyfriend would put his arm around her and squeeze, she felt nothing. At these times and others she kept fighting a temptation to shut her eyes and fantasize, imagining what it would be like if she were well again. A fiancé, a sports car, long hikes in the woods, a place on a college lacrosse team—the possibilities were endless. But they were also worthless, and Joni realized that dwelling on them did not relieve her suffering and only delayed the process of self-acceptance.

Joni soon learned that "normal" people often feel uncomfortable around the disabled. When conversing with her, some people would lean over her wheelchair and speak loudly, using simple words, as if she were mentally deficient. Sometimes, as she was being pushed along a sidewalk, pedestrians would allow a five-foot berth, stepping off the curb to let the wheelchair pass, though the sidewalk was plenty wide enough. Joni came to realize why some disabled people in hospitals and nursing homes show no desire to leave for the outside world. Inside, *they* are the normal ones, and they live among professionals trained to understand.

Friends helped. Joni's most thrilling memory of those early days is of a crazy moment, about a year after her injury, when a friend raced her wheelchair across a sand beach and pushed her into the pounding Atlantic surf. Joni squealed with delight. She may never be able to body-surf on the breakers again, but at least she could let the waves lap against her legs and the salt spray brush her cheeks. She loved it when people treated her in that carefree spirit instead of always being gentle and cautious around her.

But even learning to sit in the wheelchair required agonizing therapy. After lying horizontal for months, Joni's body had to be gradually coaxed into a sitting position. The first time a nurse raised her to a forty-five-degree angle, she nearly collapsed from nausea and dizziness as her heart tried to adjust to the new demands.

Ugly bedsores kept developing. Around her tailbone and hips, sharp edges of bone would protrude through skin. To alleviate the pressures, doctors opened the skin further (with Joni fully conscious—she felt no pain and needed no anesthesia) and filed down sharp bones in her hips and tailbone. More weeks flat in bed followed, then a repeat of the grueling exercises before she could sit again.

In these difficult times, Joni leaned heavily on friends for emotional support. A cluster group of Christian students would visit her faithfully. Once they surprised her by smuggling a puppy into her hospital room. Joni giggled as the puppy slathered her face with his tongue.

Forty-Year Delay

At first, Joni found it impossible to reconcile her condition with her belief in a loving God. It seemed that all God's gifts, the good things she had enjoyed as an active teenager, had been stolen from her. For what reason? What did she have left? The turning to God was very gradual. A melting in her attitude from bitterness to trust dragged out over three years of tears and violent questioning.

One night especially, Joni became convinced that God did understand. Pain was streaking through her back, causing the kind of torment that is unique to those with paralysis. Healthy persons can scratch an itch, massage an aching muscle, or flex a cramped foot. The paralyzed must lie still, as victims without defense against the pain.

Cindy, one of Joni's closest friends, was beside her bed, searching desperately for some way to bring encouragement. Finally, she clumsily blurted out, "Joni, you aren't the only one. Jesus knows how you feel—why, he was paralyzed too."

Joni glared at her. "What? What are you talking about?"

Cindy continued, "It's true. Remember, he was nailed on a cross. His back was raw from beatings, and he must have yearned for a way to move to change positions, or shift his weight. But he couldn't. He was paralyzed by the nails."

The thought intrigued Joni and, for a moment, took her mind off her own pain. It had never occurred to her that God might have felt the same piercing sensations that now racked her body. The realization was profoundly comforting.

§   God became incredibly close to me. I felt myself being transformed by the persistent love of my friends and family. And eventually I began to understand that, yes, God too loved me.

Few of us have the luxury—it took me forever to think of it as that—to come to ground zero with God. Before the accident, my questions had always been, "How will God fit into this situation? How will he affect my dating life? My career plans? The things I enjoy?" Many of those options were now gone. I had only a helpless body, and God. Maybe that's the kind of state the mystics strive for; I got mine unwillingly.

I had no other identity but God, and gradually he became enough. I became overwhelmed with the phenomenal possibility of a personal God, the same God who created the universe, living in my life. Perhaps he could make me attractive and worthwhile. I knew I could not do it without him.

§ The first months, even years, I was obsessed with the question of what God was trying to teach me. Secretly, I probably hoped that by figuring out God's ideas, I could learn my lesson and then he'd heal me.

I suppose every Christian with a similar experience goes back to the book of Job for answers. Here was a righteous man who suffered more than even I could imagine. But strangely, I could not find answers to the "Why?" of tragedies anywhere in the book of Job. What I found was that Job clung to God regardless, and God rewarded him.

"Is that what God wants?" I wondered. My focus changed from demanding an explanation from God to humbly depending on him. Okay, I am paralyzed. It's terrible. I don't like it. But can God still use me, paralyzed? Can I, paralyzed, still worship God and love him? He began to teach me that I could.

Maybe God's gift to me is dependence. I will never reach a place of self-sufficiency that crowds God out. I am aware of his grace every moment. My need for help is obvious every day when I wake up, flat on my back, waiting for someone to come dress me. I can't even comb my hair or blow my nose alone!

But I do have friends who care. I have the beauty of the scenery I paint. I can even support myself financially—the dream of every disabled person. Peace is internal, and God has lavished me with that peace.

There's one more thing. I have hope for the future now. The Bible speaks of our bodies being "glorified" in heaven. In high school that always seemed a hazy, foreign concept to me. But I now realize that I will be healed. I haven't been cheated out of being a complete person—I'm just going through a forty- or fifty-year delay, and God stays with me even through that.

I now know the meaning of being "glorified." It's the time, after my death here, when I'll be on my feet dancing.

It will be a while before Joni can dance again, but after two years of rehabilitation, she did learn to maneuver a motorized wheelchair well enough to drag race down hospital hallways.

Years later she learned to drive, and now she has her own van, with customized controls.

She eventually became a public speaker much in demand, and with good reason. Joni captivates an audience. She is immaculately dressed, with every blonde hair neatly in place. As she speaks, she often retraces the events of the accident and her long recovery. Her words flow articulately. Audiences most appreciate Joni's zest for life and her enthusiasm. Her limbs stay motionless, but her eyes and face sparkle with expression.

Joni moved to California some years ago, and has added the spectacular scenery of the American West to her repertoire of paintings. "Though I can no longer splash in a creek and ride horses," she says, "I can sit outside, and my senses are flooded with smells and textures and beautiful sights." She reproduces those scenes, sometimes before an audience, with her remarkable mouth-artistry.

In her talks, Joni sometimes refers to the massive barn that stood just outside her studio in Maryland. It was Joni's favorite building on the farm, for it housed her fondest memories: the sweet-smelling hay, the rustling sounds of restless horses, and the dark corners she explored as a child.

Joni describes its enchantment, its beauty, and her father's pride in its workmanship. But then she describes the nightmarish memory of a fire set by vandals that utterly destroyed the barn. That terrifying scene is etched in her mind: the wild screams of her pet horses, the smell of burning flesh, the frantic efforts of her family and neighbors to contain the fire.

The story does not end there, however. Her father, stooped and twisted from arthritis, began again the arduous task of reconstructing the barn by hand. The foundation remained, and on top of it he fitted new boulders, new beams, and new boards. The second barn, the re-created one, was even grander than the first.

"I am like that barn," Joni says. "I thought my life had been crushed beyond repair. But, with the help of God and my friends, it has been rebuilt. Now can you understand why I'm so happy? I've recovered what I thought would always elude me—life in all its fullness."

Two Who Suffer

Joni Eareckson Tada and Brian Sternberg represent those unfortunate persons for whom pain seems to be in revolt. Quadriplegics, cancer victims, parents of children with birth defects—these people of uncommon suffering may well cringe from a concept like "the gift of pain." To them, the phrase must sound hollow and sadistic; pain has left its natural cycle and become a Frankenstein.

One gained fame because of her suffering, the other lost fame because of his. After several decades, both are still incapacitated in body. Yet in their individual ways both Brian and Joni have found strength to continue, and even to grow, and their trust in God is an integral part of that process of healing wounded spirits.

Brian squarely faces the question of causation. Is God responsible? He and his parents are convinced that his condition is as abhorrent to God as it is to them. His conclusions run counter to some themes in this book, for he disallows such thoughts as the transforming value of suffering. Although he recognizes that God has providentially used his pain to bring good, he rejects the notion that God might allow such a condition to continue for the rest of his life. He has gambled his faith, and almost his theology, on the hope for healing.

Yet even that position, which seems more and more untenable to the Sternbergs' friends, signifies a turning toward God. Brian has held to a trust and belief in a loving, worthy God despite a level of torment that few will ever experience. In heaven, Brian will surely walk with the confident stride of a Job or a Habakkuk or a Jeremiah, who saw the world at its worst and still believed.

Joni Eareckson Tada's pain, except for brief flashes, has been mostly psychological, the pain of loss. Yet her life has been marked by a dominant grace note of triumph and joy. She wrestled with God, yes, but she did not turn away from him. She emerged with a spiritual depth and maturity that has brought inspiration to millions. I do not imply that every afflicted person can duplicate the success story of Joni Eareckson Tada. They cannot; Joni has unique and multiple gifts and talents. But in the way that she has used them, she has achieved something else: she has "dignified" suffering.

At first Joni received a flood of letters urging her to pray for healing, or berating her for lack of faith. She did pray for healing, of course. In the summer of 1972, after an intimate service of healing with about fifteen people present, she became convinced that in the next few weeks her spinal cord would miraculously regenerate. She even called friends and warned them, "Watch for me standing on your doorstep soon; I'm going to be healed."

It did not turn out that way. And in her books Joni explains why she was forced to the difficult conclusion that she would not receive physical healing. Joni now calls her accident a "glorious intruder," and claims it was the best thing that ever happened to her. God used it to get her attention and direct her thoughts toward him. Apart from the accident, she says, she probably would have lived a typical middle-class life: aimless, comfortable, with two divorces under her belt by now.

The injury changed all that. Over time God's grace in Joni's life became so evident that she now stands as an emblem strong enough to silence puerile arguments about faith. *Does lack of healing mean lack of faith? But what about Joni Eareckson Tada?* More, Joni became a striking demonstration of transformed or "redeemed" suffering. After succeeding admirably as an author, actress, singing star, and artist, she decided to devote herself instead to her area of greatest expertise: her disability. Today, Joni directs a ministry called "Joni and Friends" that sponsors conferences and seminars, and funds worthy projects for the disabled.

It is Joni's dream to awaken the church to the needs of the disabled, and to equip Christians to perform a healing role in all society. The crowds are smaller now. Far fewer people turn out to hear a seminar on helping the disabled than to hear a personal testimony. But, step by step, Joni is bringing hope to those who are disabled, and enlightenment to those who are not.

Thank God, very few of us will endure the trials of Joni or Brian. But in different ways, they have each lived out the truth of John 9: "Neither this man nor his parents sinned, but this happened so that the work of God might be displayed in his life." Following the pattern of the blind man of Jesus' day, two modern-day quadriplegics, one from Seattle and one from Baltimore, have brightly displayed the work of God.

It is by those who have suffered that the world has been advanced.
Leo Tolstoy

11

Other Witnesses

In his book *Creative Suffering* the Swiss physician and counselor Paul Tournier recalls his surprise upon reading an article entitled "Orphans Lead the World." The article, which appeared in a respected medical journal, surveyed the lives of 300 leaders who had had a great impact on world history. After searching for some common thread, the author discovered that all these leaders had grown up as orphans—either actually, through the death of or separation from parents, or emotionally, as a result of severe childhood deprivation. His list included such names as Alexander the Great, Julius Caesar, Robespierre, George Washington, Napoleon, Queen Victoria, Golda Meir, Hitler, Lenin, Stalin, and Castro.

"So there we are," writes Tournier, "giving lectures on how important it is for a child's development to have a father and a mother performing harmoniously together their respective roles towards him. And all at once we find that this is the very thing that those who have been most influential in world history have not had!"[1]

Tournier himself was an orphan, and he pondered the orphan phenomenon soon after the death of his wife, when he felt orphaned once again in old age. Previously, he had judged each major event of life, success or tragedy, as either good or evil. But now he began to perceive that circumstances, whether fortunate or unfortunate, are morally neutral. They simply are what they are; what matters is how we respond to them. Good and evil, in the moral sense, do not reside in things, but always in persons.

This insight changed the way Tournier approached medicine, and led to his theory of the whole person. "Only rarely are we the masters of events," he says, "but (along with those who help us) we are responsible for our reactions. . . . suffering is never beneficial in itself, and must always be fought against. What counts is the way a person reacts in the face of suffering. That is the real test of the person: What is our personal attitude to life and its changes and chances? Here is a man, sick or in the grip of some tragedy, who confides in me: What is he going to make of the grievous blow that has struck him? What is his personal reaction going to be? A positive, active, creative reaction which will develop his person, or a negative one that will stunt it? . . . The right help given at the right moment may determine the course of his life."[2]

In his medical practice, Tournier saw wounded people every day, and he was quick to admit that suffering may push a person toward brokenness and not toward personal growth. That, in fact, was why he moved away from the traditional pattern of diagnosis and treatment and began to address his patients' emotional and spiritual needs as well. He felt an obligation to help them channel suffering as a transforming agent.

Tournier used the analogy of a nutcracker. Unforeseen calamities apply force that can break through the hard outer shell of personal security. The act of breaking will cause pain, of course, but it need not destroy. To the contrary, in the right environment the disarray can lead to creative growth: when old routines and behavioral patterns no longer work, the patient, exposed and vulnerable, must seek new ones.

The role of the doctor, nurse, social worker, minister, or loving friend is simply this: to keep the nutcracker of circumstances from destroying, and to help the sufferer see that even the worst hardships open up the potential for growth and development.

A Movement of Creative Suffering

"What doesn't destroy me makes me stronger," Martin Luther King, Jr., used to say. In our calamitous century King, Gandhi, Solzhenitsyn, Sakharov, Tutu, Mandela, and many others have offered living demonstrations of Tournier's theory of creative suffering. Out of circumstances that should have merely destroyed, these courageous ones emerged with a strength that confounded whole nations.

Martin Luther King, Jr., for example, deliberately sought out the meanest southern sheriffs for his scenes of confrontation. He accepted beatings, jailings, and other brutalities because he believed a complacent nation would rally around his cause only when they saw the evil of racism in its ugliest extreme. "Christianity," he said, "has always insisted that the cross we bear precedes the crown we wear. To be a Christian one must take up his cross, with all its difficulties and agonizing and tension-packed content, and carry it until that very cross leaves its mark upon us and redeems us to that more excellent way which comes only through suffering."[3]

In the end that principle was what brought the civil rights movement the victory sought for so long. It was the sight of civil rights marchers being brutalized by policemen and sheriffs that finally aroused a nation. Just one week after the police assault on the bridge at Selma, Congress took up the Voting Rights Act of 1965. With each bloody confrontation King had become stronger, not weaker.

The principle that operates on large scale in someone like Martin Luther King, Jr., also pertains to the "little people" who followed him in the marches for freedom and justice. I think back to one unlikely hero in rural Mississippi, a man whose photo never appeared in newsmagazines. I interviewed Mr. Buckley in the early 1970s, a time when much of the South was still actively resisting the civil rights movement. When I left Mr. Buckley's house, I felt I had left the presence of a saint.

Mr. Buckley's house was the nicest black home I visited in Simpson County, Mississippi. It was brick on the outside and wood-paneled on the inside, and included four or five large rooms. At the age of ninety, though, Mr. Buckley seemed oblivious to his surroundings. He spent most of his time sitting in a wooden rocker by the kitchen fireplace, the way he used to sit around Home Comfort stoves in the one-room shacks of rural Mississippi. That's where I found him—rocking, reminiscing, scratching his close-cropped gray hair, and chuckling over how life used to be. His eyes were rheumy, his skin thick and leathery, burnt that way by nine decades of Mississippi sun.

In one interview, Mr. Buckley decided to recollect all his memories of childhood. After talking for three and a half hours into a cassette recorder, he paused and asked for a glass of water. He took a good long sip, swished it around in his mouth, and announced, "Well, that brings us up to 1901."

He was born one generation after slavery, and he grew up during the bitter days of Reconstruction. He lived through the fear-filled reign of the Ku Klux Klan, listening to their threats, watching crosses burn, hearing reports of lynchings and burnings. And after seventy-five years of being banned from white restaurants, white motels, white bathrooms, and white polling booths, Mr. Buckley joined the civil rights movement in the mid-1960s. Believing God could use him, he began working for the Rev. John Perkins in a voter registration drive. In a county with over 5,000 black adults, only 50 were then registered to vote.

Federal marshals set up registration lines around the rear loading docks of the post office, and Mr. Buckley helped organize a caravan of buses and vans. Each name added to voter lists was carved out in fear. A hostile crowd of whites would sometimes appear, shouting insults and threats. Some blacks who registered lost their jobs. But still they came. Strong black men, bowed from carrying cotton sacks on their backs, formed a courageous line through downtown Mendenhall to ask for their vote. Eventually 2,300 were registered.

During his years as a leader in the black community near Mendenhall, Mr. Buckley walked with God, and the wounds he suffered for it made him a deeper, stronger person. He demonstrated to me how the poor and the oppressed could indeed, as Jesus said, be blessed. Faith in God was all he had when days were dark and nights were filled with sleepless fear. And in the end God resided in him with evident ease and familiarity.

Mr. Buckley's faith was tested most severely one night just after he and his wife moved into their new home. At last, in their eighties, the Buckleys had a comfortable home to live in, one that still smelled like fresh paint and looked neat and clean. But Mr. Buckley suddenly awoke at two o'clock in the morning, smelling smoke. He jumped out of bed just in time: The hallway of their house was ablaze, and flames were creeping along the baseboard to their bedroom. He and his wife escaped, barely, but lost all their possessions. The fire had been set by their neighbors.

Mr. Buckley told me, "Well, I reckon we been through a lot. I lost two of my three children, and I lost my first wife, and we almost got ourselves killed that night, fo' sure. But the Lord say he won't put more on us than we can stand. If we can't take it, he'll be right there beside us giving stren'th we didn't know we had."

Mr. Buckley died in 1986, at the age of ninety-seven. He spent his last years helping to found a new church in Mendenhall. He said, "I want a church where anyone is welcome, no matter their color, a church where people pray and expect answers to their prayers. I want a church where people are known by their love for one another." By his example, Mr. Buckley showed what kind of church he wanted.

The Great Reversal

"What doesn't destroy me makes me stronger," Martin Luther King, Jr., had said. Mr. Buckley's peaceful, wrinkled face seemed to prove it. Like a tough old oak that had weathered thunderstorms, blizzards, and forest fires, Mr. Buckley exuded a quality of strength such as most of us sheltered Americans will never experience. There's something unique about having only God to lean on in times of trial.

After the hours I spent with Mr. Buckley, I finally understood Jesus' strange, paradoxical words in the Beatitudes. I realized that I had always viewed the words "Blessed are the poor . . . those who mourn . . . the meek . . . the persecuted" as a kind of sop Jesus threw to the unfortunates. *Well, since you aren't rich, and your health is bad, and your face is wet with tears, I'll toss out a few nice phrases and a promise of future rewards. Maybe you'll feel better.* But some of the promises are expressed in present tense—"theirs *is* the kingdom"—and my meetings with poor blacks in Mississippi showed me how the poor and the oppressed can indeed be blessed. Mr. Buckley demonstrated a quality of life I had encountered in few other people. His faith was solid, aged, and worn.

The apostle Paul uses a strange phrase, "His [God's] strength is made perfect in weakness." It is a phrase misunderstood and sometimes ridiculed by those who denounce God for allowing pain and suffering in this world. But in representatives like Paul and like Mr. Buckley, the phrase has the ring of truth. Even of Jesus it was said, "He learned obedience from what he suffered" (Hebrews 5:8).

We who stand alongside, observing suffering people, expect to find anger and bitterness. We wait for them to turn on God and lash out against him for the inequities of life. Remarkably, they often find instead a solace in him that puts us to shame. It is no accident that some of the most inspiring stories of faith come from those often considered "losers" by the rest of the world.

Hesitantly, C. S. Lewis concludes: "I am not convinced that suffering . . . has any natural tendency to produce such evils [anger and cynicism]. I did not find the front-line trenches of the C.C.S. more full of hatred, selfishness, rebellion, and dishonesty than any other place. I have seen great beauty of spirit in some who were great sufferers. I have seen men, for the most part, grow better not worse with advancing years, and I have seen the last illness produce treasures of fortitude and meekness from most unpromising subjects . . . If the world is indeed a 'vale of soul-making,' it seems on the whole to be doing its work."[4]

What is there in the nature of suffering to cause this reversal whereby pain can fortify instead of destroy? Jesus plainly taught that the world as seen from God's viewpoint is tilted in favor of the poor and the oppressed. This teaching, sometimes called the "theology of reversal," emerges in the Sermon on the Mount and in other statements of Jesus: the first will be last (Matthew 19:30; Mark 10:31; Luke 13:30); he who humbles himself will be exalted (Luke 14:11; 18:14); the greatest among you should be like the youngest, and the one who rules like the one who serves (Luke 22:26). The parables of the Good Samaritan and the rich man and Lazarus also point to this reversal of the world's order.

But why? Why would God single out the poor and oppressed for special attention over any other groups? What makes the weak so deserving of God's concern?

I came across a thought-provoking list of "advantages" to being poor proposed by a Catholic nun named Monica Hellwig. I have adapted her list, broadening it to include all who suffer.[5]

§   1. Suffering, the great equalizer, brings us to a point where we may realize our urgent need for redemption.

2. Those who suffer know not only their dependence on God and on healthy people but also their interdependence with one another.

3. Those who suffer rest their security not on things, which often cannot be enjoyed and may soon be taken away, but rather on people.

4. Those who suffer have no exaggerated sense of their own importance, and no exaggerated need of privacy. Suffering humbles the proud.

5. Those who suffer expect little from competition and much from cooperation.

6. Suffering helps us distinguish between necessities and luxuries.

7. Suffering teaches patience, often a kind of dogged patience born of acknowledged dependence.

8. Suffering teaches the difference between valid fears and exaggerated fears.

9. To suffering people, the gospel sounds like good news and not like a threat or a scolding. It offers hope and comfort.

10. Those who suffer can respond to the call of the gospel with a certain abandonment and uncomplicated totality because they have so little to lose and are ready for anything.

Reading over this list, I began to realize why so many Christian saints have endured much suffering. Dependence, humility, simplicity, cooperation, abandon—these are qualities greatly prized in the spiritual life, but extremely elusive for people who live in comfort.

My understanding of the Beatitudes has undergone a radical change. I no longer see them as a sop thrown by Jesus to the unfortunates of the world. I view them not as patronizing slogans, but as profound insights into the mystery of human existence. The poor, the hungry, the mourners, and those who suffer truly are blessed. Not because of their miserable states, of course—Jesus spent much of his life trying to remedy those miseries. Rather, they are blessed because of an innate advantage they hold over people more comfortable and self-sufficient.

Self-sufficiency, which first reared its head in the Garden of Eden, is the most fatal sin because it pulls us as if by a magnet away from God. The suffering and the poor have the advantage that their *lack* of self-sufficiency is obvious to them every day. They must turn somewhere for strength, and sometimes they turn to God. People who are rich, successful, and beautiful may go through life relying on their natural gifts. But there's a chance, just a chance, that people who lack such natural advantages may cry out to God in their time of need.

In summary, through no choice of their own—they may urgently wish otherwise—suffering and oppressed people find themselves in a posture that befits the grace of God. They are needy, dependent, and dissatisfied with life; for that reason they may welcome God's free gift of love.

Poverty and suffering can serve as instruments to teach us the value of dependence, and unless we learn dependence we will never experience grace. The apostle Paul gave the Corinthians an autobiographical example of this very principle. He battled against a "thorn in the flesh," an unidentified ailment for which many possibilities have been proposed: epilepsy, eye disease, chronic depression, malaria, sexual temptation. I am glad that Paul left the ailment vague, for the process he outlines in 2 Corinthians 12 applies to all of us with all our various thorns in the flesh.

At first Paul could see no benefit in his thorn in the flesh. Hardly able to "count it all joy," he instead resented the tormenting affliction. It interfered with his busy ministry schedule and caused him to question God. Three times he pleaded for a miracle of healing. Three times his request was refused. Finally, he received the lesson that God wanted him to learn through the affliction: "My grace is sufficient for you, for my power is made perfect in weakness."

The physical weakness was, in fact, being used for Paul's own benefit. The sins of spiritual pride, arrogance, and conceit represented far greater dangers, and this nagging physical weakness kept him relying on God, and not himself, for strength. When he finally saw that, Paul's attitude moved from one of resistance to one of transforming acceptance: instead of begging God to remove the thorn, he prayed that the pain would be redeemed or transformed to his benefit.

Once Paul had learned this lesson, in typical fashion he began shouting it to the world, "boasting" about his weaknesses. To the Corinthians, a sophisticated audience impressed by power and physical appearance, he bragged about God's pattern of choosing the lowly and despised people of the world to confound the wise, the weak to confound the strong. Paul had learned the lesson of the Beatitudes: poverty, affliction, sorrow, and weakness can actually be means of grace if we turn to God with a humble, dependent spirit. "For when I am weak, then I am strong," Paul concluded. The weaker we feel, the harder we may lean.

Sometimes I went so far as to thank destiny for the privilege of such loneliness [in Siberia], for only in solitude could I have scrutinized my past so carefully, or examined so closely my interior and outward life. What strong and strange new germs of hope were born in my soul during those memorable hours! I weighed and decided all sorts of issues, I entered into a compact with myself to avoid the errors of former years and the rocks on which I had been wrecked.

Fyodor Dostoyevski
The House of the Dead

12

Extreme Cases

Over the years I have read scores of accounts by survivors of concentration camps. They hold a certain fascination for me, perhaps because they present the issues of life at their most extreme. In the camps all marks of individuality are erased. Prisoners are given identical clothing and identical haircuts. They are addressed by number and not by name. They eat the same food and keep the same schedules. There are no differences of class. The barbed wire encloses humanity in its most basic, atavistic form.

In the hands of skilled—or sadistic—administrators, the concentration camps can become a laboratory of suffering. As Terrence Des Pres has pointed out, the aim of the camps was "to reduce inmates to mindless creatures whose behavior could be predicted and controlled absolutely. The camps have so far been the closest thing on earth to a perfect [B. F.] Skinner box. They were a closed, completely regulated environment, a 'total' world in the strict sense. Pain and death were the 'negative reinforcers,' food and life the 'positive reinforcers,' and all these forces were pulling and shoving twenty-four hours a day at the deepest stratum of human need."[1]

Yet if the accounts by Bettelheim, Frankl, Wiesel, Levi, Wiesenthal, Solzhenitsyn, Sharansky, and the like prove anything, they prove that the great behaviorist experiment failed. Stripped of all apparent dignity, these survivors nevertheless managed to emerge with their humanity intact while still possessing a sharply honed moral consciousness. To take just one example, a "rehabilitated" Solzhenitsyn cried out so loudly he was expelled from his homeland, but not before he had almost single-handedly dismantled the myth of Stalinism.

Similarly, if you attend a meeting of Jewish survivors of the Holocaust today, you will not find defeated, useless human beings who walk about like zombies. You will find politicians, doctors, lawyers, virtually a cross section of society in general. Children raised under a regime that approached absolute evil yet matured into men and women who personify courage and compassion.

Taken together, the survivors demonstrate that even suffering at its most diabolical extreme can be transformed in the lives of individual human beings. As Bruno Bettelheim summarized the lesson from the camps: "Our experience did not teach us that life is meaningless, that the world of the living is but a whorehouse, that one ought to live by the body's crude claims, disregarding the compulsions of culture. It taught us that, miserable though the world in which we live may be, the difference between it and the world of the concentration camps is as great as that between night and day, hell and salvation, death and life. It taught us that there is meaning to life, difficult though that meaning may be to fathom—a much deeper meaning than we had thought possible before we became survivors."[2]

George Mangakis, who was tortured and sentenced to eighteen years' imprisonment by the military junta in Greece, ended up feeling pity for his torturer, not himself.

> I have experienced the fate of a victim. I have seen the torturer's face at close quarters. It was in a worse condition than my own bleeding, livid face. The torturer's face was distorted by a kind of twitching that had nothing human about it. . . .
>
> In this situation, I turned out to be the lucky one. I was humiliated. I did not humiliate others. I was simply bearing

a profoundly unhappy humanity in my aching entrails. Whereas the men who humiliate you must first humiliate the notion of humanity within themselves. Never mind if they strut around in their uniforms, swollen with the knowledge that they can control the suffering, sleeplessness, hunger and despair of their fellow human beings, intoxicated with the power in their hands. Their intoxication is nothing other than the degradation of humanity. The ultimate degradation. They have had to pay very dearly for my torments.

I wasn't the one in the worst position. I was simply a man who moaned because he was in great pain. I prefer that. At this moment I am deprived of the joy of seeing children going to school or playing in the parks. Whereas they have to look their own children in the face.[3]

Dr. Viktor Frankl, a Jewish psychiatrist, learned through his own imprisonment that human life does have meaning and individuals have an inherent freedom that cannot be smothered even in the inhuman camp conditions. His conclusion summarizes the experience of many inmates:

The experiences of camp life show that man does have a choice of action. There were enough examples, often of a heroic nature, which proved that apathy could be overcome, irritability suppressed. Man *can* preserve a vestige of spiritual freedom, of independence of mind, even in such terrible conditions of psychic and physical stress . . . everything can be taken from man but one thing: the last of human freedoms—to choose one's attitude in any given set of circumstances, to choose one's own way. . . .

In the final analysis it becomes clear that the sort of person the prisoner became was the result of an inner decision, and not the result of camp influences alone. Fundamentally, therefore, any man can, even under such circumstances, decide what shall become of him—mentally and spiritually.[4]

The Ultimate Question

If they answered certain basic questions about humanity, the concentration camps, and most notably Hitler's Holocaust against the Jews, prompted desperate questions about God. The question of this book, "Where is God when it hurts?" almost defined the Jewish experience during the Holocaust. How could he sit by, silent, and watch the immolation of six million of his chosen people? How could he let evil rule with such apparent sovereignty?

During the 1970s a man named Reeve Robert Brenner surveyed one thousand survivors of the Holocaust, inquiring especially about their religious faith. How had the experience of the Holocaust affected their beliefs about God? Somewhat astonishingly, almost half claimed that the Holocaust had no influence whatever on their beliefs about God. But the other half told a different story. Of the total number surveyed, eleven percent said they had rejected all belief in the existence of God as a direct result of their experience. After the war, they never regained faith. Analyzing their detailed responses, Brenner noted that their professed atheism seemed less a matter of theological belief and more an emotional reaction, an expression of deep hurt and anger against God for abandoning them.

Yet Brenner also discovered that a smaller number, about five percent of his overall sample, actually changed from atheists into believers because of the Holocaust. After living through such abominations, they simply had nowhere else to turn.[5]

Within a two-month period I read two poignant accounts by survivors of the Holocaust. These two authors, Elie Wiesel and Corrie ten Boom, typify the radically different responses of faith under such conditions. Their books, both best-sellers, are among the most readable works in the vast Holocaust literature.

Night, by Elie Wiesel, affected me as much as any book I have ever read. In a terse style, his sentences tightly packed with images, Wiesel describes the world in which he spent his teenage years. All the Jews in his village were first herded together into a ghetto, then stripped of possessions and loaded into cattle cars. Almost a third of them died in transit to the death camps.

The first night Wiesel's train pulled up at Birkenbau, coils of ominous black smoke billowed from a massive oven, and for the first time in his life Elie smelled the scent of burning human flesh: "Never shall I forget that night, seven times cursed and seven times sealed. Never shall I forget that smoke. Never shall I forget the little faces of the children, whose bodies I saw turned into wreaths of smoke beneath a silent blue sky. Never shall I forget that nocturnal silence which deprived me, for all eternity, of the desire to live. Never shall I forget those moments which murdered my God and my soul and turned my dreams to dust. Never shall I forget these things, even if I am condemned to live as long as God Himself. Never."[6]

Wiesel saw his mother, a younger sister, and eventually all his family forced into an extermination oven. He saw babies pitchforked, children hanged, prisoners murdered by their cellmates over a piece of bread. Elie himself escaped death only on account of an administrative error. His books drum out different variations on the same story of senseless, hopeless tragedy.

In a foreword to *Night,* fellow Nobel laureate François Mauriac describes the meeting with Wiesel when he first heard his story.

> It was then that I understood what had first drawn me to the young Israeli: that look, as of a Lazarus risen from the dead, yet still a prisoner within the grim confines where he had strayed, stumbling among the shameful corpses. For him, Nietzsche's cry expressed an almost physical reality: God is dead, the God of love, of gentleness, of comfort, the God of Abraham, of Isaac, of Jacob, has vanished forevermore, beneath the gaze of this child, in the smoke of a human holocaust exacted by Race, the most voracious of all idols. And how many pious Jews have experienced this death! . . .
>
> Have we ever thought about the consequence of a horror that, though less apparent, less striking than the other outrages, is yet the worst of all to those of us who have faith: the death of God in the soul of a child who suddenly discovers absolute evil?[7]

A Deep Pit

I sometimes feel an aching desire to remain with Wiesel, overwhelmed by human tragedy. After undergoing such monstrosity, how can anyone begin living again? Can words like hope, happiness, and joy regain meaning? How can anyone speak of the character-building value of suffering?

After reading *Night* and several other books by Elie Wiesel, I read *The Hiding Place,* by Corrie ten Boom. The setting was by then familiar. Although not a Jew herself, Corrie was arrested in Holland for sheltering Jews and was transported to the death camps in Germany. She too felt the sting of a whip, saw prisoners disappear into the ovens, and watched her sister die. She too sensed the defilement of all virtue in a world of sovereign evil. Her books ask the same questions as Wiesel's, and sometimes her anger blazes against God.

But there is another element in *The Hiding Place*, the element of hope and victory. Woven throughout her story are the threads of small miracles, along with Bible studies, hymn-sings, and numerous acts of compassion and sacrifice. Throughout their ordeal, the two sisters continued to trust in a God who watched over them in love. As Corrie said, "However deep the pit, God's love is deeper still."

I must confess that, although my sympathies lie entirely with Corrie's view of life and I believe in her God of love, I had to fight thinking her book shallow compared to Wiesel's. Something dark and sonorous was tugging inside me, pulling me away from hope, toward despair.

Wiesel himself expressed his doubt as an act of liberation. "I was the accuser, and God the accused. My eyes were open and I was alone—terribly alone in a world without God and without man. Without love or mercy. I have ceased to be anything but ashes, yet I felt myself to be stronger than the Almighty, to whom my life had been tied for so long."[8] A force within urged me to stand proud beside Elie Wiesel as God's accuser and to throw off the confining shackles of belief.

One thing alone keeps me from standing as God's accuser. My reason for continuing to believe, ironically, is best expressed in a scene described by Wiesel himself, an episode that took place while he, at age fifteen, was imprisoned at Buna.

A cache of arms had been discovered at the Buna camp. They belonged to a Dutchman, who was immediately shipped away to Auschwitz. But the Dutchman also had a *pipel*, a young boy who served him, and the guards began torturing the young boy. The *pipel* had a refined and beautiful face that the camp had not yet ruined—the face, said Wiesel, "of a sad little angel."

When the *pipel* refused to cooperate with his interrogators, the SS sentenced him to death, along with two other prisoners who had been caught with arms.

One day when we came back from work, we saw three gallows rearing up in the assembly place, three black crows. Roll call, SS all around us, machine guns trained: the traditional ceremony. Three victims in chains—and one of them the little servant, the sad-eyed angel.

The SS seemed more preoccupied, more disturbed than usual. To hang a young boy in front of thousands of spectators was no light matter.

The head of the camp read the verdict. All eyes were on the child. He was lividly pale, almost calm, biting his lips. The gallows threw its shadow over him.

This time the *Lagerkapo* refused to act as executioner. Three SS replaced him.

The three victims mounted together onto the chairs.

The three necks were placed at the same moment within the nooses.

"Long live liberty!" cried the two adults.

But the child was silent.

"Where is God? Where is He?" someone behind me asked.

At a sign from the head of the camp, the three chairs tipped over.

Total silence throughout the camp. On the horizon, the sun was setting.

"Bare your heads!" yelled the head of the camp. His voice was raucous. We were weeping.

"Cover your heads!"

Then the march past began. The two adults were no longer alive. Their tongues hung swollen, blue-tinged. But the third rope was still moving; being so light, the child was still alive. . . .

For more than half an hour he stayed there, struggling between life and death, dying in slow agony under our eyes. And we had to look him full in the face. He was still alive when I passed in front of him. His tongue was still red, his eyes not yet glazed.

Behind me, I heard the same man asking: "Where is God now?"

And I heard a voice within me answer him, "Where is He? Here He is—He is hanging here on this gallows. . . ."

That night the soup tasted of corpses.[9]

Wiesel lost his faith in God at that concentration camp. For him, God literally hung to death on the gallows, never to be resurrected. But in fact the image that Wiesel evokes so powerfully contains within it the answer to his question. Where was God? The voice within Elie Wiesel spoke truth: in a way, God did hang beside the young *pipel*. God did not exempt even himself from human suffering. He too hung on a gallows, at Calvary, and that alone is what keeps me believing in a God of love.

God does not, in the comfortable surroundings of heaven, turn a deaf ear to the sounds of suffering on this groaning planet. He joined us, choosing to live among an oppressed people—Wiesel's own race—in circumstances of poverty and great affliction. He too was an innocent victim of cruel, senseless torture. At that moment of black despair, the Son of God cried out, much like the believers in the camps, "God, why have you forsaken me?"

Jesus, the Son of God on earth, embodied all that I have been trying to say about pain. Like Job, an innocent sufferer who preceded him, he did not receive an answer to the questions of *cause*: "Why? . . . why?" he called out from the cross, and heard nothing but the silence of God. Even so, he responded with faithfulness, turning his attention to the good that his suffering could produce: ". . . for the joy set before him [Christ] endured the cross" (Hebrews 12:2). What joy? The transformation, or redemption, of humanity.

The Gospel writers stress that Jesus' suffering was not a matter of impotence; he could have called on a legion of angels. Somehow he had to go through it for fallen creation to be redeemed. God took the Great Pain of his own Son's death and used it to absorb into himself all the minor pains of earth. Suffering was the cost to God of forgiveness.

Human suffering remains meaningless and barren unless we have some assurance that God is sympathetic to our pain, and can somehow heal that pain. In Jesus, we have that assurance.

Thus the Christian message encompasses the full range of anger and despair and darkness expressed so eloquently in a book like *Night*. It offers a complete identification with the suffering world. But Christianity takes a further step as well. It is called the Resurrection, the moment of victory when the last enemy, death itself, is defeated. A seeming tragedy, Jesus' crucifixion, made possible the ultimate healing of the world.

Did God desire the Holocaust? Ask the question another way: Did God desire the death of his own Son? Obviously, because of his character he could not possibly desire such atrocities. And yet both happened, and the question then moves from the unanswerable "Why?" to another question, "To what end?"

At the instant of pain, it may seem impossible to imagine that good can come from tragedy. (It must have seemed so to Christ at Gethsemane.) We never know in advance exactly how suffering can be transformed into a cause for celebration. But that is what we are asked to believe. Faith means believing in advance what will only make sense in reverse.

The Chaplain of Dachau

Not long after reading the books by Elie Wiesel and Corrie ten Boom, I visited the site of one of the Nazi concentration camps. On the grounds of the Dachau camp near Munich, I met with a man who survived the Holocaust and who has taken on a life mission of announcing to the world that God's love is deeper than the sloughs of human depravity. He helped me understand how Corrie ten Boom's hopeful view of life was even possible in such a place.

The man, Christian Reger, spent four years as a prisoner in Dachau. His crime? He had belonged to the Confessing Church, the branch of the German state church which, under the leadership of Martin Niemöller and Dietrich Bonhoeffer, opposed Hitler. Reger, turned over to the authorities by his church organist, was arrested and shipped hundreds of miles away to Dachau.

Since liberation, Reger and other members of the International Dachau Committee have worked hard to restore the concentration camp as a lasting monument and lesson to all humanity. "Never Again" is their slogan. Nonetheless, the camp is difficult to find, since the locals are understandably reluctant to call attention to it.

The day I visited Dachau was gray, chill, and overcast. Morning fog hung low, close to the ground, and as I walked droplets of moisture gathered on my face and hands. Thirty barracks once stood on the site, and concrete foundation blocks a foot high mark out their location. One has been restored, and placards point out that sometimes 1,600 people were pressed into this barrack designed for a crowded 208. The cremation ovens are originals, left standing by the Allied liberators.

The fog, the pervasive grayness, and the unfinished ghost buildings added up to an eerie, solemn scene. A child was dancing along the foundation blocks of the barracks. Alongside the barbed wire fences, lilacs bloomed.

I found Christian Reger in the Protestant Chapel, which stands near a Catholic convent and a Jewish memorial. He wanders the grounds, searching out tourists to converse with in German, English, or French. He answers questions, and freely reminisces about his days there as an inmate.

During the final winter, when coal supplies ran low, the ovens were finally shut off. Prisoners no longer had to put up with the constant stench of burning comrades. Many died of exposure, however, and the bodies were stacked naked in the snow like cordwood, a number stenciled on each with a blue marker. Reger will tell such horror stories if you ask. But he never stops there. He goes on to share his faith, and how even at Dachau he was visited by a God of love.

"Nietzsche said a man can undergo torture if he knows the Why of his life," Reger told me. "But here at Dachau, I learned something far greater. I learned to know the Who of my life. He was enough to sustain me then, and is enough to sustain me still."

It was not always so. After his first month in Dachau, Reger, like Elie Wiesel, abandoned all hope in a loving God. From the perspective of a prisoner of the Nazis, the odds against God's existence seemed too great. Then, in July 1941, something happened to challenge his doubt.

Each prisoner was allowed only one letter a month, and exactly one month from the date of his incarceration Christian Reger received the first news from his wife. In the fragments of the letter, which had been carefully clipped into pieces by a censor, she chatted about the family and assured him of her love. At the very bottom Reger's wife printed a Bible reference: Acts 4:26–29.

Reger, who had smuggled in a Bible, looked up the verses, which formed part of a speech delivered by Peter and John just after their release from prison. "The kings of the earth take their stand, and the rulers gather together against the Lord and against his Anointed One. Indeed Herod and Pontius Pilate met together with the Gentiles and the people of Israel in this city to conspire against your holy servant Jesus, whom you anointed. They did what your power and will had decided beforehand should happen. Now, Lord, consider their threats and enable your servants to speak your word with great boldness."

That afternoon Reger was to undergo interrogation, the most terrifying experience in the camp. He would be called on to name other Christians in the Confessing Church outside. If he succumbed, those Christians would be captured and possibly killed. But if he refused to cooperate, there was a good chance he would be beaten with clubs or tortured with electricity. He knew firsthand about "rulers gathering together against the Lord," but other than that, the verses meant little to him. How could God possibly help him at a time like this?

Reger moved to the waiting area outside the interrogation room. He was trembling. The door opened, and a fellow minister whom Reger had never met came out. Without looking at Reger or changing the expression on his face, he walked over to him, slipped something into Reger's coat pocket, and walked away. Seconds later SS guards appeared and ushered Reger inside the room. The interrogations went well; they were surprisingly easy and involved no violence.

When Reger arrived back at the barracks, he was sweating despite the cold. He breathed deeply for several minutes, trying to calm himself, then crawled into his bunk, covered with straw. Suddenly he remembered the odd encounter with the other minister. He reached in his pocket and pulled out a matchbox. *Oh,* he thought, *what a kind gesture. Matches are a priceless commodity in the barracks.* He found no matches inside, however, just a folded slip of paper. Reger unfolded the paper, and his heart beat hard against his chest. Neatly printed on the paper was this reference: Acts 4:26–29.

To Reger, it was a miracle, a message directly from God. That minister could not possibly have seen the letter from Reger's wife—the man was a stranger. Had God arranged the event as a demonstration that he was still alive, still able to strengthen, still worthy of trust?

Christian Reger was transformed from that moment. It was

a small miracle, as miracles go, but sufficient to anchor his faith in bedrock that could not be shaken, not even by the atrocities he would witness over the next four years in Dachau.

"God did not rescue me and make my suffering easier. He simply assured me that he was alive, and knew I was here. We Christians drew together. We formed a church here, among other convicted pastors and priests—a forced ecumenical movement, we called it. We found our identity as one flesh, as part of Christ's body.

"I can only speak for myself. Others turned from God because of Dachau. Who am I to judge them? I simply know that God met me. For me he was enough, even at Dachau."

As long as he has health, Christian Reger will stiffly pace the grounds of Dachau, speaking to tourists in his warm, thickly accented voice. He will tell them where God was during the long night at Dachau.

Part 4

How Can We Cope with Pain?

I do not ask the wounded person how he feels,
I myself become the wounded person.
                                        Walt Whitman
                                        Song of Myself

13

Frontiers of Recovery

To learn about suffering, I have explored the lives of people who are almost defined by it: Brian Sternberg, Joni Eareckson Tada, survivors of the Holocaust. For most of us, suffering comes for briefer periods and with less intensity. But one fact holds true of afflictions major and minor: people respond differently.

I have known people with rheumatoid arthritis who find it difficult to talk about anything else, while others will only admit their pain after much prodding and questioning. What makes the difference? Is there a way to predict a person's response to pain and suffering? Can we learn how to prepare for pain in such a way as to lessen its impact?

Pain itself, which may seem reflexive, does not work like a simple cause-and-effect response. True, neurons fire off whenever they sense a disturbance that represents danger, but all such messages are filtered through and interpreted by the brain. A person's predisposition and understanding of pain can dramatically alter his or her experience of it. You will respond quite differently to a sudden blow to the face than will a professional boxer, who is paid a huge purse to undergo fifteen rounds of pummeling.

The medical community now freely admits that in a larger

sense a person's attitude is one of the chief factors in determining the effect of all suffering. Dr. Robert Ader, a professor of psychiatry and psychology at Rochester School of Medicine, acknowledges that practically all illnesses have emotional factors. He concludes, "The germ theory simply can't account for why people get sick, because if it could—I don't know how big your office is, but if somebody gets the flu then I don't understand why everybody doesn't get it."[1]

Albert Schweitzer used to say that diseases tended to leave him rapidly because they found so little hospitality in his body. Or, as one observer commented less felicitously, "Sometimes it is more important to know what kind of fellah has a germ than what kind of germ has a fellah." Preparations, what we bring in advance, can have a decisive impact on our experience of pain and suffering. And knowing about them can teach us how to minister to others in pain when we ourselves are not suffering.

This book opened with the story of Claudia Claxton, my friend who suddenly found herself battling Hodgkin's disease. I asked Claudia and her husband John why that crisis seemed actually to pull them together, whereas more frequently a life-threatening crisis creates tension and pushes a couple apart.

"I was working as a chaplain's assistant in a hospital at the time," John replied. "I had seen sick and dying patients. In the movies, couples who have fought for years suddenly in the face of danger forget their differences and come together. But it doesn't work that way in real life.

"When a couple encounters a crisis, it magnifies what's already present in the relationship. Since Claudia and I happened to love each other deeply, and had worked on open communication, the crisis drove us to each other. Feelings of blame and anger against each other did not creep in. The crisis of her illness merely brought to the surface and intensified feelings already present."

According to John, the best way to prepare for suffering is to work on a strong, supportive life when you're healthy. You cannot suddenly fabricate foundations of strength; they must have been building all along.

The School of Suffering

The only people who can teach us about suffering—both for the sake of our own preparations and our attempts to comfort others—are the sufferers themselves. Yet someone else's sickness, especially terminal sickness, affronts our own health. It tends to bring out the worst in us: eyes averted out of fear, nervous twitches, empty promises ("Call me if you need anything"), conversation reduced to prattle. What can we *say*? Is anything worth saying?

I confess that it is not easy for me to be around suffering people. I cannot imagine a less likely candidate for hospital visitation. I begin to clam up as soon as I open the extra-wide glass doors—because of the smell, I think. Smell has a direct sensory pathway into the brain, and those antiseptic odors trigger in me deep-seated memories of a childhood tonsillectomy. When a nurse in the hallway smiles and nods, I see a giant phantom nurse leaning over me with a plastic bag to smother me and steal my breath.

After several years of professional schizophrenia—writing and talking about pain while feeling personally helpless around it—I decided I should set aside my awkwardness and force myself to be near suffering people on a regular basis. About this time, a friend discovered he had one of the rarest, most severe forms of cancer. In medical history, the doctors told Jim, only twenty-seven people had been treated with his specific condition. The other twenty-six had all died. Jim was charting new territory, alone.

He was thirty-three years old, and had been married only ten months. Earlier that year he and his wife had spent their honeymoon sailing in the Caribbean. Jim cared primarily about his career, his passion for downhill skiing, and his young marriage. Suddenly, he faced the prospect of dying, and he needed help.

At Jim's invitation I began accompanying him to a therapy group at a nearby hospital. People join therapy groups for a variety of reasons: to improve self-image, to learn how to relate to others, to overcome an addiction. This therapy group, called Make Today Count, consisted of people who were dying. They used the euphemism "life-threatening illnesses" for their congeries of cancer, multiple sclerosis, hepatitis, muscular dystrophy, and other such diseases. Each member of the group knew that his or her life had boiled down to two issues: surviving and, failing that, preparing for death.

The first meeting was very hard for me. We met in an open

waiting room area, sitting on cheap molded plastic chairs of a garish orange color doubtless chosen to create an atmosphere of institutional cheer. Bored-looking orderlies rolled stretchers up and down the hallways. Elevator doors opened and closed. I tried to ignore a nearby loudspeaker that periodically crackled with an announcement or a doctor's page.

Most people were in their thirties. That age group, usually so oblivious of death, seemed to have the deepest need to talk about its unexpected intrusion. The meeting began with each person "checking in." Someone had died in the month since the last meeting, and the social worker provided details of his last days and the funeral. Jim whispered to me that this was the one depressing aspect of the group: Its members were always disappearing.

I had expected a somber tone at the meeting, but found the opposite. Tears flowed freely, of course, but these people talked easily and comfortably about disease and death. The group served as the one place where they could talk so freely and still count on an empathetic response. They described the sad, almost bizarre manner in which most friends skirted the one thing that mattered most, the fact of their illness. Here in the group, they could lower all protective barriers.

Nancy showed off a new wig purchased to cover her baldness, a side effect of chemotherapy treatments. She joked that she had always wanted straight hair and now her brain tumor had finally given her an excuse to get it. Steve, a young black man, admitted he was terrified of what lay ahead. He had battled Hodgkin's disease as a teenager and had apparently won, but now, ten years later, symptoms were unexpectedly returning. He didn't know how to break the news to his fiancée. Lorraine, afflicted with tumors on her spinal cord, lay on the floor throughout the meeting and rarely talked. She had come to cry, she said, not to talk.

I was most affected by the one elderly person in the room, a handsome, gray-haired woman with the broad, bony face of an Eastern European immigrant. Speaking in simple declarative sentences wrapped in a thick accent, she expressed her loneliness. The group asked if she had any family. She replied that an only son was trying to get emergency leave from the Air Force in Germany. And her husband? She swallowed hard a few times and then said, "He came to see me just once. I was in the hospital. He brought me my bathrobe and a few things. The doctor stood in the hallway and told him about my leukemia." Her voice started to crack and she dabbed at her eyes before continuing. "He went home that night, packed up all his things, and left. I never saw him again."

"How long had you been married?" I asked after a pause. The group gasped aloud at her answer: "Thirty-seven years." (I later learned that some researchers report a seventy percent breakup rate in marriages in which one of the partners has a terminal illness. In this group of thirty people, no marriages remained intact longer than two years—including my friend Jim's.)

I met with that group for a year. Each person in it lived with the peculiar intensity that only death can bring. Certainly I cannot say I "enjoyed" the meetings; that would be the wrong word. Yet they became for me one of the most meaningful events of each month. In contrast to a party, where participants try to impress each other with signs of status and power and wit, in this group no one was trying to impress. Clothes, fashion, apartment furnishings, job titles, new cars—what do these things mean to people who are preparing to die?

The Make Today Count meetings seemed to confirm the "megaphone value" of suffering. More than any other people I had met, they concentrated on ultimate issues. They could not deny death, for every day they were, in Augustine's phrase, "deafened by the clanking chains of mortality." I found myself wishing that some of my shallow, hedonistic friends would attend a meeting.

Among these people, I, who had the audacity to write a book on the subject, felt ignorant. For a year I learned as a servant at the feet of teachers in the school of suffering. Most of what I will write in the next few chapters about preparing for suffering, and helping others, I gleaned from my experiences in that group.

What Helps Most

What can we do to help those who hurt? And who can help us when we suffer?

I begin with some discouraging good news. The discouraging aspect is that I cannot give you a magic formula. There is nothing much you can *say* to help suffering people. Some of the brightest minds in history have explored every angle of the problem of pain, asking why people hurt, yet still we find ourselves stammering out the same questions, unrelieved.

As I've mentioned, not even God attempted an explanation of cause or a rationale for suffering in his reply to Job. The great king David, the righteous man Job, and finally even the Son of God reacted to pain much the same as we do. They recoiled from it, thought it horrible, did their best to alleviate it, and finally cried out to God in despair because of it. Personally, I find it discouraging that we can come up with no final, satisfying answer for people in pain.

And yet viewed in another way that nonanswer is surprisingly good news. When I have asked suffering people, "Who helped you?" not one person has mentioned a Ph.D. from Yale Divinity School or a famous philosopher. The kingdom of suffering is a democracy, and we all stand in it or alongside it with nothing but our naked humanity. All of us have the same capacity to help, and that is good news.

No one can package or bottle "the appropriate response to suffering." And words intended for everyone will almost always prove worthless for one individual person. If you go to the sufferers themselves and ask for helpful words, you may find discord. Some recall a friend who cheerily helped distract them from the illness, while others think such an approach insulting. Some want honest, straightforward confrontation; others find such discussion unbearably depressing.

In short, there is no magic cure for a person in pain. Mainly, such a person needs love, for love instinctively detects what is needed. Jean Vanier, founder of l'Arche movement, says it well: "Wounded people who have been broken by suffering and sickness ask for only one thing: a heart that loves and commits itself to them, a heart full of hope for them."[2]

In fact, the answer to the question, "How do I help those who hurt?" is exactly the same as the answer to the question, "How do I love?" If you asked me for a Bible passage to teach you how to help suffering people, I would point to 1 Corinthians 13 and its eloquent depiction of love. That is what a suffering person needs: love, and not knowledge and wisdom. As is so often his pattern, God uses very ordinary people to bring about healing.

Nevertheless, love itself breaks down into specific and practical acts. We meet suffering people in every school, in every church, in every public building, as well as in every hospital. All of us will one day join them. As I've listened to what they have to say, I have come up with four "frontiers" where every suffering person will do battle: the frontiers of fear, helplessness, meaning, and hope. Our response to suffering depends largely on the outcome of our struggle in those frontiers.

I have seen the moment of my greatness flicker,
And I have seen the eternal Footman hold my coat,
*   and snicker,*
And in short, I was afraid.
                    T. S. Eliot
                    The Love Song of J. Alfred Prufrock

14

Fear

Fear is the universal primal response to suffering. And yet beyond doubt it is also the single greatest "enemy of recovery."

John Donne knew fear well. He wrote his meditations in a day when waves of bubonic plague, the Black Death, were sweeping through his city of London. The last epidemic alone killed 40,000 people. Thousands more fled to the countryside, transforming whole neighborhoods into ghost towns. For six weeks Donne lay at the threshold of death, believing he had contracted the plague. The prescribed treatments were as vile as the illness: bleedings, strange poultices, the application of vipers and pigeons to remove evil vapors.

After noting signs of fear in his attending physician, Donne set down this description:

> Fear insinuates itself in every action or passion of the mind, and as gas in the body will counterfeit any disease, and seem the stone, and seem the gout, so fear will counterfeit any disease of the mind. . . . A man that is not afraid of a lion is afraid of a cat; not afraid of starving, and yet is afraid of some joint of meat at the table presented to feed him. . . . I know not what fear is, nor I know not what it is that I fear now; I fear not the hastening of my death, and

171

yet I do fear the increase of the disease; I should belie nature if I should deny that I feared this.[1]

One would think that the advances in medicine since John Donne's day would vastly reduce our fears. Not so. Modern hospitals place patients in private rooms in which they lie all day with little to occupy their minds other than their unwell state. Sophisticated machines whir and hum, some with tentacles probing inside the patient's own body. In the hallway outside, physicians and nurses discuss a prognosis in lowered voices, going over complex graphs and figures. The patient is poked and studied and bled and charted, "for your own good," of course. All in all, a perfect breeding ground for fear, which grows like a staph infection in hospital corridors.

The Pain Augmenter

We speak of fear as an emotion, but actually it operates more like a reflex action, with immediate physiological effects. Muscles tense up and contract involuntarily, often increasing pressure on damaged nerves and producing more pain. Blood pressure changes too, and we may go pale, or flush red. A very frightened person may even experience vascular collapse and faint. All animals sense fear—even an amoeba flees heat and pain—but humans seem especially susceptible. A spastic colon, for example, a common sign of human anxiety, is virtually unknown in other species.[2]

As the emotion of fear, based in the mind, filters down into the lower recesses of the body, it alters the perception of pain. A person with an exaggerated fear of hypodermic needles quite literally feels more pain from an injection than does a diabetic who has learned to take injections every day. The physiology is the same in both persons; fear makes the difference.

Asenath Petrie, a researcher at the University of Chicago, developed a system of classifying people into three categories according to their responses to pain (as discussed in her book, *The Individuality of Pain and Suffering*). "Augmenters" have a low threshold of pain and tend to exaggerate all pain. "Reducers," who demonstrate a higher threshold of pain, can tolerate much more without noticeable disturbance. "Moderates" fall in between. Petrie found that fear is the single factor that best describes the augmenters' approach toward pain.

During World War II Henry K. Beecher of the Harvard Medical School studied soldiers in Italy who had been wounded in battle. With astonishment he observed that only one in three soldiers with severe wounds asked for morphine. Many said they felt no pain, or the pain was minor. This pattern contrasted sharply with what Beecher had seen as an anesthesiologist in private practice: eighty percent of those patients, who had wounds very similar to the soldiers', begged for morphine or other pain-killers.

Morphine works its magic primarily by reducing the patient's fear and anxiety levels. Evidently, the soldiers' fears had been replaced, either by a feeling of pride in the significance of the wound, or, in some cases, by relief at being away from the battlefield. Beecher concluded, "There is no simple direct relationship between the wound per se and the pain experienced. The pain is in very large part determined by other factors."[3]

For most of us, the fears that accompany suffering are easy to identify. We fear the experience of pain, and the unknown. We may also fear death. Am I a burden? What am I missing out on? Do I have a future? Will I ever be healthy again? Am I being punished?

People who are suffering, whether from physical or psychological pain, often feel an oppressive sense of aloneness. They feel abandoned, by God and also by others, because they must bear the pain alone and no one else quite understands. Loneliness increases the fear, which in turn increases the pain, and downward the spiral goes.

One night a member of the Make Today Count group brought to the meeting a book filled with drawings made by sick children. Their stick figures and simple words vividly expressed these primary fears. One boy drew a large, ugly military tank, bristling with weapons. Just in front of the tank, at the end of the gun barrel, he placed a tiny stick figure—himself—holding up a red stop sign.

Another boy drew an oversized hypodermic needle with a barbed fishhook on the end. An eight-year-old girl drew herself lying in a hospital bed, with the caption, "I'm lonely. I wish I was in my own bed. I don't like it in here. It smells funny." A few pages later, the same girl had another drawing, this time in the setting of a doctor's office. The chair, examining table, and filing cabinets were drawn on a giant scale. The girl portrayed herself as very small, sitting on the edge of the table. A balloon coming out of her mouth contained two words: "I'm scared."

Disarming Fear

In a sense, the entire first half of this book represents my own attempt to "disarm" fear. Knowledge about pain and an understanding of the role it plays in life help to diminish my fear. I now view pain not as an enemy I must overcome, but rather as a protective signal I must reach accommodation with. I marvel at the incredible design that went into the nervous system. I visualize pain not as a soiled spot I must somehow bleach out but as an example of my body talking to me about a subject of vital importance.

Pain is by far the most effective way for my body to get my attention. Thus I start by listening to my pain. Now that I understand its value, suffering is much less fearful. I have also found that along with such knowledge comes *gratitude,* one of my most effective emotional weapons in fighting fear.

At another level, the spiritual level, my study of the Bible has convinced me that the fact of suffering does not mean God is against me. Mainly through the example of Jesus, I have learned to see that God is on our side; Paul calls him, appropriately, "the Father of compassion and the God of all comfort" (2 Corinthians 1:3).

The Bible is a Christian's guidebook, and I believe its wisdom about suffering offers a great antidote to fear. "Perfect love drives out fear"—personal knowledge of the God of perfect love can conquer fear as light destroys darkness. I need not engage in frenzied efforts to "muster up faith." God is already full of loving concern, and I need not impress him with spiritual calisthenics.

The Christian has many resources available to help stave off fear. Just as the emotion of fear filters down from the mind to cause direct physiological changes, so the act of prayer can counter those same effects by fixing my attention away from my body to a consciousness of soul and spirit. Prayer cuts through the sensory overload and allows me to direct myself to God. As I do so my body grows still, and calm. Visceral muscles tightened by fear begin to relax. An inner peace replaces tension.

These same results can be achieved through meditation exercises, of course, but prayer to God offers additional benefits. It helps fight the isolation of pain by moving my focus away from my self and my own needs as I strive to consider the needs of others. Remember how the tolling of the bell prompted John Donne to think of his neighbor who had died of plague.

Donne's *Devotions,* in fact, offers a wonderful model of a Christian learning to disarm fear. As the quotation early in this chapter shows, Donne knew fear well. Most of the time he battled such fears alone, for in those days victims of contagious disease were subject to quarantine. As he lay on his bed he wondered if God, too, was participating in the quarantine. Where was God's promised presence?

Donne's real fear was not of the tinny clamor of pain cells all over his body; he feared God. He asked the "Why me?" question over and over again. Calvinism was still new then, and he wondered if God was behind the plague after all. Guilt from his spotted past lurked like a demon nearby. Perhaps he was indeed suffering as a result of some previous sin.

Donne never really resolves the "Why me?" questions in his book, but *Devotions* does record, step by step, how he came to resolve his fears. Obsessed, he reviews every biblical occurrence of the word *fear.* As he does so, it dawns on him that life will always include circumstances that incite fear: if not illness, financial hardship, if not poverty, rejection, if not loneliness, failure. In such a world, Donne has a choice: to fear God, or to fear everything else.

In a passage reminiscent of Paul's litany in Romans 8 ("For I am convinced that neither death nor life, neither angels nor demons . . . will be able to separate us from the love of God. . . ."), Donne checks off his potential fears. Great enemies? They pose no threat, for God can vanquish any enemy. Famine? No, for God can supply. Death? Even that, the worst human fear, is no permanent barrier to those who fear God.

Donne determines that his best course is to cultivate a proper fear of the Lord, for that fear can supplant all others. Finally he prays, ". . . as thou hast given me a repentance, not to be repented of, so give me, O Lord, a fear, of which I may not be afraid." In the most important sense, it did not matter whether his sickness was a chastening or merely a natural accident. In either case he would trust God, for in the end *trust* represents the proper fear of the Lord.

In *Devotions,* Donne likens the process to his changing attitude toward physicians. Initially, as they probed his body for new symptoms and discussed their findings in hushed tones outside his room, he could not help feeling afraid. But in time, seeing their compassionate concern, he became convinced that they deserved his trust. The same pattern applies to God. We often do not understand his methods or the reasons behind them. But the underlying issue is whether he is a trustworthy "physician." Donne decided yes.

What is the right way to approach a God we fear? In answer, Donne holds up a phrase from Matthew's story of the women who discovered Jesus' empty tomb: they hurried away from the scene "with fear and yet great joy." Donne sees in their "two legs of fear and joy" a pattern for himself.

Fear was surely in the air at the time of the Resurrection. How could they not fear a God of such awesome power? The women had, after all, met Jesus standing at the edge of the garden, alive again. Strange things were happening. They ran from the scene on legs of fear, yes, but also on legs of joy, for the strange happenings were signs of the best possible news: Jesus had conquered even death. And with that same hope John Donne found at last a fear of which he need not be afraid.

Availability

A different situation arises when it is not I who suffer, but someone else whom I want to help. What can I do to alleviate their fear? I have learned that simple availability is the most powerful force we can contribute to help calm the fears of others.

Instinctively, I shrink back from people who are in pain. Who can know whether they want to talk about their predicament or not? Do they want to be consoled, or cheered up? What good can my presence possibly do? My mind spins out these rationalizations and as a result I end up doing the worst thing possible: I stay away.

Again and again suffering people, especially my friends in Make Today Count, have stressed how much it means when healthy people make themselves available. It is not our words or our insights that they want most; it is our mere presence. By being alongside at a time of need we convey the same comfort that a parent gives a confused and wounded child: "It's all right, it's all right." *The world will go on. I am with you in this scary time.*

Tony Campolo tells the story of going to a funeral home to pay his respects to the family of an acquaintance. By mistake he ended up in the wrong parlor. It held the body of an elderly man, and his widow was the only mourner present. She seemed so lonely that Campolo decided to stay for the funeral. He even drove with her to the cemetery.

At the end of the graveside service, as he and the woman were driving away, Campolo finally confessed that he had not known her husband. "I thought as much," said the widow. "I didn't recognize you. But it doesn't really matter." She squeezed his arm so hard it hurt. "You'll never, ever, know what this means to me."

I have mentioned that no one offers the name of a philosopher when I ask the question, "Who helped you most?" Most often they answer by describing a quiet, unassuming person. Someone who was there whenever needed, who listened more than talked, who didn't keep glancing down at a watch, who hugged and touched, and cried. In short, someone who was available, and came on the sufferer's terms and not their own.

One woman, a cancer patient in the Make Today Count group, mentioned her grandmother. A rather shy lady, she had nothing to offer but time. She simply sat in a chair and knitted while her granddaughter slept. She was available to talk, or fetch a glass of water, or make a phone call. "She was the only person there on my terms," said the granddaughter. "When I woke up frightened, it would reassure me just to see her there."

We rightly disparage Job's three friends for their insensitive response to his suffering. But read the account again: When they came, they sat in silence beside Job for seven days and seven nights before opening their mouths. As it turned out, those were the most eloquent moments they spent with him.

Jewish people practice a custom called *shiva* after a death in the community. For eight days friends, neighbors, and relatives practically take over the house of the mourning person, bringing their own fruit crates to sit on. They provide food, clean up, carry on conversation, and, in short, force their presence on the griever. The grieving person who desires tranquillity or privacy may find the presence of so many guests irritating. But the message comes through loudly: *We will not leave you alone. We will bear this pain with you.* Fear, which thrives on loneliness, wilts away.

In one highly symbolic meal, the visitors feed the mourner like a baby, with their own forks and spoons. Wisdom of the ages has taught their culture this ritual of enforced availability, for the mourner needs the presence of others whether or not he or she acknowledges the need.

A story is told about the great composer Beethoven, a man not known for social grace. His deafness made conversation difficult and humiliating for him. When he learned of the death of a friend's son, Beethoven, overcome with grief, hurried to the griever's home. He had no words of comfort to offer. But he saw a piano in the room, and went to it. For the next half hour he played the piano, pouring out his emotions in the most expressive way he knew. After he had finished playing, he left. The friend later remarked that no one else's visit had meant so much.

God's Agents

Besides personal presence, what else can we offer? What does one say at such a time? Consistently I have gotten the same answer from suffering people: it matters little what we say—our concern and availability matter far more. If we can offer a listening ear, that may be the most appreciated gift of all.

Betsy Burnham, in a book written shortly before her death from cancer, told about one of the most meaningful letters she received during her illness:

> Dear Betsy,
>
> I am afraid and embarrassed. With the problems you are facing, what right do I have to tell you I am afraid? I have found one excuse after another for not coming to see you. With all my heart, I want to reach out and help you and your family. I want to be available and useful. Most of all, I want to say the words that will make you well. But the fact remains that I am afraid. I have never before written

anything like this. I hope you will understand and forgive me.

Love,
Anne[4]

Anne could not find the personal strength needed to make herself available to her friend. But at least she shared her honest feelings with Betsy and made herself vulnerable. That too was a form of availability.

Another woman, reflecting on letters that she and her husband received in the midst of a family tragedy, told me that the letters' very clumsiness made them meaningful to her. Many writers would apologize for their ineptness in not knowing what to say. But to her the anguished groping for words was the whole point: their "sheer floundering confusion" best expressed what she and her family were feeling too.

The suffering person will probably expect from you the same kind of friendship you had before. Close relationships rarely develop between suffering people and strangers. Instead, the crisis forces them back to relationships they had built in health. Offer the same qualities you shared in healthy times. If you normally tell jokes, do so. If it would be natural for you to read the Bible and pray together, do that. If your previous relationship consisted of light conversation and a little gossip, start at that level until you feel comfortable to move on. Everything else has changed in a sick person's world; he or she needs assurance that friendship has not changed.

Time restrictions put limits on us, of course, and not all of us have the freedom to set aside other demands and offer large blocks of time. But we can all pray, a powerful form of availability. And we can offer regular, consistent tokens of our care. Suffering people say that fear and loneliness steal in at unexpected moments, and regularity is often more important than the quantity of time a person can give. Regularity becomes increasingly important with illnesses that tend to drag out over long periods of time, such as Parkinson's disease.

One man told me the most helpful person during his long illness was an office colleague who called every day, just to check. His visits, usually twice a week, never exceeded fifteen minutes, but the consistency of his calls and visits became a fixed point, something he could count on when everything else in his life seemed unstable.

There are limits, of course, on what mere friendship can accomplish. Out of self-pity, suffering people may erect barriers against you. "You'll never understand; you've never been through something like this," they may say. In such cases a person who has been through a similar experience may be best qualified to help, especially with the problem of fear.

Joni Eareckson Tada was jarred out of her self-pity by a hospital visit from a cheerful, radiant quadriplegic (she now continues the chain by ministering to others). Father Damien bore no fruit in his work among those with leprosy in Molokai, Hawaii, until he contracted the disease himself and could relate to them as a fellow-sufferer. Recognizing this principle, hospitals wisely cooperate with programs in which a woman facing a mastectomy, for example, can receive "friendship counseling" from another who has lived through the experience.

Make Today Count itself represents such a program. Its founder, Orville Kelly, realized that no one fully understood his fear except other cancer patients. As a result, he organized the first mutual support network for people with life-threatening illnesses. Now the American Cancer Society sponsors a twenty-four-hour-a-day phone line open for counseling cancer patients.

Still, those who stand alongside with no special skills at all need not feel useless. Nothing else—no learned "how-to" program, no expensive gift—is worth more to the sufferer than the comfortable assurance of your physical presence. Let me say this carefully, but say it nonetheless. I believe we in the body of Christ are called to show love *when God seems not to*.

Suffering people often have the sense that God has left them. No one expressed this better than C. S. Lewis in the poignant journal he kept after his wife's death (*A Grief Observed*). Lewis said that at the moment of his most profound need, God, who had always been available to him, suddenly seemed absent. Lewis felt fear, and abandonment, and in the end it was the community of other Christians who helped to restore him.

Remember, too, the Bible studies that saw Corrie ten Boom through Nazi concentration camps, and the stranger who slipped a simple word of encouragement to Christian Reger.

God made his presence known to them through his agents, other human beings. Likewise, those of us who stand alongside must sometimes voice prayers that the suffering person cannot yet pray. In moments of extreme suffering or grief, very often God's love is best perceived through the flesh of ordinary people like you and me. In such a way we can indeed function as the body of Jesus Christ.

*The doctor said: this-and-that indicates that this-and-that is wrong
with you, but if an analysis of this-and-that does not confirm our
diagnosis, we must suspect you of having this-and-that, then . . . and
so on. There was only one question Ivan Ilyich wanted answered: was
his condition dangerous or not? But the doctor ignored that question
as irrelevant.*

Leo Tolstoy
The Death of Ivan Ilyich

15

Helplessness

Dr. Curt Richter, a psychologist from Johns Hopkins University, used two wild rats in a rather perverse experiment. He dropped Rat One, the "control" animal, into a tank of warm water and timed the reaction. Since rats are good swimmers, the creature paddled and thrashed around for sixty hours before it finally succumbed to exhaustion and drowned.

Richter added a step with Rat Two, holding the animal tightly in his hands for a few minutes until it ceased struggling. When he dropped it in the water, it reacted very differently. After splashing around for a few minutes, Rat Two passively sank to the bottom of the tank and died. Richter theorizes that it simply "gave up." The futility of the struggle in his hands had convinced the rat that its fate was hopeless even before it hit the water. In effect, Rat Two died of resigned helplessness.[1]

Other experiments demonstrate that the feeling of helplessness, like fear, can actually change physiology. Two different groups of rats are subjected to the same electrical shocks. The animals in Group One, which have a measure of control, soon learn to turn off the current by manipulating a lever. Group Two, however, has no lever. After a while, simply because of stress—the voltage is harmless—the immune system carried by their blood undergoes radical changes, and rats in the second group become much more vulnerable to disease.

Experiments on humans, not quite so perverse, likewise show that the feeling of helplessness alters not merely a person's psychological attitude but the actual perception of pain itself. The threshold of pain can be raised as much as forty-five percent by simple diversion tactics.

In one series of experiments, researchers tried to divert the subject's attention by ringing bells, repeatedly touching his hand, reading an adventure story aloud, and having the subject read a column of numbers. When the scientists used such tactics during a test of heat tolerance, they had to apply forty-five percent more heat for the preoccupied subject to notice the pain. The researchers were startled to see blisters swelling up unnoticed on their subjects' arms as those subjects concentrated on counting from fifty to one, backwards. On the other hand, if the subject had nothing to do but think about his pain (as is true in many hospitals and nursing homes), he showed much greater sensitivity.[2]

Losing a Sense of Place

People in my Make Today Count group talked about a syndrome they labeled "pre-mortem dying," in effect an advanced case of helplessness. It develops when well-intentioned relatives and friends try to make the dying person's last months more bearable. The syndrome starts with comments like these: "Oh, you mustn't do that! I know you have always taken out the garbage, but *really,* not in your condition. Let me do it." "Don't burden yourself with balancing the checkbook. It would just create an unnecessary worry for you. I'll take care of it from now on." "I think you'd better stay home. Your resistance is so low."

Gradually, inexorably, everything that has given a person a sense of place, a role in life, is taken away. A mother encourages her single daughter to sell her house and move back home. The daughter does so, but soon discovers that in the process of being helped she has also lost her independent identity. Feelings of worth and value, made precarious by the illness, slide further away. As one man told me, "All my life I've gotten feedback—grades in school, performance appraisals at work, pep talks from athletic coaches. Suddenly I have no way to measure my performance in life. If I have a to-do list, I'm the only one who cares whether it gets done."

Obviously, a very sick person must sometimes depend on others to help manage the practical matters of life. But as I learned from the group members, we bystanders can too easily slip into a pattern that, if unchecked, may eradicate everything that gives a person dignity. Dr. Eric Cassell, an internist at Cornell University, concluded about his patients, "If I had to pick the aspect of illness that is most destructive to the sick, I would choose the loss of control."[3]

Suffering people already have misgivings about their place in the world. Often they must stop working, and the fatigue brought on by illness or treatment makes every action more difficult and tedious. And yet, like all of us, they need to cling to some assurance that they have a place, that life would not go on without a bump if they simply disappeared, that the checkbook would go unbalanced except for their expert attention. Wise companions learn to seek out the delicate balance between offering help and offering too much help.

Modern society greatly compounds this problem of a sense of place, for it has no natural "place" for sick people. We put them out of sight, behind the institutional walls of hospitals and nursing homes. We make them lie in beds, with nothing to occupy them but the remote control devices that operate the television sets. They live according to other people's schedules, not their own: a nurse wakes them up, the hospital decides when to feed them, visitors drop by, a nurse turns out the light at night. (For this reason, many patients who welcome visitors prefer that they call first before dropping by—it gives them more a feeling of control over their schedule.)

I have made a kind of study of card racks, sometimes visiting new drug stores and card shops just to browse. The cards for sick people fall into distinct categories: schmaltzy cards with pictures of flowers and treacly poems, racy cards with messages about all the wild parties the recipient is missing, sincere cards with a solemn expression of sympathy, clever cards illustrated by *New Yorker* cartoonists. All have the same implicit message, expressed in their title: "get-well cards."

One card has on the cover, "Get well soon," and then inside, "otherwise somebody might steal your job." Another says, "Everybody hopes you feel better soon, except me," and inside, "I hope you feel better right now!" "This is no time to be sick," says one of Boynton's hippos from a hospital bed, "the weekend's coming up." What complaint could I have against these clever expressions of sympathy? The subtle, underlying message: *You are out of commission, useless. You don't fit, at work, at parties. You are missing out. You are not OK. Only get well, and then you can rejoin life.*

My friends in the Make Today Count group, none of whom will likely get well, impressed upon me that something as innocuous as a greeting card can deepen the devastating sense of feeling out of place, with no valid role in life.

I sometimes dream of producing my own line of get-well cards. I already have an idea for the first one. The cover would have huge letters, perhaps with fireworks in the background, spelling out CONGRATULATIONS!!! Inside, this message: ". . . to the 98 trillion cells in your body that are still working smoothly and efficiently."

I would look for ways to communicate the message that a sick person is not a *sick person,* but rather a person of worth and value who happens to have some bodily parts that are not functioning well. Perhaps the exercise of writing a series of cards like that would help me fight my own tendency of mentally labeling individuals as sick and disabled, thus complicating their battle against helplessness.

In an address to German deaconesses involved with disabled people, theologian Jürgen Moltmann attacked the modern distinction that tends to distance healthy people from the disabled or handicapped. In reality there is no such thing as a non-handicapped life, he said; only the ideal of health set up by a society of the capable condemns a certain group of people to be called handicapped. Our society arbitrarily defines health as the capacity for work and the capacity for enjoyment, but "true health is something quite different. True health is the strength to live, the strength to suffer, and the strength to die. Health is not a condition of my body; it is the power of my soul to cope with the varying condition of that body." In that respect, every human life is limited, vulnerable, and weak.[4]

Fighting Back

Norman Cousins, longtime editor of *Saturday Review*, waged a one-man crusade against modern health-care systems that foster helplessness. Hospitalized for a mysterious condition of creeping paralysis (diagnosed as ankylosing spondylitis, a degeneration of connective tissue in the spine), Cousins found that the hospital seemed perfectly designed to immobilize not only his body but his spirit. "The will to live is not a theoretical abstraction, but a physiological reality with therapeutic characteristics," he wrote in *Anatomy of an Illness*. But the hospital environment tended to stifle that will to live.

Medication fogged over his consciousness of reality. Confinement to bed made him restless and depressed. Nurses and doctors invaded his body orifices and stole away fluids. Unable to work and shut away from his most intimate relationships, he felt a gradual loss of control over his destiny.

Cousins sought to identify the obstacles facing him, as shown in this partial list:

> There was first of all the feeling of helplessness—a serious disease in itself.
>
> There was the subconscious fear of never being able to function normally again. . . .
>
> There was the reluctance to be thought a complainer.
>
> There was the desire not to add to the already great burden of apprehension felt by one's family; this added to the isolation.
>
> There was the conflict between the terror of loneliness and the desire to be left alone.
>
> There was the lack of self-esteem, the subconscious feeling perhaps that our illness was a manifestation of our inadequacy.
>
> There was the fear that decisions were being made behind our backs, that not everything was made known that we wanted to know, yet dreaded knowing.
>
> There was the morbid fear of intrusive technology, fear of being metabolized by a data base, never to regain our faces again.
>
> There was resentment of strangers who came at us with needles and vials—some of which put supposedly magic substances in our veins, and others which took more of our blood than we thought we could afford to lose.

There was the distress of being wheeled through white corridors to laboratories for all sorts of strange encounters with compact machines and blinking lights and whirling discs.

And there was the utter void created by the longing—ineradicable, unremitting, pervasive—for warmth of human contact. A warm smile and an outstretched hand were valued even above the offerings of modern science, but the latter were far more accessible than the former.[5]

Norman Cousins knew that doctors could not "heal" him; at best they could harness the vitality that existed in his body's cells. But he felt that vitality ebbing away. In an attempt to regain control over his own destiny and revive his will to live, he launched an all-out campaign against helplessness. As his book records, he employed some rather unorthodox tactics.

First, Cousins posted a sign on his door limiting hospital personnel to one blood specimen every three days, which they had to share. They had been taking as many as four blood samples in a day, simply because it was more convenient for each hospital department to obtain their own samples. What seemed to hospital staff a case of patient revolt was to Cousins an important step in asserting control over his own body.

Cousins also borrowed a movie projector and scheduled time each day to watch movies by the Marx Brothers and Charlie Chaplain. He figured that since negative emotions demonstrably produce chemical changes in the body, perhaps positive emotions might counteract them. He made the "joyous discovery that ten minutes of genuine belly laughter would give me at least two hours of painfree sleep."

As soon as his health would permit, Cousins moved from his hospital room to a nearby hotel room. It cost one-third as much, provided a more serene (and more luxurious) environment, and allowed him to schedule meals and wake-up calls at his convenience, no one else's.

Although Norman Cousins warns against making his regimen a model for other people, his results were impressive indeed. At the onset, his doctor had given him one chance in five hundred of a full recovery; some paralysis seemed inevitable. But he recovered completely, extended his life by several more happy decades, and, long after the age most people retire, took up a new career of lecturing on health matters.

Helpless No More

The changes Norman Cousins suggests would call for a complete overhaul of modern health care systems, something that is unlikely to happen soon. But we can make small steps toward his goal of "humanizing" health care, helping ourselves as patients to feel less like a chip in a computer and more like a partner in recovery.

Some solutions are simple. In a 1984 study reported in *Science*, Roger S. Ulrich found that gall-bladder patients who looked out over a cluster of trees instead of a brick wall had shorter post-operative stays and took fewer moderate painkillers. Ideally, he concluded, hospitals should be built next to public parks, or in a scenic environment. More and more architects today are taking account of such environmental factors as they design medical facilities.

In an attempt to recruit patients as partners in the battle against helplessness, some pain clinics negotiate "contracts" with their patients. First they get the patient to articulate his or her goals: to learn to walk, to lift an arm high without pain, to get a part-time job. Then they break down those goals into stages and assign weekly goals: standing for five minutes, then ten minutes; walking across the room with a cane, and then without a cane. Medical personnel chart each patient's weekly progress, and enthusiastically praise each new level of achievement.

Why must we rely on paid professionals for such encouragement? Friends and relatives can accomplish the very same thing by forming a "contract" with the recovering person and then rewarding any slight victory over helplessness.

We can also make certain the recovering patient has meaningful diversions. Just as the perception of pain increases in intensity when a research subject has no other diversions, the feeling of helplessness heightens when a patient lies alone, with nothing to do or think about except pain. I cannot imagine a more challenging place to combat pain than in a hospital room. Yet even in that sterile environment can be found sources for diversion.

In hospitals, so little happens that you must attend to small details. Instead of gulping from the paper cup, swallow slowly, with an awareness of the glottal muscles and of the texture and taste of water in your mouth. Stare at individual petals of the flowers in the room, searching for subtle patterns of design. Run your hands over sheets and bed and blankets to feel the textures.

A resilient human spirit can find extraordinary ways of combating isolation and deprivation. Benjamin Weir was a Presbyterian missionary in Beirut, Lebanon, kidnapped by Shiite Moslems. For sixteen months he was held in the most depressing of circumstances. He had no view of trees out a window; blindfolded most of the time, he had no view at all. His hands manacled, he had no freedom to run his fingers over various textures.

Weir had no control over his schedule, his food, or anything else in his daily routine. And yet even in those circumstances he was able to call upon sufficient reserves of spirit to overcome the deadening sense of helplessness. He had no one to call on but God himself. This is his report on one of the early days of captivity.

> I awoke refreshed by my nap. What other gifts would God show me in addition to sleep, a blanket, and a spirit of resistance and survival? Once again I lifted my blindfold and began examining the room. What was here that could bring me close to the sustaining presence of God? I let my imagination have total freedom.
>
> Looking up, I examined an electric wire hanging from the ceiling. The bulb and socket had been removed so that it ended in an arc with three wires exposed. To me, those wires seemed like three fingers. I could see a hand and an arm reaching downward—like the Sistine Chapel in Rome, Michelangelo's fresco of God reaching out his hand and finger toward Adam, creating the first human being. Here God was reaching toward me, reminding me, saying, "You're alive. You are mine; I've made you and called you into being for a divine purpose."
>
> What else? I began counting the horizontal slats of the shutters outside the French doors. There were 120. What could those horizontal pieces of wood stand for, so many of them? That's it! Many of them, a crowd! A cloud of witnesses past and present, who through times of trial have observed the faithfulness of God. . . . This recital of the

basics of my faith sent a chill through me. What a message! I desperately needed it in my present setting.

Then my eyes lighted on two white circles near the ceiling, one on the right-hand wall, the other on the left. Everybody in Lebanon knows what they are, plastic covers for electrical connections. Yet what could they be for me? What comes in a pair? Ears! They were the ears of God. The Lord hears the groaning of the saints. *So listen to me, dear God; I also surrender to your care and will.*[6]

By the end of the day, Weir was humming the hymn, "Count your many blessings, name them one by one." He counted: health, life, food, mattress, pillow, blanket, his wife, his family, faith, hope, prayer, Jesus, Holy Spirit, Father's love. Thirty-three things in all. In the process of reviewing these blessings, he found that his feelings of fear and helplessness had melted away. As the light through the shutter faded, he relaxed and began to get ready for the night.

Reaching Out

In the frontier of helplessness, Norman Cousins fought his battle against an insensitive medical establishment. Benjamin Weir fought his more lonely, internal battle against isolation and despair. For people who have long-term disabilities, one of the best things we can do is to provide tools that allow them to resume "normal" activity.

With computer-driven devices, a fully paralyzed person can now operate a wheelchair, type, and turn on a TV or stereo, all by various combinations of sucking and blowing on an air tube. Such devices can spell the difference between feelings of helplessness and hope, and even between recovery and defeat. Brian Sternberg's amateur radio hobby and Joni Eareckson Tada's artwork probably contribute more to their mental well-being than even the support of caring friends.

Barbara Wolf wrote a book, *Living with Pain*, about her long struggle against chronic pain. She found that the only times in a day when she completely forgot about the pain were the hours she spent teaching English. Then, her brain's active involvement drowned out all other sensations. She learned to channel that same concentration at other times. When a flash of pain hit in the middle of the night, she would organize her next day, work on a lecture, or plan an entire dinner, including all the recipes.

Sometimes going against her own nature, Wolf began forcing herself toward activities that required complete concentration. Distraction, she found, was her single best weapon against pain. "Distraction is inexpensive and non-habit-forming; it does not require a doctor's prescription."[7] In addition to her English teaching, she poured herself into hobbies that demanded her full attention: parties, pets, sports, politics, writing.

Of the various avenues of distraction open to her, Wolf found that involvement with others was the most effective in quelling her pain. Often, suffering people find a most meaningful sense of place when they learn to reach out to others who hurt. Joni Eareckson Tada claims that the people who helped her most were other quadriplegics who devoted themselves to helping her through the roughest times.

A psychologist in Atlanta told me that he meets two kinds of people. The unhealthy ones go through life crying, "Please love me, please love me." The other group consists of people healthy enough to give, not just receive, love. He says that the best cure for the first group is to help them attain a place of wholeness where *they* can be lovers and helpers of others. If so, they will automatically fill the deep needs for attention and love inside them.

Similarly, counselors among the suffering strive to get their patients to view themselves as helpers and givers, instead of always being receivers. Joni Eareckson Tada described to me her surprise at learning that many disabled persons in her rehabilitation home stayed there voluntarily. It seemed easier than risking the "outside" world with all its prejudices and dangers. Joni became a leader to them, working at her exercises, inspiring hope, and *wanting* to be released. The very process of investing in their needs proved therapeutic. She became stronger as her self-concept improved and she stopped thinking of herself as an object of pity.

The French have a saying: "To suffer passes; to have suffered never passes." Too often we think about a ministry of helps as a one-way street in which I, the healthy person, reach out in compassion to assist the wounded. But people who have suffered are the very best equipped to help, and a person crosses the final barrier of helplessness when he or she learns to use the experience of suffering itself as a means of reaching out to others.

Rabbi Harold Kushner cites an old Chinese tale about a woman overwhelmed by grief after the death of her son. When she goes to the holy man for advice, he tells her, "Fetch me a mustard seed from a home that has never known sorrow. We will use it to drive the sorrow out of your life." The tale recounts how the woman goes from house to house, asking if the home has known sorrow. Each one has, of course, and the woman lingers to comfort her hosts until at last the act of ministering to others drives the sorrow from her life.

I know personally of two small-scale ministries, run out of private homes, that put this principle into practice. The first came into being when a woman in California discovered her son, the apple of her eye, was homosexual and was dying of AIDS. She found almost no sympathy and support from her church and community. She felt so alone and needy that she decided to start a newsletter that now joins together a network of parents of gay people. She offers little professional help, and promises no magic cures, but I have read scores of letters from other parents who see this courageous woman as a lifesaver. Having been through the sorrow and grief herself, she now seeks to be available for someone else.

Another woman, in Wisconsin, lost her only son in a Marine Corps helicopter crash. For the first time, she began noticing how frequently helicopter crashes were reported in the news. Now, whenever a military helicopter crashes, she sends a packet of letters and helpful materials to an officer in the Defense Department, who forwards the packet on to the affected families. About half the families strike up a regular correspondence, and in her retirement this Wisconsin woman leads her own "community of suffering." The activity has not solved the grief over her son, of course, but it has given her a sense of place, and she no longer feels helpless against that grief.

A wise sufferer will look not inward, but outward. There is no more effective healer than a wounded healer, and in the process the wounded healer's own scars may fade away.

It is not so much the suffering as the senselessness of it that is unendurable.

Friedrich Nietzsche

16

Meaning

Merlin Olsen, former professional football player, has a well-defined philosophy of pain:

> Man is an adaptable creature. One finds out what you can or cannot do. It's like walking into a barnyard. The first thing you smell is manure. Stand there for about five minutes and you don't smell it anymore. The same thing is true of a knee. You hurt that knee. You're conscious of it. But then you start to play at a different level. You change your run a little bit. Or you drive off a different leg. Maybe you alter your stance.
>
> After surgery on my knee, I had to have the fluid drained weekly. Finally, the membrane got so thick they almost had to drive the needle in it with a hammer. I got to the point where I just said, "Damn it, get the needle in there, and get that stuff out."[1]

All participants in a sport like football are subjected to the same body checks, helmet spears, and pileups, and society lavishly rewards them for undergoing such pain. Thus pain from some sources—not only football, but also mountain climbing, a triathlon race, Marine Corps boot camp, torture by an enemy

195

interrogator—individuals are willing to accept. In previous centuries some even honored self-inflicted pain as a sign of great devotion: the coarser the hair shirt and harsher the flagellation, the more pious the worshiper.

Even more remarkably, human beings deliberately inflict pain on themselves for the sake of simple vanity. For centuries Chinese women bound their feet injuriously in order to appear beautiful. Modern women, in addition to wearing too-narrow shoes, also pluck their eyebrows, expose themselves to harmful ultraviolet rays, and undergo plastic surgery on faces, breasts, and buttocks—all to meet cultural standards of beauty. We enhance personal prestige by enduring these voluntary pains, for society ascribes to them a certain meaning that makes them worth pursuing.

Compare two intense pains: the ordeal of a difficult breech delivery and the pain of kidney stones. Considering the number of nerve cells affected and the intensity and duration of pain, the two probably rank fairly close. For childbirth, however, meaning comes implicit in the event. "A woman giving birth to a child has pain because her time has come; but when her baby is born she forgets the anguish because of her joy that a child is born into the world," observed Jesus (John 16:21). A mother's pain produces something with meaning—a new life—and for that reason she can even contemplate repeating the experience. But for the person with kidney stones, what meaning is there?

More than any society in history, our modern one struggles with the meaning of suffering. We no longer view it as a judgment of the gods, but what is it? We grant a measure of meaning to lesser pains, such as those we take on voluntarily, but what meaning does a birth-defective child have? Or cystic fibrosis? Or mental retardation? For us, suffering is something to treat and get over with; but what about suffering that never goes away?

Mostly we see only a negative meaning in suffering: it interrupts health, and slams an unwelcome brake on our pursuit of life, liberty, and happiness. As I've mentioned, any card shop gives the message unmistakably. All that we can wish for suffering people is that they "Get well!" Yet, as one woman with terminal cancer told me, "None of those cards apply to the people in my ward. None of us will get well. We're all going to die here. To the rest of the world, that makes us invalids. Think about that word. Not valid."

What is the meaning of terminal cancer?

I received a letter from a pastor in the Midwest who recorded what happens when meaning begins to unravel. This man's suffering was emotional rather than physical. A "nervous breakdown" his doctors called it, but really it was more a breakdown in meaning.*

> The most painful part of it was the seeming silence of God. I prayed, I thought, to a silent darkness. I have thought a lot about this. He only *seemed* silent. The problem was partly my depression and partly the Christian community. For most Christians I was an embarrassment. Nothing they said dealt with what I endured. One pastor prayed for me in generalities and pieties that were utterly unrelated to the situation. *They would not feel my pain.*
>
> Other people just avoided me. Ironically, Job's friends were probably a help to him, psychologically. At least they forced out feelings, even if angry ones. Their pronouncements were useless, but they did deal with the questions and gave Job the impression that maybe God was around somewhere. No one in the Christian community, except my wife, helped me even to that degree.

Honoring Pain

One of the most important things we can do for a suffering person is to restore a sense of meaning or significance to the experience.

Actually, the problem is that we already convey meaning, though on a relative scale. When I give seminars on pain, I sometimes illustrate this by calling for audience participation. I ask for the Roman "thumbs up" or "thumbs down" signal: thumbs up if the pain I mention is acceptable, an affliction that attracts sympathy, and thumbs down if the pain is unacceptable and gets little sympathy. Typically, I get these responses:

Broken leg from skiing. Thumbs up all the way. What started

*Emotional pain, such as acute depression, represents a huge area of suffering that I cannot begin to mention in this book focusing on physical pain. I recommend *A Season of Suffering,* by John H. Timmerman (Multnomah Press, 1987) as a sensitive account of one family's struggle with depression.

out as a stumble on the rope tow ends up, after many retellings, as a double somersault free-fall off a cliff. Friends sign the cast with funny remarks, and the sufferer becomes a virtual hero. The attention is almost worth the pain.

Leprosy. Thumbs down. In my work with Dr. Paul Brand, I have gotten to know leprosy patients. They lobby strongly for the name "Hansen's disease" for one simple reason: the way people respond to the image of leprosy. Although the disease differs in virtually every respect from its stereotype, a person with leprosy still gets judgment and not sympathy. Loneliness is one of the disease's worst aspects.

Influenza. Mixed response. Some people hold thumbs down because no one really *likes* fevers, vomiting, and body aches. On the other hand, the flu, being universal, attracts much sympathy. We all know how it feels. "Take it easy," we say. "Stay at home a few extra days. Get your strength back."

Mumps. Response depends on the age you're talking about. Children with mumps get plenty of sympathy. They're fawned over and indulged, perhaps granted extra television viewing time and ice cream. I still remember my childhood mumps experience with nostalgia. But an adult with mumps is something of a joke—even though to an adult mumps represents a far worse danger.

The list goes on. *Hemorrhoids:* a very painful condition, but socially a laughing matter. *AIDS:* what kind of response does an AIDS victim get? I know a few persons with AIDS, and they hear a very clear message from the church: "You get no sympathy from me. You deserve your suffering as God's punishment. Keep away." I cannot think of a more terrifying disease than AIDS, or one that provokes a less compassionate response.

Migraine headache, whiplash, cancer—each of these has a different "image," and in subtle and sometimes blatant ways we communicate to the sufferer an assessment of meaning that can make coping easier or harder.

I have come to believe that the chief contribution Christians can make is to keep people from suffering for the wrong reasons. We can "honor" pain. In the most important sense, all pain is pain; it does not matter whether the pain comes from migraine headaches or strep throat or acute depression. The first step in helping a suffering person (or in accepting our own pain) is to acknowledge that pain is valid, and worthy of a sympathetic response. In this way, we can begin to ascribe meaning to pain.

At a different level, Christians apply a further set of values to suffering. Like the visitors to Claudia Claxton's bedside, we can heap coals of fire on the suffering. We can add guilt: "Haven't you prayed? Have you no faith that God will heal you?" Or confusion: "Is Satan causing this pain? Just natural providence? Or has God specially selected you as an example to others?" Pain is a foolproof producer of guilt, I have learned. We all do things we shouldn't, and when pain strikes, it's easy to blame ourselves for what has happened.

In a context of intense suffering, even well-intended comments may produce a harmful effect. "God must have loved your daughter very much to take her home so soon," we may be tempted to say, leaving the bereaved parents to wish that God had loved their daughter less. "God won't give you a burden heavier than you can bear"; the suffering person may wish for weaker faith that might merit a lighter burden.

I have interviewed enough suffering people to know that the pain caused by this kind of bedside response can exceed the pain of the illness itself. One woman well known in Christian circles poignantly described the agony caused by TMJ (temporomandibular joint dysfunction). The pain dominates her entire life. Yet, she says, it hurts far worse when Christians write her with judgmental comments based on their pet formulas of why God allows suffering. Perhaps the chief contribution a Christian can make is to keep people from suffering for the wrong reasons. We can "honor" their pain.

Buried Treasure

Following the biblical pattern, our search for meaning should move in a forward-looking direction, toward the results of suffering, rather than dwelling on its cause.

Frankly, to me much suffering would remain meaningless if we spent all our efforts on the unanswerable "Why?" questions. Why did Solzhenitsyn have to spend eight years in a hard labor camp just for making a casual criticism of Stalin in a letter to a friend? Why did millions of Jews have to die to fulfill the whims of a crazed dictator? Such suffering is meaningless in itself, and will remain so unless the sufferer, like a miner searching for diamonds in a vein of coal, finds in it a meaning.

Viktor Frankl, who spent time in one of Hitler's camps, said, "Despair is suffering without meaning." Frankl and Bruno Bettelheim extracted meaning from the senseless suffering of the Holocaust: observing the behavior of human beings in the extreme conditions of the camps gave them insights that formed the basis for all their later work. For Elie Wiesel and others, "bearing witness" became the meaning. They now devote themselves to honoring those who did not survive.

In prison Dostoyevski pored over the New Testament and the lives of the saints. Prison became, for him and later for his countryman Solzhenitsyn, a crucible of religious faith. Both describe a process in which, first, the blunt reality of human evil convinced them of the need for redemption. Then, through the living witness of believers in the camps, they saw the possibility of transformation. As Solzhenitsyn elegantly expressed it in his classic *One Day in the Life of Ivan Denisovich*, faith in God may not get you out of the camp, but it is enough to see you through each day.

Although my own suffering seems trivial in comparison with these pioneers, I too strive to extract meaning from it. I begin with the biblical promise that suffering can produce something worthwhile in me. I go through a list like that in Romans 5, where Paul mentions perseverance, character, hope, and confidence. "How does suffering accomplish these?" I ask myself. It produces perseverance, or steadiness, by slowing me down and forcing me to turn to God; it produces character by calling on my reserves of inner strength. I continue through the list, asking how God can be involved in bringing meaning to the suffering process.

John Donne spoke of suffering as a kind of "treasure in bullion." Because it is not coined into currency, the bullion does not always help us defray expenses here on earth. But as we get nearer and nearer our home, heaven, the treasure "that may lie in his bowels, as gold in a mine" takes on eternal value, a weight of glory.[2] If we turn to God in trust, the affliction itself can be redeemed, by helping to form our character in Christ's own image.

We might use a more contemporary analogy to express the same thought. Suffering can be what economists call a "frozen asset." It may not look remotely like an asset at the time, but gradually we can find meaning in it, an enduring meaning that will help to transform the pain.

Shared Meaning

Earlier in this chapter I quoted a letter from a pastor whose depression had brought on a breakdown in meaning. He could make no sense of his suffering, and the Christian community failed to help him in the process. Eventually that pastor had to commit himself to a mental institution for treatment. His family stood with him, though, and with their support and professional help, he finally climbed back to a place of health.

Years later that same pastor, with renewed mental health, faced another crisis. A week-old grandson died, plunging the extended family into confusion and grief. Now he was supposed to be the strong one for his children, and he didn't know if he could. The Sunday after the funeral, preaching in his new church, he began reading Psalm 145 from the pulpit. He tried to focus on the words before him, but concentration failed. His tongue got thick, his chin trembled, his tear ducts opened wide. He could not continue reading the serene words about God's goodness and fairness.

The pastor set aside his sermon notes and, with a choked voice, he told the silent congregation about his grandson's death. Even while he was speaking his mind flashed back to his time at the former church, to his feelings of helplessness and failure. He was afraid.

But this time was different. "As people left the church," he remembers, "they said two important and helpful things:

"1. 'Thank you for sharing your pain with us.'

"2. 'I grieve with you.' This simple statement was the most helpful thing said. I did not feel alone. Unlike during the time of my depression before, I was not abandoned by God and his people. They embraced my grief."

Using very few words, and no special wisdom, that second congregation communicated to their pastor a sense of shared meaning. That his pain was important to them they demonstrated by taking it on themselves.

The search for meaning in suffering will always be a lonely search. No one but I can discern the meaning of my suffering.

And yet by embracing grief and standing beside the hurting person, we can indeed aid another's search for meaning.

The skill of helping another person find meaning involves recognizing various stages along the path to healing. Sharon Fischer describes her own process in dealing with ovarian cancer:

> I needed time to digest what was happening in my life and to absorb the changes forced on my daily routine, my emotional stability and my plans for the future. Perhaps the greatest way to give suffering people time is being patient with them—giving them room to doubt, cry, question and work out strong and often extreme emotions.
>
> I found that not everything in my experience could be absorbed at once, and I needed to feel free to take the time I needed to work through feelings. Elisabeth Kübler-Ross has outlined five stages grieving people often pass through, either in facing their own deaths or in dealing with the death of a loved one. These stages—denial, anger, bargaining, depression and acceptance—are not always experienced in that sequence, and not everyone goes through all of them, but they exemplify the time it can take to process a traumatic experience. . . .
>
> I am not by nature one who shares feelings easily. So it was not always easy for me to explain, even to those people closest to me, the complexity of my feelings and the depth of my reaction to the experience. But I needed good listeners—people willing to take an hour or two when I was ready to talk and just listen. Fortunately I had faithful friends, a neighbor who is a skilled counselor and family members who were available. I don't know what I would have done without people to listen.[3]

Fischer goes on to say that the least helpful people were those who came with suggested answers for her. One woman offered the opinion that diet—Sharon enjoyed hamburgers and chocolate chip ice cream—was the reason for Sharon's illness. Others urged her to rely less on medical treatment and more on prayer for healing.

I cannot emphasize too strongly how destructive such formulaic answers can be. "Rejoice with those who rejoice, and weep with those who weep," advised the apostle Paul (Romans

12:15), wise words that apply especially in times of crisis. The book of Proverbs is more blunt about inappropriate responses:

Like one who takes away a garment on a cold day,
or like vinegar poured on soda,
is one who sings songs to a heavy heart. (25:20)

At the very time I was working on this book I received a phone call from a friend in another city who had just been diagnosed with AIDS. Wallowing in guilt over past sexual sins, he felt remorse, unworthiness, self-hatred, and rejection by God. He had lost all will to live. He needed help desperately.

Some people see AIDS as a direct punishment by God, a specific, targeted message of judgment. I do not. I see it, rather, as part of a general message, a principle of health: Just as abuse of alcohol and tobacco exposes the body to certain risks, so does sexual promiscuity. But, regardless, *even if* I am wrong and the disease has come as a direct punishment, what is my responsibility as his Christian friend?

My responsibility is to dispense grace, to show him how tenderly Jesus treated people with sexual sins, to assure him of God's love and forgiveness. In short, my role is to move his focus away from the backward glance and direct it forward. Even his guilt is a signal. He can lie in a hospital bed all day and grovel in his sins. Or he can bring that guilt to God, who has promised to put confessed sin behind him, "as far as the east is from the west."

The shared meaning of guilt is not judgment, but forgiveness. The shared meaning of suffering is restoration, and union with the sufferer.

God's Question Marks

Sometimes the only meaning we can offer a suffering person is the assurance that their suffering, which has no apparent meaning for them, has a meaning for us.

Henri Nouwen's slim book with the wonderful title *The Wounded Healer* poses the question of lonely, abandoned people. What possible meaning can one bring to their pain? He gives the example of a young minister who has no suggested meaning to offer an old man facing surgery—none but his own loving concern. "No man can stay alive when nobody is waiting for him," says Nouwen. "Everyone who returns from a long and difficult trip is looking for someone waiting for him at the station or the airport. Everyone wants to tell his story and share his moments of pain and exhilaration with someone who stayed home, waiting for him to come back."[4]

My wife works with some of the poorest people in the city of Chicago, directing a program of LaSalle Street Church, which intentionally seeks out lonely and abandoned senior citizens no one else cares for. Many times I have seen her pour herself into a senior citizen's life, trying to convince the senior that it *matters* whether he or she lives or dies. In such a way she "graces" their suffering.

One man Janet works with, ninety-year-old Mr. Kruider, refused cataract surgery for twenty years. At age seventy he had decided that nothing much was worth looking at and, anyhow, God must have wanted him blind if he made him that way. Maybe it was God's punishment for looking at girls as a youngster, he said.

It took my wife two years of cajoling, arguing, persisting, and loving to convince Mr. Kruider to have cataract surgery. Finally, Mr. Kruider agreed, for one reason only: Janet impressed on him that it mattered to her, Janet, that he regain his sight. Mr. Kruider had given up on life; it held no meaning for him. But Janet transferred a meaning. It made a difference to someone that even at age ninety-two Mr. Kruider not give up. At long last the old man agreed to the surgery.

In a literal sense, Janet shared Mr. Kruider's suffering. By visiting so often she convinced him that someone cared, and that it mattered whether he lived or died or had sight or not. That principle of shared suffering is the thesis of Nouwen's book on the *wounded* healer, and perhaps the only sure contribution we can make to the meaning of suffering. In doing so, we follow God's pattern, for he too took on pain. He joined us and lived a life of more suffering and poverty than most of us will ever know. Suffering can never ultimately be meaningless, because God himself has shared it.

At times, though, despite our best efforts to honor others' pain, we encounter suffering that seems utterly devoid of meaning. I am thinking especially of a man with Alzheimer's disease; the daughter tries to tend to his needs, but every day her heart is broken by the sad shell of what used to be her father. Or I think of a severely disabled child with an IQ in the 30–40 range. The child may live a long life lying motionless in a crib, unable to talk, unable to comprehend, soaking up hours of expensive professional care.

Where is there meaning in such a senile adult and in such a child? I have received great help on this question from the compassionate work of Christians in East Germany. These people, who have grown up in a society more acquainted with suffering than ours in the West, have set an example to us all of reaching out to those least "valuable" or "useful" members of modern society.

"What is the point of their lives? Do their lives have any meaning?" asked Dr. Jürgen Trogisch, a pediatrician who works among the severely mentally handicapped. He could treat the externals, but what was going on inside, within such damaged brains?

For many years Dr. Trogisch could not answer the question of meaning. He performed his medical tasks anyway, but he had no answer. Then he ran an introductory course to train new helpers for the center, and at the end of the one-year training period, he asked the young helpers to fill out a survey. Among the questions was this one, "What changes have taken place in your life since you became totally involved with disabled people?" Here is a sampling of their answers:

§ —For the first time in my life I feel I am doing something really significant.

—I feel I can now do things I wouldn't have thought myself capable of before.

—During my time here I have won the affection of Sabine. Having had the opportunity to involve myself with a disabled person, I no longer think of her as disabled at all.

—I am more responsive now to human suffering and it arouses in me the desire to help.

—It's made me question what is really important in life.

—Work has assumed a new meaning and purpose. I feel I'm needed now.

§   —I've learned to be patient and to appreciate even the slightest sign of progress.

—In observing the disabled, I've discovered myself.

—I've become more tolerant. My own little problems don't seem so important any longer, and I've learned to accept myself with all my inadequacies. Above all I've learned to appreciate the little pleasures of life, and especially I thank God that he has shown me that love can achieve more than hate or force.

As Dr. Trogisch read over these and other responses, he realized with a start the answer to his question. The meaning of the suffering of those children was being worked out in the lives of others, his helpers, who were learning lessons that no sophisticated educational system could teach. He thought of two patients he had worked with for years, in whom he had seen little progress. "Could it be that Daniel and Monika have come into this world just for me? Are their deep and insistent questions perhaps God's questions to me? Are these two severely disabled children an answer—God's answer to me?"⁵

All that the downtrodden can do is go on hoping. After every disappointment they must find fresh reason for hope.

Alexander Solzhenitsyn

17

Hope

Pharmaceuticals today are tested by the "double blind" method, meaning the administering doctors themselves do not know which is the true drug and which the inert, "control" drug. They must be tested that way for one simple reason: the power of human hope. Before double blind testing, virtually all new drugs showed spectacular results, regardless of their chemical content. Mystified researchers eventually found the doctor's demeanor to be the key factor in the new drugs' success: By smile, voice, and attitude, the doctor would unknowingly convey confidence and hope, convincing patients of the probability of improvement.

Dozens of studies have verified the healing power of hope—as well as the dangers of its opposite. The University of Rochester School of Medicine found that open heart surgery patients were far more likely to die after surgery if they showed signs of depression.[1] Another famous study, called "Broken Heart," surveyed the mortality rate of 4,500 widowers within six months of their wives' deaths. The widowers, most of them depressed, had a mortality rate forty percent higher than other men the same age.

Prisoner-of-war accounts indicate that some POWs may die for no apparent reason other than a loss of hope. Consider the experience of Major F. J. Harold Kushner, an army medical officer held by the Vietcong for five and a half years.

> Kushner got to know one POW, a tough young marine who had already survived two years of prison camp life. The marine was a model POW, keeping himself in good health and leading the camp's thought-reform group, mainly because the camp commander had promised to release those who cooperated. As time passed, however, the marine gradually discerned that his captors had lied to him. When the full realization of this fact sunk in, he became a zombie, refusing all work and rejecting all offers of food and encouragement. He simply lay on his cot sucking his thumb. In a matter of weeks he was dead.[2]

Writing about the young marine, Dr. Martin Seligman of the University of Pennsylvania says that a strictly medical explanation of his decline isn't adequate. "Hope of release sustained him," Seligman says. "When he gave up hope, when he believed that all his efforts had failed and would continue to fail, he died."

As the noted physiologist Harold G. Wolf puts it, "Hope, faith and a purpose in life, is medicinal. This is not merely a statement of belief but a conclusion proved by meticulously controlled scientific experiment."[3]

The Elusive Gift

At long-term care facilities the patients tend to divide into two categories: the *hopers,* who endeavor to beat back their affliction and resume normal life, and the *defeatists.* On a visit to the Menninger Clinic, pastor and author Bruce Larson asked the staff to identify the single most important ingredient in the treatment of the mentally disturbed. They were unanimous in singling out hope as the most important factor, but went on to confess they didn't really know how to "dispense" hope to a patient. It is a quality of the spirit, and thus an elusive gift. Yet they could tell right away when a patient turned the corner in treatment and for the first time believed that the future did not have to be the same as the troubled present.[4]

As the staff at the Menninger Clinic discovered, such courageous hope cannot be taught. But it can sometimes be caught. We can seek ways to awaken courage in suffering people.

The organization Amnesty International offers a good illustration of infectious hope. The founder, a political prisoner at the brink of despair, was given a matchbook with a single word written on it, "Courage!" That small gesture of shared humanity renewed his hope enough to keep him alive. When the man finally attained freedom, he devoted himself to building an organization based on the simplest principle imaginable. People in free countries write letters to prisoners who are being held and tortured for political reasons. For thousands of prisoners, the mere knowledge that someone else cares—even an unknown letter-writer—has kindled the flame of hope.

Sometimes hope seems irrational and pointless. It must have seemed so to inmates in concentration camps. Yet, as Solzhenitsyn insists in the quotation that heads this chapter, people without reasonable hope must still find a source for hope; like bread, it sustains life. For Solzhenitsyn, hope was a matter of choice, a mechanism of survival that fed his will to live. Later, he compiled the stories in *The Gulag Archipelago* both to honor and to bring hope to his fellow-prisoners. For Dostoyevski, hope of release, the sense of not being *"not at home,* but on a visit,"* became a parable for all of life, and helped convince him of an afterlife beyond this one.[5]

In his book *Experiences of God,* the theologian Jürgen Moltmann tells how hope kept him alive in a camp. Captured as a German war prisoner, he was shuffled among prisons in Belgium, Scotland, and England. Besides the normal hardships of prison life—no heat, little food, constant illness—he also had to deal with the despair that came from seeing his nation go down to defeat and learning of atrocities that had been committed in Germany's name. "I saw how other men collapsed inwardly, how they gave up all hope, sickening for the lack of it, some of them dying. The same thing almost happened to me. What kept me from it was a rebirth to new life thanks to a hope for which there was no evidence at all."[6]

That hope for Moltmann was a Christian hope. He had taken two books with him to war: Goethe's poems and the works of Nietzsche. Neither of these gave him any comfort. After experiencing the death of all the mainstays that had sustained his life up to then, he turned to a New Testament given him by a well-meaning army chaplain. The Psalms, printed at the back in an appendix, opened his eyes to "the God who is with those 'that are of a broken heart.'"

After his release in 1948, Moltmann abandoned his field of physics and went on to become a leading theologian, known best for his ground-breaking book *The Theology of Hope*.

The inspiring example of other people may represent the only way for a person to climb out of hopeless despair. Throughout this book I have used illustrations of people who have "successfully coped" with suffering. There are, of course, many contrary examples, of people destroyed by pain. But hope is such a crucial ingredient in coping with pain that I wonder if realistic "success stories" can ever be overemphasized. Someone in despair needs a person or an idea, something to grasp onto that may provide a lifeline out of the currents of gloom.

Healthy people may tire of the "disabled person finds happiness and usefulness" stories in *Reader's Digest* and *Guideposts*. But the disabled people I've talked with take those stories much more seriously. The survivors challenge their self-pitying tendencies. And some such stories—John Merrick (*The Elephant Man*), Helen Keller, Christy Brown (*My Left Foot*)—challenge all of us.

Hope means simply the belief that something good lies ahead. It is not the same as optimism or wishful thinking, for these imply a denial of reality. Often, I think, those of us who stand alongside suffering people tend to confuse hope and optimism. We look for signs of encouragement to administer like nostrums. "Yes, it's true that your memory is fading, Mother, but after all, what does memory matter?" "Your sight is failing, but you can still hear me OK. That's good, isn't it?" "I know this week has been hard for you, but perhaps the pain will go away next week."

My time among the people in the Make Today Count group taught me the limitations of optimism. Most of the above statements would strike dying people as insults, not grounds for hope. They need something beyond Pollyanna optimism. For them, hope resembles courage more than cheerfulness. It involves a leap, much like faith: ". . . hope that is seen is no hope at all" said the apostle Paul. "Who hopes for what he already has? But if we hope for what we do not yet have, we wait for it patiently" (Romans 8:24–25).

Yet hope saves us from pessimism also, the belief that the universe is a chaos without final meaning. True hope is honest. It allows a person to believe that even when she falls down and the worst has happened, still she has not reached the end of the road. She can stand up and continue.

Realistic hope permits a dying person to confront reality, but at the same time gives strength to go on living. Orville Kelly, the founder of Make Today Count, expressed this quality of courageous hope well: "I do not consider myself dying of cancer, but living despite it. I do not look upon each day as another day closer to death, but as another day of life, to be appreciated and enjoyed."

Long-suffering

The people in my hospital therapy group had long-term illnesses, the kind that will never go away, and such conditions call for a special kind of availability from the rest of us. In older days waves of typhoid, smallpox, or yellow fever would bring death quickly; nowadays the terminal illness is more likely to linger. People who struggle with long-term suffering report that a fatigue factor sets in. At first, no matter what the illness, they get a spurt of attention from well-wishers and friends. Cards fill their mailboxes, and flowers fight for space on the countertops. But over time, attention fades.

Many people are embarrassed and troubled by problems that do not go away. One Christian woman told me that with each successive reappearance of her cancer fewer visitors came to see her. As the illness dragged on she felt even more vulnerable and afraid, and she also felt more alone. Some Christians seemed resentful that their prayers for healing had gone unanswered, acting almost as if they blamed her. They lost faith and stayed away, leaving her with guilt and self-hatred to cope with in addition to her pain.

Parents of children with birth defects echo this woman's complaint. A flurry of sympathetic response follows the birth, but soon fades. Thus as the parents' needs and emotional difficulties increase, offers of help tend to decrease. Unlike a person facing a terminal illness, the parents of a severely disabled child have no end in sight. They accept the task of care-giving for life and, to complicate matters, they must also worry about how the child will manage after their own deaths.

In his list of fruits of the Spirit, Paul includes one that we translate with the archaic word "long-suffering." We would do well to revive that word, and concept, in its most literal form to apply to the problem of long-term pain.

Some Christians would far rather talk about miraculous healing than long-suffering, and I should mention why I have mostly avoided this important aspect of the problem of pain. I haven't emphasized miraculous healing in this book for two reasons. First, there are many good books available on miraculous healing, ranging from personal testimonies to theological treatises. Second, I'm writing about people who feel trapped in pain and who are questioning God. Healing is one way out of the dilemma, but in truth we must acknowledge that not everyone finds miraculous healing. Ask Brian Sternberg.

I don't mean to downplay physical healing. But as I have already mentioned, everyone who has been healed (and also those who have been used to heal others) eventually dies. So healing does not remove the problem of pain; it merely delays it.

The possibility of miraculous healing offers tremendous hope for the Christian. Yet if healing does not come, that dashed hope can be a great impediment to faith and can lead to feelings of betrayal and despair. Barbara Sanderville, a young paraplegic writer in Minnesota, described this process in a letter to me:

> Someone told me just after I became a Christian that God would heal me. This seemed too good to be true, and I didn't know if I dared believe it. But seeing nothing in the Bible that contradicted it, I began to hope, and then to believe. But my faith was shaky, and when Christians came along and said, "God doesn't heal everyone," or "Affliction is a cross we must bear," my faith would waver. Then last fall it just seemed to die. I gave up believing God would heal me.
>
> At that point in my life I knew I couldn't face spending the rest of my life in the wheelchair. Knowing that God had the power to heal me but wouldn't (or so I thought) made me very bitter. I would read Isaiah 53, and 1 Peter 2:24, and accuse God of holding the promise of healing before me like a piece of meat before a starving dog. He tempted me by showing the potential but never quite allowing me

to reach it. This in turn produced deep guilt feelings because from the Bible I knew God was a loving God and answerable to no man. I had such a conflict in me that my mental state was precarious and I thought of suicide many times.

I began to take tranquilizers just to get through the day as my guilt and resentment built a higher and higher wall between God and me. About this time I began having headaches and problems with my eyes. An ophthalmologist could find no physical reason.

I was still praying because I knew God was alive, but I usually ended up crying and railing out at God. I'm afraid I experienced a lot of self-pity, which was very destructive. And over and over I asked God why He wouldn't heal me when it so plainly says that healing is a part of the redemption plan.

Barbara eventually found a mental healing that swept away the bitterness. She is still awaiting physical healing.

Because of experiences like Barbara's, I believe a hope for healing should be presented realistically. It is just that—a "hope," not a guarantee. If it comes, a joyous miracle has happened. If it doesn't come, God has not let you down. He can use even the infirmity to produce good. He does promise that, without fail.

Final Hope

As with the other frontiers of recovery—fear, helplessness, meaning—the Christian has certain unique resources available in the struggle for hope. The last section of this book will deal with specific contributions that Christian faith can make. But I would be remiss if I did not mention in this chapter as well the final hope of resurrection, the hope for a new world in which the "problem of pain" will seem like a distant memory.

The Christian believes that, no matter how bleak things look at the present, something good really does lie ahead. Bruno Bettelheim, survivor of Hitler's camps, acknowledges that such belief translates into actual help: "It is a well-known fact of the concentration camps that those who had strong religious and moral convictions managed life there much better than the rest.

Their beliefs, including belief in an afterlife, gave them a strength to endure which was far above that of most others."[7]

Joni Eareckson Tada tells of a time when she visited a home for the mentally retarded. Usually when she visits a care facility and recounts her life story, speaking from a wheelchair, she keeps her audience spellbound. These patients, however, of varying ages but all with undeveloped minds, had trouble with attention span. When Joni reached the part about imagining what heaven would be like, she could tell she had lost their interest entirely.

It was a warm day, and Joni could feel perspiration rolling down her body as she struggled to continue. Finally, in desperation, she said this, "And heaven will be the place where all of you will get new minds." As soon as the words came out, she regretted them—what if they sounded paternalistic, or cruel? But instantly the atmosphere in the room changed. Spontaneously, the patients started cheering, with loud applause.

Joni had tapped into their deepest hope. They, more than anyone, knew their minds were incomplete, unfulfilled. But she had held out the Christian promise of a place where such weaknesses would not carry over, a place of final healing. "But our citizenship is in heaven," Paul reminded the Philippians (3:20–21). "And we eagerly await a Savior from there, the Lord Jesus Christ, who, by the power that enables him to bring everything under his control, will transform our lowly bodies so that they will be like his glorious body."

We Western Christians in our increasing sophistication have, I think, grown a little ashamed of our faith's emphasis on immortality and rewards to come. I hear few sermons these days on the crown of life or crown of righteousness. Our culture announces to us that suffering is the reality and an afterlife of immortality is just a pipe dream.

But do we have any other sure hope to offer for the quadriplegic or the mother of a brain-damaged baby? And is the hope of an afterlife and eternal healing a worthy hope? To answer that question, I must tell you the story of Martha, one of the members of the Make Today Count group. In a sense, her story summarizes everything I learned about pain in my year with the group.

Martha caught my eye at the very first meeting. Other

people there showed obvious symptoms of illness: thinning hair, a sallow complexion, a missing limb, an uncontrolled trembling. But Martha showed no such signs. She was twenty-six, and very attractive. I wondered if she, like me, was visiting with a friend.

When it was Martha's turn to speak, she said she had just contracted ALS, or Lou Gehrig's disease. Her father had died of the same disease a year before, and two years before that her uncle had died of it. ALS rarely shows hereditary connections, and very rarely attacks young women, but somehow she had cruelly defied the odds.

ALS destroys nerves. It first attacks voluntary movements, such as control over arms and legs, then hands and feet. It progresses on to involuntary movements, and finally inhibits breathing enough to cause death. Sometimes a person's body succumbs quickly, sometimes not. Martha's relatives had lived through two years of degeneration before death. Martha knew the disease's pattern in excruciating detail.

My first meeting with the group took place in March. In April, Martha arrived in a wheelchair. She could walk only with great difficulty, and because of that had just been fired from her job at a university library.

By May Martha had lost use of her right arm, and could no longer use crutches. A physical therapist had taught her to pick things up off the floor by using a broomstick-and-masking-tape contraption. She operated the manual wheelchair with great difficulty.

By June she had lost use of both arms and could barely move the hand controls on a new electric wheelchair. Needing round-the-clock care, she moved into a rehabilitation hospital.

I began visiting Martha at her rehabilitation hospital. I took her for short rides in her wheelchair, and sometimes picked her up for the group meetings. I learned about the indignity of her suffering. I learned to check her toes before putting on her shoes—if they were curled, they would jam painfully in the shoe—and to close her hand and guide it carefully into the sleeve of her jacket. I also had to watch for her dangling arms before setting her down on the car seat. It is not easy to position a 125-pound body of dead weight inside a compact car.

Martha needed help with every move: getting dressed, arranging her head on the pillow, cleaning her bedpan. When she cried, someone else had to wipe her tears and hold a tissue to her nose. Her body was in utter revolt against her will. It would not obey any of her commands.

Sometimes we talked about death and about hope. I confess to you readily that the great Christian hopes of eternal life, ultimate healing, and resurrection sounded hollow and frail and thin as smoke when held up to someone like Martha. She wanted not angel wings, but an arm that did not flop to the side, a mouth that did not drool, and lungs that would not collapse. I confess that eternity, even a pain-free eternity, seemed to have a strange irrelevance to the suffering Martha felt.

She thought about God, of course, but she could hardly think of him with love. She held out against any deathbed conversion, insisting that, as she put it, she would only turn to God out of love and not out of fear. And how could she love a God who did this to her?

It became clear around October that ALS would complete its horrible cycle quickly in Martha. She soon had to practice breathing with a toy-like plastic machine, blowing with all her might to make little blue balls rise in the pressure columns. Between gasps for breath, she talked about what she preferred losing first, her voice or her breath. Ultimately she decided she would rather her lungs quit first; she preferred dying to dying mute, unable to express herself.

Because of reduced oxygen supply to her brain, Martha tended to fall asleep in the middle of conversations. Sometimes at night she would awake in a panic, with a sensation like choking, and be unable to call for help.

Despite logistical difficulties, Martha managed to make one last trip to a favorite summer cabin in Michigan, and to her mother's home nearby. She was making final preparations, saying farewells.

In that process, Martha badly wanted at least two weeks back in her own apartment in Chicago as a time to invite friends over, one by one, in order to say good-bye and to come to terms with her death. But the two weeks in her apartment posed a huge problem. How could she stay at home in view of the need for round-the-clock care? Some government aid could be found to keep her in a hospital room, but not at home, not with the intensive service she needed just to stay alive.

Only one group in all of Chicago offered the free and loving personal care that Martha needed: Reba Place Fellowship, a Christian community in Evanston. Included among the members of Reba Place was a paraplegic named Sara who knew well the agony of living in a body that did not function properly. Partly due to Sara's influence, the entire community adopted Martha as a project and volunteered all that was necessary to fulfill her last wishes.

Sixteen women rearranged their lives for her. They divided into teams, adjusted their schedules, traded off baby-sitting duties for their own children, and moved into her apartment, one pair per shift. Seventeen other people signed on as a support team to pray for Martha and the care-givers. They prayed for her miraculous healing, but they also prayed for those who would minister to her if the disease continued its deadly course.

The sixteen women stayed with Martha, listened to her ravings and complaints, bathed her, helped her sit up, moved her, sat beside her all night to listen to her breathing, prayed for her, and loved her. They were available to calm her fears. They gave her a sense of place so that she no longer felt helpless, and gave meaning to her suffering. To Martha they were God's body.

The Reba Place women also explained to Martha the Christian hope. And finally Martha, seeing the love of God enfleshed in his body—at a time when God himself seemed to her uncompassionate, even cruel—came to that God in Christ. She presented herself in trust to the one who had died for her. She did not come to God in fear; she had found his love at last. In a very moving service in Evanston, she feebly gave a testimony and was baptized.

On the day before Thanksgiving of 1983, Martha died. Her body, crumpled, misshapen, atrophied, was a pathetic imitation of its former beauty. When it finally stopped functioning, Martha left it. But today Martha lives, in a new body, in wholeness and triumph. She lives because of the victory that Christ won and because of his body at Reba Place, who made that victory known to her. And if we do not believe that, and if our Christian hope, tempered by sophistication, does not allow us to offer that truth to a dying, convulsing world then we are indeed, as the apostle Paul said, of all men most miserable.

Part 5

How Does
Faith Help?

God weeps with us so that we may one day laugh with him.
Jürgen Moltmann

18

Seeing for Himself

Every religion, whether Buddhist, Hindu, Muslim, or New Age, must somehow address the problem of pain. Much of what I have presented so far—pain's value to the human body, how to prepare for and help one another through suffering—applies to all people, regardless of religious belief. But what difference does Christian faith make, specifically? What resources can Christians fall back on?

By asking that we have, in a sense, circled back to the opening question, "Where is God when it hurts?" It is a question that C. S. Lewis asked, as did Claudia Claxton, and the movie actress whose lover rolled off a boat, and Joni Eareckson Tada and Brian Sternberg, and the survivors of the concentration camps. It is a question that every suffering person eventually asks. Where is God? How does he feel about my plight? Does he care?

The lark's on the wing
The snail's on the thorn
God's in his heaven
All's right with the world.

221

Robert Browning wrote those words in the mid-nineteenth century, an era of boundless optimism. But after two world wars and two atomic bomb attacks, the Holocaust, and numerous genocides and mass famines around the globe, few people would now dare to say, "All's right with the world." Worse, God seems to stay in his heaven despite all that's wrong with the world. Why doesn't he do something?

A Farmhand's Cry

Hear a modern-day complaint against God from the mouth of a migrant farmhand mother (as recorded by psychiatrist and author Robert Coles).

§ Last year we went to a little church in New Jersey. . . . We had all our children there, the baby included. The Reverend Jackson was there, I can't forget his name, and he told us to be quiet, and he told us how glad we should be that we're in this country, because it's Christian, and not "godless."

. . . Then my husband went and lost his temper; something happened to his nerves, I do believe. He got up and started shouting, yes sir. He went up to the Reverend Mr. Jackson and told him to shut up and never speak again—not to us, the migrant people. He told him to go back to his church, wherever it is, and leave us alone and don't be standing up there looking like he was nice to be doing us a favor.

Then he did the worst thing he could do: He took the baby, Annie, and he held her right before his face, the minister's, and he screamed and shouted and hollered at him, that minister, like I've never seen anyone do. I don't remember what he said, the exact words, but he told him that here was our little Annie, and she's never been to a doctor, and the child is sick . . . and we've got no money, not for Annie or the other ones or ourselves.

Then he lifted Annie up, so she was higher than the reverend, and he said why doesn't he go and pray for Annie and pray that the growers will be punished for what they're doing to us, all the migrant people. . . . And then my

§ husband began shouting about God and His neglecting us while He took such good care of the other people all over.

Then the reverend did answer—and that was his mistake, yes it was. He said we should be careful and not start blaming God and criticizing Him and complaining to Him and like that, because God wasn't supposed to be taking care of the way the growers behave and how we live, here on this earth. "God worries about your future"; that's what he said, and I tell you, my husband near exploded. He shouted about ten times to the reverend, "Future, future, future." Then he took Annie and near pushed her in the reverend's face and Annie, she started crying, poor child, and he asked the reverend about Annie's "future" and asked him what he'd do if he had to live like us, and if he had a "future" like ours.

Then he told the reverend he was like all the rest, making money off us, and held our Annie as high as he could, right near the cross, and told God He'd better stop having ministers speaking for Him, and He should come and see us for Himself, and not have the "preachers"—he kept calling them the "preachers"—speaking for Him.

. . . He stopped after he'd finished talking about the "preachers" and he came back to us, and there wasn't a sound in the church, no sir, not one you could hear—until a couple of other men said he was right, my husband was . . . and everyone clapped their hands and I felt real funny.[1]

This migrant family sums up the problem of suffering about as well as it can be expressed. Why does God allow a world of sick children and no money and no hope? Their dilemma is not abstract and philosophical, but intensely personal: their child Annie hurts, and they can see no solution. Does God even care?

Nothing that I can say in this or any book would solve the problems of this farmhand family. They cry out for a response of compassionate love, not a theoretical solution. But in his zeal the angry farmhand unwittingly pointed to Christianity's chief contribution to the problem of pain. Holding his child in front of the reverend's face, up near the cross, he demanded that God come down and see for himself what this world is like. It's not enough, he said, for God to keep having the preachers speak for him.

The fact is, God did come. He entered this world in human flesh, and saw and felt for himself what this world is like. Apart from the Incarnation, our faith would have little to say to the farmhand.

Keeping His Own Rules

Old Testament characters like Job and Jeremiah sometimes wondered aloud if God had "plugged his ears" to their cries of pain. Jesus put an abrupt and decisive end to such speculation. Not only had God not plugged his ears, he suddenly took on ears—literal, eardrum-ossicle-cochlea human ears. On the cracked and dusty plains of Palestine, God's Son heard firsthand the molecular vibrations of human groans: from the sick and the needy, and from others who groaned more from guilt than from pain.

Clear your mind and reflect for a moment on Jesus' life. He was the only person in history able to plan his own birth. Yet he humbled himself, trading in a perfect heavenly body for a frail body of blood and sinew and cartilage and nerve cells. The Bible says there is no temptation known to man that Jesus did not experience. He was lonely, tired, hungry, personally assaulted by Satan, besieged by leeching admirers, persecuted by powerful enemies.

As for physical appearance, there's only one description of Jesus in the Bible, one written hundreds of years in advance by the prophet Isaiah: "He had no beauty or majesty to attract us to him, nothing in his appearance that we should desire him. He was despised and rejected by men, a man of sorrows, and familiar with suffering. Like one from whom men hide their faces . . ." (Isaiah 53:2–3).

When Jesus first began his ministry, the people hooted, "Can anything good come from Nazareth?" An ancient ethnic joke: Jesus, the hick, the country bumpkin from Nazareth. In keeping with that reputation, he seemed to gravitate toward other rejects: those quarantined with leprosy, prostitutes, tax collectors, paralytics, notorious sinners.

Jesus' neighbors once ran him out of town and tried to kill him. His own family questioned his sanity. The leaders of the day proudly reported that not one authority or religious leader believed in him. His followers were a motley crew of fishermen and peasants, among whom the migrant farmhand would have felt comfortably at home. But in the end, even these forsook him when Jesus' countrymen traded his life for that of a terrorist.

No other religion—not Judaism, not Hinduism, not Buddhism or Islam—offers this unique contribution of an all-powerful God who willingly takes on the limitations and suffering of his creation. As Dorothy Sayers wrote,

> For whatever reason God chose to make man as he is— limited and suffering and subject to sorrows and death— He had the honesty and courage to take His own medicine. Whatever game He is playing with His creation, He has kept His own rules and played fair. He can exact nothing from man that He has not exacted from Himself. He has Himself gone through the whole of human experience, from the trivial irritations of family life and the cramping restrictions of hard work and lack of money to the worst horrors of pain and humiliation, defeat, despair, and death. When He was a man, He played the man. He was born in poverty and died in disgrace and thought it well worthwhile.[2]

The fact that Jesus came to earth where he suffered and died does not remove pain from our lives. But it does show that God did not sit idly by and watch us suffer in isolation. He became one of us. Thus, in Jesus, God gives us an up-close and personal look at his response to human suffering. All our questions about God and suffering should, in fact, be filtered through what we know about Jesus.

How did God-on-earth respond to pain? When he met a person in pain, he was deeply moved with compassion (from the Latin words *pati* and *cum,* "to suffer with"). Not once did he say, "Endure your hunger! Swallow your grief!" When Jesus' friend Lazarus died, he wept. Very often, every time he was directly asked, he healed the pain. Sometimes he broke deep-rooted customs to do so, as when he touched a woman with a hemorrhage of blood, or when he touched outcasts, ignoring their cries of "Unclean!"

The pattern of Jesus' response should convince us that God is not a God who enjoys seeing us suffer. I doubt that Jesus' disciples tormented themselves with questions like "Does God care?" They had visible evidence of his concern every day: they simply looked at Jesus' face.

And when Jesus himself faced suffering, he reacted much like any of us would. He recoiled from it, asking three times if there was any other way. There was no other way, and then Jesus experienced, perhaps for the first time, that most human sense of abandonment: "My God, my God, why have you forsaken me?" In the gospel accounts of Jesus' last night on earth, I detect a fierce struggle with fear, helplessness, and hope—the same frontiers all of us confront in our suffering.

The record of Jesus' life on earth should forever answer the question, How does God feel about our pain? In reply, God did not give us words or theories on the problem of pain. He gave us himself. A philosophy may explain difficult things, but has no power to change them. The gospel, the story of Jesus' life, promises change.

The Execution

> Love's as hard as nails
>   Love is nails:
> Blunt, thick, hammered through
> The medial nerves of One
> Who, having made us, knew
> The thing He had done,
> Seeing (with all that is)
> Our cross and his.
>   (C. S. Lewis, "Love's as Warm as Tears")

There is one central symbol by which we remember Jesus. Today that image is coated with gold and worn around the necks of athletes and beautiful women, an example of how we can gloss over the crude reality of history. The cross was, of course, a mode of execution. It would be no more bizarre if we made jewelry in the shape of tiny electric chairs, gas chambers, and hypodermic needles, the preferred modern modes of execution.

The cross, the most universal image in the Christian religion, offers proof that God cares about our suffering and pain. He died of it. That symbol stands unique among all the religions of the world. Many of them have gods, but only one has a God who cared enough to become a man and to die.

The scene, with the beatings and the sharp spikes and the slow torment of suffocation, has been recounted so often that we, who shrink from a news story on the death of a race horse or of baby seals, flinch not at all at its retelling. Unlike the quick, sterile executions we know today, this one stretched on for hours in front of a jeering crowd.

The promises Jesus made must have seemed especially empty to the people of his day. This man a king? A mock king if ever there was one, with his brier crown. Someone had thrown a fine purple robe over him, but blood from Pilate's beatings clotted on the cloth.

More unlikely—this man God? Even for his disciples, who had pursued him three years, it was too much to believe. They hung back in the crowd, afraid to be identified with the mock king. Their dreams of a powerful ruler who could banish all suffering turned into nightmares.

Jesus' death is the cornerstone of the Christian faith, the most important fact of his coming. The Gospels bulge with its details. He laid out a trail of hints and bald predictions throughout his ministry, predictions that were only understood after the thing had been done. What possible contribution to the problem of pain could come from a religion based on an event like the cross, where God himself succumbed to pain?

The apostle Paul called the cross a "stumbling block" to belief, and history has proved him out. Jewish rabbis question how a God who could not bear to see Abraham's son slain would allow his own Son to die. The Koran teaches that God, much too gentle to allow Jesus to go to the cross, substituted an evildoer in his place. Even today, U.S. television personality Phil Donahue explains his chief objection to Christianity: "How could an all-knowing, all-loving God allow His Son to be murdered on a cross in order to redeem my sins? If God the Father is so 'all-loving,' why didn't He come down and go to Calvary?"

All of these objectors have missed the main point of the gospel, that in some mysterious way it *was* God himself who came to earth and died. God was not "up there" watching the tragic events conspire "down here." God was *in Christ*, reconciling the world to himself. In Luther's phrase, the cross showed

"God struggling with God." If Jesus was a mere man, his death would prove God's cruelty; the fact that he was God's Son proves instead that God fully identifies with suffering humanity. On the cross, God himself absorbed the awful pain of this world.

To some, the image of a pale body glimmering on a dark night whispers of defeat. What good is a God who does not control his Son's suffering? But another sound can be heard: the shout of a God crying out to human beings, "I LOVE YOU." Love was compressed for all history in that lonely figure on the cross, who said that he could call down angels at any moment on a rescue mission, but chose not to—because of us. At Calvary, God accepted his own unbreakable terms of justice.

And thus the cross, a stumbling block to some, became the cornerstone of Christian faith. Any discussion of how pain and suffering fit into God's scheme ultimately leads back to the cross.

At the end of the book of Job, God responded to questions about suffering by delivering a splendid lecture on his power. After Calvary, the emphasis shifts from power to love:

> For God so loved the world that he gave his one and only Son, that whoever believes in him shall not perish but have eternal life. (John 3:16)

> If God is for us, who can be against us? He who did not spare his own Son, but gave him up for us all—how will he not also, along with him, graciously give us all things? (Romans 8:31–32)

Why It Matters

I once talked with a priest who had just performed the funeral of an eight-year-old girl. His parish had prayed and wept and shared the family's agony for more than a year as the girl fought a futile battle against cancer. The funeral had strained the emotions, the energy, and even the faith of the priest. "What can I possibly say to her family?" he confided in me. "I have no solution to offer them. What can I say?" He paused for a moment, and added this, "I have no solution to their pain; I have only an answer. And Jesus Christ is that answer."

The death and resurrection of Jesus Christ provide more than an abstract theological answer to the problem of pain. They also offer us actual, practical help in our own struggles with suffering. I have identified at least four ways in which those events, now two millennia old, have a direct impact on my own suffering.

I learn to judge the present by the future.

A wise man named Joe Bayly once said, "Don't forget in the darkness what you have learned in the light." Yet sometimes the darkness descends so thickly that we can barely remember the light. Surely it seemed that way to Jesus' disciples.

In his most intimate encounter with them, during the meal known as the Last Supper, Jesus made the ringing declaration, "In this world you will have trouble. But take heart! I have overcome the world" (John 16:33). I can imagine the chill bumps on the backs of the eleven men who heard that assertion from the lips of God in flesh. At that moment, eleven of the twelve would gladly have given their lives for him; later that evening Simon Peter actually pulled a sword in Jesus' defense.

Yet by the next day all eleven had lost faith. Those triumphant words from the previous night must have cruelly haunted them as they watched him—safely, at a distance— anguish on the cross. It appeared as though the world had overcome God. All of them slipped away in the darkness. Peter swore with an oath he'd never known the man.

The disciples' problem, of course, was a matter of perspective. Yes, the memory of light from the past had been extinguished, but a few days later those same men would encounter the dazzling light of Easter. On that day, they learned that no darkness is too great for God. They learned what it means to judge the present by the future. Ignited by Easter hope, those former cowards went out and changed the world.

Today half the world celebrates the back-to-back holidays Good Friday and Easter. That darkest Friday is now called Good because of what happened on Easter Sunday; and because it happened Christians have hope that God will someday restore this planet to its proper place under his reign. The miracle of Easter will enlarge to cosmic scale.

It is a good thing to remember, when we encounter dark, disturbing times, that we live out our days on Easter Saturday. As the apostle Paul expressed it, "I consider that our present sufferings are not worth comparing with the glory that will be revealed in us" (Romans 8:18). It was no accident, I believe, that Jesus spoke his triumphant words, I HAVE OVERCOME THE WORLD, even as Roman soldiers were buckling on weapons for his arrest. He knew how to judge the present by the future.

I learn the pattern of transformed pain.

Christianity contains within it paradoxes that would make little sense apart from Jesus' life and death. Consider one paradox I have already alluded to in this book: although poverty and suffering are "bad things" that I rightly spend my life fighting against, yet at the same time they can be called "blessed." This pattern of bad transmuted into good finds its fullest expression in Jesus. By taking it on himself, Jesus dignified pain, showing us how it can be transformed. He gave us a pattern he wants to reproduce in us.

Jesus Christ offers the perfect example of all the biblical lessons about suffering. Because of Jesus, I can never say about a person, "She must be suffering because of some sin she committed"; Jesus, who did not sin, also felt pain. God has never promised that tornadoes will skip our houses on the way to our pagan neighbors' and that microbes will flee from Christian bodies. We are not exempt from the tragedies of this world, just as God himself was not exempt. Remember, Peter earned Jesus' strongest rebuke when he protested against the need for Christ to suffer (Matthew 16:23–25).

We feel pain as an outrage; Jesus did too, which is why he performed miracles of healing. In Gethsemane, he did not pray, "Thank you for this opportunity to suffer," but rather pled desperately for an escape. And yet he was willing to undergo suffering in service of a higher goal. In the end he left the hard questions ("if there be any other way . . .") to the will of the Father, and trusted that God could use even the outrage of his death for good.

As Cornelius Plantinga, Jr., has said, "We do not refer each other to the cross of Christ to explain evil. It is not as if in pondering Calvary we will at last understand throat cancer. We rather lift our eyes to the cross, whence comes our help, in order to see that God shares our lot and can therefore be *trusted*."[3] In the ultimate alchemy of all history, God took the worst thing that could possibly happen—the appalling execution of his innocent Son—and turned it into the final victory over evil and death. It was an act of unprecedented cunning, turning the design of evil into the service of good, an act that holds within it a promise for all of us. The unimaginable suffering of the cross was fully redeemed: it is by his *wounds* that we are healed (Isaiah 53:5), by his weakness that we are made strong.

How would the world be different if Jesus had come as a Superman figure, immune to all pain? What if he had not died, but merely ascended to heaven during his trial before Pilate? By not making himself exempt, but by deliberately taking on the worst the world has to offer, he gives us the hope that God can likewise transform the suffering each of us must face. Because of his death and resurrection, we can confidently assume that no trial—illness, divorce, unemployment, bankruptcy, grief—extends beyond the range of his transforming power.

The four gospels record only one instance of Jesus' disciples addressing him as God directly. It comes at the end of John, after Jesus' death and resurrection. All the disciples now believe in the risen Christ but one—doubting Thomas. An empiricist, Thomas insists that he will not be convinced unless he can put his fingers on the scars in Jesus' hands and side. Before long Jesus appears, despite the locked doors, and offers just that opportunity. "My Lord and my God!" Thomas cries out. The wounds were proof of a miracle beyond miracles.

I learn a new level of meaning to suffering.

In the Old Testament, faithful believers seemed shocked when suffering came their way. They expected God to reward their faithfulness with prosperity and comfort. But the New Testament shows a remarkable change—its authors expect just the opposite. As Peter advised suffering Christians, "This suffering is all part of the work God has given you. Christ, who suffered for you, is your example. Follow in his steps" (1 Peter 2:21 LB).

Other passages go further, using phrases I will not attempt to explain. Paul speaks of "sharing in his [Christ's] sufferings" and says he hopes to "fill up in my flesh what is still lacking in regards to Christ's afflictions." In context, all these passages show that suffering can gain meaning if we consider it as part of the "cross" we take on in following Jesus.

Although Christ does not always remove our pains, he fills them with meaning by absorbing them into his own suffering.

We are helping to accomplish God's redemptive purposes in the world as co-participants with him in the battle to expel evil from this planet.

Harry Boer, who served four years as a chaplain during World War II, spent the final days of that war among marines in the Pacific Theater. "The Second Division saw much action, with great losses," he writes. "Yet I never met an enlisted man or an officer who doubted for a moment the outcome of the war. Nor did I ever meet a marine who asked why, if victory was so sure, we couldn't have it immediately. It was just a question of slogging through till the enemy gave up."[4]

I see a parallel situation in the veiled words about participating in Christ's sufferings. A far greater war is being fought on this planet, which will determine the destiny of all creation. And that war will involve certain casualties.

According to Paul, at the cross Christ triumphed over the cosmic powers—defeating them not with power but with self-giving love. The cross of Christ may have assured the final outcome, but battles remain for us to fight. Significantly, Paul prayed "to know Christ and the power of his resurrection and the fellowship of sharing in his sufferings"—embracing both the agony and the ecstasy of Christ's life on earth (Philippians 3:10).

It helps, though, to realize that the casualties we sustain are wounds of honor that will one day be rewarded. We will never know, in this life, the full significance of our actions here, for much takes place invisible to us. Christ's cross offers a pattern for that too: what seemed very ordinary, one more dreary feat of colonial "justice" in a Roman outpost, made possible the salvation of the entire world.

When a pastor in South Africa goes to prison for his peaceful protest, when a social worker moves into an urban ghetto, when a couple refuses to give up on a difficult marriage, when a parent waits with undying hope and forgiveness for the return of an estranged child, when a young professional resists mounting temptations toward wealth and success—in all these sufferings, large and small, there is the assurance of a deeper level of meaning, of a sharing in Christ's own redemptive victory. "The creation waits in eager expectation for the sons of God to be revealed" (Romans 8:19).

I gain the confidence that God truly understands my pain.

Because of Jesus, I need never cry into the abyss, "Hey, you up there—do you even care?" The presence of suffering does not mean that God has forsaken me. To the contrary, by joining us on earth God gave solid, historical proof that he hears our groans, and even groans them with us. When we endure trials, he stands beside us, like the fourth man in the fiery furnace.

Why did Jesus have to suffer and die? The question deserves an entire book, and has prompted many books, but among the answers the Bible gives is this most mysterious answer: Suffering served as a kind of "learning experience" for God. Such words may seem faintly heretical, but I am merely following phraseology from the book of Hebrews.

Hebrews was written to a Jewish audience saturated in the Old Testament. The author strives to show that Jesus is "better"—a key word throughout the book. How is he better than the religious system they were used to? More powerful? More impressive? No, Hebrews emphasizes that Jesus is better because he has spanned the chasm between God and us. "Although he was a son, he learned obedience from what he suffered" (5:8). Elsewhere, that book tells us that the author of our salvation was made perfect through suffering (2:10).

These words, full of fathomless mystery, surely mean at least this: the Incarnation had meaning for God as well as for us. Human history revolves around not our experience of God, but his experience of us. On one level, of course, God understood physical pain, for he designed the marvelous nervous system that warns against harm. But had he, a Spirit, ever felt physical pain? Not until the Incarnation, the wrinkle in time when God himself experienced what it is like to be a human being.

In thirty-three years on earth Jesus learned about hardship and rejection and betrayal. And he learned too about pain: what it feels like to have an accuser leave the red imprint of his fingers on your face, to have a whip studded with metal lash across your back, to have a crude iron spike pounded through muscle, tendon, and bone. On earth, the Son of God learned all that.

In some incomprehensible way, because of Jesus, God hears our cries differently. The author of Hebrews marvels that whatever we are going through, God has himself gone through. "For we do not have a high priest who is unable to sympathize with our weaknesses, but we have one who has been tempted in every way, just as we are—yet was without sin" (4:15).

We have a high priest who, having graduated from the school of suffering, "is able to deal gently with those who are ignorant and are going astray, since he himself is subject to weakness" (5:2). Because of Jesus, God understands, truly understands, our pain. Our tears become his tears. We are not abandoned. The farmhand with the sick child, the swollen eight-year-old with leukemia, the grieving relatives in Yuba City, the leprosy patients in Louisiana—none has to suffer alone.

T. S. Eliot wrote in one of his *Four Quartets*:

> *The wounded surgeon plies the steel*
> *That questions the distempered part;*
> *Beneath the bleeding hands we feel*
> *The sharp compassion of the healer's art*
> *Resolving the enigma of the fever chart.*[5]

The surgery of life hurts. It helps me, though, to know that the surgeon himself, the Wounded Surgeon, has felt every stab of pain and every sorrow.

Those who have known pain profoundly are the ones most wary of uttering the clichés about suffering. Experience with the mystery takes one beyond the realm of ideas and produces finally a muteness or at least a reticence to express in words the solace that can only be expressed by an attitude of union with the sufferer.

John Howard Griffin

19

The Rest of the Body

During three years of public ministry God's Son put his emotions on public display. Anyone could come to Jesus with problems of suffering. Anyone could follow him and, by observing his reactions to sick and needy people, go away with a clear answer to the question, "How does God feel about my pain?"

But of course Jesus did not stay on earth, and for nearly two thousand years the church has been without Christ's visible presence. We cannot now fly to Jerusalem, rent a car, and schedule a personal appointment with him at the King David Hotel. What about those of us who live today? How can we sense God's love?

Authors of the New Testament, still adjusting to the fact of Jesus' departure, addressed this issue with a certain urgency. They give two main suggestions.

Romans 8 contains one: "The Spirit helps us in our weakness. We do not know what we ought to pray for, but the Spirit himself intercedes for us with groans that words cannot express." The Gospels reveal *the God alongside,* a God who took on flesh and heard humanity's groans with human ears; the

235

Epistles reveal *the God within,* an invisible Spirit who lives inside us and gives expression to our wordless pain.

Because I write about pain and disappointment, I get letters from people who pour out their private groans. I know well the helpless feeling of not knowing what I ought to pray, as I imagine every Christian sometimes does. How to pray for a dead-end marriage that seems to represent only stuntedness, not growth? Or for a parent of a child diagnosed with terminal cancer? Or for a Christian in Nepal imprisoned for her faith? What can we ask for? How can we pray?

Romans 8 announces the good news that we need not figure out how to pray. We need only groan. As I read Paul's words, an image comes to mind of a mother tuning in to her child's wordless cry. I know mothers who, through years of experience, have learned to distinguish a cry for food from a cry for attention, an earache cry from a stomachache cry. To me the sounds are identical, but not to the mother, who instinctively discerns the meaning of the helpless child's cry.

The Spirit of God has resources of sensitivity beyond those of even the wisest mother. Paul says that Spirit lives inside us, detecting needs we cannot articulate and expressing them in a language we cannot comprehend. When we don't know what to pray, he fills in the blanks. Evidently, it is our very helplessness that God, too, delights in. Our weakness gives opportunity for his strength.

For this reason—the new intimacy of a compassionate God living within—Jesus informed his disciples it was actually good that he was going away. "Unless I go away," he said, "the Counselor will not come to you" (John 16:7). Now the Holy Spirit lives inside us as a personal seal of God's presence. Elsewhere, he's called a "deposit," a guarantee of better times to come.

But the Holy Spirit is just that—a spirit: invisible, quick as the wind, inaccessible to human touch. And heaven lies off in the future somewhere. What about right now? What can reassure us physically and visibly of God's love here on earth?

The New Testament's second answer centers around "the body of Christ," a mysterious phrase used more than thirty times. Paul, especially, settled on that phrase as a summary image of the church. When Jesus left, he turned over his mission to flawed and bumbling men and women. He assumed the role of head of the church, leaving the tasks of arms, legs, ears, eyes, and voice to the erratic disciples—and to you and me. The French poet Paul Claudel expressed the change this way, "Since the incarnation, Jesus has only one desire: to recommence the human life he lived. That's why he wants additional human natures, people who'll let him start all over again."[1]

A careful reading of the four gospels shows that this new arrangement was what Jesus had in mind all along. He knew his time on earth was short, and he proclaimed a mission that went beyond even his death and resurrection. "I will build my church," he declared, "and the gates of hell will not prevail against it" (Matthew 16:18 KJV).

Jesus' decision to operate as the invisible head of a large body with many members affects our view of suffering. It means that he often relies on us to help one another cope. The phrase "the body of Christ," expresses well what we are called to do: to represent in flesh what Christ is like, especially to those in need.

The apostle Paul must have had something like that process in mind when he wrote these words: "[God] comforts us in all our troubles, so that we can comfort those in any trouble with the comfort we ourselves have received from God. For just as the sufferings of Christ flow over into our lives, so also through Christ our comfort overflows" (2 Corinthians 1:4–5). And all through his ministry Paul put that principle into practice, taking up collections for famine victims, dispatching assistants to go to troubled areas, acknowledging believers' gifts as gifts from God himself.

United by Pain

Nothing unites the individual parts of a body like the pain network. An infected toenail announces to me that the toe is important, it is mine, it needs attention. If you step on my toe, I may yell "That's me!" I know it's me, because your foot is at that moment resting on pain sensors. Pain defines me, gives me borders.

Wolves have been known to gnaw off one of their own hind legs once it has grown numb in the winter cold. The numbness interrupts the unity of the body; evidently they no longer perceive the leg as belonging to them.

Remember the baby who chewed off her own finger?

Unable to feel pain, she had no acute sense that the finger was hers, and needed protection. Alcoholics and people with leprosy, diabetes, and other problems of insensitivity face a constant battle to keep in touch with their extremities.

In my work with Dr. Brand, especially, I have become aware of the body's vital need to sense pain. In the human body, blood cells and lymph cells rush pell-mell to the sight of any invasion. The body shuts down all nonessential activities and attends to the injury. And physical pain lies at the heart of this unified response.

Pain is the very mechanism that forces me to stop what I'm doing and pay attention to the hurting member. It makes me stop playing basketball if I sprain an ankle, change my shoes if they're too tight, go to the doctor if my stomach keeps hurting. In short, the healthiest body is the one that feels the pain of its weakest parts.

In the same way, we members of Christ's body should learn to attend to the pains of the rest of the body. In so doing we become an incarnation of Christ's risen body.

Dr. Paul Brand has developed this idea as a key part of his personal philosophy.

> Individual cells had to give up their autonomy and learn to suffer with one another before effective multicellular organisms could be produced and survive. The same designer went on to create the human race with a new and higher purpose in mind. Not only would the cells within an individual cooperate with one another, but the individuals within the race would now move on to a new level of community responsibility, to a new kind of relationship with one another and with God.
>
> As in the body, so in this new kind of relationship the key to success lies in the sensation of pain. All of us rejoice at the harmonious working of the human body. Yet we can but sorrow at the relationships between men and women. In human society *we are suffering because we do not suffer enough.*
>
> So much of the sorrow in the world is due to the selfishness of one living organism that simply doesn't care when the next one suffers. In the body if one cell or group of cells grows and flourishes at the expense of the rest, we call it cancer and know that if it is allowed to spread the

body is doomed. And yet, the only alternative to the cancer is absolute loyalty of every cell to the body, the head. God is calling us today to learn from the lower creation and move on to a higher level of evolution and to participate in this community which He is preparing for the salvation of the world.[2]

Cries and Whispers

It would be much easier for us to avoid people in need. Yet ministering to the needy is not an option for the Christian, but a command. We—you, I—are part of God's response to the massive suffering in this world. As Christ's body on earth we are compelled to move, as he did, toward those who hurt. That has been God's consistent movement in all history.

The Middle East, South Africa, Northern Ireland—these are loud cries of pain from the body of Christ. The scandals of some Christian leaders. Third World poverty. Do we listen to them, hear them, respond? Or do we grow numb and ignore the pain signals, in effect sacrificing a limb of the body of Christ? Not all cries of pain are so far away: there are some in every church and office. The unemployed, divorced, widowed, bedridden, homeless, aged—are we attending to them?

The Christian church, by all accounts, has done a mixed job of acting as Christ's body through the ages. Sometimes it has seemed to devour itself (the Inquisition, religious wars). Yet in his commitment to human freedom Christ still relies upon us to communicate his love to the world. And despite its failures the church has indeed responded in part. In every major city in the U.S., you can find hospitals with names like Lutheran General, Christ Hospital, St. Mary's, Good Samaritan, Baptist Hospital. These institutions, although often run as secular businesses, had their origins in a group of believers who believed healing was part of their calling as Christ's body.

In a nation like India, less than three percent of the population call themselves Christian, but Christians are responsible for more than eighteen percent of the health care. If you say the word "Christian" to an Indian peasant—who may never have heard of Jesus Christ—the first image to pop into his mind may well be that of a hospital, or of a medical van that stops by his village once a month to provide free, personal care in Christ's name. It's certainly not the whole of the gospel, but it's not a bad place to start.

In Western countries, much health care has been taken over by other sectors, but a new problem has arisen in major cities, that of homelessness. Will our society respond to the cries of pain from millions of homeless who spend the night in city parks, under expressway bridges, on heating grates? Once again, churches have been among the first to respond, organizing shelters and soup kitchens.

I received a copy of a letter from a woman in Grand Rapids who experienced the healing touch of the body of Christ on a smaller scale, one-on-one. For seven years she ministered to her husband, a well-known church musician afflicted with ALS, or Lou Gehrig's disease. He died, and on the first anniversary of his death, the widow sent out a letter of gratitude to her many friends at church. It read, in part:

> Ever since the first symptoms of ALS appeared over eight years ago, you have surrounded us with love and support. You have cheered us with innumerable notes and letters and cards, some hilarious, some profound, some just warm and caring, but all greatly valued.
>
> You visited and you phoned, often from faraway places. . . . Many of you prepared and brought marvelous food which nourished our spirits as well as our bodies. You shopped and ran errands for us and repaired our broken and out-of-order things while yours waited. You swept and shoveled our walks, brought our mail, dumped our trash. It was possible for us to be a part of our church services because you recorded them. And you brought gifts of love, too many to count, to brighten our hours.
>
> You "doctored" . . . and even repaired a tooth right here in our home. You did ingenious things that made life easier for both of us, like the "coughing jacket" and signal switch that Norm was able to use until the last few days of his life. You shared Scripture verses with us and some of you made it your ministry to pray for those who came to our home regularly to give respiratory treatments. You made him feel like he was still a vital part of the music industry and of the church music ministry.
>
> And how you prayed!!! Day after day, month after month, even year after year! Those prayers buoyed us up, lifted us through particularly hard places, gave us strength

that would have been humanly impossible to have, and helped us to reach out on our own for God's resources. Someday we'll understand why Norm's perfect healing did not take place here. But we do know that he was with us much longer and in much better condition than is the norm for an ALS victim. Love is not a strong enough word to tell you how we feel about you!

I could go back through Part 4 ("How Can We Cope with Pain?") and show how this widow's fellow church members had, by instinct, done everything recommended in this book. They became the presence of God for her. Because of their loving concern, she was not tormented by doubts over whether God loved her. She could sense his love in the human touch of Christ's body, her local church.

Bearing Burdens

Listen to one who understands loyalty to the body: "Who makes a mistake and I do not feel his sadness? Who falls without my longing to help him? Who is spiritually hurt without my fury rising against the one who hurt him?" (2 Corinthians 11:29 LB). Or again: "Think too of all who suffer as if you shared their pain" (Hebrews 13:3 PHILLIPS).

Or yet another voice, that of John Donne:

The church is catholic, universal, so are all her actions; all that she does belongs to all. When she baptizes a child, that action concerns me; for that child is thereby connected to that body which is my head too, and ingrafted into that body whereof I am a member. And when she buries a man, that action concerns me: all mankind is of one author, and is one volume. . . .

No man is an island, entire of itself; every man is a piece of the continent, a part of the main. If a clod be washed away by the sea, Europe is the less, as well as if a promontory were, as well as if a manor of thy friend's or of thine own were; any man's death diminishes me, because I am involved in mankind, and therefore can never send to know for whom the bell tolls; it tolls for thee.[3]

Bear one another's burdens, the Bible says. It is a lesson about pain that we all can agree on. Some of us will not see pain as a gift; some will always accuse God of being unfair for allowing it. But, the fact is, pain and suffering are here among us, and we need to respond in some way. The response Jesus gave was to bear the burdens of those he touched. To live in the world as his body, his emotional incarnation, we must follow his example.

The image of the body accurately portrays how God is working in the world. Sometimes he does enter in, occasionally by performing miracles, and often by giving supernatural strength to those in need. But mainly he relies on us, his agents, to do his work in the world. We are asked to *live out* the life of Christ in the world, not just to refer back to it or describe it. We announce his message, work for justice, pray for mercy . . . and suffer with the sufferers.

Alan Paton, South African author of *Cry the Beloved Country,* holds up St. Francis of Assisi as a Christlike model of human response. One of the transforming moments of Francis Bernardone's life occurred when he was riding a horse as a young nobleman and came across a person with leprosy. Francis was bitter toward God at the time, and felt a certain revulsion at the diseased man. But something within him overcame both those reactions. He dismounted from his horse, walked over, and embraced the beggar, kissing him full on the lips.

St. Francis could have cursed either God or the man with leprosy, says Paton. He did neither. Rather than spending his energy in accusing God for allowing the wound to creation, he chose instead to make his life an instrument of God's peace. That act transformed both the giver and receiver: "What had seemed bitter to me was changed into sweetness of body and soul," said St. Francis.[4]

St. Francis's response was the very same response Alyosha gave to his brother Ivan in *The Brothers Karamazov.* He could not resolve Ivan's or his own questions about the problem of pain. But he chose to put himself beside the sufferers, and embrace them. And, pointedly, Dostoyevski portrayed Jesus giving that very same response to his enemy, the Grand Inquisitor.

If the church followed the pattern consistently, and responded to questions of suffering not with arguments but with love, perhaps those questions would not be asked with such troubled intensity. The united strength of Christ's body can be a powerful force on behalf of the lonely, suffering, and deprived. It can be like the tree in the gospel that grows so large that birds begin to nest in its branches.

In my visits in hospitals, I have been impressed by the huge difference between the measure of comfort that can be offered by believers ("We're praying for you") and unbelievers ("Best of luck—we'll keep our fingers crossed"). Today, if I had to answer the question "Where is God when it hurts?" in a single sentence, I would make that sentence another question: "Where is the church when it hurts?" We form the front line of God's response to the suffering world.

"This is how we know what love is: Jesus Christ laid down his life for us. And we ought to lay down our lives for our brothers. If anyone has material possessions and sees his brother in need but has no pity on him, how can the love of God be in him? Dear children, let us not love with words or tongue but with actions and in truth" (1 John 3:16–18).

Grief melts away
Like snow in May,
As if there were no such cold thing.
George Herbert
The Flower

20

A Whole New World Outside

For the person who suffers, Christianity offers one last contribution, the most important contribution of all. As we have seen, the entire Bible, representing 3000 years of history and culture and human drama, focuses like a magnifying glass on the execution at Calvary. It is the crux of history, the cornerstone. But death is decidedly not the end of the story.

After three days in a dark tomb, Jesus was reported alive again. Alive! Could it be? The news was too good to be true. Not even the disciples dared believe the rumors until he came to them and let them touch his new body with their own fingers. More, he promised that one day each of them would receive a resurrection body as well.

The resurrection and its victory over death brought a decisive new word to the vocabulary of pain and suffering: temporary. Jesus Christ holds out the startling promise of an afterlife without pain. Whatever anguish we feel now will not last.

The Christian's final hope, then, is hope in a painless future, with God. Yet today, astonishingly, people are almost embarrassed to talk about belief in an afterlife. The notion seems quaint, cowardly, an escape from this world's problems.

Black Muslims have a funeral custom that symbolically expresses the modern view. When the body is laid out, close friends and family encircle the casket and stand quietly, looking at the dead person. There are no tears, no flowers, no singing. Muslim sisters pass around small trays from which everyone takes a thin, round peppermint candy. At a given signal the onlookers pop the candies into their mouths, and as the candies slowly melt the funeral-goers reflect on the sweetness of the life they are commemorating. When the candy is gone, that too has meaning, for it symbolizes the end of life. When it simply dissolves, there is no more.

Actually, most moderns cope with death by avoiding it altogether. We hide its blunt reminders—mortuaries, intensive care rooms, cemeteries—behind high walls. But when death cannot be avoided, the modern response differs little from that of the Black Muslims. A creeping paganism invites us to view death as the last phase of the cycle of life on earth, not as a violent transition into an ongoing life. Elisabeth Kübler-Ross defined five stages in preparing for death, with the clear implication that the final stage of "acceptance" is the most appropriate. Ever since, health workers have been helping patients strive toward that ideal.

I remember one evening in my Make Today Count group when a woman named Donna, who was in the final stages of leukemia, mentioned how much she was anticipating heaven. The comment provoked an awkward response from the group: a long silence, a cleared throat, a few rolled eyes. The social worker then steered the discussion toward how Donna could overcome her fears and progress toward the acceptance stage.

I left that meeting with a heavy heart. Our materialistic, undogmatic culture was asking its members to defy their deepest feelings. Donna had, by sheer primal instinct, struck upon a foundation stone of Christian theology. Death is an enemy, a grievous enemy, the last enemy to be destroyed. How could members of a group who each month saw bodies deteriorate before their eyes wish for a spirit of bland acceptance? I could think of only one appropriate response to Donna's impending death: "Damn you, death!"

Not long after that I came across a quote from Blaise Pascal, who lived during an era when thinkers first began scorning "primitive" beliefs in a soul and the afterlife. Pascal said of such people, "Do they profess to have delighted us by telling us that they hold our soul to be only a little wind and smoke, especially by telling us this in a haughty and self-satisfied tone of voice? Is this a thing to say gaily? Is it not, on the contrary, a thing to say sadly, as the saddest thing in the world?"[1]

What inversion of values has led us to commend a belief in annihilation as brave and dismiss a hope for blissful eternity as cowardly? How can it be noble to agree with the Black Muslims, materialists, and Marxists that this world, malignant with evil and suffering, is the designed end for man? Such a notion only appeared after 7000 years of recorded history. Every known primitive society and every ancient culture included elaborate beliefs in an afterlife. (Apart from such beliefs, archaeologists would have a very difficult task, for the ancients buried their cultural clues, conveniently, in sealed tombs.)

In great contrast, the Bible refers to the afterlife with a spirit of joy and anticipation, not embarrassment. This is a groaning planet, and Christians expectantly await a world where every tear will be wiped away.

Easter Faith

We have only shadow notions of that future state, longings that the untroubled joy eluding us now will one day fill us. We are locked in a dark room, like the setting of Sartre's play *No Exit*. But chinks of light are seeping through—virtue, glory, beauty, compassion, hints of truth and justice—suggesting that beyond those walls there exists another world, a world worth all enduring.

Christian faith does not offer us a peaceful way to come to terms with death. No, it offers instead a way to overcome death. Christ stands for Life, and his resurrection should give convincing proof that God is not satisfied with any "cycle of life" that ends in death. He will go to any extent—he *did* go to any extent—to break that cycle.

In October of 1988 one of my closest friends died in a scuba diving accident in Lake Michigan. The very afternoon Bob was making his last dive I was sitting, oblivious, in a university coffee shop reading *My Quest for Beauty*, a book by the famous therapist and author Rollo May. The book tells of Rollo May's lifelong search for beauty, and among the experiences he recounts is a visit to Mt. Athos, a peninsula of Greece inhabited exclusively by monks.

Rollo May was beginning to recover from a nervous breakdown when he visited Mt. Athos. He happened to arrive just as the monks were celebrating Greek Orthodox Easter, a ceremony thick with symbolism, thick with beauty. Icons were everywhere. Incense hung in the air. And at the height of that service the priest gave everyone present three Easter eggs, wonderfully decorated and wrapped in a veil. "Christos Anesti!" he said—"Christ is Risen!" Each person there, including Rollo May, responded according to custom, "He is risen indeed!"

Rollo May was not a believer. But he writes in his book, "I was seized then by a moment of spiritual reality: what would it mean for our world if He had truly risen?"[2] I returned home shortly after reading that chapter, and was met at the door by my wife who conveyed the news of Bob's death. Rollo May's question came back to me many times in the next few days. What does it mean for the world if Christ has truly risen?

I spoke at my friend's funeral, and there I asked Rollo May's question in a different way, in the context of the grief that pressed in on us from all sides. What would it mean for us if Bob rose again? We sat in a chapel, numbed by three days of sadness. I imagined aloud what it would be like to walk outside to the parking lot and there, to our utter amazement, find Bob. *Bob!* With his bounding walk, his big grin, and clear gray eyes.

That conjured image gave me a hint of what Jesus' disciples felt on Easter Sunday. They too had grieved for three days. But on Sunday they caught a glimpse of something else, a glimpse of the future.

Apart from Easter, apart from a life that continues beyond this one, apart from a new start, a recreated earth—apart from all that, we could indeed judge God less-than-powerful or less-than-loving or even cruel. The Bible stakes God's reputation on his ability to restore creation to its original state of perfection.

I confess that I too used to be embarrassed by talk about heaven and an afterlife. It seemed a cop-out, a crutch. We ought to make our way in the world as if that is all there is, I thought. But I've changed over the years, mainly as I've watched people die. What kind of God would be satisfied forever with a world like this one, laden with suffering and death? If I had to stand by and watch lives like Bob's get cut off—suddenly vanish, vaporize—with no hope of future, I doubt I'd believe in God.

A passage in the New Testament, 1 Corinthians 15, expresses much the same thought. Paul first reviews his life, a difficult life that included jailings, beatings, shipwrecks, and gladiator-style contests with wild beasts. Then he says, in so many words, I'd be crazy to go through all this if it ended at my death. "If only for this life we have hope in Christ, we are to be pitied more than all men." Along with Paul, I stake my hope on resurrection, a time when Christ "will transform our lowly bodies so that they will be like his glorious body" (Philippians 3:21).

Home Beyond

Scottish author and theologian George MacDonald once wrote a letter of consolation to his stepmother after the death of her good friend. "God would not let it [death] be the law of His Universe if it were what it looks to us," he said.[3] It's up to us believers to tell the world what death looks like from the perspective of One who faced it—with fear and dread—but then came back to life.

The tangible help this belief can give to a dying person is starkly portrayed in the documentary film *Dying* shown on the Public Broadcasting System. Producer-Director Michael Roemer obtained permission to follow around several terminally ill cancer patients during their last months. "People die in the way they have lived. Death becomes the expression of everything you are, and you can bring to it only what you have brought to your life," said Roemer after the filming. Two Boston families, especially, show the extremes of despair and hope.

Harriet and Bill, thirty-three, are seen struggling with a failure of nerve. In one scene Harriet, anxious about her own future as a widow with two sons, lashes out at her dying husband. "The longer this is dragged out, the worse this is going to be for all of us," she tells him.

"What happened to the sweet girl I married?" Bill asks in reply. Harriet turns to the interviewer, "The sweet girl is being tortured by his cancer. Who's gonna want a widow and eight- and ten-year-old sons? I don't wish him dead, but if he's gotta go why doesn't he go now?"

In the last weeks of their life together, this family tears apart, unable to cope with their fears. They whine and shout, attacking each other, shattering all remaining love and trust. The specter of death looms too large.

The response of Rev. Bryant, fifty-six, the dying pastor of a black Baptist church, provides an amazing contrast. "Right now I'm living some of my greatest moments," he says. "I don't think Rockefeller could be happy as I am."

The camera crew records Rev. Bryant as he preaches on death to his congregation, reads the Bible to his grandchildren, and takes a trip South to visit his birthplace. He displays calm serenity and a confidence that he is merely heading home, to a place without pain.

At his funeral, the Baptist choir sings "He's Asleep." And as mourners file past the bier, some reach down to grasp his hand or pat his chest. They are losing a beloved friend, but only for a while. They believe that Rev. Bryant faces a beginning, not an end.

The film clips from Rev. Bryant's church seem authentic to me because of my wife's experience among senior citizens in Chicago. About half are white and half are black. All of them, in their seventies and eighties, live in constant awareness of death. Yet Janet has noted a striking difference in the way the whites in general and the blacks in general face death.

Many of her white clients become increasingly more fearful and uptight. They complain about their lives, their families, and their failing health. The blacks, in contrast, maintain a good humor and triumphant spirit even though most of them have more apparent reason for bitterness and despair. (Most lived in the South just one generation after slavery, and suffered a lifetime of economic oppression and injustice. Many were senior citizens before the first Civil Rights bills were passed.)

What causes the difference in outlooks? Janet has concluded the answer is hope, a hope that traces directly to the blacks' bedrock belief in heaven. "This world is not my home, I'm just a passin' through," they say. These words and others like them ("Swing low, sweet chariot, comin' for to carry me home") came out of a tragic period of history, when everything in this world looked bleak. But somehow black churches managed to instill a vivid belief in a home beyond this one.

If you want to hear up-to-date images of heaven, attend a

few black funerals. The preachers paint word pictures of a life so serene and sensuous that everyone in the congregation starts fidgeting to go there. The mourners feel grief, naturally, but in its proper place: as an interruption, a temporary setback in a battle whose end has already been determined.

It is, of course, wrong to use heaven as an excuse to avoid relieving poverty and misery here on earth. But is it not equally wrong to deny an authentic hope in heaven for someone whose life is ending?

One Foot in the Air

Belief in a future home beyond this one should affect more than how we die. It should also affect how we live.

J. Robertson McQuilkin, former president of Columbia Bible College, was once approached by an elderly lady facing the trials of old age. Her body was in decline, her beauty being replaced by thinning hair, wrinkles, and skin discoloration. She could no longer do the things she once could, and she felt herself to be a burden on others. "Robertson, why does God let us get old and weak? Why must I hurt so?" she asked.

After a few moments' thought McQuilkin replied, "I think God has planned the strength and beauty of youth to be physical. But the strength and beauty of age is spiritual. We gradually lose the strength and beauty that is temporary so we'll be sure to concentrate on the strength and beauty which is forever. It makes us more eager to leave behind the temporary, deteriorating part of us and be truly homesick for our eternal home. If we stayed young and strong and beautiful, we might never want to leave!"

If there is a secret to handling suffering, the one most often cited by those I interviewed was along this line. To survive, the spirit must be fed so that it can break free beyond the constraints of the body. Christian faith does not always offer resources to the body. Neither Brian Sternberg nor Joni Eareckson Tada has been healed, despite thousands of prayers. Yet God does promise to nourish the spirit that will one day rejoin a perfected body. Brian will leap again—like a calf released from the stall, says Malachi; Joni will be on her feet dancing.

"Do not be afraid of those who can only kill your body; they cannot kill your soul," Jesus said as he sent out his followers. Because physical death is not the end, we need not fear it inordinately. But because it is the enemy of Life, we need not welcome it either.

In short, because of our belief in a home beyond, Christians can be realistic about death without becoming hopeless. Death is an enemy, but a defeated enemy. As Martin Luther told his followers, "Even in the best of health we should have death always before our eyes [so that] we will not expect to remain on this earth forever, but will have one foot in the air, so to speak."

Having that one foot in the air gives one a new perspective on the problems of pain and suffering. Any discussion of suffering is incomplete without this view from the vantage point of eternity.

A skilled polemicist could defend pain as a good thing, better than any of the alternatives God might have allowed. Perhaps. But actually pain and suffering are far less than half the picture.

How to imagine eternity? It's so much longer than our brief life here that it's hard even to visualize. You can go to a ten-foot blackboard and draw a line from one side to another. Then, make a one-inch dot in that line. That dot, to a microscopic germ cell undulating in its midst, would seem enormous. The cell could spend its lifetime exploring the dot. But if you, a human, step back to view the entire blackboard, you'll be struck by the hugeness of that ten-foot line compared to the tiny dot the germ cell calls home.

Eternity compares to this life in the same way. Seventy years is a long time, long enough for us to concoct many theories about God and why he sometimes appears indifferent to human suffering. But is it fair to judge God and his plan for the universe by the swatch of time we spend on earth? No more fair than for that germ cell to judge a whole blackboard by the tiny smudge of chalk on which it spends its life.

Are we missing the perspective of the universe and of timelessness? Would we complain about life on earth if God permitted a mere hour of suffering in an entire seventy-year lifetime of comfort? Now, our lifetime does include suffering, but that lifetime represents a mere hour of eternity. As St. Teresa of Avila audaciously expressed it, from heaven the most miserable earthly life will look like one bad night in an inconvenient hotel.[4]

In the Christian scheme of things, this world and the time spent here are not all there is. Earth is a proving ground, a dot in eternity—albeit an important dot, for Jesus said our destiny depends on our obedience here. Next time you want to cry out to God in anguished despair, blaming him for a miserable world, remember: less than one-millionth of reality has been presented, and that millionth is being lived out under a rebel flag.

To view the role of pain and suffering properly, one must await the whole story. Promises of it abound in the Bible: "And the God of all grace, who called you to his eternal glory in Christ, after you have suffered a little while, will himself restore you and make you strong, firm and steadfast" (1 Peter 5:10). "These troubles and sufferings of ours are, after all, quite small and won't last very long. Yet this short time of distress will result in God's richest blessing upon us forever and ever! So we do not look at what we can see right now, the troubles all around us, but we look forward to the joys in heaven which we have not yet seen. The troubles will soon be over, but the joys to come will last forever" (2 Corinthians 4:17–18 LB).

I have always been curious about one detail often over-looked at the end of Job, that great story of human suffering. The author takes pains to point out that in the end Job received double all he had lost in his time of trials: 14,000 sheep to replace the 7000; 6000 camels to replace 3000; a thousand oxen and donkeys to replace 500. There is one exception: previously Job had seven sons and three daughters, and in the restoration he got back seven sons and three daughters—the same number, not double. Could the author have been silently hinting at the eternal perspective? From that view Job did indeed receive double, ten new children here to go with the ten he would one day rejoin.

Death and Birth

An irony: death, the one event that causes the greatest emotional pain, in reality opens a doorway into the great joy of eternity. Speaking of his own death, Jesus used the analogy of a woman in the labor of childbirth: she travails until the moment of delivery, when suddenly ecstasy replaces anguish (John 16:21).

Death like birth—the analogy goes deep. Imagine birth from the perspective of the fetus.

Your world is dark, safe, secure. You are bathed in a warm, cushioning liquid. You do nothing for yourself. You are fed automatically, and a murmuring heartbeat assures you that someone larger than you is meeting all your needs. Life consists of simple waiting—you're not sure what to wait for, but any change seems faraway and scary. You encounter no sharp objects, no pain, no dangers. A fine, serene existence.

One day you feel a tug. The walls seem to press in. Those soft padded walls are now pulsing wildly, crushing you downward. Your body is bent double, your limbs twisted and wrenched. You're falling, upside down. For the first time in your life, you feel pain. You're in a sea of roiling matter. There is more pressure, almost too intense to bear. Your head is squeezed flat, and you are pushed harder, harder into a dark tunnel. Oh, the pain. Noise. More pressure.

You hurt all over. You hear a groaning sound and an awful, sudden fear rushes in on you. It is happening—your world is collapsing. You're sure it's the end. You see a piercing, blinding light. Cold, rough hands grasp at you, pull you from the tunnel and hold you upside down. A painful slap. Waaaahhhhh!

Congratulations, you have just been born.

Death is like that. On this end of the birth canal, it seems a scary, dark tunnel we are being sucked toward by an irresistible force. None of us looks forward to it. We're afraid. It's full of pressure, pain, darkness . . . the unknown.

But beyond the darkness and the pain lies a whole new world outside. When we awaken after death in that bright new world, our tears and hurts will be mere memories.[5]

Do you sometimes think God does not hear? That your cries of pain fade off into nothing? God is not deaf. He is as grieved by the world's trauma as you are. After all, his only Son died here.

Let history finish. Let the symphony scratch out its last mournful note of discord before it bursts into song. As Paul said, "In my opinion whatever we may have to go through now is less than nothing compared with the magnificent future God has planned for us. The whole creation is on tiptoe to see the wonderful sight of the sons of God coming into their own. . . .

"It is plain to anyone with eyes to see that at the present time all created life groans in a sort of universal travail. And it is plain, too, that we who have a foretaste of the Spirit are in a state of painful tension, while we wait for that redemption of our bodies which will mean that at last we have realized our full sonship in him" (Romans 8:18–19, 22–23 PHILLIPS).

As we look back on the speck of eternity that was the history of this planet, we will be impressed not by its importance, but by its smallness. From the viewpoint of the Andromeda galaxy, the holocaustic destruction of our entire solar system would be barely visible, a match flaring faintly in the distance, then imploding in permanent darkness. Yet for this burnt-out match, God sacrificed himself.

Pain can be seen, as Berkouwer puts it, as the great "not yet" of eternity. It reminds us of what we are now, and fans in us a thirst for what we will someday become. I can believe with confidence that one day every bruise and every leukemia cell, every embarrassment and every hurt will be set right, and all those grim moments of hoping against hope will find their reward at last.

At the height of his suffering, Job spoke:

How I wish someone would record what I am saying
Or with a chisel carve my words in stone,
   and write them so they would last forever.
But I know there is someone in heaven
   who will come at last to my defense.
I will see him with my own eyes,
   and he will not be a stranger.
            (Job 19:23ff. JOB FOR MODERN MAN)

Where Is God When It Hurts?

For a good portion of my life, I shared the perspective of those who rail against God for allowing pain. Suffering pressed in too close. I could find no way to rationalize a world as toxic as this one.

As I visited people whose pain far exceeded my own, though, I was surprised by its effects. Suffering seemed as likely to reinforce faith as to sow agnosticism. And as I visited those with leprosy, particularly, I became aware of pain's underlying value.

The problem of pain will have no ultimate solution until God recreates the earth. I am sustained by faith in that great hope. If I did not truly believe that God is a Physician and not a Sadist, and that he, in George MacDonald's phrase, "feels in Himself the tortured presence of every nerve that lacks its repose," I would abandon all attempts to plumb the mysteries of suffering.

My anger about pain has melted mostly for one reason: I have come to know God. He has given me joy and love and happiness and goodness. They have come in unexpected flashes, in the midst of my confused, imperfect world, but they have been enough to convince me that my God is worthy of trust. Knowing him is worth all enduring.

Where does that leave me when I stand by a hospital bed the next time a close friend gets Hodgkin's disease? After all, this search started at a bedside. It leaves me with faith in a Person, a faith so solid that no amount of suffering can erode it.

Where is God when it hurts?

He has been there from the beginning, designing a pain system that, even in the midst of a fallen world, still bears the stamp of his genius and equips us for life on this planet.

He transforms pain, using it to teach and strengthen us, if we allow it to turn us toward him.

With great restraint, he watches this rebellious planet live on, in mercy allowing the human project to continue in its self-guided way.

He lets us cry out, like Job, in loud fits of anger against him, blaming him for a world we spoiled.

He allies himself with the poor and suffering, founding a kingdom tilted in their favor. He stoops to conquer.

He promises supernatural help to nourish the spirit, even if our physical suffering goes unrelieved.

He has joined us. He has hurt and bled and cried and suffered. He has dignified for all time those who suffer, by sharing their pain.

He is with us now, ministering to us through his Spirit and through members of his body who are commissioned to bear us up and relieve our suffering for the sake of the head.

He is waiting, gathering the armies of good. One day he will unleash them, and the world will see one last terrifying moment of suffering before the full victory is ushered in. Then, God will create for us a new, incredible world. And pain shall be no more.

> Listen, I tell you a mystery: We shall not all sleep, but we will all be changed—in a flash, in the twinkling of an eye, at the last trumpet. For the trumpet will sound, the dead will be raised imperishable, and we will be changed. For the perishable must clothe itself with the imperishable, and the mortal with immortality. When the perishable has been clothed with the imperishable, and the mortal with immortality, then the saying that is written will come true: "Death has been swallowed up in victory."
> "Where, O death, is your victory?
> Where, O death, is your sting?"
> (1 Corinthians 15:51–55)

Sources

CHAPTER 1: A PROBLEM THAT WON'T GO AWAY

1. C. E. M. Joad, *God and Evil* (New York: Harper & Brothers, 1943), 28.

CHAPTER 2: THE GIFT NOBODY WANTS

1. R. J. Christman, *Sensory Experience* (Scranton, Pa.: Intext Educational Publishers, 1971), 359.
2. Ibid., 361.
3. Maurice Burton, *The Sixth Sense of Animals* (New York: Taplinger Publishing Company, 1972), 9.
4. Thomas Lewis, *Pain* (New York: The Macmillan Company, 1942).

CHAPTER 3: PAINLESS HELL

1. Ronald Melzack, *The Puzzle of Pain* (New York: Basic Books, Inc., 1973), chapter 1.

CHAPTER 4: AGONY AND ECSTASY

1. Augustine of Hippo, *The Confessions of St. Augustine,* translated by John K. Ryan (Garden City, N.Y.: Image Books, 1960), 186.

CHAPTER 5: THE GROANING PLANET

1. G. K. Chesterton, *Orthodoxy* (Garden City, N.Y.: Doubleday and Company, 1959), 144.
2. Ibid., 78.
3. C. S. Lewis, *The Problem of Pain* (New York: The Macmillan Company, 1962), 93.
4. Blaise Pascal, *Pensées* (New York: E. P. Dutton & Co., 1958), 55–56.
5. Chesterton, 80.
6. John Donne, *Devotions* (Ann Arbor, Mich.: University of Michigan Press, 1959), 108.
7. Ibid., 141.

CHAPTER 6: WHAT IS GOD TRYING TO TELL US?

1. "A Luckless City Buries Its Dead," *Time* (June 7, 1976).

2. Klaus Kloch, "Is There a Doctrine of Retribution in the Old Testament?" in *Theodicy in the Old Testament,* James L. Crenshaw, ed. (Philadelphia: Fortress Press, 1983), passim.

CHAPTER 7: WHY ARE WE HERE?

1. C. G. Jung, *Answer to Job* (Princeton, N.J.: Princeton Publishing/ Bollingen Series, 1973), 15ff.
2. C. S. Lewis, 39–42.
3. John Hick, *Philosophy of Religion* (Englewood Cliffs, N.J.: Prentice-Hall, 1963), chapter 3.
4. Bernard Seeman, *Man Against Pain* (New York: Chilton Books, 1962), 96.
5. Albert Camus, *The Plague* (New York: Vintage Books, 1972), 203.
6. Daniel Defoe, *Journal of a Plague Year* (New York: Penguin Books, 1966), 33.
7. "In Tornados, Some Trust God," *Psychology Today* (August 1974, 36).
8. Anita and Peter Deyneka, Jr., "A Salvation of Suffering: The Church in the Soviet Union," *Christianity Today* (July 16, 1982): 20.
9. David Watson, *Fear No Evil* (Wheaton, Ill.: Harold Shaw Publishers, 1984), 7.

CHAPTER 8: ARMS TOO SHORT TO BOX WITH GOD

1. Harold Kushner, *When Bad Things Happen to Good People* (New York: Schocken Books, 1981), 43–44.
2. Frederick Buechner, *Wishful Thinking* (San Francisco: Harper & Row, 1973), 46.
3. Quoted in William James, *The Varieties of Religious Experience* (New York: The Modern Library, 1936), 281.

CHAPTER 9: AFTER THE FALL

1. Brian Sternberg with John Poppy, "My Search for Faith," *Look* (March 10, 1964): 79–80.
2. Ibid.

CHAPTER 11: OTHER WITNESSES

1. Paul Tournier, *Creative Suffering* (San Francisco: Harper & Row, 1982), 2.
2. Ibid., 29, 37.
3. Quoted in David J. Garrow, *Bearing the Cross* (New York: William Morrow and Co., 1986), 532.
4. C. S. Lewis, 108.

5. Monica Hellwig, "Good News to the Poor: Do They Understand It Better?" in *Tracing the Spirit*, James E. Hug, ed. (Mahwah, N.J.: Paulist Press), 145.

CHAPTER 12: EXTREME CASES

1. Terrence Des Pres, *The Survivor* (New York: Oxford University Press, 1976), 162–63.
2. Bruno Bettelheim, *Surviving and Other Essays* (New York: Alfred A Knopf, 1979), 313–14.
3. George Mangakis, "Letter in a Bottle," *Atlantic Monthly* (October 1971): 253.
4. Viktor Frankl, *Man's Search for Meaning* (New York: Washington Square Press, 1959), 103–5.
5. Reeve Robert Brenner, *The Faith and Doubt of Holocaust Survivors* (New York: The Free Press, 1980), 94–95, 103–4.
6. Elie Wiesel, *Night* (New York: Avon Books, 1969), 44.
7. Ibid., 8–9.
8. Ibid., 79.
9. Ibid., 75–76.

CHAPTER 13: FRONTIERS OF RECOVERY

1. Quoted in Douglas Colligan, "That Helpless Feeling: The Dangers of Stress," *New York* (July 14, 1975): 32.
2. Jean Vanier, "Hearts Awakened by the Poor," *Sojourners* (January, 1982): 17.

CHAPTER 14: FEAR

1. Donne, 36.
2. Steven Brena, *Pain and Religion* (Springfield, Ill.: Charles C. Thomas, 1972), 78–81.
3. Melzack, 29–30.
4. Betsy Burnham, *When Your Friend Is Dying* (Grand Rapids: Chosen Books/Zondervan, 1982), 71–72.

CHAPTER 15: HELPLESSNESS

1. Colligan, 28.
2. James D. Hardy and Harold G. Wolff and Helen Goodell, *Pain Sensations and Reactions* (New York: Haffner Publishing Co., 1967), 117.
3. Eric J. Cassell, M.D., *The Healer's Art: A New Approach to the Doctor-Patient Relationship* (New York: Harper & Row, 1976), 44.
4. Jürgen Moltmann, *The Power of the Powerless* (San Francisco: Harper & Row), 142.

5. Norman Cousins, *Anatomy of an Illness* (New York: W. W. Norton, 1979), 153–54.

6. Benjamin M. and Carol Weir, with Dennis Benson, *Hostage Bound, Hostage Free* (Westminster/John Knox Press, 1987) as excerpted in *Leadership* (Winter 1989): 54.

7. Barbara Wolf, *Living with Pain* (New York: Seabury Press, 1977), 107.

CHAPTER 16: MEANING

1. Quoted in Mark Krum, "The Face of Pain," *Sports Illustrated* (March 8, 1976): 62.

2. Donne, 109.

3. Sharon Fischer, "What to Do When You Don't Know What to Do," *Worldwide Challenge* (June 1983): 20.

4. Henri Nouwen, *The Wounded Healer* (Garden City, N.Y.: Doubleday & Company/Image Books, 1979), 66.

5. Jürgen Trogisch, "Congenital Subnormality," in *God and the Handicapped Child* (London: Christian Medical Fellowship Publications, 1982), 41–45.

CHAPTER 17: HOPE

1. Armand Mayo Nicholi II, "Why Can't I Deal with Depression?" *Christianity Today* (November 11, 1983): 41.

2. Colligan, 30.

3. Quoted in Nicholi, 40.

4. Bruce Larson, *There's a Lot More to Health Than Not Being Sick* (Waco, Tex.: Word Books, 1981), 90.

5. Quoted in Joseph Frank, *Dostoyevsky: The Years of Ordeal* (Princeton, N.J.: Princeton University Press, 1983), 157.

6. Moltmann, *Experiences of God* (Philadelphia: Fortress Press, 1980), 7.

7. Bettelheim, 296.

CHAPTER 18: SEEING FOR HIMSELF

1. Robert Coles, *Children of Crisis, Vol. 2: Migrants, Mountaineers, and Sharecroppers* (Boston: Atlantic Monthly Press, 1967–71), 612–13.

2. Dorothy L. Sayers, *Christian Letters to a Post-Christian World* (Grand Rapids, Mich.: William B. Eerdmans Publishing Company, 1969), 14.

3. Cornelius Plantinga, Jr., "A Love So Fierce," *The Reformed Journal* (November 1986): 6.

4. Harry R. Boer, "And a Sword. . . ." *The Reformed Journal* (December 1984), 3.

5. T. S. Eliot, *Collected Poems 1904–1962* (New York: Harcourt, Brace & World), 187.

CHAPTER 19: THE REST OF THE BODY

1. Quoted in Brennan Manning, *Lion and Lamb: The Relentless Tenderness of Jesus* (Old Tappan, N.J.: Fleming H. Revell/Chosen Books, 1986), 77.
2. Dorothy Clarke Wilson, *Ten Fingers for God* (Grand Rapids, Mich.: Zondervan, 1989), 145ff.
3. Donne, 107–9.
4. Alan Paton, et al., *Creative Suffering, The Ripple of Hope* (Kansas City, Mo.: National Catholic Reporter Publishing Company, 1970), 17.

CHAPTER 20: A WHOLE NEW WORLD OUTSIDE

1. Pascal, 57.
2. Rollo May, *My Quest for Beauty* (Dallas: Saybrook Publishing Company, 1985), 60.
3. William Raeper, *George MacDonald* (London: Lion Publishing, 1987), 133.
4. Peter Kreeft, *Making Sense Out of Suffering* (Ann Arbor, Mich.: Servant Books, 1986), 139.
5. Joseph Bayly was the essential source for this analogy.

DISAPPOINTMENT
WITH GOD

For my brother,
who is still disappointed

Contents

Foreword

AFTER I HAD BEGUN WORK on this project, I received phone calls from a few people in my church who had heard about it. "Is it true you're writing a book about disappointment with God?" the callers would ask. "If so, I'd like to talk. I haven't told anyone before, but my life as a Christian has included times of great disappointment." I did interview some of those callers, and their stories helped set the direction of this book.

I found that for many people there is a large gap between what they *expect* from their Christian faith and what they actually experience. From a steady diet of books, sermons, and personal testimonies, all promising triumph and success, they learn to expect dramatic evidence of God working in their lives. If they do not see such evidence, they feel disappointment, betrayal, and often guilt. As one woman said, "I kept hearing the phrase, 'personal relationship with Jesus Christ.' But I found to my dismay that it is unlike any other personal relationship. I never saw God, or heard him, or felt him, or experienced the most basic ingredients of a relationship. Either there's something wrong with what I was told, or there's something wrong with me."

Disappointment occurs when the actual experience of something falls far short of what we anticipate. For that reason, the first half of this book explores the Bible to see what we can rightfully expect from God. I hesitated to start there since I know that some people, especially disappointed people, have little tolerance for the Bible. But what better place to begin than by letting God speak for himself? I tried to rid myself of preconceptions and read the Bible like a story, with a "plot." What I found there astonished me. It was very different from the story I had been told most of my life.

Actually, I set out to write two different books, and did so; but I ended up putting them both between the same covers. Book II moves to more practical, existential issues and applies the ideas I have developed to actual situations—the kinds of situations that foster disappointment with God. Ultimately, I concluded that the two approaches belonged in the same book; either would be incomplete on its own.

Once as I explained this project to a friend, he frowned and shook his head. "I guess I've never tried to psychoanalyze God before," he said. I hope that's not what I'm attempting! But I do wish to understand God better, to learn why he sometimes acts in such mysterious ways—or does not seem to act at all.

A few words of caution, however. This is not a book of apologetics, so I will not travel the path of pointing out evidences for God. Others have done that effectively, and, besides, I am dealing with doubts that are more emotional than intellectual. Disappointment implies a hoped-for relationship that somehow has not worked out.

Nor will I debate the question, "Does God ever perform miracles?" I take for granted that he has supernatural power and has used it. Yes, God can intervene; so why doesn't he do so more often? Why handicap himself among sincere skeptics who would like to believe, if only they had a sign? Why permit injustice and suffering to thrive on earth? Why aren't God's interventions "ordinaries" rather than "miracles"?

One last caution: by no means am I presenting a balanced view of the Christian faith. I am, after all, writing for people who have, at one time or another, heard the silence of God. Studying someone like Job as an example of faith is a little like studying the history of civilization by examining only the wars. On the other hand, there are many Christian books that leave out any mention of the wars and promise nothing but victory. This is a book about faith, but it looks at faith through the eyes of those who doubt.

And finally, I should explain the way I have chosen to handle

Bible references. I resisted putting them in footnotes or parentheses within the text: that creates an awkwardness in reading not unlike listening to someone with a stutter. Instead, I have indicated the sources of direct citations at the end of each chapter. True sleuths should be able to track down the correct passage.

Awake, O Lord! Why do you sleep?
Rouse yourself! Do not reject us forever.
Why do you hide your face?

—Psalm 44:23–24

BOOK I

GOD WITHIN
THE SHADOWS

You do not have to sit outside in the dark.
If, however, you want to look at the stars,
you will find that darkness is required.
The stars neither require it nor demand it.
                                        —Annie Dillard

Part One

Hearing the Silence

Chapter 1

A Fatal Error

E VER SINCE my book *Where Is God When It Hurts?* was published, I have received letters from people disappointed with God.

A young mother wrote that her joy had turned to bitterness and grief when she delivered a daughter with *spina bifida,* a birth defect that leaves the spinal cord exposed. In page after page of tiny, spidery script she recounted how medical bills had soaked up the family savings and how her marriage had cracked apart as her husband came to resent all the time she devoted to their sick child. As her life crumbled around her, she was beginning to doubt what she had once believed about a loving God. Did I have any advice?

A homosexual spilled out his story gradually, in a succession of letters. For more than a decade he had sought a "cure" for his sexual orientation, trying charismatic healing services, Christian support groups, and chemical treatment. He even underwent a form of aversion therapy in which psychologists applied electrical shocks to his genitals when he responded to erotic photos of men. Nothing worked. Finally he surrendered to a life of gay promiscuity. He still writes me occasionally. He insists that he wants to follow God but feels disqualified because of his peculiar curse.

A young woman wrote, with some embarrassment, about her ongoing depression. She has no reason to be depressed, she said. She is healthy, earns a good salary, and has a stable family background. Yet most days when she wakes up she cannot think of a single reason to go on living. She no longer cares about life or God, and when she prays, she wonders if anyone is really listening.

These and other letters I have received over the years all lead up to the same basic question, phrased in different ways. It goes something like this: "Your book is about physical pain. But what about pain like mine? Where is God when I hurt emotionally? What does the Bible say about that?" I answer the letters as best I can, sadly conscious of the inadequacy of words on paper. Can a word, any word, ever heal a wound? And I must confess that after reading these anguished accounts I ask the very same questions. Where is God in our emotional pain? Why does he so often disappoint us?

Disappointment with God does not come only in dramatic circumstances. For me, it also edges unexpectedly into the mundaneness of everyday life. I remember one night last winter, a cold, raw Chicago night. The wind was howling, and sleet slanted out of the skies, coating the streets with darkly shining ice. That night my car stalled in a rather ominous neighborhood. As I raised the hood and hunched over the engine, the sleet stinging my back like tiny pebbles, I prayed over and over, *Please help me get this car started.*

No amount of fiddling with wires and tubes and cables would start the car, and so I spent the next hour in a dilapidated diner waiting for a tow truck. Sitting on a plastic chair, my drenched clothes forming a widening pool of water around me, I wondered what God thought about my plight. I would miss a scheduled meeting that night and would probably waste many hours over the next few days trying to wring fair, honest work out of a service station set up to prey upon stranded motorists. Did God even care about my frustration or the waste of energy and money?

Like the woman embarrassed over her depression, I feel ashamed even to mention such an unanswered prayer. It seems petty and selfish, maybe even stupid, to pray for a car to start. But I have found that petty disappointments tend to accumulate over time, undermining my faith with a lava flow of doubt. I start to wonder whether God cares about everyday details—about me. I am tempted to pray less often, having concluded in advance that it won't matter. Or will it? My emotions and my faith waver. Once those doubts seep in, I am even less prepared for times of major crisis. A neighbor is dying of cancer; I pray diligently for her. But even as I pray, I wonder. Can God be trusted? If so many small prayers go unanswered, what about the big ones?

One morning in a motel room I switched on the television and the square, jowly face of a well-known evangelist filled the screen. "I'm mad at God!" he said, glowering. It was a remarkable confession from a man who had built his career around the notion of "seed faith" and absolute confidence in God's personal concern. But God had let him down, he said, and went on to explain. God had commanded him to build a large ministry complex; and yet the project proved to be a financial disaster, forcing him to sell off properties and cut back programs. He had kept his part of the bargain, but God had not.

A few weeks later I again saw the evangelist on television, this time exuding faith and optimism. He leaned toward the camera, his craggy face splitting into a big grin, and jabbed his finger toward a million viewers. "Something *good* is going to happen to you this week!" he said, coaxing three syllables out of the word "good." He was at his salesman best, utterly convincing. A few days later, however, I heard on the news that his son had committed suicide. I could not help wondering what the evangelist said to God in his prayers that fateful week.

Such struggles seem almost to mock the triumphant slogans

about God's love and personal concern that I often hear in Christian churches. Yet no one is immune to the downward spiral of disappointment. It happens to people like the televangelist and to people like the letter writers, and it happens to ordinary Christians: first comes disappointment, then a seed of doubt, then a response of anger or betrayal. We begin to question whether God is trustworthy, whether we can really stake our lives on him.

I have been thinking about this topic of disappointment with God for a long time, but I hesitated to write about it for two reasons. First, I knew I would have to confront questions that have no easy answers—that may, in fact, have no answers. And second, I did not want to write a book that would, by focusing on failure, dampen anyone's faith.

Some Christians, I know, would reject the phrase "disappointment with God" out of hand. Such a notion is all wrong, they say. Jesus promised that faith the size of a grain of mustard seed can move mountains; that anything can happen if two or three gather together in prayer. The Christian life is a life of victory and triumph. God wants us happy, healthy, and prosperous, and *any* other state simply indicates a lack of faith.

During a visit among people who believe exactly this, I finally reached the decision to write this book. I was investigating the topic of physical healing for a magazine assignment, and the research led me to a rather infamous church headquartered in rural Indiana. I had learned of the church from a *Chicago Tribune* series and from a special report on ABC's "Nightline" program.

Members of this church believed that simple faith could heal any disease and that to look elsewhere for help—for example, to medical doctors—demonstrated a lack of faith in God. The *Tribune* articles told of parents who had looked on helplessly as their children fought losing battles with meningitis or pneumonia or a common flu virus—diseases that easily could have been treated. On a map of the United States, a *Tribune* artist had drawn tiny tombstone symbols to mark where people had died after refusing medical treatment in accordance with church teaching. There were fifty-two tombstones in all.

According to the reports, pregnant women in that church died in childbirth at a rate eight times the national average, and young children were three times more likely to die. Yet the church was growing and had established branches in nineteen states and five foreign countries.

I visited the mother church in Indiana on a sweltering August day. Heat waves shimmied off the asphalt roads, and parched brown cornstalks drooped in the fields. The building sat unmarked in the midst of one of those cornfields—huge, isolated, like a misplaced barn. In the parking lot I had to talk my way past two ushers with walkie-talkies; the church was nervous about publicity, especially since former members had recently filed lawsuits.

I suppose I expected a sign of fanaticism during the service: a swooning, hypnotic sermon delivered by a Jim Jones–type preacher. I saw nothing like that. For ninety minutes, seven hundred of us sitting in a large semicircle sang hymns and studied the Bible.

I was among simple people. The women wore dresses or skirts, no slacks, and used little makeup. The men, dressed in shirts and ties, sat with their families and helped keep the children in line.

Children were far more conspicuous here than in most churches; they were everywhere. Keeping quiet for ninety minutes stretches the limits of a small child's endurance, and I watched the parents try to cope. Coloring books abounded. Mothers played games with their children's fingers. Some had brought along a treasure trove of toys in oversized pocketbooks.

If I had come looking for sensationalism, I went away disappointed. I had seen a slice of old-fashioned Americana where the traditional family was still alive and well. Parents there loved their children as much as any parents on earth.

And yet—the map with the tiny tombstones leaped to mind—some of those same parents had sat by the bedsides of their dying youngsters and done nothing. One father told the *Tribune* of his prayer vigil as he watched his fifteen-month-old son battle a fever for two weeks. The illness first caused deafness, then blindness. The pastor of the church urged even more faith and persuaded the father not to call a doctor. The next day the boy was dead. An autopsy revealed that he had died from an easily treatable form of meningitis.

By and large, the members of the Indiana church do not blame God for their miseries, or at least they do not admit to doing so. Instead, they blame themselves for weak faith. Meanwhile, the tombstones multiply.

I went away from that Sunday service with a profound conviction that what we think about God and believe about God matters—*really* matters—as much as anything in life matters. Those people were not ogres or child-murderers, and yet several dozen of their children had died because of an error (I believe) in theology. (Actually, the teaching of the Indiana church is not so different from what I hear in many evangelical churches and on religious television and radio; they simply apply the extravagant promises of faith more consistently.)

Because of those sincere people in Indiana, along with the questioning people who had written to me, I decided to confront issues I am sorely tempted to avoid. Thus, this book of theology. Not a technical book by any means, but a book about the nature of God and why he sometimes acts in puzzling ways and sometimes does not act.

We dare not confine theology to seminary coffee shops where professors and students play mental badminton. It affects all of us. Some people lose their faith because of a sharp sense of disappointment with God. They expect God to act a certain way, and God "lets them down." Others may not lose their faith, but they too experience a form of disappointment. They believe God will intervene, they pray for a miracle, and their prayers come back unanswered. Fifty-two times, at least, it happened that way in the Indiana church.

Chapter 2

Up in Smoke

O NE AFTERNOON my phone rang and the caller identified himself as a theology student at Wheaton College Graduate School. "My name is Richard," he said. "We haven't met, but I feel a kinship with you because of some of your writings. Do you have a minute?"

Richard proceeded to tell me about his life. He had become a Christian as a university student when an InterVarsity worker befriended him and introduced him to the faith. Yet Richard hardly talked like a new Christian. Although he asked for my recommendations of Christian books, I found that he had already read each one I mentioned. We had a pleasant, wandering conversation, and not until the end of the call did I learn his real purpose in contacting me.

"I hate to bother you with this," he said nervously. "I know you're probably busy, but there is one favor I'd like to ask. You see, I wrote this paper on the Book of Job, and my professor told me I should make a book out of it. Is there a chance you could take a look and see what you think?"

I said yes, and the manuscript arrived within a few days. In truth, I did not expect much. Graduate school papers do not normally make compelling reading, and I doubted whether a relatively recent convert could come up with fresh insights on the daunting Book of Job. But I was wrong. The manuscript showed real promise, and over the next few months Richard and I discussed by phone and mail how the paper could be reshaped into book form.

A year later, with a finished manuscript and a signed contract in hand, Richard called to ask if I would write a foreword. I had still never met Richard, but I liked his enthusiasm, and he had written a book I could easily endorse.

Six months passed, during which the book went through final editing and revision. Then, shortly before its publication date, Richard called yet again. His voice sounded different: tense, edgy. To my surprise he fended off questions about his forthcoming book. "I need to see you, Philip," he said. "There's something I feel obligated to tell you, and it should be in person. Could I come over some afternoon this week?"

Hot, hazy rays of sunlight streamed into my third-floor apartment. The open French doors had no screens, and flies buzzed in and out of the room. Richard, dressed in white tennis shorts and a T-shirt, sat on a couch across from me. Sweat glistened on his forehead. He had driven for an hour in heavy Chicago traffic for this meeting, and he first gulped down a glass of iced tea, trying to cool off.

Richard was lean and in good physical shape—"pure ectomorph," as an aerobics instructor might say. A bony face and short-cropped hair gave him the severe, intense look of a God-haunted monk. If body language speaks, his was voluble: his fists clenched and unclenched, his tanned legs crossed and uncrossed, and his facial muscles often tightened with tension.

He skipped the small talk. "You've a right to be furious with me," he began. "I don't blame you a bit if you feel snookered."

I had no idea what he meant. "About what?"

"Well, it's like this. The book you helped me with—it's coming out next month, including your foreword. But the truth is, I don't believe what I wrote in that book anymore, and I feel I owe you an explanation."

He paused for a moment, and I watched the lines of tension working in his jaw. "I hate God!" he suddenly blurted out. "No, I don't mean that. I don't even believe in God."

I said nothing. In fact, I said very little for the next three hours as Richard told me his story, beginning with his parents' breakup. "I did everything I could to prevent the divorce," he said. "I'd just become a Christian at the university, and I was naive enough to believe that God cared. I prayed nonstop day and night that they'd get back together. I even dropped out of school for a while and went home to try to salvage my family. I thought I was doing God's will, but I think I made everything worse. It was my first bitter experience with unanswered prayer.

"I transferred to Wheaton College to learn more about the faith. I figured I must be doing something wrong. At Wheaton I met people who used phrases like 'I spoke with God,' and 'the Lord told me.' I sometimes talked like that too, but never without a twitch of guilt. Did the Lord really tell me anything? I never heard a voice or had any proof of God I could see or touch. Yet I longed for that kind of closeness.

"Each time I faced a crucial decision I would read the Bible and pray for guidance, like you're supposed to. Whenever I felt right about the decision, I would act on it. But, I swear, I ended up making the wrong choice every time. Just when I really thought I understood God's will, then it would backfire on me."

Street noises drifted in, and I could hear neighbors going up and down the stairs, but these sounds did not distract Richard. He kept talking, and I nodded occasionally, though I still did not understand the reason for his almost violent outburst against God. Lots of families break up; lots of prayers go unanswered. What was the true source of his molten rage?

He next told me about a job opportunity that had fallen through. The employer reneged on a promise to him and hired someone less deserving, leaving Richard with school debts and no source of income. About the same time, Richard's fiancee jilted him. With no warning she broke off contact, refusing to give any explanation for her abrupt change of heart. Sharon, the fiancee, had played a key role in Richard's spiritual growth, and as she left him, he felt some of his faith leach away as well. They had often prayed together about their future; now those prayers seemed like cruel jokes.

Richard also had a series of physical problems, which only added to his sense of helplessness and depression. Wounds of rejection, suffered when his parents had separated, seemed to reopen. Had God merely been stringing him along—like Sharon? He visited a pastor for advice. He felt like a drowning man, he said. He wanted to trust God, but whenever he reached out he grasped a fistful of air. Why should he keep believing in a God so apparently unconcerned about his well-being?

The pastor was barely sympathetic, and Richard got the clear impression that his own complaints did not measure up to the man's normal fare of broken marriages, cancer patients, alcoholics, and parents of wayward children. "When something straightens out with your girlfriend, you'll straighten out with God, too," the pastor said with a condescending smile.

To Richard, the problems were anything but minor. He could not understand why a loving heavenly Father would let him suffer such disappointment. No earthly father would treat his child like that. He continued going to church, but inside him a hard lump of cynicism began forming, a tumor of doubt. The theology he had learned in school and had written about in his book no longer worked for him.

"It was odd," Richard told me, "but the more anger I directed at God, the more energy I seemed to gain. I realized that for the last several years I had shrunken inside myself. Now, as I started doubting, and even hating the school and other Christians around me, I felt myself coming back to life."

One night something snapped. Richard attended a Sunday evening church service where he heard the usual testimonies and praise, but one report in particular rankled him. Earlier that week a plane carrying nine missionaries had crashed in the Alaskan outback, killing all aboard. The pastor solemnly related the details and then introduced a member of the church who had survived an unrelated plane crash that same week. When the church member finished describing his narrow escape, the congregation responded, "Praise the Lord!"

"Lord, we thank you for bringing our brother to safety and for having your guardian angels watch over him," the pastor prayed. "And please be with the families of those who died in Alaska." That prayer triggered revulsion, something like nausea, in Richard. You can't have it both ways, he thought. If God gets credit for the survivor, he should also get blamed for the casualties. Yet churches never hear testimonies from the grievers. What would the spouses of the dead missionaries say? Would they talk about a "loving Father"?

Richard returned to his apartment greatly agitated. Everything was coming to a head around one question: "Is God even there?" He had not seen convincing evidence.

Richard interrupted his story at this point. The sun had strayed behind a large building to the west, gauzily softening the room's shadows and streaks of light. Richard closed his eyes and chewed on his lower lip. He pressed on his eyes with his thumbs, hard. He seemed to be setting a mental picture, as if to get it just right.

"What happened next?" I asked, after a few minutes of silence. "Was that the night you lost your faith?"

He nodded and resumed speaking, but in a subdued tone. "I stayed up late that night, long after my neighbors had gone to bed—I live on a quiet street in the suburbs—and it seemed like I was alone in the world. I sensed something important was about to happen. I was hurt. So many times God had let me down. I hated God, and yet I was afraid too. I was a theology student, right? Maybe God was there and I had it all wrong. How could I know? I

31

went back over my whole Christian experience, from the very beginning.

"I remembered the first flush of faith at the university. I was young then, and vulnerable. Maybe I had just learned a few upbeat phrases and talked myself into believing in 'an abundant life.' Maybe I had been mimicking other people and living off their experiences. Had I deluded myself about God?

"Still, I hesitated to cast aside all that I believed. I felt I had to give God one last chance.

"I prayed that night as earnestly and sincerely as I knew how. I prayed on my knees, and I prayed stretched out flat on the oak floor. 'God! Do you care?' I prayed. 'I don't want to tell you how to run your world, but please give me some sign that you're really there! That's all I ask.'

"For four years I'd been straining for 'a personal relationship with God,' as the phrase goes, and yet God had treated me worse than any of my friends. Now everything narrowed down to one final question: How can you have a personal relationship if you're not sure the other person even exists? With God, I could never be sure.

"I prayed for at least four hours. At times I felt foolish, at times utterly sincere. I had the sensation of stepping off a ledge in the darkness with no idea where I might land. That was up to God.

"Finally, at four o'clock in the morning, I came to my senses. Nothing had happened. God had not responded. Why continue torturing myself? Why not just forget God and get on with life, like most of the rest of the world?

"Instantly I felt a sense of relief and freedom, like I had just passed a final exam or gotten my first driver's license. The struggle was over. My life was my own.

"It seems silly now, but this is what I did next. I picked up my Bible and a couple other Christian books and walked downstairs and out the back door. I shut the door softly behind me, so as not to wake anyone. In the backyard was a brick barbecue grill, and I piled the books on it, sprayed them with lighter fluid, and struck a match. It was a moonless night, and the flames danced high and bright. Bible verses and bits of theology curled, blackened, then broke off in tiny crumbs of ash and floated skyward. My faith was going up with them.

"I made another trip upstairs and brought down another armload of books. I did this maybe eight times over the next hour. Commentaries, seminary textbooks, the rough draft of my book on Job—all of them went up in smoke. I might have burned every book I owned if I hadn't been interrupted by an angry fireman in a yellow rain slicker who ran toward me, shouting, 'What do you think you're doing!' Someone had phoned in an alarm. I fumbled around for an excuse and finally told him I was just burning trash.

"After the fireman had squirted some chemicals on my bonfire and shoveled dirt over it, he let me go. I climbed the stairs and sank into bed, smelling of smoke. It was almost dawn by then, and at last I had peace. A great weight had lifted. I had been honest with myself. Any pretense was gone, and I no longer felt the pressure to believe what I could never be sure of. I felt converted—but converted *from* God."

I'm glad I don't make my living as a professional counselor. When I sit across from someone spilling his guts like Richard did, I never know what to say. I said little that afternoon, and maybe that was best. It would not have helped for me to find fault with the "tests" Richard had devised for God.

He seemed especially concerned about the book on Job due out within the next few weeks. The publisher knew about his change of heart, he said, but the first edition was already on the presses. I assured him my endorsement of the book still held. It was the content of the book I was endorsing, more than his personal attachment. "Besides, I've certainly changed my mind about some things I've written in the last ten years," I told him.

Richard was exhausted after talking so long, but he seemed more relaxed as he stood to leave. "Maybe all my problems started with my study of Job," he said. "I used to love Job—he wasn't afraid to be honest with God. He took God on. I guess the difference between us is what happened at the end. God came through for Job, after all his pain. He didn't come through for me."

Dusk had fallen, and a photocell had already switched on the stairway lights. As Richard shook my hand and disappeared down the steps, I felt very sad. He was young and tanned and healthy. Some would say he had no real reason to despair. But listening to him, watching his hands clenching and the lines of tension in his face, I had recognized at last the source of his rage.

Richard was feeling a pain as great as any that a human being experiences: the pain of betrayal. The pain of a lover who wakes up and suddenly realizes *it's all over*. He had staked his life on God, and God had let him down.

Chapter 3

The Questions No One Asks Aloud

S OMETIMES the most important questions, those that float in vague suspension for much of our lives, can crystallize in a single moment. Richard's visit provided such a moment for me. In one respect his complaints—broken home, health problems, failed romance, lost job—hardly ranked as world-class disappointments. And yet that night by the barbecue grill he had, with theatrical finality, acted on the doubts that plague almost all of us. Does God really care? If so, why won't he reach down and fix the things that go wrong—at least some of them?

Absorbed in his anger and pain, Richard had not given voice to his doubts in a systematic way; he experienced them more as feelings of betrayal than as matters of faith. As I brooded over our conversation, however, I kept returning to three large questions about God that seemed to lurk just behind the thicket of his feelings. The longer I pondered them, the more I realized that these questions are lodged somewhere inside all of us. Yet few people ask them aloud, for they seem at best impolite, at worst heretical.

Is God unfair? Richard had tried to follow God, but his life fell apart anyway. He could not reconcile his miseries with the biblical promises of rewards and happiness. And what about the people who openly deny God yet prosper anyway? This is an old complaint, as old as Job and the Psalms, but it remains a stumbling block to faith.

Is God silent? Three times, as he faced crucial choices in his education, career, and romance, Richard begged God for clear direction. Each time he thought he had God's will figured out, only to have that choice lead to failure. "What kind of Father is he?" Richard asked. "Does he enjoy watching me fall on my face? I was told that God loves me and has a wonderful plan for my life. Fine. So why doesn't he tell me what that plan is?"

Is God hidden? This question, above all, obsessed Richard. It seemed to him an irreducible minimum, a theological bottom line, that God should somehow prove himself: "How can I have a relationship with a Person I'm not even sure exists?" Yet it seemed that God deliberately hid himself, even from people who sought him out. And when Richard's late-night vigil provoked no response, he simply gave up on God.

I thought about these three questions often on a subsequent writing assignment in South America. In Peru, a missionary pilot flew me to a small Shipibo Indian village. He landed the floatplane, taxied to the riverbank, and guided me along a jungle trail to the main "street" in town: a dirt path surrounded by a dozen huts built on stilts and covered with palm-frond roofs. He had brought me there to show me a thriving, forty-year-old church. But he also showed me a granite marker just off the main path and told me the story of the young missionary who had helped found that church.

When his six-month-old son died from a sudden onset of vomiting and diarrhea, the young missionary seemed to crack. He hewed a marker by hand from local stone—the marker we were looking at—buried the baby's body, and planted a tree beside the grave. At the hottest part of each day, when everyone else sought shade, the missionary walked to the river and hauled back a jug of water for the tree. Then he stood beside the grave, his shadow falling across it, as if to shield it from the blazing equatorial sun. Sometimes he would weep, sometimes pray, and sometimes just stand there with a vacant gaze. His wife, the Indian church members, and other missionaries all tried to comfort him, but to no avail.

Eventually, the missionary himself got sick. His mind wandered; he had constant diarrhea. He was flown to Lima, where doctors probed him for any sign of amoeba or other tropical organisms, but found nothing. None of the drugs they tried were effective. They diagnosed his problem as "hysterical diarrhea" and sent him and his wife back to the United States.

As I stood beside the crumbling granite marker, which the Indian women now used as a place to rest their water pots, I tried to put myself in that young missionary's place. I wondered what he had prayed as he stood there in the noonday sun, and Richard's three questions kept coming to mind. My guide had said the man was tormented by the question of unfairness. His baby had done nothing wrong. The missionary had brought his family to serve God in the jungle—was this their reward? He had also prayed for some sign of God's presence, or at least a word of comfort. But he felt none. As if distrustful of God's own sympathy, the missionary took on a form of sympathetic suffering in his own body.

True atheists do not, I presume, feel disappointed in God. They expect nothing and receive nothing. But those who commit their lives to God, no matter what, instinctively expect something in return. Are those expectations wrong?

I did not see my friend Richard for a long time. I prayed for him regularly, but all my efforts to contact him proved futile. His phone had been disconnected, and I heard he had moved out of the area. His publisher eventually sent me a copy of his book on Job, and it sat on my shelf as a potent warning against writing too hastily on matters of faith.

Then one day, about three years later, I bumped into Richard in downtown Chicago. He looked good: by putting on a little weight and letting his hair grow a few inches longer, he had lost the haunted, severe mien. He seemed glad to see me, and we scheduled a lunch.

"Last time I met with you, I guess I was in the pits," he said with a smile as he joined me in a Mexican restaurant a few days later. "Life is treating me much better now." He had a promising job and had long since put the failed romance behind him.

Soon our conversation turned to God, and it quickly became evident that Richard had not fully recovered. A thick scab of cynicism now covered the wounds, but he was as angry at God as ever.

The waitress poured a fresh cup of coffee, and Richard wrapped both hands around the cup and stared at the dark, steaming liquid. "I've gained some perspective on that crazy period," he said. "I think I've figured out what went wrong. I can tell you the exact hour and minute I began doubting God, and it wasn't at Wheaton or in my room that night I stayed up praying." He then related an incident that had occurred very early in his Christian life.

"One thing bugged me from the very beginning: the notion of faith. It seemed a black hole that could gobble up any honest question. I'd ask the InterVarsity leader about the problem of pain, and he would spout something about faith. 'Believe God whether you feel like it or not,' he'd say. 'The feelings will follow.' I faked it, but I can now see that the feelings never followed. I was just going through the motions.

"Even back then I was searching for hard evidence of God as an alternative to faith. And one day I found it—on television, of all places. While randomly flipping a dial, I came across a mass healing service being conducted by Kathryn Kuhlman. I watched for a few minutes as she brought various people up on the stage and interviewed them. Each one told an amazing story of supernatural healing. Cancer, heart conditions, paralysis—it was like a medical encyclopedia up there.

"As I watched Kuhlman's program, my doubts gradually melted away. At last I had found something real and tangible. Kuhlman asked a musician to sing her favorite song, 'He Touched

Me.' That's what I needed, I thought: a touch, a personal touch from God. She held out that promise, and I lunged for it.

"Three weeks later when Kathryn Kuhlman came to a neighboring state, I skipped classes and traveled half a day to attend one of her meetings. The atmosphere was unbelievably charged—soft organ music in the background; the murmuring sound of people praying aloud, some in strange tongues; and every few minutes a happy interruption when someone would stand and claim, 'I'm healed!'

"One person especially made an impression, a man from Milwaukee who had been carried into the meeting on a stretcher. When he walked—yes, walked—onstage, we all cheered wildly. He told us he was a physician, and I was even more impressed. He had incurable lung cancer, he said, and was told he had six months to live. But now, tonight, he believed God had healed him. He was walking for the first time in months. He felt great. Praise God!

"I wrote down the man's name and practically floated out of that meeting. I had never known such certainty of faith before. My search was over; I had seen proof of a living God in those people on the stage. If he could work tangible miracles in them, then surely he had something wonderful in store for me.

"I wanted contact with the man of faith I had seen at the meeting, so much so that exactly one week later I phoned Directory Assistance in Milwaukee and got the physician's number. When I dialed it, a woman answered the phone. 'May I please speak to Dr. S_____,' I said.

"Long silence. 'Who are you?' she said at last. I figured she was just screening calls from patients or something. I gave my name and told her I admired Dr. S_____ and had wanted to talk to him ever since the Kathryn Kuhlman meeting. I had been very moved by his story, I said.

"Another long silence. Then she spoke in a flat voice, pronouncing each word slowly. 'My . . . husband . . . is . . . dead.' Just that one sentence, nothing more, and she hung up.

"I can't tell you how that devastated me. I was wasted. I half-staggered into the next room, where my sister was sitting. 'Richard, what's wrong?' she asked. 'Are you all right?'

"No, I was not all right. But I couldn't talk about it. I was crying. My mother and sister tried to pry some explanation out of me. But what could I tell them? For me, the certainty I had staked my life on had died with that phone call. A flame had flared bright for one fine, shining week and then gone dark, like a dying star."

Richard stared into his coffee cup. Marimba music playing in the background sounded tinny and jarringly loud. "I don't quite understand," I said. "That happened long before you went to Wheaton and got a theology degree and wrote a book—"

"Yeah, but it all started back then," he interrupted. "Everything that followed—Wheaton, the book on Job, the Bible study groups—was a grasping attempt to prove wrong what I should have learned from that one phone call. Nobody's out there, Philip. And if by some chance God does exist, then he's toying with us. Why doesn't he quit playing games and show himself?"

Richard soon changed the topic of conversation, and we spent the rest of the lunch catching up on the past three years. He kept insisting that he was happy. He may have been protesting too strongly, but he did indeed seem more content.

Toward the end, as we were digging into our ice cream desserts, he brought up our last meeting, three years before. "You must have thought I was half-crazy, charging in there and blurting out my whole life story when I'd never even met you."

"Not at all," I said. "In a strange sort of way, I've never been able to get that conversation out of my mind. Actually, your complaints against God helped me better understand my own."

I then told Richard about the three questions. After I had explained them, I asked if they summed up his complaints against God.

"Well, my doubt was more like a feeling—I felt jilted, like God had strung me along just to watch me fall. But you're right, as

I think about it; those questions were behind my feelings. God was certainly unfair. And he always seemed hidden, and silent. Yeah, that's it. That's it exactly!" he said.

"Why on earth doesn't God answer those questions!" Richard had raised his voice and was waving his arms like a politician—like an evangelist. Fortunately, the restaurant had emptied. "If only God answered those questions—if only he answered *one* of them. If, say, he would just speak aloud one time so that everyone could hear, then I would believe. Probably the whole world would believe. Why doesn't he?"

Chapter 4

What If

I F ONLY," Richard had said. If only God solved those three problems, then faith would flourish like flowers in springtime. Wouldn't it?

The same year I met Richard in the Mexican restaurant, I happened to be studying the books of Exodus and Numbers. And even though Richard's questions were still buzzing about in my mind, it took a while for me to notice a curious parallel. Then one day it suddenly jumped out from the page: Exodus described the very world Richard wanted! It showed God stepping into human history almost daily. He acted with utter fairness and spoke so that everyone could hear. Behold, he even made himself visible!

The contrast between the days of the Israelites and our days, the twentieth century, got me thinking about how God runs the world, and I went back to the three questions. If God has the power to act fairly, speak audibly, and appear visibly, why, then, does he seem so reluctant to intervene today? Perhaps the record of the Israelites in the wilderness contained a clue.

Question: Is God unfair? Why doesn't he consistently punish evil people and reward good people? Why do awful things happen to people good and bad, with no discernible pattern?

Imagine a world designed so that we experience a mild jolt of pain with every sin and a tickle of pleasure with every act of virtue. Imagine a world in which every errant doctrine attracts a lightning bolt, while every repetition of the Apostles' Creed stimulates our brains to produce an endorphin of pleasure.

The Old Testament records a "behavior modification" experiment almost that blatant: God's covenant with the Israelites. In the Sinai Desert, God resolved to reward and punish his people with strict, legislated fairness. He signed the guarantee with his own hand, making it dependent on the one condition that the Israelites had to follow the laws he laid down. He then had Moses outline the terms of this guarantee to the people:

Results of Obedience	Results of Disobedience
Prosperous cities and rural areas	Violence, crime, and poverty everywhere
No sterility among men, women, or livestock	Infertility among people and livestock
Assured success in farming	Crop failure; locusts and worms
Dependable weather conditions	Scorching heat, drought, blight, and mildew
Guaranteed military victories	Domination by other nations
Total immunity to diseases	Fever and inflammation; madness, blindness, confusion of mind

If they were obedient, Moses said, God would set them "high above all the nations on earth"; they would "always be at the top, never at the bottom." In effect, the Israelites were promised protection from virtually every kind of human misery and disappointment. On the other hand, if they disobeyed they would become "a thing of horror and an object of scorn and ridicule to all the nations where the Lord will drive you. . . . Because you did not serve the Lord your God joyfully and gladly in the time of prosperity, therefore in hunger and thirst, in nakedness and dire poverty, you will serve the enemies the Lord sends against you."

I read on, scanning the books of Joshua and Judges to see the

44

results of this covenant based on a "fair" system of rewards and punishment. Within fifty years the Israelites had disintegrated into a state of utter anarchy. Much of the rest of the Old Testament recounts the dreary history of the predicted curses—not blessings—coming true. Despite all the lavish benefits of the covenant, Israel failed to obey God and meet its terms.

Years later when New Testament authors looked back on that history, they did not hold up the covenant as an exemplary model of God relating to his people with absolute consistency and fairness. Rather, they said the old covenant served as an object lesson, demonstrating that human beings were incapable of fulfilling a contract with God. It seemed clear to them that a new covenant ("testament") with God was needed, one based on forgiveness and grace. And that is precisely why the "New Testament" exists.

Question: Is God silent? If he is so concerned about our doing his will, why doesn't he reveal that will more plainly?

Various people claim to hear the word of God today. Some of them are crazy, like the wild man who on "God's orders" attacked Michelangelo's *Pietà* with a hammer, or the political assassin who claimed God told him to shoot the president. Others seem sincere but misguided, like the six strangers who reported to author Joni Eareckson that God had instructed them to marry her. Still others seem to carry on the authentic tradition of the prophets and apostles, delivering the word of God to his people. So then, how can we know whether what we have heard is truly a word from God?

God simplified matters of guidance, I discovered, when the Israelites camped in the Sinai wilderness. *Should we pack up our tent and move today or stay put?* For the answer, an inquisitive Israelite need only glance at the cloud over the tabernacle. If the cloud moved, God wanted his people to move. If it stayed, that meant stay. (You could conveniently check God's will around the clock; at night the cloud glowed like a tower of fire.)

God set up other ways, like the casting of lots and the Urim and Thummim, to directly communicate his will, but most issues were pre-decided. He had spoken his will for the Israelites in a set of rules, codified into 613 laws that covered the complete range of behavior, from murder to boiling a young goat in its mother's milk. Few people complained about fuzzy guidance in those days.

But did a clear word from God increase the likelihood of obedience? Apparently not. "Do not go up and fight [the Amorites]," said God, "because I will not be with you. You will be defeated by your enemies." The Israelites promptly went up and fought the Amorites and were defeated by their enemies. They marched when told to sit tight, fled in fear when told to march, fought when told to declare peace, declared peace when told to fight. They made a national pastime out of inventing ways to break the 613 commands. Clear guidance became as much of an affront to that generation as unclear guidance is to ours.

I also noticed a telling pattern in the Old Testament accounts: the very clarity of God's will had a stunting effect on the Israelites' faith. Why pursue God when he had already revealed himself so clearly? Why step out in faith when God had already guaranteed the results? Why wrestle with the dilemma of conflicting choices when God had already resolved the dilemma? In short, why should the Israelites act like adults when they could act like children? And act like children they did, grumbling against their leaders, cheating on the strict rules governing manna, whining about every food or water shortage.

As I studied the story of the Israelites, I had second thoughts about crystal-clear guidance. It may serve some purpose—it may, for example, get a mob of just-freed slaves across a hostile desert—but it does not seem to encourage spiritual development. In fact, for the Israelites it nearly eliminated the need for faith at all; clear guidance sucked away freedom, making every choice a matter of obedience rather than faith. And in forty years of wilderness wanderings, the Israelites flunked the obedience test so badly that God was forced to start over with a new generation.

Question: Is God hidden? Why doesn't he simply show up sometime, visibly, and dumbfound the skeptics once and for all?

What the Soviet cosmonaut wanted when he looked for God in the dark void outside his spacecraft window, what my friend Richard wanted, alone in his room at two in the morning, is the hungering desire of our age (for those who still hunger). We want proof, evidence, a personal appearance, so that the God we have heard about becomes the God we see.

What we hunger for happened once. For a time God did show up in person, and a man spoke to him face to face as he might speak with a friend. They met together, God and Moses, in a tent pitched just outside the Israelite camp. The rendezvous was no secret. Whenever Moses trudged over to the tent to talk with God, the whole camp turned out to watch. A pillar of cloud, God's visible presence, blocked the entrance to the tent. No one except Moses knew what transpired inside; no one wanted to know. The Israelites had learned to keep their distance. "Speak to us yourself and we will listen," they said to Moses. "But do not have God speak to us or we will die." After each meeting Moses would emerge glowing like a space alien, and the people turned their faces away until he covered himself with a veil.

There were few, if any, atheists in those days. No Israelites wrote plays about waiting for a God who never arrived. They could see clear evidence of God outside the tent of meeting or in the thick storm clouds hovering around Mount Sinai. A skeptic need only hike over to the trembling mountain and reach out a hand to touch it, and his doubts would vanish—one second before he did.

And yet what happened during those days almost defies belief. When Moses climbed the sacred mountain stormy with the signs of God's presence, those people who had lived through the ten plagues of Egypt, who had crossed the Red Sea on dry ground, who had drunk water from a rock, who were digesting the miracle of manna in their stomachs at that moment—those same people got bored or impatient or rebellious or jealous and apparently forgot all about their God. By the time Moses descended from the mountain, they were dancing like heathens around a golden calf.

God did not play hide-and-seek with the Israelites; they had every proof of his existence you could ask for. But astonishingly—and I could hardly believe this result, even as I read it—God's directness seemed to produce the very *opposite* of the desired effect. The Israelites responded not with worship and love, but with fear and open rebellion. God's visible presence did nothing to improve lasting faith.

I had distilled Richard's complaints about God into three questions. But Exodus and Numbers taught me that quick solutions to those three questions may not solve the underlying problems of disappointment with God. The Israelites, though exposed to the bright, unshaded light of God's presence, were as fickle a people as have ever lived. Ten different times on the melancholy pathless plains of the Sinai they rose up against God. Even at the very border of the Promised Land, with all its bounty stretching out before them, they were still keening for the "good old days" of slavery in Egypt.

These dismal results may provide insight into why God does not intervene more directly today. Some Christians long for a world well-stocked with miracles and spectacular signs of God's presence. I hear wistful sermons on the parting of the Red Sea and the ten plagues and the daily manna in the wilderness, as if the speakers yearn for God to unleash his power like that today. But the follow-the-dots journey of the Israelites should give us pause. Would a burst of miracles nourish faith? Not the kind of faith God seems interested in, evidently. The Israelites give ample proof that signs may only addict us to signs, not to God.

True, the Israelites were a primitive people emerging out of slavery. But the biblical accounts have a disturbingly familiar ring to them. The Israelites tended to behave, in Frederick Buechner's phrase, "just like everybody else, only more so."

I came away from my study of them both surprised and confused: surprised to learn how little difference it made in people's lives when three major reasons for disappointment with God—unfairness, silence, and hiddenness—were removed; confused by the questions stirred up about God's actions on earth. Has he changed? Has he pulled back, withdrawn?

As Richard sat in my living room telling me his story that first time, he had looked up suddenly and said in a fierce voice, "God doesn't know what the HELL he's doing with this world!" What is God doing? What is the human experiment all about? What does he want from us, after all, and what can we expect from him?

Without somehow destroying me in the process, how could God reveal himself in a way that would leave no room for doubt? If there were no room for doubt, there would be no room for me.
— Frederick Buechner

Bible references: Deuteronomy 9, 7, 28; Romans 3; Galatians 3; Exodus 28, 40; Deuteronomy 1–2; Exodus 19–20, 32–33; Deuteronomy 1.

Chapter 5

The Source

F OR TWO WEEKS I holed up in a Colorado cabin to ponder
Richard's three questions in light of what I had seen in the
Old Testament. I brought along a suitcase full of books to study,
but during my entire time there I opened only a Bible.

I started at Genesis late the first afternoon, a day of heavy
snowfall. It was a perfect setting for reading the story of creation.
Clouds lifted in time for a spectacular alpenglow sunset, with puffs
of snow pluming off the tops of the mountain peaks, like pink
cotton candy. At night the clouds closed in again, and snow blew
furiously.

I read straight through the Bible, slowly, cover to cover. By
the time I reached Deuteronomy, snow covered the bottom step;
when I hit the Prophets it had crept up the mailbox post; and
when I finally made it to Revelation I had to call for a snowplow
to unbury the driveway. Over seventy-two inches of fresh powder
fell during the two weeks I spent in a loft reading the Bible and
looking out the window at sugar-coated evergreens.

It struck me forcefully there that our common impressions of God may be very different from the God the Bible actually portrays. What is he really like? In church and at a Christian college I had learned to think of God as an unchanging, invisible spirit who possesses such qualities as omnipotence, omniscience, and impassibility (incapable of emotion). These doctrines, which are supposed to help us understand God's point of view, can be found in the Bible, but they are well buried.

Simply reading the Bible, I encountered not a misty vapor but an actual Person. A Person as unique and distinctive and colorful as any person I know. God has deep emotions; he feels delight and frustration and anger. In the Prophets he weeps and moans with pain, even comparing himself to a woman giving birth: "I cry out, I gasp and pant." Again and again God is shocked by the behavior of human beings. When the Israelites commit infant sacrifice, he seems stunned by actions which—an omniscient God is speaking here—"I did not command or mention, nor did it enter my mind." He explains the need to punish by asking plaintively, "What else can I do?" I know, I know, the word "anthropomorphism" is supposed to explain all those humanlike characteristics. But surely the images God "borrows" from human experience point to an even stronger reality.

As I read through the Bible in my winter aerie, I marveled at how much God lets human beings affect him. I was unprepared for the joy and anguish—in short, the passion—of the God of the Universe. By studying "about" God, by taming him and reducing him to words and concepts that could be filed away in alphabetical order, I had lost the force of the passionate relationship God seeks above all else. The people who related to God best—Abraham, Moses, David, Isaiah, Jeremiah—treated him with startling familiarity. They talked to God as if he were sitting in a chair beside them, as one might talk to a counselor, a boss, a parent, or a lover. They treated him like a person.

That Colorado trip put my three questions about disappointment with God in a new light. They are not puzzles awaiting solution, such as you would encounter in the field of mathematics or computer programming or even philosophy. Rather, they are problems of relationship between human beings and a God who wants desperately to love and be loved by us.

I saw few people during my two-week retreat. Mostly I huddled indoors, behind the wall of snow, and read. Perhaps it was this aloneness, this isolation, that cleared the way for the conclusion that I reached: I had always considered just one point of view, the human point of view. I have shelves full of books presenting the dilemma of being human. Some are funny, some anguished, some sarcastic, some densely philosophical, but all express the same basic viewpoint: "Here's what it feels like to be a human being." People disappointed with God likewise focus on the human point of view. When we ask our questions—Why is God unfair? Silent? Hidden?—we're really asking, Why is God unfair *to me*? Why does he seem silent *with me,* and hidden *from me?*

I tried to set aside my existential questions, my personal disappointments, and consider instead God's point of view. Why does he seek contact with human beings in the first place? What is he pursuing in us, and what interferes with that pursuit? I turned to the Bible again, trying to hear God's words as if for the first time. He speaks for himself there, and I realized that I had not often paid attention. I had been too preoccupied with my feelings to listen attentively to *his* feelings.

I came away from Colorado with a very different mental image of God. After two weeks of studying the Bible, I had a strong sense that God doesn't care so much about being analyzed. Mainly, he wants to be loved. Nearly every page of his Word rustles with this message. And I returned home knowing I must somehow explore the relationship between a passionate God— hungry for the love of his people—and the people themselves. All feelings of disappointment with God trace back to a breakdown in that relationship. Thus, I determined to look for the answer to a question I had never before considered: "What does it feel like to be God?"

The reason the mass of men fear God, and at bottom dislike Him, is because they rather distrust his heart, and fancy Him all brain like a watch.

—Herman Melville

Bible references: Isaiah 42; Jeremiah 19, 9.

Part Two

Making Contact:
The Father

Chapter 6

Risky Business

T O UNDERSTAND how it feels to be God, there is only one
place to begin: the moment of creation. Often Genesis 1
gets read as a prelude, as our minds speed ahead to the major
disruption in chapter 3 or to the modern debate over the process
used in creation. But Genesis 1 says nothing of that process or of
the tragedy to follow. It lays out the barest sketch of our world—
sun and stars, oceans and plants, fish and beasts, man and
woman—along with God's own comment on each new work.

"And God saw that it was good"—five times the understatement beats in cadence like a drum. And when he had finished,
"God saw all that he had made, and it was very good." Other parts
of the Bible recall the time with more exuberance. "The morning
stars sang together and all the angels shouted for joy," God
reported with pride to Job. Proverbs expands on the upbeat mood:
"I was the craftsman at his side. I was filled with delight day after
day, rejoicing always in his presence, rejoicing in his whole world
and delighting in mankind."

Creation as it felt to God—since then every artist has felt an echo, a sympathetic vibration: a craftsman who squints at his finished product and reckons, "Very good"; a performer who cannot suppress a grin when the audience stands and cheers; even a child with her glued-together Popsicle sticks.

Anthropologist and essayist Loren Eiseley tells of a day when he felt the joy of original creation. An old man then, walking a deserted beach, he found shelter from damp fog under the prow of a wrecked boat and promptly fell asleep. When he opened his eyes, he was looking at the two small neat ears and inquisitive face of a young fox, so young that it had not learned to fear. There, under the boat's shadow, the distinguished naturalist and the fox pup stared at one another. And then the tiny fox, a vast and playful humor in his face, selected a chicken bone from a pile and shook it in his teeth. On impulse Eiseley bent over and grabbed the other end, and the frolic began.

Loren Eiseley: "It has been said repeatedly that one can never, try as he will, get around to the front of the universe. Man is destined to see only its far side, to realize nature only in retreat. Yet here was the thing in the midst of the bones, the wide-eyed innocent fox inviting me to play. The universe was swinging in some fantastic fashion around to present its face, and the face was so small that the universe itself was laughing. It was not a time for human dignity.

"For just a moment I had held the universe at bay by the simple expedient of sitting on my haunches before a fox den and tumbling about with a chicken bone." It was "the gravest, most meaningful act I shall ever accomplish," he later concluded, for in it he had caught at last a glimpse of the universe as it begins for all things. "It was, in reality, a child's universe, a tiny and laughing universe."[1]

Despite the awesome emptiness of our universe, despite the pain that haunts it, something lingers, like a scent of old perfume, from that moment of beginnings in Genesis 1. I too have sensed it. The first time I rounded a bend and saw Yosemite Valley spread out before me, its angel-hair waterfalls spilling over the snow-glazed granite. On a small peninsula of Ontario where five million migrating monarch butterflies stop to rest, their papery wings adorning every tree with shimmering, translucent orange. In the children's zoo in Chicago's Lincoln Park, where every beast born—gorilla, aardvark, or hippopotamus—begins life mischievous and full of play.

Eiseley is right: at the heart of the universe is a smile, a pulse of joy passed down from the moment of creation. A new parent who holds a baby, *my* baby, close against flesh for the first time knows it. And that is the feeling God had when he looked over what he had made and pronounced it good. In the beginning, the very beginning, there was no disappointment. Only joy.

Adam and Eve

Genesis 1 does not tell the whole story of creation, however. To understand what follows, you must create something for yourself.

Every creator, from a child with Play-Doh to Michelangelo, learns that creation involves a kind of self-limiting. You produce something that did not exist before, yes, but only by ruling out other options along the way. Stick the curved clay trunk on the front of the elephant; now it cannot go on the rear or on the side. Pick up a pencil and start drawing; now you limit yourself to black and white, not color.

No artist, no matter how great, escapes this limitation. Michelangelo knew that no *trompe l'oeil* would give the Sistine Chapel ceiling the three-dimensional reality he had achieved in his sculptures. When he decided on a medium, paint on plaster, he limited himself.

When God created, he invented the media as he went, calling into being what had existed only in his imagination, and along with every free choice came a limitation. He chose a world of time and space, a "medium" with peculiar restrictions: first A happens, then B happens, and then C. God, who sees future, past, and present all at once, selected sequential time as an artist selects a canvas and palette, and his choice imposed limits we have lived with ever since. (Hasidic scholars have a wonderful word for God's self-limitation: *zimsum*, they call it.)

"And God said, 'Let the water teem with living creatures.'" Behind that sentence lay a thousand decisions: fish with gills and not lungs, scales not fur, fins not feet, blood not sap. At every stage God the Creator made choices, eliminating alternatives.

Genesis tells of God's final set of choices, then pauses, backs up, and retells it in more detail. On the sixth day of creation, man and woman came into being, two creatures unlike all others. God designed them in his own image, desiring to recognize something of himself in them. They were like a mirror, reflecting back his own likeness.

But Adam and Eve had another distinction as well: alone of all God's creatures, they had a moral capacity to rebel against their creator. The sculptures could spit at the sculptor; the characters in the play could rewrite the lines. They were, in a word, free.

"Man is God's risk," said one theologian. Another, Søren Kierkegaard, put it this way: "God has, so to speak, imprisoned himself in his resolve." Nearly everything theologians say about human freedom sounds somehow right and somehow wrong. How can a sovereign God take risks or imprison himself? Yet God's creation of man and woman approached that kind of astonishing self-limitation.

Consider a rather fanciful rendition of creation by William Irwin Thompson:

> Imagine God in Heaven surrounded by the choirs of adoring angels singing hosannahs unendingly . . . "If I create a perfect world, I know how it will turn out. In its absolute perfection, it will revolve like a perfect machine, never deviating from My absolute will." Since God's imagination is perfect, there is no need for Him to create such a universe: it is enough for Him to imagine it to see it in all its details. Such a universe would not be very interesting to man or God, so we can assume that the Divinity continued His meditations. "But what if I create a universe that is free, free even of me? What if I veil My Divinity so that the creatures are free to pursue their individual lives without being overwhelmed by My overpowering Presence? Will the creatures love Me? Can I be loved by

60

creatures whom I have not programmed to adore me forever? Can love arise out of freedom? My angels love me unceasingly, but they can see Me at all times. What if I create beings in My own image as a Creator, beings who are free? But if I introduce freedom into this universe, I take the risk of introducing Evil into it as well, for if they are free, then they are free to deviate from My will. Hmmm. But what if I continue to interact with this dynamic universe, what if I and the creatures become the creators together of a great cosmic play? What if out of every occasion of evil, I respond with an unimaginable good, a good that overwhelms evil by springing out of the very attempts of evil to deny the Good? Will these new creatures of freedom then love Me, will they join with Me in creating Good out of Evil, novelty out of freedom? What if I join with them in the world of limitation and form, the world of suffering and evil? Ahh, in a truly free universe, even I do not know how it will turn out. Do even I dare to take that risk for love?"[2]

Why would Adam and Eve want to rebel? They lived in a garden paradise, and if they had a complaint they could talk it over with God as with a friend. But there was that one forbidden tree, the one with the enticing name, "the tree of the knowledge of good and evil." Apparently God was keeping something from them. What secret lay behind that name? And how would they ever know unless they tried? Adam and Eve made their own "creative" choice: they ate the fruit, and earth has never been the same.

Genesis 3 shows exactly what God felt when Adam and Eve disobeyed: sadness over the broken relationship; anger at their denials; and an emotion surprisingly like alarm. "The man has now become like one of us, knowing good and evil. He must not be allowed to reach out his hand and take also from the tree of life and eat, and live forever."

Creation, which seems like pure freedom, involves limitation. And as Adam and Eve soon learned, rebellion, which also seems like freedom, involves limitation as well. By their choice they put distance between themselves and God. Before, they had walked and talked with God. Now when they heard his approach, they hid in the shrubbery. An awkward separation had crept in to spoil the intimacy. And every quiver of disappointment in our own relationship with God is an aftershock from their initial act of rebellion.

Perhaps we do not realize the problem, so to call it, of enabling finite free wills to co-exist with Omnipotence. It seems to involve at every moment almost a sort of "divine abdication."
—C. S. Lewis

[1]Loren Eiseley, *The Star Thrower*, 64–65.
[2]William I. Thompson, *The Time Falling Bodies Take to Light*, 24–25.

Bible references: Job 38; Proverbs 8; Genesis 1–3.

Chapter 7

The Parent

A FTER MY RETURN from Colorado, I read Genesis over and over, searching the book of beginnings for some clue into what God had in mind for this world. Even after that first landmark rebellion against him, God did not cast off his creation. Genesis tells amazing stories of his continuing personal encounters with humanity.

If I had to reduce the "plot" of Genesis to one sentence, it would be something like this: God learns how to be a parent.* The disruption in Eden changed the world forever, destroying the intimacy Adam and Eve had known with God. In a kind of warm-

---

*A phrase like "God learns" may seem strange because we normally think of learning as a mental process, moving in sequence from a state of not-knowing to a state of knowing. God, of course, is not bound by time or ignorance. He "learns" in the sense of taking on new experiences, such as the creation of free human beings. Using the word in a similar sense, Hebrews says that Jesus "learned obedience from what he suffered."

up to history, God and human beings had to get used to each other. The humans set the pace by breaking all the rules, and God responded with individualized punishments. What did it feel like to be God? What does it feel like to be the parent of a two-year-old?

No one could accuse God of being shy to intervene in the early days. He seemed a close, even hovering parent. When Adam sinned, God met with him in person, explaining that all creation would have to adjust to the choice he, Adam, had made. Just one generation later a new kind of horror—murder—appeared on earth. "What have you done?" God demanded of Cain. "Listen! Your brother's blood cries out to me from the ground." Once again God met with the culprit and custom-designed a punishment.

The state of the earth and, indeed, the entire human race continued to deteriorate toward a point of crisis which the Bible sums up in the most poignant sentence ever written: "The Lord was grieved that he had made man on the earth, and his heart was filled with pain." Behind that one statement stands all the shock and grief God felt as a parent.

What human parent has not experienced at least a pang of such remorse? A teenage son tears away in a fit of rebellion. "I hate you!" he cries, fumbling for words that will cause the most pain. He seems bent on twisting a knife in the belly of his parents. That rejection is what God experienced not just from one child, but from the entire human race. As a result, what God had created, God destroyed. All the joy of Genesis 1 vanished under the churning waters of the Flood.

But there was Noah, that one man of faith who "walked with God." After the remorse expressed in Genesis 3 through 7, you can almost hear God sigh with relief as Noah, in his first act back on land, worships the God who had saved him. *At last, someone to build on.* (Years later, in a message to Ezekiel, God would mention Noah as one of his three most righteous followers.) With the whole planet freshly scrubbed and sprouting life anew, God agreed to a covenant or contract that bound him not just to Noah but to every living creature. It promised one thing only: that God would never again destroy all creation.

64

The Parent

You could view the covenant with Noah as the barest minimum of a relationship: one party agrees not to obliterate the other. And yet even in that promise God limited himself. He, the sworn enemy of all evil in the universe, pledged to endure wickedness on this planet for a time—or, rather, to solve it through some means other than annihilation. Like the parent of a runaway teenager, he forced himself into the role of The Waiting Father (as Jesus' story of the Prodigal Son expresses so eloquently). Before long another mass rebellion, at a place called Babel, tested God's resolve, and he kept his promise not to destroy.

In earliest history, then, God acted so plainly that no one could grouse about his hiddenness or silence. Yet those early interventions shared one important feature: each was a punishment, a response to human rebellion. If it was God's intention to have a mature relationship with free human beings, he certainly met with a series of rude setbacks. How could he ever relate to his creation as adults when they kept behaving like children?

The Plan

Genesis 12 marks a momentous change. For the first time since the days of Adam, God stepped in not to punish, but to set into motion a new plan for human history.

There was no mystery about what he had in mind. He told Abraham forthrightly: "I will make you into a great nation, with many people bearing your name, and from that nation I will bless all peoples on earth." The plan appears in some form in Genesis 13, 15, 16, and 17 as well as dozens of other Old Testament passages. Rather than trying to restore the whole earth at once, God would begin with a pioneer settlement, a new race set apart from all others. Abraham, dazzled by God's promises, left home and migrated hundreds of miles to the land of Canaan.

Despite the honor accorded him as the father of this new race, however, Abraham emerges as the Bible's first example of a person severely disappointed in God. Miracles, he had. Abraham entertained angels in his home and dreamed mystical visions of smoking fire pots. But there was one nagging problem: after the promise, after the blaze of revelation, came silence—long years of bewildering silence.

"Go, claim the land I have for you," God said. But Abraham found Canaan dry as bone, its inhabitants dying of famine. To stay alive, he fled to Egypt.

"You'll have descendants as countless as the stars in the sky," God said. No promise could have made Abraham happier. At age seventy-five he still anticipated a tent filled with the sounds of children at play. At eighty-five he worked out a backup plan with a female servant. At ninety-nine the promise seemed downright ludicrous, and when God showed up to confirm it, Abraham laughed in his face. A father at ninety-nine? Sarah in maternity clothes at ninety? They both cackled at the thought.

A laugh of ridicule and also of pain. God had dangled a bright dream of fertility before a barren couple and then sat on his hands and watched as they advanced toward tottery old age. What kind of game was he playing? Whatever did he want?

God wanted faith, the Bible says, and that is the lesson Abraham finally learned. He learned to believe when there was no reason left to believe. And although he did not live to see the Hebrews fill the land as the stars fill the sky, Abraham did live to see Sarah bear one child—just one—a boy, who forever preserved the memory of absurd faith, for his name Isaac meant "laughter."

And the pattern continued: Isaac married a barren woman, as did his son Jacob. The esteemed matriarchs of the covenant—Sarah, Rebekah, and Rachel—all spent their best childbearing years slender and in despair. They too experienced the blaze of revelation, followed by dark and lonely times of waiting that nothing but faith would fill.

A gambler would say God stacked the odds against himself. A cynic would say God taunted the creatures he was supposed to love. The Bible simply uses the cryptic phrase "by faith" to describe what they went through. Somehow, that "faith" was what God valued, and it soon became clear that faith was the best way for humans to express a love for God.

Joseph

If you read Genesis in one sitting, you cannot help noticing a change in how God related to his people. At first he stayed close by, walking in the garden with them, punishing their individual sins, speaking to them directly, intervening constantly. Even in Abraham's day he sent extraterrestrial messengers on house calls. By Jacob's time, however, the messages were far more ambiguous: a mysterious dream about a ladder, a late-night wrestling match. And toward the end of Genesis, a man named Joseph received guidance in the most unexpected ways.

Genesis slows down when it gets to Joseph, and it shows God working mostly behind the scenes. God spoke to Joseph not through angels, but through such means as the dreams of a despotic Egyptian pharaoh.

If anyone had a valid reason to be disappointed in God, it was Joseph, whose valiant stabs at goodness brought him nothing but trouble. He interpreted a dream to his brothers, and they threw him in a cistern. He resisted a sexual advance and landed in an Egyptian prison. There, he interpreted another dream to save a cell mate's life, and the cell mate promptly forgot about him. I wonder, as Joseph languished for his virtue in an Egyptian dungeon, did questions like Richard's—Is God unfair? Silent? Hidden?—occur to him?

But shift for a moment to the perspective of God the parent. Had he deliberately "pulled back" to allow Joseph's faith to reach a new level of maturity? And could this be why Genesis devotes more space to Joseph than to any other person? Through all his trials, Joseph learned to trust: not that God would prevent hardship, but that he would redeem even the hardship. Choking back tears, Joseph tried to explain his faith to his murderous brothers: "You intended to harm me, but God intended it for good. . . ."

The central idea of the great part of the Old Testament may be called the idea of the loneliness of God.

—G. K. Chesterton

Bible references: Genesis 1–11; Hebrews 5; Ezekiel 14; Genesis 12–21, 25, 30; Hebrews 11; Genesis 37, 39–41, 45.

Chapter 8

Unfiltered Sunlight

G ENESIS CLOSES with a single family, small enough for the
Bible to name all its sons, settling into the friendly haven
of Egypt. The next book, Exodus, opens with a swarm of Israelites
toiling as slaves under a hostile pharaoh. Nowhere in the Bible
will you find an account of what happened during the intervening
four hundred years.

I have heard many sermons on the life of Joseph, and many
more on Moses and the miracle of the Exodus. But I have never
heard a sermon on the four-hundred-year gap between Genesis
and Exodus. (Could some of our feelings of disappointment stem
from a habit of skipping over times of silence in favor of the
Bible's stories of victory?) We tend to speed ahead to the
exhilarating stories of liberation from slavery. But think of it! For
an ellipsis of time twice as long as the U.S.A. has been in
existence, heaven was silent. Surely the Hebrew slaves in Egypt
felt profound disappointment with God.

You are a Hebrew, a descendant of Abraham. You grew up hearing about the wonderful promises God gave that great man. "Someday your race will become a mighty nation and will live at peace in their own land"—God swore that in person, first to Abraham, and then to Isaac and Jacob. As a child you obediently memorized those promises. But they now seem like fairy tales. Independent nation? You and your neighbors serve the most powerful empire on earth; daily, you suffer the insults and feel the whips of Egyptian taskmasters. Your own infant brother was slaughtered by the pharaoh's soldiers.*

As for the vaunted Promised Land, it lies somewhere to the east, divided under the dominion of a dozen kings.

Four hundred years of silence, until Moses, when suddenly anything a skeptic might have wished for happened. First, God appeared in a burning bush, introducing himself to Moses by name. He spoke aloud. "My people have suffered enough," said God. "Now you will see what I will do." Next, he let loose with the most bravura display of divine power the world has ever seen. Ten times he intervened on a scale so massive that not a single person in Egypt could doubt the existence of the God of the Hebrews. Billions of frogs, gnats, flies, hailstones, and locusts gave empirical proof of the Lord of all creation.

For the next forty years, the years of wilderness wanderings, God carried his people "as a father carries his son." He fed the Israelites, clothed them, planned their daily itinerary, and fought their battles.

Is God unfair? Silent? Hidden? Such questions must have troubled the Hebrews until, in Moses' lifetime, God took off the wraps. He punished evil and rewarded good. He spoke audibly. And he made himself visible, first to Moses in a burning bush and then to the Israelites in a pillar of cloud and fire.

The response of the Israelites to such direct intervention

offers an important insight into the inherent limits of all power. Power can do everything but the most important thing: it cannot control love. The ten plagues in Exodus show the power of God over a pharaoh. But the ten major rebellions recorded in Numbers show the impotence of power to bring about what God desired most, the love and faithfulness of his people. No pyrotechnic displays of omnipotence could make them trust and follow him.

We do not need the ancient Israelites to teach us this fact. We can see it today in societies where power runs wild. In a concentration camp, as so many witnesses have told us, the guards possess nearly unlimited power. By applying force, they can make you renounce your God, curse your family, work without pay, eat human excrement, kill and then bury your closest friend or even your own mother. All this is within their power. Only one thing is not: they cannot force you to love them.

The fact that love does not operate according to the rules of power may help explain why God sometimes seems shy to use his power. He created us to love him, but his most impressive displays of miracle—the kind we may secretly long for—do nothing to foster that love. As Douglas John Hall has put it, "God's problem is not that God *is not able* to do certain things. God's problem is that God loves. Love complicates the life of God as it complicates every life."[1]

And when his own love is spurned, even the Lord of the Universe feels in some way helpless, like a parent who has lost what he values most. The Bible records a kind of diary of God's tender relationship with the Israelites:

> On the day you were born your cord was not cut, nor were you washed with water to make you clean, nor were you rubbed with salt or wrapped in cloths. No one looked on you with pity or had compassion enough to do any of these things for you. Rather, you were thrown out into the open field, for on the day you were born you were despised.
>
> Then I passed by and saw you kicking about in your blood, and as you lay there in your blood I said to you, "Live!"

71

I made you grow like a plant of the field. You grew up and developed and became the most beautiful of jewels. Your breasts were formed and your hair grew, you who were naked and bare.

Later I passed by, and when I looked at you and saw that you were old enough for love, I spread the corner of my garment over you and covered your nakedness. I gave you my solemn oath and entered into a covenant with you, declares the Sovereign Lord, and you became mine.

I bathed you with water and washed the blood from you and put ointments on you. I clothed you with an embroidered dress and put leather sandals on you. I dressed you in fine linen and covered you with costly garments. I adorned you with jewelry: I put bracelets on your arms and a necklace around your neck, and I put a ring on your nose, earrings on your ears and a beautiful crown on your head.

Yet God, all-seeing, knew the ultimate, tragic destiny of the Israelites: "I know what they are disposed to do, even before I bring them into the land," he said. As his people gathered beside the Jordan River, in an upbeat mood for a change, God allowed a remarkable glimpse into what it feels like to be God. He did not share the spirit of anticipation in the camp, and he visited Moses in the Tent of Meeting to explain why.

More than anything, God longed for the covenant to succeed: "Oh, that their hearts would be inclined to fear me and keep all my commands always, so that it might go well with them and their children forever!" But the repeated rebellions in the wilderness had taken a toll. God predicted a terrible disobedience to come and foretold his own response: "I will certainly hide my face on that day." He spoke with rueful resignation, like the parent of a drug addict, helpless to stop his own child from self-destructing; like the husband of an alcoholic who hears a blubbering promise to do better tomorrow or the next day, a promise his wife has already broken too many times to mention.

Then God gave Moses a very odd assignment. "Write down a song," he said, "and make the Israelites learn it as a witness to history." The song set God's point of view to music: the lament of a lover grieved to the point of desertion. Thus at the birth of their nation, euphoric over the crossing of the Jordan River, the Israelites premiered a kind of national anthem—the strangest that has ever been sung. It had virtually no words of hope, only doom.

They sang first of the favored times, when God found them in a howling wasteland and treasured them as the apple of his eye. They sang of the awful betrayal to come, when they would forget the God who gave them birth. They sang of the curses that would afflict them, the wasting famine, deadly plague, and arrows drunk with blood. With this bittersweet music ringing in their ears, the Israelites marched into the Promised Land.

Like a bloodhound on a trail, I keep zigzagging back to the wanderings in the wilderness to poke around for clues. The tabernacle luminous with God's presence, the miraculous breakfast food, the throng of unhappy Israelites shuffling along in the desert sand—somewhere between the bright promise and the blighted futility of those forty years lies the mystery of disappointment with God. What went wrong?

I have often longed for God to act in a direct, closeup manner. If only he would show himself! But in the Israelites' dreary stories of failure I can perceive certain "disadvantages" to God acting so directly. One problem they encountered immediately was the lack of personal freedom. For the Israelites to live in proximity to a holy God, nothing—not sex, menstruation, the content of clothing fabric, or dietary habits—could fall outside the purview of his laws. Being a "chosen people" had a cost. Just as God found it nearly impossible to live among sinful people, the Israelites found it nearly impossible to live with a holy God in their midst.

Petty things seemed to bother the Israelites most—witness their constant complaints about food. With a few exceptions, they ate the same thing every day for forty years: *manna* (meaning, literally, "What is it?") that appeared like dew on the ground each morning. A monotonous diet may seem a trivial exchange for liberation from slavery, but listen to the grumbling: "We remember the fish we ate in Egypt at no cost—also the cucumbers, melons, leeks, onions and garlic. But now we have lost our appetite; we never see anything but this manna!"

In addition to these mundane issues, a far more serious problem arose. The closer God drew toward his people, paradoxically, the more distant they felt from him. Moses laid down an amazing elaboration of rituals necessary to approach God, and no margin for error. The Israelites could see clear evidence of God's presence in the Most Holy Place—but no one dared enter. If you want to know what kind of "personal relationship with God" the Israelites enjoyed, listen to the words of the worshipers themselves: "We will die! We are lost, we are all lost! Anyone who even comes near the tabernacle of the Lord will die." And again, "Let us not hear the voice of the Lord our God nor see this great fire anymore, or we will die."

Once, as an experiment, the great scientist Isaac Newton stared at the image of the sun reflected in a mirror. The brightness burned into his retina, and he suffered temporary blindness. Even after he hid for three days behind closed shutters, still the bright spot would not fade from his vision. "I used all means to divert my imagination from the sun," he writes, "but if I thought upon him I presently saw his picture though I was in the dark." If he had stared a few minutes longer, Newton might have permanently lost all vision. The chemical receptors that govern eyesight cannot withstand the full force of unfiltered sunlight.

There is a parable in Isaac Newton's experiment, and it helps illustrate what the Israelites ultimately learned from the wilderness wanderings. They had attempted to live with the Lord of the Universe visibly present in their midst; but, in the end, out of all the thousands who had so gladly fled Egypt, only two survived God's Presence. If you can barely endure candlelight, how can you gaze at the sun?

"Who of us can dwell with the consuming fire?" asked the prophet Isaiah. Is it possible that we should be grateful for God's hiddenness, rather than disappointed?

[1]Douglas John Hall, *God and Human Suffering*, 156.

Bible references: Exodus 1–12; Deuteronomy 1; Ezekiel 16; Deuteronomy 31, 5, 31–32; Numbers 11, 17; Deuteronomy 18; Isaiah 33.

Chapter 9

One Shining Moment

NINE-YEAR-OLD Leo Tolstoy, convinced God would help him fly, dove headfirst out a third-floor window and had his first major crisis of disappointment with God. Fortunately, Tolstoy survived the crash landing and, years later, could laugh at his childish test of faith.

What child has not fantasized about supernatural powers? *Lord, help me walk across this lake. Help me beat up that bully. Make me smart without having to study.* And if God ever saw fit to answer some of those prayers, if, like a genie in a bottle, he granted us any wish we wanted, wouldn't we then try to please him out of gratitude? In my dark hours of disappointment, I instinctively think like that: *If God can get me out . . . if things calm down . . . if I get well . . . then I'll follow God.*

My friend Richard believed that anyone would, like a faithful puppy, follow a God who acted fairly, spoke clearly, and made himself obvious. The wilderness wanderings of the Israelites prove him wrong. But, some might argue, their faith faltered in a harsh land, a place remembered by Moses as a "vast and dreadful desert, that thirsty and waterless land, with its venomous snakes and scorpions." Who wouldn't lose heart in those circumstances. Were there happier times, when God seemed close *and* granted his people their desires?

The tone of the Old Testament brightens when the name David shows up. "Then the Lord awoke as from sleep, as a man wakes from the stupor of wine," Psalm 78 says about those days. God had at last found a man after his own heart, the kind of person he could build a nation around. Lusty King David broke every law on the books save one: he loved God with all his heart, all his mind, and all his soul. With David installed as king over Israel, dreams of the covenant came surging back.

And when David's son Solomon took the throne, God pulled out all the stops. What children only dream of, Solomon got. God offered him any wish—long life, riches, anything at all—and when Solomon chose wisdom God added bonus gifts of wealth, honor, and peace. He would rule over a Golden Age, a shining moment of tranquillity in the long, tormented history of the Hebrews.

Solomon

He took over the throne of Israel as a teenager and soon became the richest person of his time. The Bible says that silver was as common in Jerusalem as stones. A fleet of trading ships sought out exotica for the king's private collections—apes and baboons from Africa—and ivory and gold by the ton. Solomon had artistic talent as well: he wrote 1005 songs and 3000 proverbs.

Rulers traveled hundreds of miles to test Solomon's wisdom firsthand and to see the great city he had built. One such ruler, the queen of Sheba, said to him:

> The report I heard in my own country about your achievements and your wisdom is true. But I did not believe these things until I came and saw with my own eyes. Indeed, not even half was told me; in wisdom and wealth you have far

exceeded the report I heard. How happy your men must be! How happy your officials, who continually stand before you and hear your wisdom! Praise be to the Lord your God, who has delighted in you and placed you on the throne of Israel.

Impressive words from a queen who, as a farewell gift, gave Solomon four and a half tons of pure gold.

And what did God feel during these halcyon days? Relief, pleasure, delight—the Bible hints at all these. Israel's chronic grumblers had died off, and Solomon went out of his way to make God feel loved. He lavished the wealth of his kingdom on a tremendous temple, fashioned by 200,000 workmen, that ranked as one of the wonders of the world. From a distance, it shone like a snowcapped mountain.

Old Testament history reached a high-water mark on the day Solomon dedicated that temple to God. Think of a movie scene of the most blinding encounter with an extraterrestrial being. Something like that happened in Jerusalem, only this was no illusion staged by special-effects crews. Thousands of people were looking on in a huge public ceremony. When the glory of the Lord came down to fill the temple, even the priests were driven back by the blast.

God was making Solomon's temple the center of his activity on earth, and the crowd spontaneously decided to stay another two weeks to celebrate. Kneeling on a bronze platform, Solomon prayed aloud, "I have indeed built a magnificent temple for you, a place for you to dwell forever." Then he caught himself in astonishment. "But will God really dwell on earth? The heavens, even the highest heaven, cannot contain you. How much less this temple I have built!"

Later, God responded: "I have heard the prayer and plea you have made before me; I have consecrated this temple. . . . My eyes and my heart will always be there." God had done it! His promises to Abraham and Moses had finally come true. The Israelites now had land, a nation with secure boundaries, and a gleaming symbol of God's presence among them. No one present on the famous day of the temple dedication could doubt God;

everyone saw the fire and the cloud of his presence. And all this came to pass not in a harsh desert full of snakes and scorpions, but in a land rich with silver and gold.

With everything imaginable working in his favor, at first it seemed Solomon would gratefully follow God. His prayer of dedication for the temple in 1 Kings 8 is one of the most majestic ever prayed. Yet by the end of his reign Solomon had squandered away nearly every advantage. The poetic man who had sung of romantic love broke all records for promiscuity: seven hundred wives in all, and three hundred concubines! The wise man who had composed so many commonsense proverbs flouted them with an extravagance that has never been equaled. And to please his foreign-born wives, the devout man who had built the temple of God took a final, terrible step: he introduced idol worship into God's holy city.

In one generation, Solomon took Israel from a fledgling kingdom dependent on God for bare survival to a self-sufficient political power. But along the way he lost sight of the original vision to which God had called them. Ironically, by the time of Solomon's death, Israel resembled the Egypt they had escaped: an imperial state held in place by a bloated bureaucracy and slave labor, with an official state religion under the ruler's command. Success in the kingdom of this world had crowded out interest in the kingdom of God. The brief, shining vision of a covenant nation faded away, and God withdrew his sanction. After Solomon's death, Israel split in two and slid toward ruin.

A quotation from Oscar Wilde might provide the best epitaph for Solomon: "In this world there are only two tragedies. One is not getting what one wants, and the other is getting it." Solomon got whatever he wanted, especially when it came to symbols of power and status. Gradually, he depended less on God and more on the props around him: the world's largest harem, a house twice the size of the temple, an army well-stocked with chariots, a strong economy. Success may have eliminated any crises of disappointment with God, but it also seemed to eliminate Solomon's desire for God at all. The more he enjoyed the world's good gifts, the less he thought about the Giver.

In the wilderness God dwelt in a pillar of fire and cloud, so nearby that his power sometimes "broke out" with destructive force. In Solomon's day God seemed to restrict that power, giving the king authority to represent him to the people. As for the Israelites, who had shrunk in fear from God in the wilderness, they simply took God for granted once his presence was centered in the temple. He became just another part of the royal landscape.

In response to this change, God quietly turned elsewhere. You can easily detect the shift by scanning the Old Testament, which gives lengthy accounts of the first three kings of Israel— Saul, David, and Solomon; but after Solomon, stories of the kings speed up into a forgettable blur. God turned instead to his prophets.

Bible references: Deuteronomy 8; 2 Samuel 7; 1 Kings 8–10.

Chapter 10

Fire and the Word

It was an unholy coincidence that many took to be divine retribution. Two weeks ago, canon David Jenkins, 59, who had publicly asserted that neither the Virgin birth nor the Resurrection need be taken too literally, was formally consecrated as Bishop of Durham in York Minster amid cries of protest. Less than three days later, in the early hours of the morning, lightning forked down on the wooden roof of the minster's 13th century south transept. By 2:30 A.M., flames were leaping from the medieval masterpiece that is the largest Gothic cathedral in Northern Europe. . . . Jenkins' detractors lost no time in claiming that their views had been vindicated. . . . a vicar who had been evicted from the minster for voicing protests in the midst of the new bishop's consecration ceremony suggested that "divine intervention" might have caused the fire. Others . . . cit[ed] the prophet Elijah, who brought down a fire from heaven, which destroyed an altar he had built in the presence of the prophets of Baal.

—*Time*, July 23, 1984

The problem with the York Minster lightning bolt, of course, is that it stands as such an exception. So fire from the heavens hits a famous church—what about all the Unitarian churches that brashly deny orthodox Christian doctrines, not to mention the Muslim mosques and Hindu temples? Why should David Jenkins provoke divine wrath when the outright blasphemer Bertrand Russell lived unpunished into cranky old age? If God consistently sent lightning bolts in response to bad doctrine, our planet would sparkle nightly like a Christmas tree.

And yet fire did fall from heaven once, almost thirty centuries ago, and ministers ever since have harked back to that scene on Mount Carmel. The story has a mythic, Tolkienesque quality to it: like Frodo on his mission to Mordor, Elijah journeyed across Israel to a rugged desert mountain to wage war, single-combat style, against 850 false prophets.

Elijah, the wildest and woolliest prophet of Israel, worked the crowd like a master magician. He doused the site with twelve large jars of water—a most precious commodity after three years of drought. And just when it seemed Elijah was perpetrating a huge national joke, it happened. A ball of fire dropped like a meteor from a clear sky. The heat was so intense it melted the stones and soil, and flames lapped up water from the trenches like fuel. The crowd dropped to the ground in fear and awe. "The Lord—he is God! The Lord—he is God!" they cried.

In a dramatic public showdown, God clobbered the forces of evil. No wonder the scene looms large in the annals of faith. No wonder the people of Jesus' day mistook him for Elijah reincarnate. Even in modern times, when lightning strikes a cathedral, some wistfully recall Mount Carmel.

Yet when I sat in a Colorado cabin and read straight through the Bible, I saw the life of Elijah in a very different light. He and his miracle-working twin Elisha emerged not as prototypes of the Old Testament prophet, but as stellar exceptions: few successors had even a trace of their ability to work miracles. If we yearn for their power, we yearn for the wrong thing. The signs and wonders of Elijah's day were a blip in history, with no long-term effect on the Israelites. No wildfire revivals broke out, and after the briefest flurry of religious fervor, the nation settled back into its long, steady slide away from God. King Ahab, himself a spectator at Mount Carmel, left a legacy as Israel's wickedest king.

Apparently the fireball on Mount Carmel had no lasting impact on Elijah either. Terrified for his life, the prophet put forty days' distance between himself and Queen Jezebel, Ahab's vengeful consort. And when God next met with Elijah, he did not appear in a fire, or in a great and powerful wind, or in an earthquake. Rather, he came in a whisper, a thin, small voice almost like silence—a preview of a striking change to come.

The Prophets

It must have been hard to follow the prophet Elijah. Not long after the showdown on Mount Carmel another prophet, Micaiah, stood before the same king, Ahab, in very similar circumstances. Elijah-like, he faced down four hundred false prophets and delivered a stinging message from God. But instead of fire falling from heaven, Micaiah got a slap in the face and a stint in jail.

After Elijah and Elisha, God seemed to rein in his supernatural power, turning from spectacle to word. Most prophets—Isaiah, Hosea, Habakkuk, Jeremiah, Ezekiel—had no stunning displays of omnipotence to dangle before an audience; they had only the power of words. And as God seemed to draw farther and farther away, these prophets themselves began to ask questions: eloquent questions, haunting questions, questions wrapped in pain. They voiced aloud the cries of a people who felt abandoned by God.

I had always misread the prophets—when I bothered to read them at all. I had seen them as finger-wagging, fusty old men who, like Elijah, called down judgment on the pagans. I discovered to my surprise that the ancient prophets' writings actually sound the most "modern" of any part of the Bible. They deal with the very same themes that hang like a cloud over our century: the silence of God, the seeming sovereignty of evil, the unrelieved suffering in the world. The prophets' questions are, in fact, the questions of this book: God's unfairness, silence, hiddenness.

More passionately than anyone in history, the prophets of

Israel gave voice to the feeling of disappointment with God. Why do godless nations flourish? they asked. Why is there such poverty and depravity in the world? Why so few miracles? Where are you, God? "Why do you always forget us? Why do you forsake us so long?" Show yourself; break your silence. For God's sake, literally, ACT!

There was the urbane voice of Isaiah, an aristocrat and adviser to kings, in personal style as far removed from Elijah as Winston Churchill was from Gandhi. "Truly you are a God who hides himself," Isaiah said. "Oh, that you would rend the heavens and come down, that the mountains would tremble before you!"

Jeremiah loudly protested the failure of "success theology." In his day, prophets were being tossed in dungeons and wells, and even sawed in half. Jeremiah compared God to a weakling, "a man taken by surprise . . . a warrior powerless to save." Voltaire himself could not have put it better: How can an all-powerful and all-loving God permit such a messed-up world?

Habakkuk challenged God to explain why, as he put it, "justice never prevails."

> How long, O Lord, must I call for help,
>   but you do not listen?
> Or cry out to you, "Violence!"
>   but you do not save?
> Why do you make me look at injustice?
>   Why do you tolerate wrong?

Like all Israelites, the prophets had been raised on victory stories. As children they had learned how God freed his people from slavery, descended to live among them, and carried them into the Promised Land. But now in visions of the future they saw, in slow-motion detail, all those victories being undone. In a stark reversal of the unforgettable scene from Solomon's day, the prophet Ezekiel watched God's glory rise, hover above the temple for a moment, and then vanish.

What Ezekiel saw in a vision, Jeremiah saw in stark reality. Babylonian soldiers entered the temple—pagans in the Most Holy Place!—looted it, then burned it to the ground. (Historians record that as they entered the temple the soldiers swept the empty air with their spears, seeking the unseen Hebrew God.) Jeremiah wandered the deserted streets of Jerusalem in a state of shock, like a survivor of Hiroshima staggering through the rubble. Israel's king was now shackled and blinded, the nation's princes slaughtered. In the final siege, Jerusalem's gentle women had cooked and eaten their own children.

How did it feel to be a prophet then? Jeremiah tells us:

> Since my people are crushed, I am crushed;
> I mourn, and horror grips me. . . .
> Oh, that my head were a spring of water
> and my eyes a fountain of tears!
> I would weep day and night
> for the slain of my people. . . .
> My heart is broken within me;
> all my bones tremble.
> I am like a drunken man,
> like a man overcome by wine.

But the most amazing feature of the prophets is not their "modern" outlook or their passionate cry of disappointment. The reason these seventeen books merit a close look is that they include God's own reply to the prophets' bracing questions.

Bible references: 1 Kings 17–19, 22; Lamentations 5; Isaiah 45, 64; Jeremiah 14; Habakkuk 1; Jeremiah 8–9, 23.

Chapter 11

Wounded Lover

G OD TALKED BACK, defending the way he ran the world. He lashed out, stormed, and wept. And this is what he said: *I am not silent; I have been speaking through my prophets.*

We tend to rank God's revelations by their dramatic effect, with spectacular personal appearances at the top, supernatural miracles just below, and the words of the prophets at the bottom. The fireball on Mount Carmel, for example, seems more convincing than one of Jeremiah's doleful sermons. But God acknowledged no such rating. In an ironic twist, he pointed to the prophets themselves—the very people who were questioning his silence—as proof of his concern. How can a nation complain about the silence of God when they have the likes of Ezekiel and Jeremiah and Daniel and Isaiah?

God did not consider "mere words" an inferior form of proof. Miracles, after all, had never had much lasting impact on the Israelites' faith; but the prophets would inscribe a permanent record, to be passed down over generations, of God's overtures toward his people. Sometimes God pointed to past miracles as proofs of his love, but more often he said something like this, in the familiar tone of an exasperated parent: "From the time your forefathers left Egypt until now, day after day, again and again I sent you my servants the prophets. But they did not listen to me or pay attention." God concluded that the people did not really want a word from the Lord, and they proved him right, warning Isaiah, "Tell us pleasant things, prophesy illusions . . . and stop confronting us with the Holy One of Israel."

I have indeed withdrawn my presence.

When the prophets complained loudly about God's hiddenness, God didn't argue. He agreed with them, and then explained why he was keeping his distance.

To Jeremiah, God expressed his disgust with what he saw in Israel: dishonest gain, the shedding of innocent blood, oppression, extortion. He covered his eyes, he said, refusing even to see hands spread out in a posture of prayer, for those hands were covered with blood.

To Ezekiel, God explained that once Israel's rebellions had passed a certain point, he simply "gave them over" to their sins. He withdrew, letting the people choose their own way and bear the consequences.

To Zechariah, he said, "When I called, they did not listen; so when they called, I would not listen."

My slowness to act is a sign of mercy, not of weakness.

When God did not punish quickly, the people of Israel presumed he had lost his power: "He will do nothing! No harm will come to us; we will never see sword or famine." They were wrong. God's restraint marked an interlude of mercy, a time of probation he was granting Israel. Reluctantly, like a parent out of options, God resorted to punishment.

For Israel, punishment took the form of foreign invasions. But the prophets also speak of a "day of the Lord" at the end of time. Sandwiched between their shining accounts of a new heaven and new earth are some of the most dreadful apocalyptic visions ever set to words. Before we can hear the last word, said Dietrich Bonhoeffer, we must listen to the next-to-the-last word. And the more I study the prophets' accounts of the last days, the more content I become with God's apparent "shyness" to intervene in human affairs.

In my own times of disappointment with God, I have called on him to act with power. I have prayed against political tyranny and unfairness and injustice. I have prayed for miracle, for proof of God's existence. But as I read the prophets' descriptions of the day when God finally will take off all the wraps, one prayer overwhelms all others: "God, I hope I'm not around then." God freely admits he is holding back his power, but he restrains himself for our benefit. For all scoffers who call for direct action from the heavens, the prophets have ominous advice: Just wait.

Though my judgments appear stern, I am suffering with you.

God exposed his deepest feelings to the prophets. For example, here is how he felt about the destruction of Moab, one of Israel's enemies:

> I wail over Moab,
>   for all Moab I cry out. . . .
> My heart laments for Moab like a flute.

As for his chosen people of Israel, whatever shame and humiliation they endured, God also endured. The Israelites watched in horror as Babylonian axmen hacked apart the cedar beams of the temple—but it was God's own house they were invading, and he felt that invasion as a personal desecration. As the temple was razed, his dwelling place was razed. As the Jews were led captive, he was led captive. And when the conquerors divided the spoils of Israel, they joked not about the Israelites but about their weakling God. "Wherever they went among the nations they profaned my holy name, for it was said of them, 'These are the Lord's people, and yet they had to leave his land.'"

A single, elegant sentence from Isaiah summarizes God's point of view: "In all their distress he too was distressed." God may have hidden his face, but that face was streaked with tears.

Despite everything, I am ready to forgive at any moment.

Often, in the midst of a stern reproof, God would stop—literally midsentence—and beg Israel to repent. Ahab, the most wicked king of Israel, got another chance after Mount Carmel, and then another, and another. "I take no pleasure in the death of the wicked," God explained to Ezekiel. "Turn! Turn from your evil ways! Why will you die, O house of Israel?" He told Jeremiah that if he could find just one honest person in Jerusalem, he would spare the whole city.

Nothing expresses God's yearning to forgive better than the Book of Jonah. It contains but one line of prophecy: "Forty more days and Nineveh will be overturned." But, to Jonah's disgust, that simple announcement of doom sparked a spiritual revival in hated Nineveh and changed God's plans for punishment. Jonah, sulking under a shriveled vine, admitted he had suspected God's soft heart all along. "I knew that you are a gracious and compassionate God, slow to anger and abounding in love, a God who relents from sending calamity." Thus the whole madcap scenario of balky prophet, ocean storm, and whale detour came about because Jonah could not trust God—could not, that is, trust him to be harsh and unrelenting toward Nineveh. As Robert Frost summed up the story, "After Jonah, you could never trust God not to be merciful again."

Passion

Although God answered the prophets' questions directly, his explanations did not satisfy Israel. Knowing the reason behind a disaster does not lessen the sense of pain and betrayal. And in truth God's rational "defense" seems tossed in almost as an aside. The prophets are not as concerned about intellectual questions as they are about God's *passion*. How does it feel to be God? To understand, consider the human images stressed again and again by the prophets: God as parent, and as lover.

Follow around some first-time parents. Their conversation seems limited to one topic: The Child. They crow that their wrinkled, ruddy baby is the most beautiful child ever born. They spend hundreds of dollars on equipment to videotape the first babbling words and the first lurching steps—ordinary skills mastered by almost all five billion people on earth. Such strange behavior expresses a new parent's pride and joy in a human relationship like no other.

In choosing Israel, God was seeking such a relationship. He wanted what any parent wants: a happy household of children who return their parent's love. His voice sings with pride as he reminisces about the early days: "Is not Ephraim my dear son, the child in whom I delight?" But the joy fades away as God abruptly shifts from the perspective of a parent to that of a lover, a wounded lover. *What have I done wrong?* he demands in a tone of sadness, and horror, and rage.

> I supplied all their needs,
>   yet they committed adultery
>   and thronged to the houses of prostitutes.
> They are well-fed, lusty stallions,
>   each neighing for another man's wife.
> Should I not punish them for this?

In reading the prophets I cannot help envisioning a counselor with God as a client. The counselor gets out one stock sentence, "Tell me how you really feel," and then God takes over.

"I'll tell you how I feel! I feel like a rejected parent. I find a baby girl lying in a ditch, near death. I take her home and make her my daughter. I clean her, pay for her schooling, feed her. I dote on her, clothe her, hang jewelry on her. Then one day she runs away. I hear reports of her debased life. When my name comes up, she curses me.

"I'll tell you how I feel! I feel like a jilted lover. I found my lover thin and wasted, abused, but I brought her home and made her beauty shine. She is my precious one, the most beautiful woman in the world to me, and I lavish on her gifts and love. And yet she forsakes me. She pants after my best friends, my enemies—anyone. She stands by a highway and under every spreading tree and, worse than a prostitute, she *pays* people to have sex with her. I feel betrayed, abandoned, cuckolded."

God does not hide his hurt. He employs shocking language, comparing Israel to "a swift she-camel running here and there, a wild donkey accustomed to the desert, sniffing the wind in her craving—in her heat who can restrain her?"

As if words alone were too weak to convey his passion, God asked one brave prophet, Hosea, to act out a living parable. On God's orders, Hosea married Gomer, a woman with a most unsavory reputation. From then on, the poor man lived a soap-opera existence. Time after time Gomer wandered off, fell for another man, and moved out. And each time, incredibly, God instructed Hosea to welcome Gomer back and forgive her.

God used Hosea's unhappy story to illustrate his own whipsaw emotions. That first blush of love when he found Israel, God said, was like finding grapes in the desert. But as Israel broke his trust again and again, he was forced to endure the awful shame of a wounded lover. His words carry a tone not far from self-pity: "I am like a moth to Ephraim, like rot to the people of Judah."

The powerful image of a jilted lover explains why, in his speeches to the prophets, God seems to "change his mind" every few seconds. He is preparing to obliterate Israel—wait, now he is weeping, holding out open arms—no, he is sternly pronouncing judgment again. Those shifting moods seem hopelessly irrational, except to anyone who has been jilted by a lover.

The words of the prophets sound like the words of a lovers' quarrel drifting through thin apartment walls. A neighbor of mine endured two years of such conflict. In November she was ready to kill her unfaithful husband. In February she forgave him and invited him back in. In April she filed for divorce. In August she stopped the proceedings and asked her husband to return again. It took two years for her to face the ugly truth that her love had been rejected forever.

And that is the precise cycle of anger, grief, forgiveness, jealousy, love, pain that God himself went through. The prophets show God struggling for a language, any language, that might break through to his people. Just as my neighbor would hang up the phone on her estranged husband, God would tell the prophets that he would no longer listen to the prayers of Israel. And just as my friend would soften, God would soften and beg his people to try again. Sometimes his love and anger seemed to collide. But at last, all alternatives exhausted, God concluded that he must give up: "What else can I do because of the sin of my people?"

My friend Richard described to me his deep sense of betrayal when God "let him down." He felt exactly as he had when his fiancee abruptly cut him off. But the prophets, and especially Hosea, communicate one message above all others: God is the betrayed one. It was Israel, not God, who had gone a-whoring. The prophets of Israel had expressed a profound disappointment in God, accusing him of acting aloof, unconcerned, silent. But when God spoke, he poured out emotions pent up for centuries. And he, not Israel, was the truly disappointed party.

"What else can I do?" God's poignant question to Jeremiah points up the dilemma of an omnipotent God who has made room for freedom. The stork in the sky knows her seasons, the ocean tide rolls in on schedule, snow always covers the high mountains, but human beings are like nothing else in nature. God cannot control them. Yet he cannot simply thrust them aside either. He cannot get humanity out of his mind.

Bible references: Jeremiah 7; Isaiah 30; Jeremiah 5; Ezekiel 20; Zechariah 7; Jeremiah 5, 48; Ezekiel 36; Isaiah 63; Ezekiel 33; Jonah 3–4; Jeremiah 31, 5, 2; Hosea 9, 5; Jeremiah 9.

Chapter 12

Too Good To Be True

Grief melts away
Like snow in May,
As if there were no such cold thing.
                    —*George Herbert, ''The Flower''*

O NE DAY when George MacDonald, the great Scottish preacher and writer, was talking with his son, the conversation turned to heaven and the prophets' version of the end of all things. "It seems too good to be true," the son said at one point. A smile crossed MacDonald's whiskered face. "Nay," he replied, "it is just so good it must be true!"[1]

Does any human emotion run as deep as hope? Fairy tales pass on through the centuries a stubborn hope in a happy ending, a belief that in the end the wicked witch will die and the brave and innocent children will somehow find a way of escape. A dozen cartoons in a row on Saturday morning television crank out a similar message to children who sit enthralled, too young to sneer at impossibly cheery endings. In real life, a mother caught in a war zone holds her infant son tight against her breast, pats his head, and whispers, illogically, "It'll be all right," even as the percussive blasts grow closer.

Where does such hope come from? Searching for words to explain the ageless attraction of fairy tales, Tolkien said:

> [Fairy tale] does not deny the existence of . . . sorrow and failure: the possibility of these is necessary to the joy of the deliverance; it denies (in the face of much evidence, if you will) universal final defeat . . . giving a fleeting glimpse of Joy, Joy beyond the walls of the world, poignant as grief.[2]

No summary of the prophets would be complete apart from one last message: their loud insistence that the world will not end in "universal final defeat," but in Joy. They spoke in foreboding times to audiences filled with fear, and often their dire predictions of droughts and locust plagues and enemy sieges fueled that fear. But always, in every one of their seventeen books, the prophets of the Old Testament got around to a word of hope. The wounded lover will recover from his pain, Isaiah promises: "For a brief moment I abandoned you, but with deep compassion I will bring you back."

Their voices soar like songbirds' when the prophets turn at last to describe the Joy beyond the walls of the world. In that final day, God will roll up the earth like a carpet and weave it anew. Wolves and lambs will feed together in the same field, and a lion graze in peace beside an ox.

One day, says Malachi, we will leap like calves released from the stall. There will be no fear then, and no pain. No infants will die; no tears will fall. Among the nations, peace will flow like a river, and armies will melt their weapons into farm tools. No one will complain about the hiddenness of God in that day. His glory will fill the earth, and the sun will seem dim by contrast.

For the prophets, human history is not an end in itself but a transition time, a parenthesis between Eden and the new heaven and new earth still to be formed by God. Even when everything seems out of control, God is firmly in control, and someday will assert himself. *

The Meantime

But what about right now? Must we wait past death for all meaningful answers to the problem of disappointment with God? After the prophets had died off, the Jewish people began to raise such questions, for once again the heavens went silent: "We are given no miraculous signs; no prophets are left, and none of us knows how long this will be. How long will the enemy mock you, O God?"

Torn from their homeland and sold once more into bondage, the Jews hung onto the prophets' promises of a deliverer and a peaceful future. As the decades, even centuries passed, empires—Babylon, Persia, Egypt, Greece, Syria, Rome—rose and fell, their armies chasing each other across the plains of Palestine. Each new empire subjugated the Jews with ease, as if scraping their feet on a doormat. Sometimes the entire race verged on extinction.

No Moses figure appeared to lead the Jews out of bondage. No Elijahs called down fireballs from heaven. No luminous glow radiated from the temple in Jerusalem. Until King Herod came along with his penchant for ostentatious buildings, the temple site remained half-finished, a pile of rubble recalling more shame than glory.

---

*Some people find no comfort in the prophets' vision of a future world. "Mere pie in the sky," they say. "The church has used that line for centuries to justify slavery, oppression, and all manner of injustice. They force-feed the hope of heaven to the poor in order to keep them from demanding too much on earth." The criticism sticks because the church has abused the prophets' vision. But you will never find that "pie in the sky" rationale in the prophets themselves. Amos, Hosea, Isaiah, and Jeremiah have scathing words about the need to care for widows and orphans and aliens, and to clean up corrupt courts and religious systems. The people of God are not merely to mark time, waiting for God to step in and set right all that is wrong. Rather, they are to model the new heaven and new earth, and by so doing awaken longings for what God will someday bring to pass.

At the end of the Old Testament, God was in hiding. He had threatened to hide his face, and when he finally did a dark shadow fell across the planet. Our disappointment with God twenty-five centuries later is a faint aftershock of what the Jews felt when God turned his back. Today, we may find some comfort in looking back on lessons from the past. We may see the "disadvantages" to God's closeup interventions: his Presence, too bright for us, leaves scorch marks; it creates distance; and worse, it doesn't even seem to foster faith. We may also find comfort in looking ahead to eternal life free of tears and pain, in a new dimension somewhere, after we're transformed into beings who can endure God's Presence. But what of the meantime? The mean times? Like the Jews, we feel God's hiddenness as a disappointment, an aching in the heart, a doubt never fully set to rest.

Four centuries separate the last words of Malachi in the Old Testament from the first words of Matthew in the New Testament. "The four hundred silent years," they are called, and that phrase marks an era bordered by disappointment with God. Did God care? Was he even alive? He seemed deaf to the Jews' prayers. Still, despite everything, they waited for a Messiah—they had no other hope.

"What else can I do?" God had asked. There was something else. What could not be won through power, he would win through suffering.

God weeps with us so that we may one day laugh with him.
                                          —*Jürgen Moltmann*

[1]Greville MacDonald, *George MacDonald and His Wife*, 172.
[2]J. R. R. Tolkien, *The Tolkien Reader*, 68–69.

Bible references: Isaiah 54; Malachi 4; Psalm 74.

Part Three

Drawing Closer:
The Son

Chapter 13

The Descent

S UPPOSE THERE WAS A KING who loved a humble maiden,"
begins a story by Kierkegaard.

*The king was like no other king. Every statesman trembled before
his power. No one dared breathe a word against him, for he had the
strength to crush all opponents. And yet this mighty king was melted by
love for a humble maiden.*

*How could he declare his love for her? In an odd sort of way, his
very kingliness tied his hands. If he brought her to the palace and
crowned her head with jewels and clothed her body in royal robes, she
would surely not resist—no one dared resist him. But would she love
him?*

*She would say she loved him, of course, but would she truly? Or
would she live with him in fear, nursing a private grief for the life she
had left behind. Would she be happy at his side? How could he know?*

*If he rode to her forest cottage in his royal carriage, with an armed
escort waving bright banners, that too would overwhelm her. He did not
want a cringing subject. He wanted a lover, an equal. He wanted her to*

forget that he was a king and she a humble maiden and to let shared love cross over the gulf between them.

"For it is only in love that the unequal can be made equal," concluded Kierkegaard. The king, convinced he could not elevate the maiden without crushing her freedom, resolved to *descend*. He clothed himself as a beggar and approached her cottage incognito, with a worn cloak fluttering loosely about him. It was no mere disguise, but a new identity he took on. He renounced the throne to win her hand.[1]

What Kierkegaard expressed in parable form, the apostle Paul expressed in these words about Jesus the Christ:

> Who, being in very nature God,
> did not consider equality with God
> something to be grasped,
> but made himself nothing,
> taking the very nature of a servant,
> being made in human likeness.
> And being found in appearance as a man,
> he humbled himself
> and became obedient to death—
> even death on a cross!

In his dealings with human beings, God had often humbled himself. I see the Old Testament as one long record of his "condescensions" ("to descend to be with"). God condescended in various ways to speak to Abraham, and to Moses, and to the nation of Israel and the prophets. But no condescension could match what came next, after the four hundred years of silence. God, like the king in Kierkegaard's parable, took on a new form: he became a man. It was the most shocking descent imaginable.

Fear Not

We hear the words every Christmas season at church pageants when children dress up in bathrobes and act out the story of Jesus' birth. "Fear not!" lisps the six-year-old angel, his bedsheet costume dragging the ground, his coat-hanger-frame wings flapping ever so slightly from the trembling of his body. He sneaks a glance at the script hidden in the folds of his sleeve. "Fear not, for I bring you good tidings of great joy." Already he has appeared to Zechariah (his older brother with a taped-on cotton beard) and to Mary (a freckled blonde from the second grade). He used the same greeting for both, "Fear not! . . ."

These were also God's first words to Abraham, and to Hagar, and to Isaac. "Fear not!" the angel said in greeting Gideon and the prophet Daniel. For supernatural beings, that phrase served almost as the equivalent of "Hello, how are you?" Little wonder. By the time the supernatural being spoke, the human being was usually lying face down in a cataleptic state. When God made contact with planet Earth, sometimes the supernatural encounter sounded like thunder, sometimes it stirred the air like a whirlwind, and sometimes it lit up the scene like a flash of phosphorous. Nearly always it caused fear. But the angel who visited Zechariah and Mary and Joseph heralded that God was about to appear in a form that would not frighten.

What could be less scary than a newborn baby with jerky limbs and eyes that do not quite focus? In Jesus, born in a barn or cave and laid in a feeding trough, God found at last a mode of approach that humanity need not fear. The king had cast off his robes.

Think of the condescension involved: the Incarnation, which sliced history into two parts (a fact even our calendars grudgingly acknowledge), had more animal than human witnesses. Think, too, of the risk. In the Incarnation, God spanned the vast chasm of fear that had distanced him from his human creation. But removing that barrier made Jesus vulnerable, terribly vulnerable.

> The child born in the night among beasts. The sweet breath and steaming dung of beasts. And nothing is ever the same again.
>
> Those who believe in God can never in a way be sure of him again. Once they have seen him in a stable, they can never be sure where he will appear or to what lengths he will go or to what ludicrous depths of self-humiliation he will descend in his wild pursuit of man. . . .

For those who believe in God, it means, this birth, that God himself is never safe from us, and maybe that is the dark side of Christmas, the terror of the silence. He comes in such a way that we can always turn him down, as we could crack the baby's skull like an eggshell or nail him up when he gets too big for that.[2]

How did Christmas day feel to God? Imagine for a moment becoming a baby again: giving up language and muscle coordination, and the ability to eat solid food and control your bladder. God as a fetus! Or imagine yourself becoming a sea slug—that analogy is probably closer. On that day in Bethlehem, the Maker of All That Is took form as a helpless, dependent newborn.

"Kenosis" is the technical word theologians use to describe Christ emptying himself of the advantages of deity. Ironically, while the emptying involved much humiliation, it also involved a kind of freedom. I have spoken of the "disadvantages" of infinity. A physical body freed Christ to act on a human scale, without those "disadvantages." He could say what he wanted without his voice blasting the treetops. He could express anger by calling King Herod a fox or by reaching for a bullwhip in the temple, rather than shaking the earth with his stormy presence. And he could talk to anyone—a prostitute, a blind man, a widow, a leper—without first having to announce, "Fear not!"

> 'Twas much, that man was made like God before,
> But that God should be made like man, much more.
> —John Donne, "Holy Sonnet 15"

[1] Paraphrase of Søren Kierkegaard, *Philosophical Fragments*, 31–43.
[2] Frederick Buechner, *The Hungering Dark*, 13–14.

Bible reference: Philippians 2.

Chapter 14

Great Expectations

E VERY YEAR around Christmastime the air vibrates with lyrical promises of the Messiah. From high school choristers to distinguished professionals, musicians trek to practices as if on a pilgrimage, clutching sheet music tattered from overuse. Nowadays you don't even have to belong to a choir to sing the famous prophecies that Handel set to music; most major cities offer a "Do-It-Yourself *Messiah*" (amazing phrase!) open to all.

And what is it that we celebrate in grand concert style? These are the words Handel lifted from the biblical prophets:

> Every valley shall be exalted, and every mountain and hill made low; the crooked straight, and the rough places plain.
>
> The people that walked in darkness have seen a great light: and they that dwell in the land of the shadow of death, upon them hath the light shined.
>
> For unto us a Child is born, unto us a Son is given, and the government shall be upon His shoulder: and His name

shall be called Wonderful, Counsellor, the Mighty God, the Everlasting Father, the Prince of Peace.

Those same words were on the lips of faithful Jews during the years of God's silence. Disappointment, even despair, metastasized throughout Israel as history, ever crueler, destroyed all hopes but one: the prophets' promise of a King of Kings. When the Messiah comes, then at last justice will roll down like a river—the Jews clung to that promise fiercely, like capsized sailors clinging to a life raft.

Four centuries after the last biblical prophet, strange rumors started circulating: first about a desert prophet named John, and then about Jesus, a carpenter's son from Nazareth. As word of Jesus' miraculous powers began to leak out, speculation spread. Could he be the One? Some insisted the Messiah truly had come. With their own eyes they had seen Jesus heal the blind and make the lame walk. "God has come to help his people!" they declared when he raised a young man from death. Others remained skeptical. Jesus fulfilled the messianic promises, but—an important but—not in the way anyone expected.

When I went through the Bible searching for signs of disappointment with God, I expected to find a decisive change when I reached the Gospels. The prophets' Messiah—as a quick scan of Handel's libretto easily shows—would seem to dispel such feelings. To the contrary, disappointment did not vanish from the earth in Jesus' day, and has not vanished yet, two thousand years later. What went wrong? Or, ask the question another way: What did Jesus' life contribute to the three questions that stalk this book?

Is God silent? "Follow me!" "This, then, is how you should pray." "We are going up to Jerusalem." In certain respects, Jesus made God's will clearer than it had ever been before. Incredibly, he opened himself to the scientific method of investigation, which is exactly what he got from Pharisees, Sadducees, and other skeptics. Anyone could walk right up to the Son of God and ask a question or debate with him. As the Gospels tell it, God broke his silence loudly and convincingly while Jesus lived on earth: the *Word* was made flesh.

Is God hidden? With Jesus, God actually took on a shape in the world, acquiring a face, a name, and an address. He was a God you could touch and smell and hear and see. "Anyone who has seen me has seen the Father," Jesus said bluntly.

And yet Jesus' visibility, his very ordinariness, introduced a new problem for Jews raised on stories of Mount Sinai and Mount Carmel. Where was the smoke, the fire, the burst of light? Jesus did not match their image of what God should look like. He was a man, for goodness' sake, one who hailed from the jerkwater town of Nazareth at that—Mary's boy, a common carpenter. Jesus' neighbors, who had watched him play in the streets with their own children, never could accept him as the Messiah. And Mark notes in a remarkable aside that even Jesus' own family once concluded, "He is out of his mind." His mother and brothers! Mary, who on seeing the angel Gabriel had spontaneously let loose with the annunciation hymn; his brothers, who had spent more time with him than anyone else—these, too, could not reconcile the strange combination of wondrous and ordinary. Jesus' skin got in the way.

Is God unfair? Perhaps this lingering question produced the most doubt about Jesus, for Jews believed the Messiah would set right all that was wrong with the world. Had not the prophets promised the Lord would swallow up death forever and wipe the tears from all faces? Indeed, Jesus did heal some people; but many more went unhealed. He raised Lazarus from the dead, but many others died during his time on earth. He did not wipe away tears from all faces.

The problem of unfairness bothers many people who are otherwise attracted to Jesus' life. The great theologian Augustine, for example, puzzled over the arbitrariness of the healings in the

Gospels. If Jesus had the power, why didn't he heal everyone? One story especially, from the Gospel of John, caught Augustine's attention.

The disabled of Jerusalem—the blind, the lame, the paralyzed—used to flock around a certain pool in the city, the Lourdes shrine of its day. Sometimes the water in the pool would ripple, and they would run, limp, or crawl to enter the water while it was astir. One day Jesus struck up a conversation with a pathetic man who lay there. He had been crippled for thirty-eight years, he told Jesus, but he had never made it to the pool. Whenever the waters stirred, someone would always push in ahead. Without batting an eye, Jesus ordered the invalid to get up and walk. "At once the man was cured; he picked up his mat and walked." After thirty-eight years of lying flat, he walked! He was the happiest man in Jerusalem.

But the storyteller, John, adds one significant detail: Jesus then slipped away, into the crowd. He ignored the rest of that great throng of disabled people, leaving all but the one unhealed. Why? Augustine wondered: "There lay so many there, and yet only one was healed, whilst He could by a word have raised them all up."[1]

Jesus' cousin was another person troubled by unfairness. John the Baptist, a true believer if there ever was one, had excited the nation's hopes about Jesus. In the early days, when people used to ask if John himself was the Messiah, he would set them straight: "After me will come one more powerful than I, the thongs of whose sandals I am not worthy to stoop down and untie." That promised one—Jesus of Nazareth—came to John for baptism, and he watched in amazement as the Spirit of God descended from the sky in the form of a dove. As if to eliminate all doubts about Jesus, a voice spoke from heaven, loud as thunder.

Two years later, however, John the Baptist had his own doubts, his own crisis of disappointment. Although he had served God faithfully, he had ended up in Herod's prison. While languishing on death row, he smuggled out a message to Jesus: "Are you the one who was to come, or should we expect someone else?" That single question—from John!—captures the ambivalence, the hope-yet-uncertainty, that swirled around Jesus.

The Kingdom Within

If Jesus had just avoided one emotionally charged word, *kingdom,* everything might have been different. As soon as he said it, images sprang to life in the minds of his audience: bright banners, glittering armies, the gold and ivory of Solomon's day, a nation restored to grandeur. But then something would happen to dash those expectations and all the feelings of disappointment would wash in again. As it turned out, the word *kingdom* meant one thing to the crowd and quite another to Jesus.

The masses wanted more than a sprinkling of miracles here and there; they wanted a visible kingdom of power and glory. But Jesus talked instead about "the kingdom of heaven," an invisible kingdom. Yes, he solved some problems in the world around him, but mainly he used his energy to battle unseen forces. He once encountered a paralytic so desperate for healing that the man had persuaded four friends to dig up a roof and lower him through the hole to Jesus. Jesus' response: "Which is easier, to say to the paralytic, 'Your sins are forgiven,' or to say, 'Get up, take your mat and walk'?" He made plain which was easier. No physical deformity could withstand his healing touch. The real battle was against invisible, spiritual powers.

Faith, the forgiveness of sins, the power of the Evil One— these were the concerns that drove Jesus to his Father in prayer each day. Such an emphasis confused the crowds, who primarily sought solutions to their problems in the physical world: poverty, illness, political oppression. In the end, Jesus failed to measure up to their expectations of a king. (Has anything changed? I know of many ministries that emphasize physical healing and prosperity, but few that direct their focus to such persistent human problems as pride, hypocrisy, and legalism—the problems that so troubled Jesus.)

Whatever notions Jesus' followers had of a new and mighty Solomon recapturing Israel evaporated as they watched what took place in Jerusalem. A few days after a "triumphal procession"—a slapstick comedy affair compared to the lavish parades of the Romans—Jesus was arrested and put on trial. He told the Roman governor that he was in fact a king, but added, "My kingdom is not of this world. If it were, my servants would fight to prevent my arrest by the Jews. But now my kingdom is from another place."

Jesus a king? A mock king if ever there was one, with his purple robe clotted with blood from the beatings and a crown of thorns jammed onto his head. The disciples ran away, their loyalty overwhelmed by their fear of immediate danger. If Jesus would not protect himself, why should he protect them? The visible world of Roman might met the invisible world of the kingdom of heaven and seemed for a time to snuff it out.

In Cat's Cradle *the contemporary novelist Kurt Vonnegut shows a physicist who helped father the atomic bomb visiting his laboratory during the Christmas season. Office employees are all standing around a crèche singing Christmas carols. "The hopes and fears of all the years are met in thee tonight," they sing. It is a scene of biting irony, a modern counterpart to Jewish disillusionment in Jesus' day. Do the carolers really believe that the hopes and fears of all the years—which will vanish in a moment if someone presses the wrong button—rest on faith in a Bethlehem newborn destined to live only thirty-three years?*

[1]Colin Brown, *Miracles and the Critical Mind*, 10.

Bible references: Luke 7; John 14; Mark 3; John 5; John 1; Matthew 11; John 18.

Chapter 15

Divine Shyness

My project is the first scientific experiment in history to settle once and for all the question of God's existence. As things presently stand, there may be signs of his existence but they point both ways and are therefore ambiguous and so prove nothing. For example, the wonders of the universe do not convince those most conversant with the wonders, the scientists themselves. Whether or not this testifies to the stupidity of scientists or to God's success at concealing himself doesn't matter.

—Walker Percy, The Second Coming

I F EVER the time was ripe to settle the question of God's existence, it was while Jesus walked on earth. Jesus had one splendid opportunity to silence the critics forever.

If, for example, my friend Richard had lived in Jesus' day, he could have demanded proof to Jesus' face. "You say you're the Son of God? Okay, show me!" We need not speculate about what would have happened, for Jesus often faced a similar challenge.

When religious experts begged him for a miraculous sign, he turned on them in anger, calling them a "wicked and adulterous generation." When a curious king asked to see a miracle, Jesus refused to cooperate though it might have saved his life.

Why the divine restraint? Perhaps a clue can be found in the first "event" in Jesus' ministry, the Temptation, a kind of final exam to prepare him for public life.

You couldn't ask for a more dramatic confrontation: Jesus versus the ultimate skeptic, Satan himself, with the cracked and wrinkled hills of Palestine serving as a backdrop. Satan wanted some proof: "If you are the Son of God . . ." He challenged Jesus to make bread from a stone, asked to see a sample of Jesus' powers of self-protection, and offered him authority over all the kingdoms of the world.

I believe that Satan's challenge was a true temptation for Jesus, not a staged, predetermined contest. A loaf of bread would tempt anyone who had fasted for forty days. A guarantee of physical safety surely held appeal for someone facing torture and execution. And the splendor of all the kingdoms of earth—had not the prophets predicted as much for the Messiah? All three of the "temptations" lay within Jesus' grasp; all three were, in fact, his prerogatives. In effect, Satan was offering him a shortcut to achieve his messianic goals.

Russian novelist Fyodor Dostoyevsky made the Temptation scene a centerpiece in his masterwork *The Brothers Karamazov*. Ivan Karamazov calls the Temptation the most stupendous miracle on earth: the miracle of restraint. If he had yielded to the Temptation, Jesus would have earned his credentials, not just with Satan but with all Israel, establishing himself beyond dispute. According to Dostoyevsky's view, Satan offered three easy means of inciting belief—miracle, mystery, and authority—and Christ refused all three. In Ivan Karamazov's words, "You would not enslave man by a miracle, and craved faith given freely, not based on miracle."[1]

As I studied Matthew's concise account of the Temptation and then Dostoyevsky's long, embellished reconstruction, a question arose, abruptly, disturbingly. How does the Temptation in the desert differ from what took place in Richard's suburban apartment? He too pleaded for a supernatural display: a light, a voice, *something* that would demonstrate God's power beyond dispute. Or, getting more personal, how does the Temptation differ from times when I beg, almost demand, that God intervene and save me from a predicament?

There are differences, of course, and my self-defense quickly fills them in. Richard was, presumably, sincere; I was needy; we were both asking God for help, not taunting him or demanding worship. And yet I cannot easily dismiss the haunting similarity between Satan's "Throw yourself down!" and Richard's "Show yourself!" In each case the challenge is the same: a demand for God to take off the wraps and prove himself. In each case, God demurred.

One more instance of divine restraint comes to mind. It occurred in Jerusalem very near the site of Satan's third challenge. Jesus looked down from a high hill and cried out, "O Jerusalem, Jerusalem, you who kill the prophets and stone those sent to you, how often I have longed to gather your children together, as a hen gathers her chicks under her wings, but you were not willing!" That wail of grief over Jerusalem has about it a quality almost like shyness. Jesus, who could destroy Jerusalem with a word, who could call down legions of angels to force subjection, instead looks over the city and weeps.

God holds back; he hides himself; he weeps. Why? Because he desires what power can never win. He is a king who wants not subservience, but love. Thus, rather than mowing down Jerusalem, Rome, and every other worldly power, he chose the slow, hard way of Incarnation, love, and death. A conquest from within.

George MacDonald summed up Christ's approach: "Instead of crushing the power of evil by divine force; instead of compelling justice and destroying the wicked; instead of making peace on the earth by the rule of a perfect prince; instead of gathering the children of Jerusalem under His wings whether they would or not, and saving them from the horrors that anguished His prophetic soul—He let evil work its will while it lived; He contented

Himself with the slow unencouraging ways of help essential; making men good; casting out, not merely controlling Satan. . . . To love righteousness is to make it grow, not to avenge it. . . . Throughout His life on earth, He resisted every impulse to work more rapidly for a lower good—strong, perhaps, when He saw old age and innocence and righteousness trodden under foot."[2]

The Miracles

I have not told the whole story about Jesus, of course. Yes, his humanity represented a kind of disguise, at least in contrast to God's glory in the Old Testament. Yes, Jesus showed restraint, refusing to overwhelm people with a brash display of power. But what about the miracles he did perform, three dozen of which are recounted in the Gospels? No one who saw him provide lunch for five thousand, or order Lazarus from his tomb, or shout down a summer squall could easily speak of a quality like "divine shyness."

Yet Jesus, who presumably could work a wonder any day of his life if he wanted, seemed curiously ambivalent about miracles. With his disciples, he used them as proof of who he was ("Believe me when I say that I am in the Father and the Father is in me; or at least believe on the evidence of the miracles themselves"). But even as he performed them, he often seemed to downplay them. When he resurrected the daughter of a Jewish VIP, he gave strict orders to keep it quiet. Mark records seven separate occasions when Jesus told a person he had healed, "Tell no one!"

Jesus knew well the shallow effect of miracles in Moses' day, and in Elijah's: they attracted crowds, yes, but rarely encouraged long-term faithfulness. He was bringing a hard message of obedience and sacrifice, not a sideshow for gawkers and sensation-seekers. (Sure enough, the true skeptics of his day—much like people today—explained away his powers. If God's voice spoke from heaven, some dismissed it as thunder. Others credited his gifts to Satan. And Jesus' staunchest enemies refused to trust him even when faced with solid evidence. Once, they assembled a formal tribunal to study a reported healing. Ignoring firsthand testimony—"One thing I do know. I was blind but now I see!"—

116

they hurled insults at the healed man and threw him out of court. Likewise, when Lazarus showed up alive after four days in a tomb, those enemies conspired to kill him off again.)

With remarkable consistency, the Bible's accounts show that miracles—dramatic, showstopping miracles like many of us still long for—simply do not foster deep faith. For proof, we need look no further than the Transfiguration, when Jesus' face shone like the sun and his clothes became dazzling, "whiter than anyone in the world could bleach them." To the disciples' astonishment, two long-departed giants of Jewish history—Moses and Elijah—appeared in a cloud with them. God spoke audibly. It was too much to take; the disciples fell down, terrified.

Yet what effect did this stupendous event have on Jesus' three closest friends, Peter, James, and John? Did it permanently silence their questions and fill them with faith? A few weeks later, when Jesus needed them the most, they all forsook him.

I have read books on signs and wonders that presume to silence doubters, as if Jesus' miracles prove he is the answer to the world's problems. But I must confess that most of these arguments strike me as irrelevant to people disappointed in God. They are more interested in the miracles Jesus did *not* perform. Why does a God who possesses the power to right what is wrong sometimes choose not to? Or, why did Jesus bother with miracles at all? Why heal one paralyzed man at Bethesda—but only one?

A hint may be found in a fanciful depiction of Jesus' life that never made it into the Bible, for good reason. The spurious *Gospel of the Infancy of Jesus Christ* purports to reveal unknown stories about Jesus' childhood. It shows Jesus as a person might *want* him to be. According to this ancient book, he would perform "tricks" on demand to impress his friends—something the real Jesus always refused to do. The apocryphal Jesus had the allure of a pet genie or a neighborhood magician. Whenever his father Joseph messed up an important carpentry assignment, Jesus would step in and magically repair the flaw.

This mythical Jesus was not afraid to use his power for revenge, either. When a neighbor woman hurt one of Jesus' playmates, she mysteriously fell into a well and died of a crushed skull. When Jesus approached a town, its idols disintegrated into mounds of sand.

These hotheaded actions are uncharacteristic of Jesus as depicted in the Gospels, who used his powers compassionately to meet human needs, not for showy tricks. Every time someone asked directly, he healed. When his audience got hungry he fed them, and when wedding guests grew thirsty he made wine. The real Jesus rebuked his disciples for suggesting that he avenge a resistant city. And when soldiers came to arrest him, he used his supernatural power only once—to restore the slashed ear of one of the arresters. In short, the miracles in the authentic Gospels are about love, not power.

Although Jesus' miracles were far too selective to solve every human disappointment, they served as *signs* of his mission, previews of what God would someday do for all creation. In Helmut Thielicke's words, the miracles were "signal fires which announce the coming kingdom of God." For people who experienced them—the paralytic lowered like a chandelier for cleaning—the healings offered convincing proof that God himself was visiting earth. For everyone else, they awakened longings that will not be fulfilled until a final restoration ends all pain and death.

The miracles did just what Jesus had predicted. To those who chose to believe him, they gave even more reason to believe. But for those determined to deny him, the miracles made little difference. Some things just have to be believed to be seen.

[1] Fyodor Dostoyevsky, *The Brothers Karamazov*, 235.
[2] George MacDonald, *Life Essential: The Hope of the Gospel*, 24.

Bible references: Matthew 12, 16; Luke 4; Matthew 23 and Luke 13; John 14, 9; Mark 9.

Chapter 16

The Postponed Miracle

W HEN CHARLEMAGNE, king of the Franks, first heard the story of Jesus' arrest and execution, he exploded in rage. Grabbing his sword and rattling it in the scabbard, he shouted, "Oh, if only I had been there; I would have slain them all with my legions!" We smile at the simple warrior loyalty of Charlemagne, or of Simon Peter, who actually drew a sword in Jesus' defense. Yet behind their outrage lies a dark, dark question. Charlemagne, after all, was not present in Gethsemane and could not have helped. But God the Father, who *could* have helped, did not lift a finger on behalf of his condemned Son.

Why didn't God act? Anyone who thinks about disappointment with God must pause at Gethsemane, and at Pilate's palace, and at Calvary—the scenes of Jesus' arrest, trial, and execution. For in those three places Jesus himself experienced a state very much like disappointment with God.

The ordeal began as Jesus prayed in a quiet, cool grove of olive trees, with three of his disciples waiting sleepily outside. Inside the garden all seemed peaceful; but outside, the forces of hell itself were loose. A disciple had turned traitor, Satan was on the prowl, and a large mob with swords and clubs was heading toward Gethsemane.

"My soul is overwhelmed with sorrow to the point of death," Jesus said to his three disciples. Although he claimed the authority to dispatch an army of angels in his own defense, Jesus did not. He had come to live in a world of skin and blood and tissue, and he would die by its rules as well. At one point he fell facedown on the ground and prayed for some way, *any* way, out. His sweat fell to the ground in large drops, like blood.

And God stayed silent.

At Pilate's palace, the restraint continued. In the most literal way, God—in Jesus—had his hands tied. "Prophesy!" some cried, taunting him with a challenge toward miracle. "Who hit you?" The Son of God did not resist as their fists fell on his blindfolded face and their spit ran down his beard.

The next scene, at Calvary, has been imagined for us so many times in passion plays and sermons and paintings that, benumbed, we can hardly imagine it for ourselves. Start by remembering your time of most acute disappointment. You staked everything on what seemed within God's power—a recovery from cancer, perhaps, or the birth of a healthy baby, or God's help in stitching a marriage together. But everything turned out wrong. The cancer killed, despite your prayers; the baby was born with brain damage; you got divorce papers in the mail. Think of Calvary as that time. Or as a time like the night Richard spent in his apartment, kneeling on the floor, pleading with God. Think of it as a time of No Miracle.

Everybody craved a miracle then: Pilate and Herod, who had heard the sensational rumors; the women who had trailed Jesus all the way from Galilee; the disciples who cowered in the shadows. One dying thief begged for a miracle; the other mocked, and spectators took up the cry, "Let him come down from the cross, and we will believe in him. . . . Let God rescue him now if he wants him."

But there was no rescue, no miracle. There was only silence. Charles Williams looks back on the scene and says, "The taunt flung at Christ, at the moment of his most spectacular impotency, was: 'He saved others; himself he cannot save.' It was a definition as precise as any in the works of the medieval schoolmen."[1]

"My God, my God, why have you forsaken me?" Jesus cried out at last. It was a quotation from the Psalms, the ultimate wail of disappointment. The Father had turned his back, or so it surely seemed, letting history take its course, letting all that was wrong with the world triumph over all that was right. Nature itself convulsed: the ground shook as in an earthquake, tombs cracked open. The solar system shuddered in the chill: the sun hid, and the sky went black.

Sunday Morning

Two days later came the Resurrection, with a sound like an earthquake and a flash like lightning. Shouldn't that have vindicated God and solved the problem of disappointment once and for all?

What a missed opportunity! If only the risen Jesus had reappeared on Pilate's porch to deliver a withering blast against his enemies—that would have showed them! But his dozen or so appearances after resurrection show a clear pattern: Christ presented himself only to people who already believed in him. So far as we know, not a single unbeliever saw Jesus after his death.

Consider two men who could have seen the risen Christ, if they had tarried long enough. These coarse Roman guards were standing outside the tomb when the Miracle of Miracles occurred. They trembled and became like dead men. Then, showing an incurably human reflex, they ran to the authorities; and later that afternoon these two, the only witnesses to the actual event of resurrection, agreed to a cover-up. Stacks of freshly minted silver seemed far more significant than the resurrection of the Son of

God. And so the two eyewitnesses of that great day, the forgotten men of Easter, died apparent unbelievers.

♪

Today, the major events of Jesus' life are marked on calendars around the world—Christmas, Good Friday, and Easter. Of the three, however, only the middle one, the Crucifixion, took place in the open for all the world to see. At the moment when God seemed downright helpless, the cameras of history were rolling, recording it all. Large crowds watched every excruciating detail. And when four men wrote up accounts of Jesus' life, they collectively devoted one- third of their Gospels to that time of apparent failure.

The spectacle of the Cross, the most public event of Jesus' life, reveals the vast difference between a god who proves himself through power and One who proves himself through love. Other gods, Roman gods, for example, enforced worship: in Jesus' own lifetime, some Jews were slaughtered for not bowing down to Caesar. But Jesus Christ never forced anyone to believe in him. He preferred to act by appeal, drawing people out of themselves and toward him.

Paradoxically, that scene of weakness inspired new hope. "If God is for us, who can be against us?" concluded the apostle Paul, resting his faith in the boundless love of a God "who did not spare his own Son, but gave him up for us all." Love is most persuasive when it involves sacrifice, and the Gospels make clear that Jesus came to die. In his own words, "Greater love has no one than this, that one lay down his life for his friends." Somehow, the possibility of eternal happiness required this time of silence and profound disappointment.

[1]Charles Williams, *He Came Down from Heaven*, 115.

Bible references: Matthew 26–27; Romans 8; John 15.

Chapter 17

Progress

"Madame," I said, "if our God were a pagan god or the god of intellectuals—and for me it comes to much the same—He might fly to His remotest heaven and our grief would force Him down to earth again. But you know that our God came to be among us. Shake your fist at Him, spit in His face, scourge Him, and finally crucify Him: what does it matter? My daughter, it's already been done to Him."

—George Bernanos, *Diary of a Country Priest*

L ET ME BE BLUNT: What difference does Jesus make to our feelings of disappointment with God? How does it help us to learn that he too tasted disappointment?

Theologians, following the apostle Paul, usually explain Christ's contribution in legal terms: justification, reconciliation, propitiation. But these words merely hint at what took place. To understand the difference Jesus makes to the problem of disappointment, we must look past such words to the underlying story of God's passionate pursuit of human beings.

Think back to one of the main images in the Prophets: an anxious father grieving over his runaway child. Jesus' story of the Prodigal Son provides a happy ending at last. The Waiting Father has waited long enough; he flings open the front door and *races* to welcome home the runaway, no questions asked.

The Torn Curtain

What difference did Jesus make? Both for God and for us, he made possible an *intimacy* that had never before existed. In the Old Testament, Israelites who touched the sacred Ark of the Covenant fell down dead; but people who touched Jesus, the Son of God in flesh, came away healed. To Jews who would not pronounce or even spell out the letters in God's name, Jesus taught a new way of addressing God: *Abba,* or "Daddy." In Jesus, God came close.

Augustine's *Confessions* describes how this closeness affected him. From Greek philosophy he had learned about a perfect, timeless, incorruptible God, but he could not fathom how an oversexed, undisciplined person like himself could relate to such a God. He tried various heresies of the day and found them all unsatisfying, until he met at last the Jesus of the Gospels, a bridge between ordinary human beings and a perfect God.

The Book of Hebrews explores this startling new advance in intimacy. First the author elaborates on what was required just to approach God in Old Testament times. Only once a year, on the Day of Atonement—Yom Kippur—could one person, the high priest, enter the Most Holy Place. The ceremony involved ritual baths, special clothing, and five separate animal sacrifices; and still the priest entered the Most Holy Place in fear. He wore bells on his robe and a rope around his ankle so that if he died and the bells stopped ringing, other priests could pull out his body.

Hebrews draws the vivid contrast: we can now "approach the throne of grace with confidence," without fear. Charging boldly into the Most Holy Place—no image could hold more shock value for Jewish readers. Yet at the moment of Jesus' death, a thick curtain inside the temple literally ripped in two from top to bottom, breaking open the Most Holy Place. Therefore, concludes Hebrews, "Let us draw near to God."

Jesus contributes at least this to the problem of disappointment with God: because of him, we can come to God directly. We need no human mediator, for God himself became one.

A Face

No one in the Old Testament could claim to know the face of God. No one, in fact, could survive a direct gaze. The few who caught a glimpse of God's glory came away glowing like extraterrestrials, and all who saw them hid in fear. But Jesus offered a long, slow look at the face of God. "Anyone who has seen me has seen the Father," he said. Whatever Jesus is, God is. As Michael Ramsey put it, "In God is no unChristlikeness at all."

People grow up with all sorts of notions of what God is like. They may see God as an Enemy, or a Policeman, or even an Abusive Parent. Or perhaps they do not see God at all, and only hear his silence. Because of Jesus, however, we no longer have to wonder how God feels or what he is like. When in doubt, we can look at Jesus to correct our blurry vision.

If I wonder how God views deformed or disabled people, I can watch Jesus among the crippled, the blind, and those with leprosy. If I wonder about the poor, and whether God has destined them to lives of misery, I can read Jesus' words in the Sermon on the Mount. And if I ever wonder about the appropriate "spiritual" response to pain and suffering, I can note how Jesus responded to his own: with fear and trembling, with loud cries and tears.

Not Yet

I could not help noticing an abrupt mood shift in the Bible around the Book of Acts. If you scour the rest of the New Testament, you will find none of the outrage of Job nor the despair of Ecclesiastes nor the anguish of Lamentations. Clearly, the writers of the New Testament were convinced that Jesus had changed the universe forever. The apostle Paul, for example, spraying sentence fragments across the page, spared no superlative: "In Christ all things hold together . . . through him he reconciled all things to himself, whether things on earth or things in heaven. . . . Christ is seated far above all rule and authority, power and dominion, and every title that can be given, not only in the present age but also in the one to come."

Yet as he was writing those very words, the Roman Empire was grinding on with its grim succession of wars and tyrants; people everywhere were still lying and stealing and killing each other; diseases continued to spread; and Christians themselves were being lashed with whips and thrown in jail. Such common reasons for doubt and disappointment did not seem to shake the apostles' confidence that Jesus would come again as he had promised, in power and great glory. It was simply a matter of time. They had doubted him once, but after the Resurrection they would not doubt him again.

The sure, settled tone of the New Testament writers creates a problem, though: the problem of why, some twenty centuries after the apostle Paul, I am devoting an entire book to the topic of disappointment with God. And the people who told me their wrenching stories—why do they lack the bold assurance of the New Testament writers? Why hasn't all our disappointment melted away?

As I think about these things, I keep coming back to the single question of unfairness. *Is God unfair?* In a remarkable way, Jesus gave a direct response to the problems of God's hiddenness and silence. But the problem of unfairness only seemed to worsen. Jesus' own life ended in the greatest unfairness of history: the best man who ever lived suffering the worst of punishments. One more victim of a cruel planet. Conditions hardly improved after his death, when Jesus' disciples received the "rewards" of prison, torture, and martyrdom. The problem of unfairness did not disappear.

Amazingly, the author of Hebrews seemed to anticipate that very situation, almost as a backhanded acknowledgment that people would continue to feel disappointed in God. Chapter 2 begins with a lofty quotation from the Psalms about God putting everything under Jesus' feet. Then follows this single, pregnant sentence: "Yet at present we do not see everything subject to him."

As an author, I know what it's like to write what I believe to be true and then wonder, as soon as I've written it, *Do I really mean that?* The author of Hebrews, after recording the gust of grand theology from the Psalms, likewise seems to pause and reconsider. Yes, it's true that Jesus is in control—but it sure doesn't look like it: "at present we do not see everything subject to him." That one sentence encompasses all unfairness: all war and violence, all hatred and lust, all triumph of evil over good, all illness and death, all tears and groans, all the disappointment and despair of this chaotic world. It may be the "truest" sentence in the Bible.

The paragraph continues, "But we see Jesus . . . who suffered death, so that by the grace of God he might taste death for everyone." Pointedly, Hebrews does not summon up a triumphant image of Jesus on the Mount of Transfiguration or in his resurrected body; it shows Jesus on the cross. Then the author goes on to use some of the most mysterious language of the New Testament. He tells of Christ "being made perfect" and "learning obedience" through the things that he suffered. Commentators often skirt these phrases, for they are not easy to reconcile with traditional notions of an unchanging, passionless God. But I must not skirt them, for they are presented in Hebrews as Jesus' direct contribution to the continuing problem of disappointment with God.

From Hebrews, it seems clear that the Incarnation had meaning for God as well as for us. It was the ultimate way for him to identify with us. He, a spirit, had never before been confined in the world of matter, had never experienced the soft vulnerability of human flesh, had never sensed the clamorous warnings from pain cells. Jesus changed all that. He went through the entire human experience, from the blood and pain of birth to the blood and pain of death.

From the Old Testament we can gain much insight into what it "feels like" to be God. But the New Testament records what happened when God learned what it feels like to be a human being. Whatever we feel, God felt. Instinctively, we want a God who not only knows about pain but shares in it; we want a God who is affected by our own pain. As the young theologian Dietrich Bonhoeffer scribbled on a note in a Nazi prison camp, "Only the Suffering God can help." Because of Jesus, we have such a God. Hebrews reports that God can now sympathize with our weaknesses. The very word expresses how it was done: "sympathy" comes from two Greek words, *sym pathos*, meaning "suffer with."

Would it be too much to say that, because of Jesus, God understands our feelings of disappointment with him? How else can we interpret Jesus' tears, or his cry from the cross? One could almost pour the three questions of this book into that dreadful cry, "My God, my God, why have you forsaken me?" God's Son "learned obedience" from his suffering, says Hebrews. A person can only learn obedience when tempted to disobey, can only learn courage when tempted to flee.

Why didn't Jesus brandish a sword in Gethsemane, or call on his legions of angels? Why did he decline Satan's challenge to dazzle the world? For this reason: if he had done so, he would have failed in his most important mission—to become one of us, to live and die as one of us. It was the only way God could work "within the rules" he had set up at Creation.

All through the Bible, especially in the Prophets, we see a conflict raging within God. On the one hand he passionately loved the people he had made; on the other hand, he had a terrible urge to destroy the Evil that enslaved them. On the cross, God resolved that inner conflict, for there his Son absorbed the destructive force and transformed it into love.

Progress

The only ultimate way to conquer evil is to let it be smothered within a willing, living, human being. When it is absorbed there, like blood in a sponge or a spear thrown into one's heart, it loses its power and goes no further.
—Gale D. Webbe, *The Night and Nothing*

Bible references: Hebrews 4, 10; John 14; Colossians 1; Ephesians 1; Hebrews 2–5.

Part Four

Turning It Over: The Spirit

Chapter 18

The Transfer

Y OUR STOMACH is churning with that first-day-on-the-job tension. *Will I make it? What if I do the wrong thing? Will the boss like me?* You glance around at the others who are squinting against the bright sun, shifting from one leg to the other, nervously carving designs in the sand with the edges of their sandals. Seventy of you received the summons to appear for a special assignment.

Jesus is giving a full-fledged speech. He looks worried, and his words convey alarm: "I am sending you out like lambs among wolves. Do not take a purse or bag or sandals; and do not greet anyone on the road." By the time he gets to the closing line, his voice has risen in timbre, commanding attention: "He who listens to you listens to me; he who rejects you rejects me; but he who rejects me rejects him who sent me." What is that supposed to mean? The group begins to disperse, and, swallowing your uncertainties, you head out with your designated partner on the assigned mission.

The next time you see Jesus, a few days later, it looks as if he has changed faces. All severity and alarm have drained away. He's grinning at your stories, urging you to elaborate. He can't seem to get enough details about the healings and the exorcisms and the transformed lives. It really did work, this perilous mission into the hill country, and Jesus is jubilant. It's a victory party. Listen to him long enough and you'll believe you can do anything: trample on snakes, scorpions, whatever.

Right in the middle of your report he holds up his hand to interrupt. He can't wait. You've never seen him so excited. "I saw Satan fall like lightning from heaven!" he announces, and though you have no clue to what he means, you are swept up in the sudden rush of enthusiasm. Some enormous breakthrough must have just occurred. Then he bends closer and says in a hushed voice, "Many prophets and kings wanted to see what you see but did not see it, and to hear what you hear but did not hear it."

Final Exam

Another scene, about six months later. This time you are dining with the rest of the Twelve in a small room in Jerusalem. A stuffy, cloistered feeling pervades the place, and you are a bit light-headed after the meal and the wine. Everything's happening too fast. Earlier this week Jesus, permitting a rare display of public acclaim, rode into the city in a triumphant procession. It seemed all your dreams would come true after all. But tonight's mood is foreboding.

First came the incident of the foot-washing, when Jesus embarrassed Peter. And even now as he talks, Jesus' mood wavers. One minute he seems nostalgic and comforting, and the next minute he suddenly rebukes you for dullness and lack of faith. He keeps alluding to a betrayal. Some of it you do not grasp. But one thing he insists on, over all protests: he is leaving. Someone else will come to take his place; someone he calls the Counselor.

There is a sudden stirring in the room, like wind over grass. For months you have waited for Jesus to take command of his kingdom. But now he says he is turning the whole thing over—to you, the Twelve! He looks around the table and says with finality, "I confer on you a kingdom, just as my Father conferred one on me."

The Transfer

Departure

Okay, you failed—all of you, even Peter, who had bragged about his loyalty just a few hours before the great denial. "I have overcome the world!" Jesus had said in the small room that night. But you simply could not reconcile his words with what happened next. Less than twenty-four hours later you saw him hanging naked on a cross, his frail body glimmering in the torchlight. This one, the Savior of your nation, the King of Kings? It was too much to ask anyone to believe.

That was Friday.

On Sunday, wild, crazy rumors shot through the close-knit community of mourners. And then later in the week you saw him. It was true! You touched him with your own hands. Jesus! He had done what no one had done before: he had walked voluntarily into death, and walked back out. You would never, never doubt him again.

For forty days Jesus appeared and disappeared seemingly at will. When he showed up, you listened eagerly to his explanations of what had happened. When he left, you and the others plotted the new kingdom. Think of it: Jerusalem free at last from Roman rule!

Friends had long mocked your stubborn obsession with this peasant preacher. Now you'd show them. No one would push you around anymore; no one would push Israel around. Peter, James, and John would naturally have the inside track on the top positions, but a kingdom would need many leaders—and, after all, you had followed Jesus for three years. The Messiah, the true Messiah, had counted you among his most intimate disciples.

During those forty days, none of the glow wore off. How could it? Every reappearance of Jesus was a new miracle. At last someone broke the question to him, the burning question you had all been debating. "Lord, are you at this time going to restore the kingdom to Israel?" You waited breathless for some sign—a call to arms perhaps, a battle plan. The Romans wouldn't walk away without a fight.

No one was prepared for Jesus' reaction. At first it seemed he hadn't heard the question well. He brushed it aside and began talking not about Israel, but about neighboring countries and other faraway places. He said you were to go there eventually as his witnesses. But for now, you should simply return to Jerusalem and wait for the Holy Spirit.

Then the most amazing thing happened. You were standing there, listening to him, when suddenly his body began to lift off the ground. He hung in midair for a moment; then a cloud hid him from sight. And you never saw Jesus again.

Three Scenes

These scenes—the Sending of the Seventy, the Last Supper, and the Ascension—all reveal something about why Jesus came to earth, and why he left. True, he came to settle divine justice and to show us what God is like. But he also came to establish a Church, a new dwelling place for the Spirit of God.

And that is why, when the seventy reported back to him, Jesus nearly erupted with joy. "He who listens to you listens to me," he had told them, and indeed the plan was working. His own mission—more, his own life—was being lived out through seventy commonplace human beings.

At the last supper with the disciples, Jesus conveyed a greater sense of urgency. They were his closest friends in all the world, and it was time to turn the entire mission over to them—these well-meaning friends so quick with their protestations of loyalty now, so quick with their denials later. "As the Father has sent me, I am sending you," he said, knowing they did not comprehend. This little band would take his message to Jerusalem, and to all Judea and Samaria, and then to places he himself had never visited—all the way to the ends of the earth.

At the Ascension, Jesus' body left the earth before his astonished disciples' eyes. But soon, very soon, at Pentecost, the Spirit of God would take up residence in other bodies. Their bodies.

Bible references: Luke 10; John 13–17; Acts 1.

Chapter 19

Changes in the Wind

A documentary film series about religion for PBS. Great. One more yawner of an assignment. "Explore images of the deity through the ages," or some such abstraction, they say. Just fine. Who comes up with these schemes? For starters, the central character is invisible.

Well, until someone finds a way to arrange an interview with God himself, they'll have to settle for vignettes *about* God.

14th Century B.C. *Begin with helicopter shot of the Sinai peaks. Uninhabited area, so no TV antennae to dismantle, etc. Zoom to a clump of Bedouin extras impersonating ancient Hebrews. Voice-over on how they eat, what they wear. In tight on a Jewish boy about twelve years old. Interrupt him from play and call him over.*

"Tell me about your God. What's he like?" narrator asks.

Boy's eyes widen. "You mean . . . you mean . . ." Can't bring himself to say the word.

"That's right, Yahweh, the God you worship."

"What's he like? Him? See that mountain over there? [*Cut to volcano. Lots of steam, smoke. Close-up of magma.*] That's where he lives. Don't go near it or you'll die! He's . . . he's . . . well, most of all he's scary. *Real* scary."

A.D. *1st Century. Pan across a broad, flat horizon of Palestine. Same Bedouins, now milling around the desert in a group. Oasis in the background. Tighten in on a clump of bystanders, then on a woman along the edge, sitting down, leaning against a desert shrub. Prompt her.*

"God? I'm still trying to figure him out. I thought I knew, but when I started following this teacher around, I got confused. He claims he's the Messiah. My friends laugh. But I was in the crowd the day he fed five thousand people—who else could do that? I ate a piece of the fish. And with my own eyes I saw him heal a blind man.

"Somehow God is like that man named Jesus, over there."

A.D. *20th Century. Move film crew to picturesque church in small town, U.S.A. Pan across the faces of people in the pews.*

Voice-over from narrator, "And what is God like now?"

The New Testament asks us to believe that the answer lies in that ordinary church, among those ordinary people in the pews. God in Christ is one thing, but in *us*? The only way to sense the shock of it is to read the Bible straight through, from Genesis to Revelation, as I did during those snowy days in Colorado.

The mighty, awesome Lord of the Universe, full of passion and fire and holiness, dominates the first nine hundred pages. Four Gospels follow, about one hundred pages long, recounting Jesus' life on earth. But after Acts, the Bible shifts to a series of personal letters. Grecians, Romans, Jews, slaves, slave owners, women, men, children—the letters address all these diverse groups, and yet each letter assumes its readers belong to an overarching new identity. They are all "in Christ."

"The Church is nothing but a section of humanity in which Christ has really taken form," said Dietrich Bonhoeffer. The apostle Paul expressed much the same thought with his phrase "the body of Christ." The way he saw it, a new species of humanity was emerging on earth, in whom God himself—the Holy Spirit—was living. They extended the arms and legs and eyes of God on earth. What's more, Paul acted as if that had been God's goal all along.

"Don't you know that you yourself are God's temple and that God's Spirit lives in you?" Paul wrote to the unruly bunch at Corinth. To the Jews, of course, the temple was an actual building, the central place on earth where the Presence of God dwelt. Was Paul claiming, to put it plainly, that God had "moved?"

Three temples appear in the Bible, and, taken together, they illustrate a progression: God revealed himself first as Father, then as Son, and finally as Holy Spirit.* The first temple was a magnificent structure built by Solomon and rebuilt by Herod. The second was the "temple" of Jesus' body ("Destroy it," he said, "and I will raise it again in three days"). And now a third temple has taken shape, fashioned out of individual human beings.

Delegation

He seems to do nothing of Himself which He can possibly delegate to His creatures. He commands us to do slowly and blunderingly what He could do perfectly and in the twinkling of an eye.

Creation seems to be delegation through and through. I suppose this is because He is a giver.[1]

The progression—Father, Son, Spirit—represents a profound advance in intimacy. At Sinai the people shrank from God, and begged Moses to approach him on their behalf. But in Jesus' day people could hold a conversation with the Son of God; they could

---

*I realize the Trinity is by no means a simple doctrine, and activities of the Son and the Spirit can be traced throughout the Old Testament. But we would probably not speak of a Trinity at all apart from the Incarnation and Pentecost. Each event revealed something about God that had not been known before, and each caused an upheaval in the way people thought about God.

touch him, and even hurt him. And after Pentecost the same flawed disciples who had fled from Jesus' trial became carriers of the Living God. In an act of delegation beyond fathom, Jesus turned over the kingdom of God to the likes of his disciples—and to us.

But enough. All these misty ideas about the Spirit must somehow accord with the glaring reality of the actual church. Look at the people in the pews of any church. Is this what God had in mind?

Delegation always entails risk, as any employer soon learns. When you turn over a job, you let go. And when God "makes his appeal through us" (Paul's phrase), he takes an awful risk: the risk that we will badly misrepresent him. Slavery, the Crusades, pogroms against the Jews, colonialism, wars, the Ku Klux Klan—all these movements have claimed the sanction of Christ for their cause. The world God wants to love, the world God is appealing to, may never see him; our own faces may get in the way.

Yet God took that risk, and because he did so the world will know him primarily through Christians. The doctrine of the Holy Spirit is the doctrine of "the church": God living in us. Such a plan is the "foolishness of God," as Paul says in one place, and writer Frederick Buechner marvels at the folly: "to choose for his holy work in the world . . . lamebrains and misfits and nitpickers and holier-than-thous and stuffed shirts and odd ducks and egomaniacs and milquetoasts and closet sensualists."[2]

"And yet," Paul continues, "the foolishness of God is wiser than men."

We who live among the flawed, ordinary people of the church, we who *are* the lamebrains and misfits and odd ducks of the church, may want to water down the Bible's extravagant statements about the body of Christ, for we know how poorly we embody him. But the Bible is unequivocal. Consider just two examples.

1. We represent God's holiness on earth. Holiness, above all else, constitutes the great distance between God and human beings. It's what made the Most Holy Place forbidden ground. But the New Testament insists that a seismic change has taken place.

A perfect God now lives inside very imperfect human beings. And because he respects our freedom, the Spirit in effect "subjects himself" to our behavior. The New Testament tells of a Spirit we can lie to, or grieve, or quench. And when we choose wrongly, we quite literally subject God to that wrong choice.

No passage illustrates this strange truth more forcefully than 1 Corinthians 6, a passage in which Paul scolds the randy members of the church at Corinth for hiring prostitutes. One by one, he smashes all their rationalizations. Then, finally, he settles on the most sobering warning of all: "Do you not know that your bodies are members of Christ himself?" Paul seems to mean this in the most literal sense, and he does not shrink from the next, astounding conclusion: "Shall I then take the members of Christ and unite them with a prostitute? Never!"

You don't have to be a biblical scholar to see the contrast. In the Old Testament, adulterers were stoned to death for disobeying God's law. But in the age of the Spirit, God delegates his reputation, even his essence, to us. We incarnate God in the world; what happens to us happens to him.

2. Human beings do the work of God on earth. Or, to be strictly accurate, God does his work through us—the tension comes into play as soon as you try to phrase it. "Without God, we cannot. Without us, God will not," said Augustine. In a similar vein, Paul wrote, "Continue to work out your salvation with fear and trembling," in one clause, and "for it is God who works in you" in the next. Whatever else they mean, such conundrums surely contradict a "Leave it up to God" attitude.

God miraculously provided food for the Israelites wandering through the Sinai desert, and even made sure their shoes would not wear out. Jesus, too, fed hungry people and ministered directly to their needs. Many Christians who read those thrilling stories look back with a sense of nostalgia, or even disappointment. "Why doesn't God act like that now?" they wonder. "Why doesn't he miraculously provide for my needs?"

But the New Testament letters seem to show a different pattern at work. Locked in a cold dungeon, Paul turned to his long-time friend Timothy to meet his physical needs. "Bring my cloak and my scrolls," he wrote, "and also bring Mark, who has always been so helpful." In other straits, Paul received "God's comfort" in the form of a visit from Titus. And when a famine broke out in Jerusalem, Paul himself led a fund-raising effort among all the churches he had founded. God was meeting the needs of the young church as surely as he had met the needs of the Israelites, but he was doing so indirectly, through fellow members of his body. Paul made no such distinction as "the church did this, but God did that." Such a division would miss the point he had made so often. The church is Christ's body; therefore if the church did it, God did it.

Paul's insistence on this truth may trace back to his first, dramatic personal encounter with God. At the time, he was a fierce persecutor of Christians, a notorious bounty hunter. But on the road to Damascus he saw a light bright enough to blind him for three days, and heard a voice from heaven: "Saul, Saul, why do you persecute me?"

Persecute you? Persecute who? I'm only after those heretics the Christians.

"Who are you, Lord?" asked Saul at last, knocked flat on the ground.

"I am Jesus, whom you are persecuting," came the reply.

That sentence summarizes as well as anything the change brought about by the Holy Spirit. Jesus had been executed months before. It was the Christians Saul was after, not Jesus. But Jesus, alive again, informed Saul that those people were in fact his own body. What hurt them, hurt him. It was a lesson the apostle Paul would never forget.

I must not leave this thought without applying its meaning in a most personal way. The doctrine of the Holy Spirit has great significance for the underlying questions of this book. My friend Richard had asked, "Where is God? Show me. I want to see him." Surely at least part of the answer to his question is this: *If you want*

to see God, then look at the people who belong to him—they are his "bodies." They are the body of Christ.

"His disciples will have to look more saved if I am to believe in their Savior," said Nietzsche to such a challenge. But maybe if Richard could find a saint, someone like Mother Teresa, to embody the qualities of love and grace, maybe then he would believe. *There—see her? That is what God is like. She is doing the work of God.*

Richard does not know Mother Teresa, but he does know me. And that is the most humbling aspect of the doctrine of the Holy Spirit. Richard probably will never hear a voice from a whirlwind that drowns out all questions. He will likely never get a personal glimpse of God in this life. He will only see me.

[1]C. S. Lewis, *The World's Last Night*, 9.
[2]Frederick Buechner, *A Room Called Remember*, 142.

Bible references: 1 Corinthians 3; John 2; 2 Corinthians 5; Philippians 2; 2 Timothy 4; 2 Corinthians 7; Romans 15; Acts 9.

Chapter 20

The Culmination

I F WE COULD, for a moment, set aside preconceptions about the Bible and simply read that huge book as an unfolding story, the plot line might emerge as something like this:

In the beginning God, a Spirit, created the vast world of matter. Of all God's remarkable works, only human beings possessed a likeness to him that could be called "the image of God." It was at once a great gift and a great burden, this image of God. Man and woman, spirit-ual beings, could commune directly with God. But of all species they alone had the freedom to rebel against him.

Rebel they did, and something died inside Adam and Eve that fateful day. Their bodies lived on for many years, but their spirits lost the free and open communion with God.

The Bible tells of God's efforts to restore that fallen spirit. He worked with individual families: first Adam's family, later Noah's, and finally Abraham's family, the central focus of most of the Old Testament. Sometimes the Bible portrays God as a parent raising a child, sometimes as a lover in passionate pursuit, but always it shows him seeking to "break through" to human beings in order to restore what had been lost.

With a few glowing exceptions, the Old Testament recounts failures. But the New Testament opens with a radical move by God: an "invasion," the birth of Jesus. Jesus represented a whole new beginning. "The second Adam" he was called, the leader of a new species. He at last tore down the barriers and made possible a truce between God and humanity.

After Jesus had left, at Pentecost the Spirit of God descended and filled individual human beings. Thus their fallen spirit was finally restored. More than walking in a garden with human beings, God was now living inside them.

You don't have to read far in the New Testament letters to catch the excitement. The apostle Paul could not have expressed it more strongly: "The creation waits in eager expectation for the sons of God to be revealed." He pictured the entire universe pausing to watch the events on earth: "[God's] intent was that now, *through the church*, the manifold wisdom of God should be made known to the rulers and authorities in the heavenly realms." Peter added breathlessly that "even angels long to look into these things."

Meanwhile, the little band of Christians spread out toward Samaria, Greece, Ethiopia, Rome, and Spain. According to the New Testament, they were engaged in the great reversal of history, helping to reclaim all of creation for God.

Why Better?

I determined from the outset of this book to be honest; I am writing, after all, for victims of overwrought promises and dashed expectations. So I must state frankly that it is difficult for disappointed people to share the enthusiasm of the New Testament writers. My friend Richard, for example, claims he lost his faith because God acts all too subtly. He longs for something more convincing, something along the lines of a burning bush, perhaps, or the parting of the Red Sea. The "manifold wisdom of God" being made known through the church? Have you been to a church lately? Jesus would have been impressive; the shekinah glory cloud would have stopped you flat; but the church?

How can we reconcile the exalted words of the New Testament with the everyday reality around us? Some people have a quick reply: "Oh, but Paul was talking about the New Testament church; we've strayed far from that ideal." I cannot agree. The Epistles were written to a motley crew of converted angel worshipers, thieves, idolaters, backbiters, and prostitutes— those were the people in whom God took up residence. Read Paul's descriptions of the supposed "ideal church" in a city like Corinth: a raucous, ornery bunch that rivals any church in history for their unholiness. And yet Paul's most stirring depiction of the church as Christ's body appears in a letter to them.

There is no way to pose the question elegantly, so I will simply ask it: What, exactly, does God's plan for the ages accomplish? If one could submit that plan to something like a "cost-benefit analysis" used by corporations, what would be the "gains" and "costs" of such a plan—for God and for us?

The church's obvious defects would seem to be the greatest cost to God. Just as he committed his name to the nation Israel and had it dragged through mud, he now commits his Spirit to flawed human beings. You don't have to look far—the church in Corinth, racism in South Africa, bloodshed in Northern Ireland, scandals among U.S. Christians—for proof that the church does not measure up to God's ideal. And the watching world judges God by those who carry his name. A large measure of disappointment with God stems from disillusionment with other Christians.

Dorothy Sayers has said that God underwent three great humiliations in his efforts to rescue the human race. The first was the Incarnation, when he took on the confines of a physical body. The second was the Cross, when he suffered the ignominy of public execution. The third humiliation, Sayers suggested, is the church. In an awesome act of self-denial, God entrusted his reputation to ordinary people.

Yet in some way invisible to us, those ordinary people filled with the Spirit are helping to restore the universe to its place under the reign of God. At our repentance, angels rejoice. By our prayers, mountains are moved. The gain to God can be seen in a passage already mentioned: Luke 10. "I saw Satan fall like lightning from heaven," Jesus exclaimed exuberantly when the seventy returned with success stories. He responded like a proud father who had just seen his children perform far above what he had ever thought possible.

We must not press the point so far as to think God "needs" our cooperation. Rather, he has chosen us as the preferred way to reclaim his creation here on earth. He uses human instruments just as my brain uses the instruments of fingers and hand and wrist to write this sentence. That is the metaphor Paul used most frequently to describe Christ's role in the world today: the Head of the body, directing its members to carry out his will.

To understand the gain to God, think back to the images from the Prophets: God as Parent and as Lover. Both those human relationships contain elements of what God has always been seeking from human beings. One word, *dependence*, holds the key—the key to what they have in common and the key to how they differ.

For a baby, dependence is everything; someone else must meet its every need or the child will die. Parents stay up all night, clean up vomit, teach toilet training, and perform other unpleasant chores out of love because they sense the child's dependence. But such a pattern cannot continue forever. An eagle stirs the nest to force its eaglets to fly; a mother covers her breast to wean her child.

No healthy parent wants a permanently dependent child on his hands. And so a father does not push his daughter around in a large carriage for life, but teaches her to walk, knowing that she may one day walk away. Good parents nudge their children from dependence toward freedom.

Lovers, however, reverse the pattern. A lover possesses complete freedom, yet chooses to give it away and become dependent. "Submit to one another," says the Bible, and any couple can tell you that's an apt description of the day-to-day process of getting along. In a healthy marriage, one submits to the other's wishes voluntarily, out of love. In an unhealthy marriage, submission becomes part of a power struggle, a tug-of-war between competing egos.

The difference between those two relationships shows, I believe, what God has been seeking in his long history with the human race. He desires not the clinging, helpless love of a child who has no choice, but the mature, freely given love of a lover. He has been "romancing" us all along.

God never got such mature love from the nation Israel. The record shows God nudging the young nation toward maturity: on the day Israel advanced into the Promised Land, the manna ceased. God had provided a new land; now it was up to the Israelites to grow their own food. In a typically childish response, Israel promptly started worshiping fertility gods. God wanted a lover; he got a permanently stunted child.

What about now, in the age of the Spirit? Does God now have a lover rather than a child? Amazingly, the New Testament seems to answer yes. This sampling of phrases from the New Testament expresses how God views us: "Christ loved the church . . . a radiant church, without stain or wrinkle or any other blemish, but holy and blameless"; "without fault in a crooked and depraved generation, in which you shine like stars in the universe"; "you who once were far away have been brought near"; "you are no longer foreigners and aliens, but . . . members of God's household . . . a dwelling in which God lives by his Spirit."

The Bible, in fact, presents the union of ordinary people with God's Spirit as the supreme achievement of creation. God's goal all along was to equip *us* to accomplish his will in the world. That slow, difficult process will one day result in the total restoration of the earth.

Our Gain

Such grand thoughts, however—agents of God, supreme achievement of creation—represent God's point of view, a vantage unavailable to us. What are the costs and gains of God's plan for us who live on earth? We still inhabit a world cursed with pain, tragedy, and disappointment. And what I have presented as a great advance in *closeness*—from the smoke of Sinai to the person of Jesus to the indwelling Holy Spirit—may, ironically, seem like God's *withdrawal* from direct involvement.

Some people pine for the "good old days" of the Old Testament when God used a more obvious, hands-on approach. The Old Testament tells of an actual contract signed by God guaranteeing physical safety and prosperity, under certain terms; the New Testament offers no such contract. The change from the visible presence of God in the wilderness to the invisible presence of the Holy Spirit involves a certain kind of loss as well. We lose the clear, sure proof that God exists. Nowadays, God does not hover over us in a cloud that we can gaze at for reassurance. For some, like Richard, this seems a great loss indeed.

In fact, God's reliance on the church almost guarantees that disappointment with God will be permanent and epidemic. In the old days, if the Hebrews wanted to know God's will about a military maneuver, or what kind of wood to use in the sanctuary, the high priests had ways of discerning the answer. But 1,275 denominations in the U.S. alone attest to the difficulty of the church agreeing on God's will about anything nowadays. The confused voice of the modern church is part of the cost, the disadvantage to living today rather than with the Hebrews in the desert or among the disciples who followed Jesus.

What, then, is the gain? The New Testament takes great pains to spell it out, especially in Hebrews, Romans, and Galatians. I can almost picture the apostle Paul, an excitable sort, responding to a question like "What is the gain?"

> What, are you crazy?! The gain? Go back and read Leviticus, Numbers, and Deuteronomy at one sitting, and then we can talk. You call those "good old days"? Who wants to live like that? Do you want to spend every day of your life worrying about your eternal destiny? Do you want to scramble all day to make sure you keep all those rules? Do you want to go through long rituals and animal sacrifices and a fancy-dressed high priest just to approach God? Hey, I spent half my life trying to measure up to those demands, and you can have

them. The difference between the Law and Spirit is the difference between death and life, between slavery and freedom, between perpetual childhood and growing up. Why would anyone want to go back to that?

To use Paul's own words, the Old Testament way was "the ministry that brought death, which was engraved in letters of stone." It was a mere "*schoolmaster* to lead us to Christ." Who wants to stay in kindergarten forever? As Paul said, "We are not like Moses, who would put a veil over his face to keep the Israelites from gazing at it while the radiance was fading away. . . . Now the Lord is the Spirit, and where the Spirit of the Lord is, there is freedom."

God's plan includes risk on both sides. For us, it means risking our independence by committing to follow an invisible God who requires of us faith and obedience. For God, it means risking that we, like the Israelites, may never grow up; it means risking that we may never love him. Evidently, he thought it a gamble worth taking.

A Trinity of Voices

Think of God's plan as a series of Voices. The first Voice, thunderingly loud, had certain advantages. When the Voice spoke from the trembling mountain at Sinai, or when fire licked up the altar on Mount Carmel, no one could deny it. Yet, amazingly, even those who heard the Voice and feared it—the Israelites at Sinai and at Carmel, for example—soon learned to ignore it. Its very volume got in the way. Few of them sought out that Voice; fewer still persevered when the Voice fell silent.

The Voice modulated with Jesus, the *Word* made flesh. For a few decades the Voice of God took on the timbre and volume and rural accent of a country Jew in Palestine. It was a normal human voice, and though it spoke with authority, it did not cause people to flee. Jesus' voice was soft enough to debate against, soft enough to kill.

After Jesus departed, the Voice took on new forms. On the

day of Pentecost, tongues—*tongues*—of fire fell on the faithful, and the church, God's body, began to take shape. That last Voice is as close as breath, as gentle as a whisper. It is the most vulnerable Voice of all, and the easiest to ignore. The Bible says the Spirit can be "quenched" or "grieved"—try quenching Moses' burning bush or the molten rocks of Sinai! Yet the Spirit is also the most intimate Voice. In our moments of weakness, when we do not know what to pray, the Spirit within intercedes for us with groans that words cannot express. Those groans are the early pangs of birth, the labor pains of the new creation.

The Spirit will not remove all disappointment with God. The very titles given to the Spirit—Intercessor, Helper, Counselor, Comforter—imply there will be problems. But the Spirit is also "a deposit, guaranteeing what is to come," Paul said, drawing on an earthy metaphor from the financial world. The Spirit reminds us that such disappointments are temporary, a prelude to an eternal life with God. God deemed it necessary to restore the spiritual link *before* re-creating heaven and earth.

In two places the New Testament compares being Spirit-filled with the state of drunkenness. Both states change the way you view life's trials, but there is a profound difference between them. Many people turn to drink to drown out the sadness of unemployment, illness, and personal tragedy. Inevitably, however, a drunk must awake from the fantasy world of inebriation and return to an unchanged reality. But the Spirit whispers of a new reality, a fantasy that is actually true, one into which we will awake for eternity.

Bible references: Romans 8; Ephesians 3; 1 Peter 1; 1 Corinthians 12; Ephesians 5; Philippians 2; Ephesians 2; 2 Corinthians 3; Galatians 3 (KJV); 2 Corinthians 3, 5.

BOOK II

SEEING
IN THE DARK

I said to my soul, be still, and let the dark
    come upon you
Which shall be the darkness of God. . . .
I said to my soul, be still, and wait without hope
For hope would be hope for the wrong thing;
    wait without love
For love would be love of the wrong thing;
    there is yet faith
But the faith and the love and the hope are all
    in the waiting.

                    —T. S. Eliot, "East Coker"

Chapter 21

Interrupted

R ATHER LATE ONE NIGHT I sat in my basement office and began to outline the next part of this book, which I intended to be a review and summation. Over the years I had filled several file folders with miscellaneous notes on the subject of disappointment with God, and I started to sift through these scraps of paper, reviewing them in light of what I had learned from the Bible.

As I worked, I thought about the original meeting with Richard in my living room, when his three large questions had first emerged. These questions about God's fairness and silence and hiddenness had become my own and had launched my search through the Bible. When I began that search, I wanted a more active God, one who would on occasion roll up his sleeves and step into my life with visible power. At the least, I thought, I wanted a God who did not stay quite so hidden and silent, one who worked in slightly *less* mysterious ways. Surely that wasn't asking too much.

But the Bible contained some surprises: notably that such

times of frequent miracles usually did not foster long-term belief. Just the opposite—most of them stand out as examples of faith*less*ness. The more I studied the Bible, the less I longed for the "good old days" of daily manna and fireballs from heaven.

Most important, in the Bible I caught a glimpse of God's point of view. God's "goal," if one can speak in such terms, is not to overpower all skeptics with a flashy miracle; he could do that in an instant if he wished. Rather, he seeks to reconcile: to love, and to be loved. And the Bible shows a clear progression in God's efforts to break through to human beings without overwhelming them: from God the Father who hovered parentally over the Hebrews; to God the Son who taught the will of God "from the bottom up," rather than by fiat, from above; and finally, to the Holy Spirit who fills us with the literal presence of God. We who live now are not disadvantaged but wonderfully privileged, for God has chosen to rely primarily on *us* to carry out his will on earth.

I reviewed these thoughts with growing enthusiasm as I worked on my outline that night. Then, shuffling through another stack of papers, I found a letter from Meg Woodson.

I have known Meg for more than a decade. She is a devout Christian, a pastor's wife, and a very fine writer. Yet I cannot think of Meg without feeling a stab of grief.

The Woodsons had two children—Peggie and Joey—both born with cystic fibrosis. Peggie and Joey stayed skinny no matter how much food they ate. They coughed constantly and labored to breathe—twice a day Meg had to pound on their chests to clear out mucus. They spent several weeks each year in a local hospital, and both grew up knowing they would probably die before reaching adulthood. *

---

*Meg has written strong, moving books about both her children: *Following Joey Home; I'll Get to Heaven Before You Do!* and *The Time of Her Life.*

Joey, a bright, happy, all-American boy, died at the age of twelve. Peggie defied the odds by living much longer. I joined Meg in desperate prayers for Peggie. Although we knew of no recorded miraculous healings of cystic fibrosis, we prayed for healing anyway. Peggie survived several health crises in high school and went away to college. She seemed to grow stronger, not weaker, and our hopes rose that she would find healing after all.

But there was no miracle: Peggie died at the age of twenty-three. And that night in my basement office I came across the letter Meg had written to me after Peggie's death.

> I find myself wanting to tell you something of how Peggie died. I don't know why except that the need to talk about it is so compelling and, since I refuse to put my friends here through it more than once, I have run out of people to tell.
>
> The weekend before she went into the hospital for the last time, Peggie came home all excited about a quotation from William Barclay her minister had used. She was so taken with it that she had copied it down on a 3 x 5 card for me: "Endurance is not just the ability to bear a hard thing, but to turn it into glory." She said her minister must have had a hard week, because after he read it he banged the pulpit and then turned his back to them and cried.
>
> After Peggie had been in the hospital for a while and things were not going well, she looked around at all the paraphernalia of death to which she was attached. Then she said, "Hey, Ma, remember that quotation?" And she looked around again at all the tubes, stuck the tip of her tongue out of the corner of her mouth, nodded her head, and raised her eyes in excitement at the experiment to which she was committing herself.
>
> Her commitment held as long as her awareness of anything in the real world held. Once, the president of her college came to see her and asked if there was anything specific he could pray for. She was too weak to talk, but nodded to me to explain the Barclay quote and ask him to pray that her hard time would be turned into glory.

I was sitting beside her bed a few days before her death when suddenly she began screaming. I will never forget those shrill, piercing, primal screams. Nurses raced into the room from every direction and surrounded her with their love. "It's okay, Peggie," one said. "Jeannie's here."

The nurses stroked her body. Eventually with their words and their touches they soothed her (though as time went on and the screaming continued, they could not). I've rarely seen such compassion. Wendy, Peggie's special nurse-friend, tells me there isn't a nurse on the floor who does not have at least one patient she would give one of her lungs to save if she could.

So, it's against this background of human beings falling apart—nurses can only stay on that floor so long—because they could not do more to help, that God, who could have helped, looked down on a young woman devoted to Him, quite willing to die for Him to give Him glory, and decided to sit on His hands and let her death top the horror charts for cystic fibrosis deaths.

I tell you, Philip, it does not help to talk of the good that results from pain. Nor does it help to talk of God almost always letting the physical process of disease run its course. Because if He ever intervenes, then at every point of human suffering He makes a decision to intervene or not, and in Peggie's case His choice was to let C.F. rip. There are moments when my only responses are grief and an anger as violent as any I have ever known. Nor does expressing it dissipate it.

Peggie never complained against God. It was no pious restraint: I don't think it ever occurred to her to complain. And none of us who lived through her death with her complained at the time either. We were upheld. God's love was so real, one could not doubt it or rail against its ways.

If I've been telling you all this in an effort to come to some kind of resolution to the problem of Peggie's and my pain, perhaps I've been brought once again to the only thing that helps me experience God's love: His stroking, His "I'm here, Meg." But, again I wonder, how could He be in a situation like that and sit on His hands?

As I think of it, I've never expressed all this to anyone before, for fear of disturbing someone's faith. Don't think you must say anything to "make me feel better." But thanks for listening. Most people have no idea how much that helps.

After reading Meg's letter, I could not work anymore that evening.

The View from Here

Old questions churned up again, my own questions about social injustices, unanswered prayers, unhealed bodies, and countless other instances of unfairness. And Richard's questions came surging back with new emotional force, a fraction of the force Meg herself must have felt as she sat helpless by her daughter's hospital bed.

I had searched the Bible for insights into what God is up to in this world and how it must feel to be God—knowing, of course, that we can never come close to comprehending such an exalted viewpoint. Meg's letter, however, pushed me in another direction and changed my whole approach to the last part of this book.

It's fine to consider God's viewing level, but what about *our* point of view? I had been exploring what it feels like to be God; Meg's letter jarred me back to what it feels like to be human. Her questions are questions of the heart, not the head. As a mother, she watched her children die slow, horrible deaths. Yet as a Christian she believes in God the loving Father. How can she fit the two together?

That night, I realized this book was not over. Theological concepts don't amount to very much unless they can speak to someone like Meg Woodson, who gropes for God's love in a world bordered by grief. I recalled a floundering minister in a John Updike novel who said, "Something's gone wrong. I have no faith. Or, rather, I have faith, but it doesn't seem to apply." How does it apply? What do we have a right to expect from God?

Then the Lord said to Satan, "Have you considered my servant Job? There is no one on earth like him; he is blameless and upright, a man who fears God and shuns evil."

—Job 1:8

Chapter 22

The Only Problem

There is one church here, so I go to it. On Sunday mornings I quit the house and wander down the hill to the white frame church in the firs. On a big Sunday there might be twenty of us there; often I am the only person under sixty, and feel as though I'm on an archaeological tour of Soviet Russia. The members are of mixed denominations; the minister is a Congregationalist, and wears a white shirt. The man knows God. Once, in the middle of the long pastoral prayer of intercession for the whole world—for the gift of wisdom to its leaders, for hope and mercy to the grieving and pained, succor to the oppressed, and God's grace to all—in the middle of this he stopped, and burst out, "Lord, we bring you these same petitions every week." After a shocked pause, he continued reading the prayer. Because of this, I like him very much.
—Annie Dillard, Holy the Firm

S O FAR, I have avoided one book in the Bible, a book that confronts the very issues raised by the Congregationalist minister, and by Richard and Meg, and almost everyone who thinks about God. Not surprisingly, then, after reading Meg's letter I found myself turning to the Book of Job.

Possibly the oldest book in the Bible, Job reads like the most modern. Its extreme portrayal—one man confronting the abyss in a universe that makes no sense—foreshadows the predicament of modern humanity. People who reject nearly everything else in the Bible keep coming back to Job for inspiration. Its recurring theme—How can a good God allow suffering?—is "the only problem worth discussing," said contemporary British novelist Muriel Spark in her book *The Only Problem.* The problem of pain is a modern obsession, the theological kryptonite of our time, and the ancient man Job expressed it as well as it has ever been expressed.

Richard complained about the loss of a fiancée and a job and a stable home life. Meg cried out in pain over the loss of a son and a daughter. Yet by any standard Job lost far more: 7000 sheep, 3000 camels, 5000 oxen, 500 donkeys, and numerous servants. Then all Job's children—seven sons and three daughters—died in one mighty gust of wind. Finally Job's health, his last consolation, failed him, as sores broke out from the soles of his feet to the top of his head. Overnight, the greatest man in all the East was reduced to the most pitiable.

Job is the Bible's prime case study of disappointment with God, and as such it seems to anticipate whatever disappointment Richard or Meg or any of us might feel. An American rabbi wrote a popular book called *When Bad Things Happen to Good People.* The Book of Job raises the ante: it portrays the very worst things happening to the very best person.

A Misreading

If you had asked me when I began my study what the Book of Job was about, I would have been quick to respond. *Job? Everybody knows what Job is about. It's the Bible's most complete treatment of the problem of suffering. It's about terrible grief and bewildering pain.* Without doubt the bulk of the book does center on the theme of suffering. Chapters 3–37 contain no action to speak of, just the opinionated dialogues of five prickly men—Job, his three friends, and the enigmatic Elihu—concerning the problem of pain. They are all trying to account for the slings and arrows of outrageous fortune that have fallen upon poor Job, who sits forlorn in the ashes of what used to be his mansion.

I now believe I misread the book—or, more accurately, didn't take into account the entire book. Despite the fact that all but a few pages of Job deal with the problem of pain, I am coming to the conclusion that Job is not really about the problem of pain. Suffering contributes the ingredients of the story, not its central theme. Just as a cake is not about eggs, flour, milk, and shortening, but uses those ingredients in the process of creating a cake, Job is not "about" suffering; it merely uses such ingredients in its larger story, which concerns even more important questions, cosmic questions. Seen as a whole, Job is primarily about *faith* in its starkest form.

I am drawn to this conclusion mainly because of the introductory "plot" in chapters 1 and 2, which reveals that Job's personal drama on earth had its origin in a cosmic drama in heaven. I once regarded Job as a profound expression of human disappointment—something on the order of Meg Woodson's letter, only longer and more detailed, and with direct biblical sanction. As I studied the book further, however, I discovered that it does not really present the human viewpoint. God is the central character in the Bible, and nowhere does this come through more clearly than in the Book of Job. I realized that I had always read it from the perspective of chapter 3 on—in other words, from Job's perspective.

Let me explain.

It helps to think of the Book of Job as a mystery play, a "whodunit" detective story. Before the play itself begins, we in the audience get a sneak preview, as if we have showed up early for a press conference in which the director explains his work (chapters 1–2). He relates the plot and describes the main characters, then tells us in advance who did what in the play, and why. In fact, he solves every mystery in the play except one: how will the main character respond? Will Job trust God or deny him?

Later, when the curtain rises, we see only the actors on stage. Confined within the play, they have no knowledge of what the director has told us in the sneak preview. We know the answer to the "whodunit" questions, but the star detective, Job, does not. He spends all his time on stage trying to discover what we already know. He scratches himself with shards of pottery and asks, "Why me? What did I do wrong? What is God trying to tell me?"

To the audience, Job's questions should be mere intellectual exercises, for we learned the answers in the prologue, the first two chapters. What did Job do wrong? Nothing. He represents the very best of the species. Didn't God himself call Job "blameless and upright, a man who fears God and shuns evil"? Why, then, is Job suffering? Not for punishment. Far from it—he has been selected as the principal player in a great contest of the heavens.

The Wager

In retrospect, I sometimes wonder how I could have misread the Book of Job so badly. Part of the reason, I think, lies in the eloquence of chapters 3–37, which express the human dilemma with such power that we can get trapped in their force field, forgetting that the questions they raise have already been answered in chapters 1 and 2. But there is yet another reason: no one knows quite what to make of the first two chapters. Even biblical scholars tend to view the prologue with embarrassment, or discount it as the addition of a later editor. The prologue shows God and Satan involved in—and you can almost see blush marks on the commentary pages—something resembling a wager. All Job's trauma traces back to, well, a kind of bet, placed by the two cosmic powers.

The trouble starts with Satan's claim that Job is a spoiled favorite, loyal only because God has "put a hedge around him." Satan scoffs that God, unworthy of love in himself, only attracts people like Job because they're "bribed" to follow him. If times ever get tough, Satan charges, such people will quickly abandon

God. When God accepts the challenge to test Satan's theory, thus consenting to let Job's response settle the issue, the calamities begin to rain down on poor, unsuspecting Job.

I would certainly not deny the strangeness of this heavenly contest. On the other hand, I cannot sidestep the account of The Wager in Job, for it offers a rare peek through the keyhole of eternity. When people experience pain, questions spill out—the very questions that tormented Job. Why me? What's going on? Does God care? Is there a God? This one time, in the raw recounting of Job's travail, we the onlookers—not Job—are granted a view behind the curtain. What we long for, the prologue to Job provides: a glimpse into how the world is run. As nowhere else in the Bible, the Book of Job shows us God's point of view, including the supernatural activity normally hidden from us.

Job has put God on trial, accusing him of unfair acts against an innocent party. Angry, satirical, betrayed, Job wanders as close to blasphemy as he can get—just to the edge. His words have a startlingly familiar ring because they are so modern. He gives voice to our most deeply felt complaints against God. But chapters 1 and 2 prove that, regardless of what Job thinks, God is not on trial in this book. Job is on trial. The point of the book is not suffering: Where is God when it hurts? The prologue dealt with that issue. The point is faith: Where is Job when it hurts? How is he responding? To understand the Book of Job, I must begin there.

To believe in the supernatural is not simply to believe that after living a successful, material, and fairly virtuous life here one will continue to exist in the best-possible substitute for this world, or that after living a starved and stunted life here one will be compensated with all the good things one has gone without: it is to believe that the supernatural is the greatest reality here and now.

—T. S. Eliot

Bible references: Job 1–2.

What is man that you make so much of him,
    that you give him so much attention,
that you examine him every morning
    and test him every moment?
Will you never look away from me,
    or let me alone even for an instant?
                  —Job 7:17–18

Chapter 23

A Role in the Cosmos

Some say that to the gods we are like flies that boys idly swat on a summer day. Others say that not a feather from a sparrow falls to the ground without the will of the Heavenly Father.
—Thornton Wilder, The Bridge of San Luis Rey

T O MY FRIEND Richard, who wrote a book about Job, that ancient man seemed a larger-than-life hero who had dared arm wrestle with God Almighty. Once, after listening to Richard expound on the valor of Job, I brought up the account of The Wager. Anger rose in his face. "All I can say," he snapped, "is that Job paid one *hell* of a price just to make God feel good!"

I, too, found it hard to avoid such sentiments at first. There is no easy way around the difficulty, for the heavenly contest played itself out in Job's life in the form of marauders, firestorms, windstorms, and boils. How can God's winning a contest, *any* contest, be worth such a price? As C. G. Jung asked in his caustic book on Job, "Is it worth the lion's while to terrify the mouse?"

167

As I studied Job further, however, I saw that I had been harboring the wrong image of what took place. Yes, there was an arm wrestling match, but not between Job and God. Rather, *Satan and God* were the chief combatants, although—most significantly—God had designated the man Job as his stand-in. The first and last chapters make clear that Job was unknowingly performing in a cosmic showdown before spectators in the unseen world.

Disturbing the Universe

The strange scene of The Wager reminded me of a few other places where the Bible affords a brief glimpse behind the curtain. Consider, for example, Revelation 12, which depicts an even more bizarre contest: a pregnant woman, wearing the sun for a dress and twelve stars for a crown, opposes a red dragon so enormous he can dislodge a third of the stars from the sky with one sweep of his tail. The dragon lies in wait, seeking to devour the pregnant woman's child at birth. And there's more: a flight into the desert, a serpent who tries to drown the woman, and a fierce war in heaven.

Biblical commentators propose as many interpretations of the details in Revelation 12 as there are commentaries, but almost all agree that the weird images point to the great disruption in the universe caused by Jesus' birth in Bethlehem. In a sense, Revelation 12 presents another side of Christmas, adding a new set of holographic images to the familiar scenes of manger and shepherds and the slaughter of the innocents. Which is the "true" story of Christmas: Luke's pastoral version or Revelation's account of the cosmos at war? They are the same story, of course; only the level of viewing differs. Luke gives the view from earth and Revelation shades in details from the unseen world.

The two worlds come together vividly in three of Jesus' most famous stories, the parables of the lost sheep, the lost coin, and the lost son. All three make the same point: great joy breaks out in heaven when a sinner repents. Today, anyone can watch a sinner repenting, for televised Billy Graham crusades portray the scene live and in color. The camera follows a young woman as she makes her way through the stands to an area set aside for repentance and conversion. But Jesus' stories imply that far more may be going on out there: beyond that stadium scene, in a place concealed from all camera lenses, a great party has erupted, a gigantic celebration in the unseen world.

Belief in an unseen world forms a crucial dividing line of faith today. Many people get up, eat, drive their cars, work, make phone calls, tend to their children, and go to bed without giving a single thought to the existence of an unseen world. But according to the Bible, human history is far more than the rising and falling of people and nations; it is a staging ground for the battle of the universe. Hence what seems like an "ordinary" action in the seen world may have an extraordinary effect on the unseen world: a short-term mission assignment causes Satan to fall like lightning from heaven (Luke 10); a sinner's repentance sets off celestial celebration (Luke 15); a baby's birth disturbs the entire universe (Revelation 12). Much of that effect, however, remains hidden from our view—except for the occasional glimpses granted us in places like Revelation, and in Job.

An ordinary person in the seen world, Job was called upon to endure a trial with cosmic consequences. He had no glimmer of light to guide him, no hint that the unseen world cared about him, or even existed. Yet like a laboratory test animal, he was handpicked to settle one of the most urgent issues of humanity and to determine a small piece of the history of the universe.

Is it absurd to believe that one human being, a tiny dot on a tiny planet, can make a difference in the history of the universe? It certainly seemed so to Job's friends. Listen to Elihu, the last of Job's comforters:

> If you sin, how does that affect him [God]?
> If your sins are many, what does that do to him?
> If you are righteous, what do you give to him,
> or what does he receive from your hand?
> Your wickedness affects only a man like yourself,
> and your righteousness only the sons of men.

Elihu, however, was flat wrong. The opening and closing chapters of Job prove that God was greatly affected by the response of one man and that cosmic issues were at stake. (Later, in a message to the prophet Ezekiel, God would point with pride to Job—along with Daniel and Noah—as one of his three favorites.)

Job's example, drawn in sharp relief, shows how life on earth affects the universe. When I began my study, I tended to avoid the "embarrassing" scene in chapter 1, but I have since come to believe that, whether drama or history, The Wager offers a message of great hope to all of us—perhaps the most powerful and enduring lesson from Job. In the end, The Wager resolved decisively that the faith of a single human being counts for very much indeed. Job affirms that our response to testing *matters*. The history of mankind—and, in fact, my own individual history of faith–is enclosed within the great drama of the history of the universe.

God has granted us "the dignity of causation," said Pascal. We may doubt, with Elihu, whether one person can make any appreciable difference. But the Bible rustles with hints that something like The Wager is played out in other believers as well. We are God's Exhibit A, his demonstration piece to the powers in the unseen world. The apostle Paul, borrowing an image from the processional of gladiators into the Colosseum, pictured himself on public display: "We have been made a spectacle to the whole universe, to angels as well as to men." And in the same letter he commented, in an astonishing aside, "Do you not know that we will judge angels?"

We humans inhabit a mere speck of a planet in the outer suburbs of a spiral galaxy that is only one of about a million million such galaxies in the observable universe, but the New Testament insists that what happens among us here will, in fact, help determine the future of that universe. Paul is emphatic: "The whole creation is on tiptoe to see the wonderful sight of the sons of God coming into their own." Natural creation, "groaning" in travail and decay, can only be set free by the transformation of human beings.

The Great Reversal

In the Christian view, all of human history takes place somewhere between the first part of Genesis and the last part of Revelation, which paint the same scene, with the same brush strokes: Paradise, a river, the luminous glory of God, and the Tree of Life. History begins and ends at the same place, and everything in between comprises the struggle to regain what was lost.*

After the fall from Paradise, history entered a new phase. Creation God had done by himself, starting with nothing and ending up with the universe in all its splendor. The new work is Re-creation, and for this God employs the very human beings who had originally spoiled his work. Creation progressed through stages: first stars, then the sky and sea, and on through plants and animals, and finally man and woman. Re-creation reverses the sequence, starting with man and woman and culminating in the restoration of all the rest.

In many ways the act of Re-creation is "harder" than creation, for it relies on flawed human beings. Surely, it has cost God more: the death of his Son. Still, God insists on healing the world from the bottom up, rather than from the top down.

As I studied Job, it struck me that The Wager was, at its heart, a stark reenactment of God's original question in creation: Will the humans choose for or against me? From God's point of view that has been the central question of history, beginning with Adam and continuing on through Job and every man and woman who has ever lived. The Wager in the Book of Job called into question the whole human experiment.

Satan denied that human beings are truly free. We have

---

*John MacQuarrie discusses our ultimate destiny in this passage from *The Humility of God:* "If the doctrine of original sin is not to have the last word, it must be confronted with a doctrine of original righteousness. After all, in the Old Testament story righteousness is more original than sin."

freedom to descend, of course—Adam and all his descendants proved that. But freedom to ascend, to believe God for no other reason than, well . . . for no reason at all? Can a person believe even when God appears to him as an enemy? Or is faith one more product of environment and circumstance? The opening chapters of Job expose Satan as the first great behaviorist: Job was *conditioned* to love God, he implied. Take away the rewards, and watch his faith crumble. The Wager put Satan's theory to the test.

I have come to see Job's trials as a crucial test of human freedom, an important issue in modern times as well. In our century, it takes faith to believe that a human being amounts to more than a combination of DNA programming, instincts of the gene pool, cultural conditioning, and the impersonal forces of history. Yet even in this behaviorist century, we want to believe differently. We want to believe that the thousand hard and easy choices we make each day somehow count. And the Book of Job insists that they do; one person's faith can make a difference. There is a role for human beings, after all, and by fulfilling that role Job set a pattern for anyone who ever faces doubt or hardship.

Very often, disappointment with God begins in Job-like circumstances. The death of a child, a tragic accident, or a loss of job may bring on the same questions Job asked. Why me? What does God have against me? Why does he seem so distant? As readers of Job's story, we can see behind the curtain to a contest being waged in the invisible world. But in our own trials, we will not have such insight. When tragedy strikes, we will live in shadow, unaware of what is transpiring in the unseen world. The drama that Job lived through will then replicate itself in our individual lives. Once again, God will let his reputation ride on the response of unpredictable human beings.

For Job, the battleground of faith involved lost possessions, lost family members, lost health. We may face a different struggle: a career failure, a floundering marriage, sexual orientation, a body shape that turns people off, not on. At such times the outer circumstances—the illness, the bank account, the run of bad luck—will seem the real struggle. We may beg God to change those circumstances. *If only I were beautiful or handsome, then*

172

everything would work out. If only I had more money—or at least a job—then I could easily believe God.

But the more important battle, as shown in Job, takes place inside us. Will we trust God? Job teaches that at the moment when faith is hardest and *least* likely, then faith is most needed. His struggle presents a glimpse of what the Bible elsewhere spells out in detail: the remarkable truth that our choices matter, not just to us and our own destiny but, amazingly, to God himself and the universe he rules.

In short, God has granted to ordinary men and women the dignity of participating in the Great Reversal which will restore the cosmos to its pristine state. All the reasons for disappointment with God that I have mentioned in this book, as well as all cancers, all deaths, all broken relationships, all the collected groanings of our savage planet—all these imperfections will be wiped away. We may at times question God's wisdom and lose patience with his timetable. (The disciples, after all, felt bitter disappointment when Jesus rejected their dream of a physical kingdom in favor of an invisible, spiritual kingdom.) But all the prophets' lavish promises will someday come true, and we, you and I, are the ones selected to help bring that about.

No one has expressed the pain and unfairness of this world more poignantly than Job; no one has voiced disappointment with God more passionately. We must still attend to Job's complaints and to God's fierce response. But the Book of Job begins not with the complaints—the human viewpoint—but with God's point of view. In the prologue, the scene of The Wager establishes a darkly shining truth: Job—and you and I—can join the struggle to reverse all that is wrong with the universe. We can make a difference.

The Book of Job gives no satisfying answers to the question "Why?" Instead, it substitutes another question, "To what end?" By remaining faithful to God through his trials Job, crotchety, sardonic old Job, helped abolish the very pain and unfairness of this world that he had protested so vigorously. And Meg Woodson, who stubbornly clings to God's love in the shadows, even after watching two children die . . . she too is helping to reverse those wrongs.

Why the delay? Why does God let evil and pain so flagrantly exist, even thrive, on this planet? Why does he let us do slowly and blunderingly what he could do in an eyeblink?

He holds back for our sakes. Re-creation involves us; we are, in fact, at the center of his plan. The Wager, the motive behind all human history, is to develop us, not God. Our very existence announces to the powers in the universe that restoration is under way. Every act of faith by every one of the people of God is like the tolling of a bell, and a faith like Job's reverberates throughout the universe.

> Our present life feels like a real fight—as if there were something really wild in the universe which we, with all our idealities and faithfulnesses, are needed to redeem.
> —William James, The Will to Believe

> I had far rather walk, as I do, in daily terror of eternity, than feel that this was only a children's game in which all the contestants would get equally worthless prizes in the end.
> —T. S. Eliot

Bible references: Job 35; 1 Corinthians 4, 6; Romans 8 PHILLIPS.

Yet when I hoped for good, evil came;
    when I looked for light, then came darkness.
The churning inside me never stops.
                                    —Job 30:26–27

Chapter 24

Is God Unfair?

T he *Road Less Traveled,* by M. Scott Peck, opens with a
blunt three-word sentence: "Life is difficult." If reduced to
a single sentence, the Book of Job would express something
similar, for the loud cry, "Life is unfair!" resounds from almost
every page.

Unfairness is no easier for us to swallow today than it was for
Job thousands of years ago. Consider the most common curse word
in the English language: "God" followed by the word "damn."
People say it not only in the face of great tragedy, but also when
their cars won't start, when a favored sports team loses, when it
rains on their picnic. That oath renders an instinctive judgment
that life *ought* to be fair and that God should somehow "do a
better job" of running his world.

The world as it is versus the world as it ought to be—the
constant tension between those two states bursts into the open in
the Book of Job. For three long, windy rounds, Job and his friends
spar in a verbal boxing match. On the ground rules, they all agree:

God should reward those who do good and punish those who do evil.

Why, then, is Job, a supposedly good man, suffering so much apparent punishment? Job's friends, confident of God's fairness, defend the world as it is. "Use your common sense," they tell Job. "God would not afflict you without a cause. You must have committed some secret sin." But Job, who knows beyond doubt he has·done nothing to deserve such punishment, cannot agree. He pleads innocent.

Gradually, however, the suffering wears down Job's most cherished beliefs. How can God be on his side? Job wonders. He is, after all, squatting in a heap of ashes, the ruins of his life. He is a broken, despairing man, "betrayed" by God. "Look at me and be astonished; clap your hand over your mouth," Job cries.

A crisis of faith brews inside him. Is God unfair? Such a notion calls into question everything Job believes, but how else can he explain what has happened? He looks around for other examples of unfairness and sees that evil people sometimes do prosper—they don't get punished, as he'd like to believe—while some godly people suffer. And many other people live happy, fruitful lives without ever giving a thought to God. For Job, the facts simply do not add up. "When I think about this, I am terrified; trembling seizes my body."

The reason the Book of Job seems so modern is that for us, too, the facts do not add up. Job's strident message of life's unfairness seems peculiarly suited to our own pain-racked century. Simply plug contemporary illustrations into his arguments: "innocent" but starving children in the Third World; faithful pastors imprisoned in South Africa; Christian leaders who die in their prime; Mafia dons and spoiled entertainers who profit obscenely from flouting God's rules; the millions in Western Europe who live quiet, happy lives and never give God a thought. Far from fading away, Job's questions about this world's unfairness have only grown louder and shriller. We still expect a God of love and power to follow certain rules on earth. Why doesn't he?

Is God Unfair?

Coming to Terms with Unfairness

At some point, every human being confronts the mysteries that caused Job to tremble in terror. Is God unfair?

One option seemed obvious to Job's wife: "Curse God and die!" she advised. Why hold on to a sentimental belief in a loving God when so much in life conspires against it? And in this Job-like century, more people than ever before have come to agree with her. Some Jewish writers, such as Jerzy Kosinski and Elie Wiesel, began with a strong faith in God, but saw it vaporize in the gas furnaces of the Holocaust. Face to face with history's grossest unfairness, they concluded that God must not exist. (Still, the human instinct asserts itself. Kosinski and Wiesel cannot avoid a tone of outrage, as if they too feel betrayed. They overlook the underlying issue of where our primal sense of fairness comes from. Why ought we even *expect* the world to be fair?)

Others, equally mindful of the world's unfairness, cannot bring themselves to deny God's existence. Instead, they propose another possibility: perhaps God agrees that life is unfair, but cannot do anything about it. Rabbi Harold Kushner took this approach in his best-selling book *When Bad Things Happen to Good People*. After watching his son die of the disease progeria, Kushner concluded that "even God has a hard time keeping chaos in check," and that God is "a God of justice and not of power."

According to Rabbi Kushner, God is as frustrated, even outraged, by the unfairness on this planet as anyone else, but he lacks the power to change it. Millions of readers found comfort in Kushner's portrayal of a God who seemed compassionate, albeit weak. I wonder, however, what those people make of the last five chapters of Job, which contain God's "self-defense." No other part of the Bible conveys God's power so impressively. If God is less-than-powerful, why did he choose the worst possible situation, when his power was most called into question, to insist on his omnipotence? (Elie Wiesel said of the God described by Kushner, "If that's who God is, why doesn't he resign and let someone more competent take his place?")

A third group of people evades the problem of unfairness by

looking to the future, when an exacting justice will work itself out in the universe. Unfairness is a temporary condition, they say. The Hindu doctrine of Karma, which applies a mathematical precision to this belief, calculates it may take a soul 6,800,000 incarnations to realize perfect justice. At the end of all those incarnations, a person will have experienced exactly the amount of pain and pleasure that he or she deserves.

A fourth approach is to flatly deny the problem and insist the world is fair. Echoing Job's friends, these people insist the world does run according to fixed, regular laws: good people will prosper and evil ones will fail. I encountered this point of view at the faith-healing church in Indiana, and I hear it virtually every time I watch religious television, where some evangelist promises perfect health and financial prosperity to anyone who asks for it in true faith.

Such lavish promises have obvious appeal, but they fail to account for all the facts. The babies who contract AIDS *in utero*, for example, or the roll call of persecuted saints in *Foxe's Book of Martyrs*—how do these fit into a doctrine of life's fairness?* There is nothing I would rather have said to Meg Woodson than, "The world is fair, and therefore if you pray hard enough, your daughter will not die." But I could not say that, any more than I can now say, "God took Peggie away because of something you did wrong." Both points of view are represented in the Book of Job; both are dismissed by God in the end.

It takes an Olympian leap of faith to argue that life is completely fair. More commonly, Christians respond to life's unfairness not by denying it outright, but by watering it down.

---

*One of the "apocryphal" books circulating among early Christians told the story of a woman named Thecla, a convert of the apostle Paul. Her faith supposedly warded off all attacks: wild beasts refused to eat her, and men suddenly stopped in the act of ravishing her. When her tormentors tried to burn her at the stake, a cloud of rain and hail appeared overhead and doused the flames. The book circulated widely, but one needs only to read other books of church history, like *Foxe's Book of Martyrs*, to see why Thecla's story was ultimately dismissed as apocryphal.

They, like Job's friends, search for some hidden reason behind suffering:

"God is trying to teach you something. You should feel privileged, not bitter, about your opportunity to lean on him in faith."

"Meditate on the blessings you still enjoy—at least you are alive. Are you a fair-weather believer?"

"You are undergoing a training regimen, a chance to exercise new muscles of faith. Don't worry—God will not test you beyond your endurance."

"Don't complain so loudly! You will forfeit this opportunity to demonstrate your faithfulness to non-believers."

"Someone is always worse off than you. Give thanks despite your circumstances."

Job's friends offered a version of each of these words of wisdom, and each contains an element of truth. But the Book of Job plainly shows that such "helpful advice" does nothing to answer the questions of the person in pain. It was the wrong medicine, dispensed at the wrong time.

And finally, there is one more way to explain the world's unfairness. After hearing all the alternatives, Job was driven to the conclusion I have suggested as the one-sentence summary of the entire book: *Life is unfair!* It came to Job more as a reflex reaction than a philosophy of life, and that is how it strikes anyone who suffers. "Why me?" we ask. "What have I done?"

A Modern Job

While working on this book, I made it a point to meet regularly with people who felt betrayed by God. I wanted to keep before me the actual look, the facial expressions, of disappointment and doubt. When it came time to write about the Book of Job, I decided to interview the one person I know whose life most resembles Job's, a man I will call Douglas.

To me, Douglas seems "righteous" in the same sense as Job: not perfect, of course, but a model of faithfulness. After years of training in psychotherapy, he had declined a lucrative career in favor of starting an urban ministry. Douglas's troubles began some years ago when his wife discovered a lump in her breast. Surgeons removed that breast, but two years later the cancer had spread to her lungs. Douglas took over many household and parental duties as his wife battled the debilitating effects of chemotherapy. Sometimes she couldn't hold down any food. She lost her hair. And always she felt tired and vulnerable to fear and depression.

One night, in the midst of this crisis, as Douglas was driving down a city street with his wife and twelve-year-old daughter, a drunk driver swerved across the center line and smashed head-on into their car. Douglas's wife was badly shaken, but unhurt. His daughter suffered a broken arm and severe facial cuts from windshield glass. Douglas himself received the worst injury, a massive blow to the head.

After the accident, Douglas never knew when a headache might strike. He could not work a full day, and sometimes he would become disoriented and forgetful. Worse, the accident permanently affected his vision. One eye wandered at will, refusing to focus. He developed double vision and could hardly walk down a flight of stairs without assistance. Douglas learned to cope with all his disabilities but one: he could not read more than a page or two at a time. All his life, he had loved books. Now he was restricted to the limited selections and the sluggish pace of recorded books.

When I called Douglas to ask for an interview, he suggested meeting over breakfast; and when the scheduled time came, I braced myself for a difficult morning. By then I had interviewed a dozen people and had heard the full range of disappointment with God. If anyone had a right to be angry at God, Douglas did. Just that week, his wife had gotten a dismaying report from the hospital: there was another spot on her lung.

As our meal was being served, we caught up on the details of our lives. Douglas ate with great concentration and care. Thick glasses corrected some of his vision problems, but he had to work hard at focusing just to guide his fork to his mouth. I forced myself to look directly at him as he talked, trying to ignore the distraction of his wandering eye. At last, as we finished breakfast and motioned to the waitress for more coffee, I described my book on disappointment with God. "Could you tell me about your own disappointment?" I asked. "What have you learned that might help someone else going through a difficult time?"

Douglas was silent for what seemed like a long time. He stroked his peppery gray beard and gazed off beyond my right shoulder. I fleetingly wondered if he was having a mental "gap." Finally he said, "To tell you the truth, Philip, I didn't feel any disappointment with God."

I was startled. Douglas, searingly honest, had always rejected easy formulas like the "Turn your scars into stars!" testimonials of religious television. I waited for him to explain.

"The reason is this. I learned, first through my wife's illness and then especially through the accident, not to confuse God with life. I'm no stoic. I am as upset about what happened to me as anyone could be. I feel free to curse the unfairness of life and to vent all my grief and anger. But I believe God feels the same way about that accident—grieved and angry. I don't blame him for what happened."

Douglas continued, "I have learned to see beyond the physical reality in this world to the spiritual reality. We tend to think, 'Life should be fair because God is fair.' But God is not life. And if I confuse God with the physical reality of life—by expecting constant good health, for example—then I set myself up for a crashing disappointment.

"God's existence, even his love for me, does not depend on my good health. Frankly, I've had more time and opportunity to work on my relationship with God during my impairment than before."*

There was a deep irony in that scene. For months I had been absorbed in the failures of faith, having sought out stories of people disappointed in God. I had chosen Douglas as my modern

---

*Douglas's answer reminded me of a statement by Dr. Paul Brand. To the question "Where is God when it hurts?" Dr. Brand replied, "He is in *you*, the one hurting, not in *it*, the thing that hurts."

Job, and had expected from him a bitter blast of protest. The last thing I anticipated was a graduate-school course in faith.

"If we develop a relationship with God *apart* from our life circumstances," said Douglas, "then we may be able to hang on when the physical reality breaks down. We can learn to trust God despite all the unfairness of life. Isn't that really the main point of Job?"

Although Douglas's strict separation of "physical reality" and "spiritual reality" bothered me, I found his notion intriguing. For the next hour, we worked through the Bible together, testing out his ideas. In the Sinai wilderness, God's guarantees of *physical* success—health, prosperity, and military victory—did nothing to help the Israelites' *spiritual* performance. And most heroes of the Old Testament (Abraham, Joseph, David, Elijah, Jeremiah, Daniel) went through trials much like Job's. For each of them, at times, the physical reality surely seemed to present God as the enemy. But each managed to hold on to a trust in him despite the hardships. In doing so, their faith moved from a "contract faith"—I'll follow God if he treats me well—to a relationship that could transcend any hardship.

Suddenly, Douglas glanced at his watch and realized he was already late for another appointment. He put his coat on hurriedly and stood up to leave, and then leaned forward with one final thought. "I challenge you to go home and read again the story of Jesus. Was life 'fair' to him? For me, the cross demolished for all time the basic assumption that life will be fair."

Douglas and I had started out discussing Job and ended up discussing Jesus, and that pattern stayed with me: in the Old Testament one of God's favorites suffered terrible unfairness, and in the New Testament God's own Son suffered even more.

When I returned home, I took Douglas's advice and went through the Gospels again, wondering how Jesus would have answered the direct question, "Is life unfair?" Nowhere did I find him denying unfairness. When Jesus encountered a sick person, he never delivered a lecture about "accepting your lot in life"; he healed whoever approached him. And his scathing words about the rich and powerful of his day show clearly what he thought

184

about social inequities. The Son of God reacted to life's unfairness much like anybody else. When he met a person in pain, he was deeply moved with compassion. When his friend Lazarus died, he wept. When Jesus himself faced suffering, he recoiled from it, asking three times if there was any other way.

God responded to the question of unfairness not with words, but with a visit, an Incarnation. And Jesus offers flesh-and-blood proof of how God feels about unfairness, for he took on the "stuff" of life, the physical reality at its unfairest. He gave, in summary, a final answer to all lurking questions about the goodness of God. (It occurred to me as I read the Gospels that if all of us in his Body would spend our lives as he did—ministering to the sick, feeding the hungry, resisting the powers of evil, comforting those who mourn, and bringing the Good News of love and forgiveness— then perhaps the question "Is God unfair?" would not be asked with such urgency today.)

The Great Unfairness

Is God unfair? The answer depends on how closely we identify God and life. Surely life on earth is unfair. Douglas was correct in saying that the Cross settled that issue forever.

Author Henri Nouwen tells the story of a family he knew in Paraguay. The father, a doctor, spoke out against the military regime there and its human rights abuses. Local police took their revenge on him by arresting his teenage son and torturing him to death. Enraged townsfolk wanted to turn the boy's funeral into a huge protest march, but the doctor chose another means of protest. At the funeral, the father displayed his son's body as he had found it in the jail—naked, scarred from the electric shocks and cigarette burns and beatings. All the villagers filed past the corpse, which lay not in a coffin but on the blood-soaked mattress from the prison. It was the strongest protest imaginable, for it put injustice on grotesque display.

Isn't that what God did at Calvary? "It's God who ought to suffer, not you and me," say those who bear a grudge against God for the unfairness of life. The curse word expresses it well: God be damned. And on that day, God was damned. The cross that held Jesus' body, naked and marked with scars, exposed all the violence and injustice of this world. At once, the Cross revealed what kind of world we have and what kind of God we have: a world of gross unfairness, a God of sacrificial love.

No one is exempt from tragedy or disappointment—God himself was not exempt. Jesus offered no immunity, no way *out* of the unfairness, but rather a way *through* it to the other side. Just as Good Friday demolished the instinctive belief that this life is supposed to be fair, Easter Sunday followed with its startling clue to the riddle of the universe. Out of the darkness, a bright light shone.

The primal desire for fairness dies hard, and it should. Who among us does not sometimes yearn for more justice in this world here and now? Secretly, I admit, I yearn for a world "fault-proof" against disappointment, a world where my magazine articles will always find acceptance and my body does not grow old and weak, a world where my sister-in-law does not deliver a brain-damaged child, and where Peggie Woodson lives into ripe old age. But if I stake my faith on such a fault-proof earth, my faith will let me down. Even the greatest of miracles do not resolve the problems of this earth: all people who find physical healing eventually die.

We need more than miracle. We need a new heaven and a new earth, and until we have those, unfairness will not disappear.

A friend of mine, struggling to believe in a loving God amid much pain and sorrow, blurted out this statement: "God's only excuse is Easter!" The language is non-theological and harsh, but within that phrase lies a haunting truth. The Cross of Christ may have overcome evil, but it did not overcome unfairness. For that, Easter is required. Someday, God will restore all physical reality to its proper place under his reign. Until then, it is a good thing to remember that we live out our days on Easter Saturday.

Is God Unfair?

To be commanded to love God at all, let alone in the wilderness, is like being commanded to be well when we are sick, to sing for joy when we are dying of thirst, to run when our legs are broken. But this is the first and great commandment nonetheless. Even in the wilderness—especially in the wilderness—you shall love him.

—Frederick Buechner

Bible references: Job 21, 2.

Surely I spoke of things I did not understand,
things too wonderful for me to know.
　　　　　　　　　　　　—Job 42:3

Chapter 25

Why God Doesn't Explain

T OWARD THE END of the Book of Job, brash young Elihu delivers a stinging address in which he ridicules Job's desire for a visit from God. "Do you think God cares about a puny creature like you? Do you imagine that Almighty God, the Maker of the Universe, will deign to visit earth and meet with you in person? Does he owe you some kind of explanation? Get serious, Job!"

As Elihu drones on, a tiny cloud appears on the horizon, just over his shoulder. And as the cloud draws closer, roiling into a full-fledged storm, a Voice like no other voice booms out. Elihu's fine speech abruptly ends, and Job begins to tremble. God himself has arrived on the scene. He has come to reply in person to Job's accusations of unfairness.

If Job serves as the Bible's main case study of disappointment with God, then surely this dramatic speech out of the whirlwind should yield important insights into all other times of confusion and doubt. What, then, does God say in his own defense?

I can think of several helpful things God could have said:

"Job, I'm truly sorry about what's happened. You've endured many unfair trials on my behalf, and I'm proud of you. You don't know what this means to me and even to the universe." A few compliments, a dose of compassion, or at the least a brief explanation of what transpired "behind the curtain" in the unseen world—any of these would have given Job some solace.

God says nothing of the kind. His "reply," in fact, consists of more questions than answers. Sidestepping thirty-five chapters' worth of debates on the problem of pain, he plunges instead into a magnificent verbal tour of the natural world. He seems to guide Job through a private gallery of his favorite works, lingering with pride over dioramas of mountain goats, wild donkeys, ostriches, and eagles, speaking as if astonished by his own creations. The beauty of the poetry at the end of Job rivals anything in world literature. Even as I marvel at God's dazzling portrayal of the natural world, however, a sense of bewilderment steals in. Of all moments, why did God choose this one to give Job a course in wilderness appreciation? Are these words relevant?

In his book *Wishful Thinking*, Frederick Buechner sums up God's speech. "God doesn't explain. He explodes. He asks Job who he thinks he is anyway. He says that to try to explain the kind of things Job wants explained would be like trying to explain Einstein to a little-neck clam. . . . God doesn't reveal his grand design. He reveals himself."[1] The message behind the splendid poetry boils down to this: *Until you know a little more about running the physical universe, Job, don't tell me how to run the moral universe.*

"Why are you treating me so unfairly, God?" Job has whined throughout the book. "Put yourself in my place."

"NO!!!" God thunders in reply. "You put yourself in *my* place! Until you can offer lessons on how to make the sun come up each day, or where to scatter lightning bolts, or how to design a hippopotamus, don't judge how I run the world. Just shut up and listen."

The impact of God's speech on Job is almost as amazing as the speech itself. Although God never answers question one about Job's predicament, the blast from the storm flattens Job. He repents in dust and ashes, and every trace of disappointment with God is swept away.

What We Cannot Know

The rest of us, however, who may never hear a voice speaking out of the whirlwind, must try to figure out what God actually said to Job. Quite frankly, for me God's evasive reply creates as many problems as it solves. I cannot simply wish the "Why?" questions away. They come up every time I talk to someone like Meg Woodson, every time my own life starts to unravel.

God's refusal to answer Job's questions does not sit well with modern minds. We don't like—*I* don't like—being told something is beyond our grasp. I own a book titled *The Encyclopedia of Ignorance* which outlines many areas of science we cannot yet explain; but scientists all over the world are doing their best to explore those areas and fill in the gaps of knowledge. Has God perhaps fenced off an area of knowledge, *The Encyclopedia of Theological Ignorance*, that no human being will ever understand?

Much as I resist, I am pushed toward such a conclusion by the Book of Job. Why is life so unfair? When does God cause suffering and when merely permit it—and what is the difference? Why does God sometimes seem silent and sometimes close and intimate? When God had the perfect opportunity to settle those issues for good, he scowled and shook his head. Why bother to explain? Not Job nor any other human being could possibly understand.

I cannot offer answers to Job's specific questions, because God offered none. I can only ask why God gives no answers, why there must be an *Encyclopedia of Theological Ignorance*. Because I am entering an area on which the Bible stays silent, what follows is pure speculation. I include it for people who are never satisfied with a non-answer, for those who cannot stop asking questions even God has declined to answer.

1. Perhaps God keeps us ignorant because enlightenment might not help us.

The same urgent questions torment almost every suffering person: Why? Why me? What is God trying to tell me? In the

Book of Job, God deflects those questions of *cause,* and focuses instead on our *response* of faith. But think what might happen if God did answer our questions forthrightly. We assume that we would bear suffering better if we only knew the reason behind it. But would we?

I find striking similarities in two biblical books: Job and Lamentations. Job stared in disbelief at the ruins of his house and possessions; the author of Lamentations stared in disbelief at the ruins of his city, Jerusalem. Both books express anger and bitterness and deep disappointment with God. In fact, many passages from Lamentations sound like paraphrases of the much older Book of Job. Yet the prophet who wrote Lamentations (probably Jeremiah) was not in the dark. He knew exactly why Jerusalem had been destroyed: the Hebrews had broken their covenant with God. Nevertheless, knowing the cause did nothing to alleviate the suffering or the feelings of despair and abandonment. "The Lord is like an enemy," he pronounced, Job-like. "Why do you always forget us? Why do you forsake us so long?" he asked of God, though he knew full well the answers—other parts of the book spell them out in exhaustive detail.

What possible explanation could comfort a Job, a Jeremiah, or a Meg Woodson? Knowledge is passive, intellectual; suffering is active, personal. No intellectual answer will solve suffering. Perhaps this is why God sent his own Son as one response to human pain, to experience it and absorb it into himself. The Incarnation did not "solve" human suffering, but at least it was an active and personal response. In the truest sense, no words can speak more loudly than the Word.

If you look to the Book of Job for an answer to the "Why?" questions, you will come away disappointed. God declined to answer, Job withdrew his questions, and the three friends repented of all their mistaken assumptions. Jesus likewise avoided the issue of the direct cause of suffering. When his disciples drew certain conclusions about a man born blind (John 9) and about two local catastrophes (Luke 13), Jesus rebuked them. From the biblical evidence, I must conclude that any hard-and-fast answers to the "Why?" questions are, quite simply, out of reach.

192

Why God Doesn't Explain

Whenever we take on one of God's prerogatives, we tread on dangerous ground. Even a well-meaning attempt to comfort a child, "God took your Dad home because he liked him so much," crosses over into an area that the Bible seems to rule out of bounds. Though catastrophes—an airplane crash, a plague, a sniper's random killings, the deliberate poisoning of medicines, a famine in Africa—cry out for some authoritative interpretation, the Book of Job offers an important reminder: God himself did not attempt an explanation.

2. Perhaps God keeps us ignorant because we are incapable of comprehending the answer.

Maybe God's majestic non-answer to Job was no ploy, no clever way of dodging questions; maybe it was God's recognition of a plain fact of life. A tiny creature on a tiny planet in a remote galaxy simply could not fathom the grand design of the universe. You might as well try to describe colors to a person born blind, or a Mozart symphony to a person born deaf, or expound the theory of relativity to a person who doesn't even know about atoms.

To appreciate the problem, imagine yourself trying to communicate with a creature on a microscope slide. The "universe" to such a creature consists of only two dimensions, the flat plane of the glass slide; its senses cannot perceive anything beyond the edges. How could you convey a concept of space or height or depth to such a creature? Looking "from above," you can understand the creature's two-dimensional world as well as the three-dimensional world surrounding it. The creature, however, "from below," can only comprehend a world of two dimensions.*
In a similar way, the unseen world exists outside our range of perception—except for rare interventions into our "plane," which

---

*Anthropologists report a very similar "perception gap" among remote cultures. If an indigenous tribesman in Papua New Guinea is shown a photograph of a forest, he sees only marks and splotches of colors on a flat paper. He must, through experience, learn to "see" that the two-dimensional photograph actually contains three-dimensional images: birds, trees, waterfalls.

we call miracles. Job, or you and I, cannot comprehend the total picture with our present faculties.

Filmmaker Woody Allen playfully explored this "two worlds" level of viewing in his movie *Purple Rose of Cairo*. We first see the hero through Mia Farrow's eyes as she watches him play a role in a movie. Then, incredibly, that hero steps out—literally—from the two-dimensional movie screen and lands in the New Jersey theater; suddenly he is in the "real" world with the flabbergasted character played by Miss Farrow.

The outside world holds many surprises for the movie actor. When someone hits him with a fist, he dutifully falls down, as he was taught to do on-screen, but rubs his jaw with amazement— those blows aren't supposed to hurt! When he and Mia kiss, he pauses, waiting for the fadeout. And when someone tries to explain the concept of God—"He's the one in control of everything. He's what the whole world is about"—the actor nods, "Oh, you mean Mr. Mayer, the owner of the movie company." His perceptions are confined to the world of the movie.

Eventually, the actor climbs back onto the two-dimensional movie screen and tries to explain the real world to the rest of the cast. They stare at him as if he belongs in a mental asylum. He's talking nonsense. There is no "other" world out there; only the world of the movie is real for them.

Woody Allen makes the same point as the analogy of the two-dimensional creature. If one world (the world of two-dimensions, or the world of the movie) exists inside another, it will only make sense from the "higher" world's point of view. And, to carry the analogy a long way, all the way back to the Book of Job, most of Job's questions concerned activity in the "higher" world, a world beyond his comprehension.

God lives on a "higher" level, in another dimension. The universe does not contain him; he created the universe. In a way we cannot fathom, he is not bound by space and time. He can step into the material world—if he did not, in fact, our senses would never perceive him—but it is for him a "stepping into," like an author who introduces himself as a character in his own play, like a person in the real world who makes a brief appearance in a movie.

A Matter of Time

There was a young lady named Bright
Whose speed was much greater than light
So she set off one day
In a relative way
And returned on the previous night.

The perception of time, especially, points up the huge difference between God's perspective (the view from above) and ours, and I have come to believe that this difference accounts for many of our unanswered questions on disappointment with God. For that reason, it merits what may seem like a diversion.

St. Augustine devoted Book 11 of *The Confessions* to a discussion of time. "What, then, is time?" he begins. "If no one asks me, I know; if I want to explain it to someone who does ask me, I do not know." When asked, "What was God doing *before* creation?" Augustine responded that since God invented time along with the created world, such a question is nonsense, and merely betrays the time-bound perspective of the questioner.* "Before" time there is only eternity, and eternity for God is a never-ending present. For God, one day is like a thousand years, and a thousand years are like a day.[2]

What would Augustine make of all that has happened since Einstein connected time and space? Now we understand time as relative, not as absolute. Perception of time, we are told, depends on the relative position of the observer. Take a recent example: on the night of February 23, 1987, an astronomer in Chile observed with his naked eye the explosion of a distant supernova, a blast so powerful that it released as much energy in one second

---

*Martin Luther was not nearly so polite. "When one asked, where God was before heaven was created? St. Augustine answered: He was in himself. When another asked me the same question, I said: He was building hell for such idle, presumptuous, fluttering and inquisitive spirits as you."

as our sun will release in ten billion years. But did that event truly occur on February 23, 1987? Only from the perspective of our planet. Actually, the supernova exploded 170,000 years prior to our 1987, but the light generated by that faraway event, traveling almost 6 trillion miles a year, took 170,000 years to reach our galaxy.

And here is where the "higher" view of eternity defies our normal understanding of time. Imagine, if you will, a very large Being, larger than the entire universe—so large that the Being exists simultaneously on earth and in the space occupied by Supernova 1987A. In 1987, *what time was it* for that Being? It depends on the perspective. From the perspective of earth, the Being would have "observed" 1987 history, which included the discovery of Supernova 1987A. But from the perspective of Supernova 1987A, the Being would have experienced what the earth will not know about for another 170,000 years! The Being thus observed both past (from earth, he saw the supernova explosion of 170,000 years before), present (the events of 1987 on earth), and future (what was happening on Supernova 1987A "now" that earthlings will not learn about for 170,000 years) simultaneously.

Such a Being, big as the universe, could, from some lookout post, see what is happening anywhere in the universe at any given time. For example, if he wants to know what is taking place on our sun right now, he can "watch" from the perspective of the sun. If he wants to see what took place on the sun eight minutes ago, he can "watch" from earth—that's what we see, after light has traveled the 93 million miles from the sun to earth.

The analogy is inexact, for it traps such a Being in space even as it frees him from time. But it may illustrate how our "first A happens, then B happens" conception of time expresses the very limited perspective of our planet. God, outside both time and space, can view what happens on earth in a way we can only guess at, and never fully comprehend.

Such notions are not mere flights of fancy. High school physics students learn about theoretical astronauts of the future who will travel into space faster than the speed of light and thus return even younger than when they left. Theories that seemed wildly speculative just a decade ago are being proved by modern researchers who bounce laser beams off the moon and send atomic clocks into space. Science is fulfilling fantasy: "It is a poor memory indeed that only works backwards!" said the White Queen to Alice in Wonderland.

God and Time

One more analogy: as a writer, I live in two different "time zones." First, there is the time zone of the real world that encompasses my daily ritual of waking, getting dressed, eating breakfast, and then moving to my office to plan out chapters, pages, and words. Meanwhile, the book itself is creating another, artificial world with its own self-contained time zone.

If I were writing a book of fiction, I might write these two sentences: "The phone rang. Immediately she got up from the couch and ran to answer it." Within the book, the time sequence goes like this: phone rings, immediate response. But outside the book, in the author's world, minutes, hours, even days may separate those two sentences. Perhaps I end one day's work with the sentence "The phone rang," and then go on vacation for two weeks. Regardless of when I return to the book, I am bound by the laws of its time zone. I could never write, "The phone rang. Two weeks later she got up and answered it." Mixing the two time zones would create an absurdity.

After I finish the book, in a way peculiar to me as its author, I carry around the entire book inside my mind. "From above," I can see the whole plot at once: beginning, middle, and end. No one else can do that—not unless they too experience it within time by plodding through it sentence by sentence.

I keep reaching for analogies because analogies are the only means we have to imagine human history as God sees it. We see history like a sequence of still frames, one after the other, as in a motion picture reel; but God sees the entire movie at once, in a flash. He sees it simultaneously from the viewpoint of a faraway star and from the viewpoint of my living room where I sit praying.

He sees it in entirety, like a whole book, rather than sentence by sentence and page by page.

We can imagine such a perspective dimly, as if through a fog. But merely recognizing our incurable time-boundedness may help us understand why God did not answer Job's "Why?" Instead, God replied by reeling off a few fundamental facts of the universe that Job could barely comprehend, and warning, "Leave the rest to me." Perhaps God keeps us ignorant because neither Job, nor Einstein, nor you or I could possibly understand the view "from above."

We cannot understand what "rules" apply to a God who lives outside of time, as we perceive it, and yet sometimes steps into time. Consider all the confusion that surrounds the word "foreknowledge." Did God know in advance whether Job would stay faithful to him and thus win The Wager? If he did, how was it a real wager? Or what about natural disasters on earth? If God knows about them in advance, isn't he to blame? In our world, if a person knows in advance that a bomb will explode in a parked car and fails to warn authorities, he or she is legally responsible. Is God therefore "responsible" for everything that happens, even tragedies, because he knows about them in advance?

But—and this may be the main message underlying God's vigorous speech to Job—we cannot apply our simplistic rules to God. The very word *fore*knowledge betrays the problem, for it expresses the B-follows-A viewpoint of someone trapped inside time. Strictly speaking, God does not "foresee" us doing things. He simply *sees* us doing them, in an eternal present. And whenever we try to figure out God's role in any given event, we necessarily see things "from below," judging his behavior by the frail standards of a time-contingent morality. One day we may see such problems as "Did God cause that airplane to crash?" in a very different light.

The church's long arguments over *fore*knowledge and *pre*destination illustrate our awkward attempts to comprehend what, to us, only makes sense as it enters time. In another dimension, we will undoubtedly view such matters very different-ly. The Bible hints at the viewpoint "from above" in some of its most mysterious passages. It says that Christ "was chosen before the creation of the world," which means before Adam and before the Fall and thus before the need for redemption at all. It says grace and eternal life were "given us in Christ Jesus before the beginning of time." How could anything be said to occur "*before* the beginning of time"? Such wording suggests the viewpoint of a God who lives outside time. Before creating time, he made provision to redeem a fallen planet that did not yet even exist! But when he "stepped into" time (as I, an author, might write myself into my own book), God had to live, and die, by the rules of our world, trapped within time.*

The Eternal Present

There is a sense in which we humans also perceive time in something like a never-ending present. True, we experience it in sequence—morning happens, then afternoon, then evening—but we do all our thinking in the present. If I think about the breakfast I ate earlier this morning, I think *in the present* about what happened in the past. If I contemplate dinner this evening, I

---

*This difference in perception may also help clarify one of the most confusing aspects of the Prophets. Often they did not bother telling whether the predicted events—invasions, earthquakes, a coming Leader, a re-created earth—would occur the next day, or a thousand years later, or three thousand years later. In fact, near and distant predictions often appear in the same paragraph, blurring together. Isaiah's famous prophecy, "Therefore the Lord himself will give you a sign: The virgin will be with child and will give birth to a son, and will call him Immanuel," fits this category. The next two verses make clear that the sign had a fulfillment in Isaiah's own day (many scholars assume the child to be Isaiah's own), and yet Matthew applies the prophecy's final fulfillment to the Virgin Mary. Biblical scholars have names for this common characteristic of the prophets: double or triple fulfillment, part-for-the-whole, creative bisociation.

For a God who encompasses all time, sequence is the least important issue. Should we be surprised, then, that incursions into time by a timeless Being would have overtones that resound in Isaiah's day, and Mary's, and also our own?

think *in the present* about what will happen in the future. Because I only exist in the present, I can only perceive the past and the future from the perspective of the present.

That insight gives a slight glimpse into the eternal present from which God "sees" the world, And it may explain the Bible's consistent pattern for people who doubt God. To such people, trapped in the present, disappointed with God, the Bible offers two cures: remember the past and consider the future. In the Psalms, in the Prophets, in the Gospels and Epistles, the Bible constantly urges us to look back and remember the great things God has done. He is the God of Abraham, Isaac, and Jacob, the One who delivered the Hebrews from slavery in Egypt. He is the God who, out of love, sent his Son to die, and who then resurrected him from death. By focusing too myopically on what we want God to do on our behalf, we may miss the significance of what he has already done.

Likewise, the Bible points us toward the future. For disappointed people everywhere—the Jews held captive in Babylon, the Christians persecuted by Rome, or by Iran or South Africa or Albania—the prophets envision a future state of peace and justice and happiness; and they call us to live in light of the future they image up. Can we live now "as if" God is loving, gracious, merciful, and all-powerful, even while the blinders of time are obscuring our vision? The prophets proclaim that history will be determined not by the past or present, but by the future.

I have taken such a long diversion into the mysteries of time because I believe there is no other answer to the question of unfairness. No matter how we rationalize, God will sometimes *seem* unfair from the perspective of a person trapped in time. Only at the end of time, after we have attained God's level of viewing, after every evil has been punished or forgiven, every illness healed, and the entire universe restored—only then will fairness reign. Then we will understand what role is played by evil, and by the Fall, and by natural law, in an "unfair" event like the death of a child. Until then, we will not know, and can only trust in a God who does know.

We remain ignorant of many details, not because God enjoys

keeping us in the dark, but because we have not the faculties to absorb so much light. At a single glance God knows what the world is about and how history will end. But we time-bound creatures have only the most primitive manner of understanding: we can let time pass. Not until history has run its course will we understand how "all things work together for good." Faith means believing in advance what will only make sense in reverse.

I have a friend who bristles at such a definition of faith: "You never blame God for the bad things and yet you give him credit for the good things!" In a curious sort of way, my friend is right. That, I believe, is also what faith sometimes requires: trusting God when there is no apparent evidence of him—as Job did. Trusting in his ultimate goodness, a goodness that exists outside of time, a goodness that time has not yet caught up with.

The Eternal may meet us in what is, by our present measurements, a day, or (more likely) a minute or a second; but we have touched what is not in any way commensurable with lengths of time, whether long or short. Hence our hope finally to emerge, if not altogether from time (that might not suit our humanity) at any rate from the tyranny, the unilinear poverty, of time, to ride it, not to be ridden by it, and so to cure that always aching wound which mere succession and mutability inflict on us, almost equally when we are happy and when we are unhappy. For we are so little reconciled to time that we are even astonished at it. "How he's grown!" we exclaim, "How time flies!" as though the universal form of our experience were again and again a novelty. It is as strange as if a fish were repeatedly surprised at the wetness of water. And that would be strange indeed; unless of course the fish were destined to become, one day, a land animal.

—C. S. Lewis, Reflections on the Psalms

[1]Frederick Buechner, *Wishful Thinking*, 46.
[2]Saint Augustine, *The Confessions of Saint Augustine*, 286–287.

Bible references: Job 36–38; Lamentations 2, 5; 1 Peter 1; 2 Timothy 1; Isaiah 7:14; Romans 8.

Why is life given to a man
    whose way is hidden,
    whom God has hedged in?
For sighing comes to me instead of food;
    my groans pour out like water.
—Job 3:23–24

Chapter 26

Is God Silent?

ONCE A FRIEND OF MINE went swimming in a large lake at dusk. As he was paddling at a leisurely pace about a hundred yards offshore, a freak evening fog rolled in across the water. Suddenly he could see nothing: no horizon, no landmarks, no objects or lights on shore. Because the fog diffused all light, he could not even make out the direction of the setting sun.

For thirty minutes he splashed around in panic. He would start off in one direction, lose confidence, and turn ninety degrees to the right. Or left—it made no difference which way he turned. He could feel his heart racing uncontrollably. He would stop and float, trying to conserve energy, and force himself to breathe slower. Then he would blindly strike out again. At last he heard a faint voice calling from shore. He pointed his body toward the sounds and followed them to safety.

Something like that sensation of utter lostness must have settled in on Job as he sat in the rubble and tried to comprehend what had happened. He too had lost all landmarks, all points of orientation. Where should he turn? God, the One who could guide him through the fog, stayed silent.

The whole point of The Wager was to keep Job in the dark. If God had delivered an inspiring pep talk—"Do this for me, Job, as a Knight of Faith, as a martyr"—then Job, ennobled, would have suffered gladly. But Satan had challenged whether Job's faith could survive with no outside help or explanation. When God accepted those terms, the fog rolled in around Job.

God ultimately "won" The Wager, of course. Though Job lashed out with a stream of bitter complaints, and though he despaired of life and longed for death, still he defiantly refused to give up on God: "Though he slay me, yet will I hope in him." Job believed when there was no reason to believe. He believed in the midst of the fog.

You could read Job's story, puzzle over The Wager, then breathe a deep sigh of relief: *Phew! God settled that problem. After proving his point so decisively, surely he will return to his preferred style of communicating clearly with his followers.* You could think so— unless, that is, you read the rest of the Bible. I hesitate to say this, because it is a hard truth and one I do not want to acknowledge, but Job stands as merely the most extreme example of what appears to be a universal law of faith. The kind of faith God values seems to develop best when everything fuzzes over, when God stays silent, when the fog rolls in.

Survivors of the Fog

A flash of light from a beacon on shore and then a long, dreadful time of silence and darkness—that is the pattern I find not only in the Book of Job, but throughout the Bible. Recall tottery old Abraham as he neared the century mark, holding feebly to the lustrous vision that he would father a great nation. For twenty-five years that vision had seemed a desert mirage until one son, just one, was born. And when God spoke again, he called Abraham to a test of faith every bit as severe as Job's. "Take your son, your only son, Isaac, whom you love," said God, in words that stabbed deep into Abraham's heart, "and sacrifice him as a burnt offering."

Then there was Joseph, who heard from God in his dreams but landed at the bottom of a well and later in an Egyptian dungeon for trying to follow that guidance. And Moses, hand-picked liberator of the Hebrew people, who hid in a desert for forty years, hunted by a pharaoh's security guards. And the fugitive David, anointed king on God's command, who spent the next decade dodging spears and sleeping in caves.

The baffling, Morse-code pattern of divine guidance—a clear message followed by a long, silent gap—is spelled out bluntly in 2 Chronicles. There we read of a rare good king, Hezekiah, who so pleased God that he was granted an unprecedented fifteen-year extension to his life. What happened next? "*God left him* to test him and to know everything that was in his heart."

Most of these Old Testament characters show up in the honor roll of Hebrews 11, a chapter some have labeled "The Faith Hall of Fame." I prefer to call that chapter, "Survivors of the Fog," for many of the heroes listed have one common experience: a dread time of testing like Job's, a time when the fog descends and everything goes blank. Torture, jeers, floggings, chains, stonings, sawings in two—Hebrews records in grim detail the trials that may befall faith-full people.

Saints become saints by somehow hanging on to the stubborn conviction that things are not as they appear, and that the unseen world is as solid and trustworthy as the visible world around them. God deserves trust, even when it looks like the world is caving in. "The world was not worthy of them," Hebrews 11 concludes about its amazing assemblage, adding this intriguing comment: "Therefore God is not ashamed to be called their God." For me, that phrase puts a reverse spin on Dorothy Sayers's remark about the three great humiliations of God—the church, in particular, has borne God shame, but it has also brought him moments of pride, and the gaunt saints of Hebrews 11 demonstrate how.

God's favorites, *especially* God's favorites, are not immune from the bewildering times when God seems silent. As Paul Tournier said, "Where there is no longer any opportunity for doubt, there is no longer any opportunity for faith either." Faith demands uncertainty, confusion. The Bible includes many proofs of God's concern—some quite spectacular—but no guarantees. A guarantee would, after all, preclude faith.

Two Kinds of Faith

My friend Richard found the word "faith" a central obstacle to belief: "Just have faith," other Christians would counsel when he doubted. What did they mean? "Faith" seemed to him a method of avoiding questions, not of answering them.

Some of the difficulty comes, I think, from the elastic way in which we use the word. First, we use it to describe great, childlike gulps of faith, when a person swallows the impossible. David exercised this kind of extravagant faith when he strode out to meet Goliath, as did the Roman centurion whom Jesus commended (he was "astonished" by the man's unflinching confidence). In our day, "faith missionaries" write stirring accounts of miracles that may result from childlike trust. This is the "seed faith" that can feed a houseful of orphans or move a mountain, and the Bible contains many proddings toward such.

But Job, along with the saints in Hebrews 11, points to a different kind of faith, the kind I have circled around in this book on disappointment with God. Childlike trust may not survive when the miracle does not come, when the urgent prayer gets no answer, when a dense gray mist obscures any sign of God's concern. Such times call for something more, and I will use the musty word "fidelity" for that hang-on-at-any-cost faith.

I interviewed a young nurse whose disappointment with God stemmed directly from confusing these two kinds of faith. Reared in a Christian home, she seldom doubted God, even through her college years. On her wall hung a painting of Jesus with a child in his arms, illustrating the poem "Footprints." That plaque portrayed faith at its most childlike: simply trust God and you will not even feel the burden. As you look back on hard times, you'll see only one set of footprints in the sand, for Jesus has carried you through.

At the age of twenty-four, this nurse was assigned to work in a cancer ward. She told me, one by one, the case histories of people she had nursed there. Some of her patients had prayed with childlike faith, crying out to God for healing and comfort, for relief from pain. Yet they died cruel, ugly deaths. And each night this nurse would come home, weighed down by the scenes of unsolvable suffering, and face the footprints plaque with its bright, alluring promise.

To get the picture vividly, simply read two psalms back-to-back. Start with Psalm 23: "The Lord is my Shepherd, I shall not be in want . . . he guides me . . . I will fear no evil . . . goodness and love will follow me all the days of my life." Then turn back one page to Psalm 22. "My God, my God, why have you forsaken me? Why are you so far from saving me? . . . I cry out by day, but you do not answer . . . I can count all my bones; people stare and gloat over me."

Psalm 23 models childlike faith; Psalm 22 models fidelity, a deeper, more mysterious kind of faith. Life with God may include both. We may experience times of unusual closeness, when every prayer is answered in an obvious way and God seems intimate and caring. And we may also experience "fog times," when God stays silent, when nothing works according to formula and all the Bible's promises seem glaringly false. Fidelity involves learning to trust that, out beyond the perimeter of fog, God still reigns and has not abandoned us, no matter how it may appear.

Paradoxically, the most perplexing, Job-like times may help "fertilize" faith and nurture intimacy with God.* The deepest faith, what I have called fidelity, sprouts at a point of contradiction, like a blade of grass between stones. Human beings grow by striving, working, stretching; and in a sense, human nature needs problems more than solutions. Why are not all prayers answered magically and instantly? Why must every convert travel the same tedious path of spiritual discipline? Because persistent prayer, and

---

*American Christians who have visited churches in places like Ethiopia and China can attest to this fact.

fasting, and study, and meditation are designed primarily for our sakes, not for God's.

Kierkegaard said that Christians reminded him of schoolboys who want to look up the answers to their math problems in the back of the book rather than work them through. I confess to such schoolboy sentiments, and I doubt that I am alone. We yearn for shortcuts. But shortcuts usually lead away from growth, not toward it. Apply the principle directly to Job: what was the final result of the testing he went through? As Rabbi Abraham Heschel observed, "Faith like Job's cannot be shaken because it is the result of having been shaken."

In an essay on prayer, C. S. Lewis suggested that God treats new Christians with a special kind of tenderness, much as a parent dotes on a newborn.[1] He quotes an experienced Christian: "I have seen many striking answers to prayer and more than one that I thought miraculous. But they usually come at the beginning before conversion, or soon after it. As the Christian life proceeds, they tend to be rarer. The refusals, too, are not only more frequent; they become more unmistakable, more emphatic."[1]

At first glance, such a suggestion seems to have it all backward. Shouldn't faith become easier, not harder, as a Christian progresses? But, as Lewis points out, the New Testament gives two strong examples of unanswered prayers: Jesus pled three times for God to "Take this cup from me" and Paul begged God to cure the "thorn in my flesh."

Lewis asks, "Does God then forsake just those who serve Him best? Well, He who served Him best of all said, near His tortured death, 'Why hast thou forsaken me?' When God becomes man, that Man, of all others, is least comforted by God, at His greatest need. There is a mystery here which, even if I had the power, I might not have the courage to explore. Meanwhile, little people like you and me, if our prayers are sometimes granted, beyond all hope and probability, had better not draw hasty conclusions to our own advantage. If we were stronger, we might be less tenderly treated. If we were braver, we might be sent, with far less help, to defend far more desperate posts in the great battle."

Is God Silent?

The Unavoidable Question

C. S. Lewis's words sound impressive. Yet I cannot simply reduce the pattern of fidelity—faith toughened through testing—to a cheery formula. This book began with the story of Richard, who was secure and well-grounded until his faith was tested. And then he felt betrayed. Why would God submit him or, for that matter, *anyone* he loves, to such a test? Richard could no longer trust such a God. I have spoken with many others whose exuberant, childlike faith likewise foundered in the time of testing.

An unavoidable question lurks just under the surface of the Book of Job. If, for the sake of a "test" of love, a husband subjected his wife to the trauma that Job had to endure, we would call him pathological and lock him away. If a mother hid herself from her children, refusing to call out directions from the shore in the fog, we would judge her an unfit mother. How, then, can we understand such behavior, such a wager, by God himself?

I offer no neat formula, only two observations.

1. We have little comprehension of what our faith means to God. In some mysterious way, Job's terrible ordeal was "worth" it to God because it went to the core of the entire human experiment. More than Job's faith, the motive behind all creation was at stake. Ever since God took the "risk" of making room for free human beings, faith—true, unbribed, freely offered faith—has had an intrinsic value to God that we can barely imagine. There is no better way for us to express love to God than by exercising fidelity to him.

It is wrong to speak of God's need of love from his creation, but remember how God himself expressed his longing for that love: like a father starved for some response, *any* response, from his rebellious children; like a jilted lover who, against all reason, gives his faithless beloved one more chance. Those are the images God summoned up again and again throughout the time of the prophets. The deepest longings we feel on earth, as parents, as lovers, are mere flickers of the hungering desire God feels for us. It is a desire that cost him the Incarnation and the Crucifixion.

209

All human metaphors fail to contain these matters, but they fail from understatement, not exaggeration. As Jesus said, at the end of history (when the fog lifts for good) only one question will matter: "When the Son of Man comes, will he find faith on the earth?" And the apostle Paul, after sketching out the scheme of the world from creation up to Jesus, concluded, "God did this so that men would seek him and perhaps reach out for him and find him, though he is not far from each one of us." Sending his Son was the "cost" to God; a faithful response from someone like Job—or you or me—represents the "reward."

I admit, it is hard for any of us with our limited vision to perceive the "reward" gained by Job's trials. C. S. Lewis may have come close in his comment about God sending us to "far more desperate posts in the great battle." According to the Bible, human beings serve as the principal foot soldiers in the warfare between unseen forces of good and evil; and faith is our most powerful weapon. Perhaps God sends us to dangerous posts with the same mixture of pride, love, anguish, and remorse that any parent feels when sending a son or daughter off to war.

Was Job's trial "worth it" to God? Only God can answer that. I have had to conclude that divine sovereignty means at least this: only God can determine what is of value to God. "Blessed are those who have not seen and yet have believed," Jesus said in a mild rebuke to doubting Thomas. Job saw the darkest side of life, heard the deepest silence of God, and still believed.

2. *God did not exempt himself from the same demands of faith.* Job's trials cannot stand apart from their louder echo in the life of Jesus. He too was tempted. He too lost everything of value, including his friends and his health. As Hebrews says, he "offered up prayers and petitions with loud cries and tears to the one who could save him from death." Finally, he lost his life.

We can never fully plumb the mystery of what took place on the cross, but it does offer the consolation that God is unwilling to put his creatures through any test that he himself has not endured. I have spoken with many suffering people over the years, and I cannot emphasize too strongly how important this fact seems to them. From famous people like Joni Eareckson Tada, from unknowns in county hospitals, from inmates in hellish Third World prisons, I have heard something like this: "At least, because of Jesus, God understands how I feel."

I think again of Richard's comment, "All I can say is that Job paid one *hell* of a price just to make God feel good!" He was thinking of Job, sitting in the ashes, scratching his sores. But as Richard said those words I was thinking of Jesus, hanging on a cross, unable to reach his wounds. I had to agree—it was a hell of a price to pay. In one sense, God tied his own hands in the wager over Job; in the most literal sense, he let his hands be tied the night of the Crucifixion. (Jesus, speaking of his death: "Now my heart is troubled, and what shall I say? 'Father, save me from this hour'? No, it was for this very reason I came to this hour. Father, glorify your name!")

In my study of the Bible, I was struck by a radical shift in its authors' attitudes about suffering, a shift that traces directly back to the Cross. When New Testament writers speak of hard times, they express none of the indignation that characterized Job, the prophets, and many of the psalmists. They offer no real explanation for suffering, but keep pointing to two events—the death and resurrection of Jesus—as if they form some kind of pictographic answer.

The apostles' faith, as they freely confessed, rested entirely on what happened on Easter Sunday, when God transformed the greatest tragedy in all history, the execution of his Son, into a day we now celebrate as Good Friday. Those disciples, who gazed at the cross from the shadows, soon learned what they had failed to learn in three years with their leader: When God seems absent, he may be closest of all. When God seems dead, he may be coming back to life.

The three-day pattern—tragedy, darkness, triumph—became for New Testament writers a template that can be applied to all our times of testing. We can look back on Jesus, the proof of God's love, even though we may never get an answer to our "Why?" questions. Good Friday demonstrates that God has not abandoned us to our pain. The evils and sufferings that afflict our lives are so real and so significant to God that he willed to share them and endure them himself. He too is "acquainted with grief." On that day, Jesus himself experienced the silence of God—it was Psalm 22, not Psalm 23, that he quoted from the cross.

And Easter Sunday shows that, in the end, suffering will not triumph. Therefore, "Consider it pure joy . . . whenever you face trials of many kinds," writes James; and "In this you greatly rejoice, though now for a little while you may have had to suffer grief in all kinds of trials," writes Peter; and "we also rejoice in our sufferings," writes Paul. The apostles go on to explain what good can result from such "redeemed suffering": maturity, wisdom, genuine faith, perseverance, character, and many rewards to come.

Why rejoice? Not for the masochistic thrill of the trial itself, but because what God did Easter Sunday on large scale he can do on small scale for each of us. The afflictions addressed by James, Peter, and Paul would likely have ignited a major crisis of faith in the Old Testament. But New Testament writers came to believe that, as Paul expressed it, "All things work together for good."

That well-known passage is often distorted. Some people interpret its meaning as "Only good things will happen to those who love God." Paul meant just the opposite, and in the very next paragraph he defines what "things" we might expect: trouble, hardship, persecution, famine, nakedness, danger, sword. Paul endured all those. Yet, he insists, "in all these things we are more than conquerors"; no amount of hardship can separate us from the love of God.

It's a matter of time, Paul says. Just wait: God's miracle of transforming a dark, silent Friday into Easter Sunday will someday be enlarged to cosmic scale.

Is God Silent?

Though thou with clouds of anger do disguise
Thy face; yet through that mask I know those eyes,
Which, though they turn away sometimes,
They never will despise.
　　　　　—John Donne, "A Hymn to Christ"

Everything difficult indicates something more than our theory
of life yet embraces.
　　　　　—George MacDonald

[1]C. S. Lewis, *The World's Last Night*, 10.

Bible references: Job 13; Genesis 22; 2 Chronicles 32; Matthew 8; Mark 14; 2 Corinthians 12; Luke 18; Acts 17; John 20; Hebrews 5; John 12; Isaiah 53 (KJV); James 1; 1 Peter 1; Philippians 3; Romans 8.

But if I go to the east, he is not there;
   if I go to the west, I do not find him.
When he is at work in the north, I do not see him;
   when he turns to the south, I catch no
   glimpse of him.

—Job 23:8–9

Chapter 27

Why God Doesn't Intervene

I KNOW WHAT my friend Richard would think about the ideas in the last few chapters. In fact, I know what he does think, because I discussed them with him at length. Richard, you may remember, had written a book on Job, so I had no need to review the story with him. I concentrated instead on the ending, speculating aloud on why God declined to answer Job. I went over my thoughts about timelessness, and Job's inability to comprehend God's perspective, and the inherent value of faith to God.

Richard listened carefully, and when I had finished meandering through my ideas, he nodded approvingly. "That's good, Philip. You may well be right. I have no problem with what you say. But there's one big difference between Job's story and mine. For all his troubles, Job finally did receive a word from God. Supposedly, he heard an actual voice out of the whirlwind. But for me, God stayed silent. And I guess that's why Job chose to believe, and I chose not to."

As we talked further, it became clear that Richard simply could not accept the notion of two worlds. Living in a seen world of trees and buildings and cars and people, he could not believe in another, unseen world existing alongside it. "I want proof," he said. "How can I be certain that God even exists if he won't enter into my world?"

The conversation took me back to a time when I too was a skeptic. Richard, ironically, lost his faith at a Christian college, surrounded by believers who professed an intimate knowledge of God; and it was in a similar environment—a Bible college no less—that I found faith most difficult.

A Skeptic's View

I ran into the same stumbling block as Richard: actions regarded as "spiritual" by the believers on campus seemed utterly ordinary to me. If the unseen world really was making contact with the seen world, where were the scorch marks, the sure signs of a supernatural Presence?

Take the matter of prayer: the believers seemed to distort events to make everything look like an answer to prayer. If an uncle sent an extra fifty dollars to help with school bills, they would grin and shout and call a prayer meeting to thank God. They accepted these "answers to prayer" as final proof that God was out there listening to them. But I could always find another explanation. Perhaps the uncle had sent *all* his nephews fifty dollars that month, and the prayers were merely coincidental. After all, I had an uncle who occasionally sent me gifts, though I never prayed for them. And what of these students' many requests that went unanswered? Prayer, it seemed to me, involved nothing more than talking to the walls and an occasional self-fulfilling prophecy.

As an experiment, I began mimicking "spiritual" behavior on campus. I prayed devoutly in prayer meetings, gave phony testimonies about my conversion, and filled my vocabulary with pious jargon. And it worked, confirming my doubts. I the skeptic soon passed for a veritable saint, just by following the prescribed formula. Could Christian experience be genuine if most of it was reproducible by a skeptic?

216

I conducted this experiment as a result of my reading in the psychology of religion. Books like *The Varieties of Religious Experience*, by William James, had persuaded me that religion was just a complex psychological reaction to the stresses of life. James examined the claims that the sincere Christian is a new creature formed out of new fabric. But, concluded James, "Converted men as a class are indistinguishable from natural men; some natural men even excel some converted men in their fruits; and no one ignorant of doctrinal theology could guess by mere every-day inspection of the 'accidents' of the two groups of persons before him that their substance differed as much as divine differs from human substance."[1] I too could see no unusual radiance, no distinguishing mark in the believers around me.

For reasons I will explain later, I did not remain a skeptic. But in honesty I must admit that even now, after two decades of rich and rewarding faith, I am vulnerable to Richard's kind of doubt. Spiritual experience does not bear introspection easily; shine a spotlight on it, and it vaporizes. If I probe my times of communion with God, I can usually uncover another, more natural explanation for what has taken place. There is no blinding difference between the natural and supernatural worlds, no gulf fixed with barbed wire separating the two.

I do not stop being a "natural" person when I pray: I get sleepy, lose concentration, and suffer the same frustrations and miscommunications while conversing with God that I do with other people. When I write on "spiritual" topics, I am not suddenly lifted heavenward by the muses; I still must sharpen pencils, cross out words, consult the dictionary, wad up and throw away countless false starts. Instances of "knowing God's will" in my life have never been as straightforward as the examples I see in the life of a Moses or Gideon. I have never heard the booming Voice from the whirlwind. I could, if I wished, do what Richard does now: explain away spiritual behavior through some combination of psychological theories.

Why, then, do I believe in an unseen world? I have received great help in this struggle from the writings of C. S. Lewis. The theme of two worlds runs like a thread through most of his work—

in the early writings, in letters to his friends, and in all his fiction, until it finally develops into a full-blown theory in an essay called "Transposition."[2] Lewis defined the problem as being "that of the obvious continuity between things which are admittedly natural and things which, it is claimed, are spiritual; the reappearance in what professes to be our supernatural life of all the same old elements which make up our natural life." Most of what follows in this chapter will simply expand on his ideas.

Looking Along the Beam

Lewis began his essay by referring to the curious phenomenon of *glossolalia* or speaking in tongues. How odd, he commented, that an undeniably "spiritual" event, the descent of the Holy Spirit at Pentecost, would express itself in the strange human phenomenon of speaking in another language. To the bystanders at Pentecost it resembled drunkenness; to many "scientific" observers today glossolalia resembles hysteria or a nervous disorder. How can such natural actions as the movement of vocal cords express the supernatural indwelling of the Holy Spirit of God?

Lewis suggested the analogy of a beam of light in a dark toolshed. When he first entered a shed, he saw a beam and looked *at* the luminous band of brightness filled with floating specks of dust. But when he moved over to the beam and looked *along* it, he gained a very different perspective. Suddenly he saw not the beam, but, framed in the window of the shed, green leaves moving on the branches of a tree outside and beyond that, 93 million miles away, the sun. Looking at the beam and looking along the beam are quite different.

Our century excels in techniques of looking *at* the beam, and "reductionism" is the word most commonly used to describe this process. We can "reduce" human behavior down to neurotransmitters and enzymes, reduce butterflies to molecules of DNA, and reduce sunsets to particle waves of light and energy. In its most extreme forms, reductionism sees religion as psychological projection, world history as evolutionary struggle, and thought itself as only the opening and shutting of billions of I/O computer gates in the brain.

This modern world, so skilled in looking at the beam from every angle, is a world hostile to "faith." Throughout most of history, all societies took for granted the existence of an unseen, supernatural world. How else could they explain such marvels as a sunrise, an eclipse, a thunderstorm? But now we can explain them, and much more. We can reduce most natural phenomena, and even most spiritual phenomena, to their component parts. As Lewis observed about glossolalia, even the most "supernatural" acts express themselves on this earth in "natural" ways.

From the theory of transposition, I draw these conclusions about living in such a world.

1. *First, we must simply acknowledge the powerful force of reductionism.* That force offers both a blessing and a curse. It blesses us with the ability to analyze earthquakes and thunderstorms and tornadoes and thus defend ourselves against them. By looking *at* the beam, we have learned to fly—all the way to the moon and back—and to tour the world while staring at a box in our living rooms, and to bring the sounds of orchestras to our ears as we jog along country lanes. By looking at the beam of human behavior, we can recognize chemical components and thus, through drugs, rescue people from severe depression and schizophrenia.

But reductionism has also brought a curse. Looking at the beam rather than along it, we risk reducing life to nothing more than its constituent parts. We will never again view the sunrise or moonrise with the same sense of awe and near-worship that our "primitive" ancestors—or even the sixteenth-century poets—felt. And if we reduce behavior to *merely* hormones and chemistry, we lose all human mystery and free will and romance. The ideals of romantic love that have inspired artists and lovers through the centuries suddenly reduce to a matter of hormonal secretions.

Reductionism may exert undue influence over us unless we recognize it for what it is: a way of looking. It is not a True or False concept; it is a point of view that informs us about the parts of a thing, but not the whole.

Spiritual acts, for example, can be viewed from both a lower and higher level. One does not supplant the other; each merely sees the same behavior differently (just as looking *at* a beam of light differs from looking *along* it). From the "lower" perspective, prayer is a person talking to himself (and glossolalia the same, only gibberish). The "higher" perspective presumes that a spiritual reality is at work, with human prayer serving as a contact point between the seen and unseen worlds.

I can attend a Billy Graham rally as a curious spectator and, selecting one person in the vast audience, theorize on all the sociological and psychological factors that might entice this one woman to be receptive to Graham's message. Her marriage is falling apart; she's looking for stability; she remembers the strength of a pious grandmother; the music takes her back to childhood church experiences. But those "natural" factors do not rule out the supernatural; to the contrary, they may be the means God chooses to prompt that person toward him. Perhaps the continuity between natural and supernatural is a continuity of design from the same Creator. That, at least, is the "higher" view of faith. The one level of viewing does not exclude the other; they are two ways of looking at the same event.

2. Oddly, the lower viewpoint may even seem superior to the higher. C. S. Lewis recalled that as a child he had first learned to appreciate orchestral music by listening to the single, undifferentiated sound produced by a primitive gramophone. He could hear the melody, but not much else. Later, when he went to live concerts, he was disillusioned. A multitude of sounds came from many instruments playing different notes! He longed for "the real thing," which to his untrained ear was the mongrel sound of the gramophone. To Lewis, at that moment, the substitute seemed superior to the reality.[3]

Similarly, a person raised on a steady diet of television might find real mountain hiking, complete with mosquitoes, shortness of breath, and annoying weather changes, inferior to the vicarious experience afforded by a *National Geographic* special.

More to the point, the lower viewpoint may seem superior in moral issues as well. The ideal of romantic love has inspired our greatest sonnets and novels and operas. But reductionists like Hugh Hefner now argue quite articulately that sex is superior when freed from the constraints of love and relationship. (Certainly, *Playboy* has more visceral appeal than the works of Elizabeth Barrett Browning.) And secularists, dismissing religion as a crutch, extol the "braver" challenge of surviving in this world without an appeal to a higher Being.

3. *The reality of the higher world is carried by the faculties of the lower world.* The word "transposition" belongs to the vocabulary of music. A song can be transposed from one musical key into another. Or a symphony score written for 110 orchestral instruments can be transposed into a version for the piano. Naturally, something will get lost in the process: ten fingers striking piano keys cannot possibly reproduce all the aural nuances of an orchestra. Yet the transposer, limited to the range of sounds made by those keys, must somehow convey the essence of the symphony through them.

C. S. Lewis cited a diary entry from Samuel Pepys regarding a rapturous musical concert. Pepys said the sound of the wind instruments was so sweet that it ravished him "and, indeed, in a word, did wrap up my soul so that it made me really sick, just as I have formerly been when in love with my wife." Try to analyze the physiology of any emotional response, said Lewis. What happens in our bodies when we experience beauty, or pride, or love? To Pepys it felt at once ravishing, yet not unlike nausea. A kick in the stomach, a flutter, a muscular contraction—he experienced the very same bodily reactions that he might at a moment of illness![4]

Looked at from the lower viewing level, our physical responses to joy and fear are almost identical. In each case the adrenal gland secretes the same hormone, and neurons in the digestive system fire off the same chemicals; but the brain interprets one message as joy and one as fear. At its lower levels, the human body has a limited vocabulary, just as a transposer has a limited number of piano keys to express the sounds of a full orchestra.

And this is where reductionism reveals its greatest weakness:

if you look only "at the beam," reducing human emotions to their most basic components (neurons and hormones), you might logically deduce that joy and fear are the same, when they are in fact near-opposites. The human body has no nerve cells specially assigned to convey a sensation of pleasure—nature is never so lavish. All our experiences of pleasure come from "borrowed" nerve cells that also carry sensations of pain and touch and heat and cold.

A Way of Life

The human brain offers a nearly perfect model of transposition. Although the brain represents the "higher" point of view within the body, there is no more isolated or helpless organ. It sits in a box of thick bone, utterly dependent on lower faculties for information about the world. The brain has never seen anything, or tasted anything, or felt anything. All messages to it arrive in the same coded form, our many sensory experiences reduced down to an electrical sequence of dots and dashes (–. – –.. –. . . – –). The brain relies totally on these Morse code messages from the extremities, which it then assembles into meaning.

As I write, I am listening to Beethoven's magnificent Ninth Symphony. What is that symphony but a series of codes transposed across time and technology. It began as a musical idea which Beethoven "heard" in his mind (an extraordinary mental feat, for the composer, by then totally deaf, had only memory to guide him and could not test his idea on musical instruments). Beethoven then transposed the symphony onto paper, using a series of codes known as musical notation.

More than a century later, an orchestra read those codes, interpreted them, and reassembled them into a glorious sound approximating what Beethoven must have "heard" in his mind. Recording engineers captured that orchestra's sound as a series of magnetic impulses on a streaming tape, and a studio transposed that code into a more mechanical form, eventuating in the tiny ripples on my record album.

My turntable is now "reading" those ripples and amplifying

the variations through loudspeakers. Molecular vibrations caused by those speakers reach my ears, setting into motion another series of mechanical acts: tiny bones beat against my eardrums, transferring the vibrations through a viscous fluid on into the Organ of Corti, where 25,000 sound receptor cells lie in wait. Once stimulated, the appropriate cells fire off their electrical message. Finally, those impulses, mere dots and dashes of code, reach my brain, where the cortical screen assembles them into a sound I recognize as Beethoven's Ninth Symphony. I experience pleasure, even joy, as I pause and listen to that great work of music—the joy being once again carried to me by "lower" faculties of my body.

Transposition is a way of life. All knowledge comes to us through a process of translating downward into code and then upward into meaning. I have just written three paragraphs on Beethoven's Ninth Symphony. These were thoughts originating in my mind that I then transposed into words and typed into a computer, which recorded them in code on a magnetic disk. Eventually, my computer will transpose that magnetic code into a binary code, and a device called a modem will transpose the binary code into digital sounds that it will send over telephone wires to a publisher. If I listen in as my modem transmits the three paragraphs on Beethoven, I will hear nothing but a cloud of static, yet that static will somehow contain my thoughts and words.

The publisher's computer, receiving the digital sounds, will translate them back into magnetic codes stored on a disk. The publisher will retranslate those codes into words visible on a screen, edit them, and then transpose the words into patterned ink marks on paper—the very ink marks you are reading right now. To your trained eye, these blobs of ink on a page form letters and words that are conveyed to your eye cells and transposed into electrical impulses that your brain is assembling into some kind of meaning.

All communication, all knowledge, all sensory experience— all of life on this planet—relies on the process of transposition: meaning travels "downward" into codes which can later be reassembled. We instinctively trust that process, believing that the lower codes really do carry something of the original meaning. I trust that the words I choose, and even the staticky transmissions of my modem, will carry my original thoughts about Beethoven's Ninth Symphony. I look at a photograph, an image of the Rocky Mountains transposed on a small, flat, glossy sheet, and mentally relive a visit there. I scratch a magazine ad to smell a perfume sample, and the image of my wife, who wears that perfume, suddenly comes to mind. The lower carries something of the higher.

Transposition of the Spirit

Should it surprise us, then, to find the same universal principle operating in the realm of the spirit?

Think back to Richard's questions posed early in this book and restated at the beginning of this chapter. Why doesn't God intervene and make himself obvious? Why doesn't he speak aloud so we can hear him? We yearn for miracle, for the supernatural in its pure, unadulterated form.

I chose the word "unadulterated" deliberately because it betrays a sentiment that is central to this issue. We moderns strive to separate natural from supernatural. The natural world that we can touch and smell and see and hear seems self-evident; the supernatural world, however, is another matter. There is nothing certain about it, no skin on it, and that bothers us. We want proof. We want the supernatural to enter the natural world in a way that retains the glow, that leaves scorch marks, that rattles the ear drums.

The God revealed in the Bible does not seem to share our desire. Whereas we cleave natural from supernatural, and seen from unseen, God seeks to bring the two together. His goal, one might say, is to rescue the "lower" world, to restore the natural realm of fallen creation to its original state, where spirit and matter dwelt together in harmony.

When we become Christians and thus establish contact with the unseen world, we are not mysteriously transported upward; we do not suddenly put on space-suit bodies that remove us from the natural world (ever since the Gnostics and Manichaeans, the church has consistently judged such notions heretical). Rather, our physical bodies reconnect with spiritual reality and we begin to listen to the code through which the unseen world transposes itself into this one. One might say our task is the very opposite of reductionism. We look for ways to re-enchant or "hallow" the world: to see in nature an engine of praise, to see in bread and wine a sacrament of grace, to see in human love a shadow of ideal Love.

Granted, we have a limited vocabulary for this higher realm. We speak to God as we would speak to another person; could anything be more commonplace, more "natural"? Praying, proclaiming the gospel, meditating, fasting, offering a cup of cold water, visiting prisoners, observing the sacraments—these everyday acts, we are told, carry the "higher" meaning. They somehow express the unseen world.

Looked at from the lower, reductionist perspective, all spiritual acts have natural "explanations." Prayer is mumbling in the void; a sinner repenting, contrived emotionalism; the Day of Pentecost, an outbreak of drunkenness. A skeptic might say that the natural faculties are an impoverished lot if that's all we have to express the exalted world beyond.

But faith, looking *along* the beam, sees such natural acts as hallowed carriers of the supernatural. From that perspective, the natural world is not impoverished, but graced with miracle. And the miracle of a natural world reclaimed reached a point of climax in the Grand Miracle, when the actual Presence of God took up residence in a "natural" body exactly like ours: the Word transposed into flesh.

In one body, Christ brought the two worlds together, joining spirit and matter at long last, unifying creation in a way that had not been seen since Eden. The theologian Jürgen Moltmann puts it this way, in a sentence that merits much reflection: "Embodiment is the end of all God's works."[5] And this is how the apostle Paul puts it: "And he is the head of the body, the church. . . . For God was pleased to have all his fullness dwell in him, and through him to reconcile to himself all things, whether things on earth or things in heaven, by making peace through his blood, shed on the cross."

When that Word-become-flesh ascended, he left behind his actual Presence in the form of his body, the church. Our goodness becomes, literally, God's goodness ("Whatever you did for one of the least of these brothers of mine, you did for me"). Our suffering becomes, in Paul's words, "the fellowship of sharing in his sufferings." Our actions become his actions ("He who receives you receives me"). What happens to us, happens to him ("Saul, Saul, why do you persecute me?"). The two worlds, seen and unseen, merge in Christ; and we, as Paul kept insisting, are quite literally "in Christ." Embodiment is the end of all God's work, the goal of all creation.

From below, we tend to think of miracle as an invasion, a breaking into the natural world with spectacular force, and we long for such signs. But from above, from God's point of view, the real miracle is one of transposition: that human bodies can become vessels filled with Spirit, that ordinary human acts of charity and goodness can become nothing less than the incarnations of God on earth.

To complete the analogy, I need search no further than the words of Paul, for the image he gives to describe Christ's role in the world today is the same image I have used to illustrate transposition. Jesus Christ, said Paul, now serves as the head of the body. We know how a human head accomplishes its will: by translating orders downward in a code that the hands and eyes and mouth can understand. A healthy body is one that follows the will of the head. In that same way, the risen Christ accomplishes his will through us, members of his body.

Is God silent? I answer that question with another question: Is the church silent? We are his mouthpiece, his designated vocal chords on this planet. A plan of such awesome transposition guarantees that God's message will sometimes seem garbled or incoherent; it guarantees that God will sometimes seem silent. But embodiment was his goal, and in that light the Day of Pentecost becomes a perfect metaphor: God's voice on earth, speaking through human beings in a manner even they could not comprehend.

The Hope

I have a bright, talented, and very funny friend in Seattle named Carolyn Martin. But Carolyn has cerebral palsy, and it is the peculiar tragedy of her condition that its outward signs—drooling, floppy arm movements, inarticulate speech, a bobbing head—cause people who meet her to wonder if she is retarded. Actually, her mind is the one part of her that works perfectly; it is muscular control that she lacks.

Carolyn lived for fifteen years in a home for the mentally retarded, because the state had no other place for her. Her closest friends were people like Larry, who tore all his clothes off and ate the institution's houseplants, and Arelene, who only knew three sentences and called everyone "Mama." Carolyn determined to escape from that home and to find a meaningful place for herself in the outside world.

Eventually, she did manage to move out and establish a home of her own. There, the simplest chores posed an overwhelming challenge. It took her three months to learn to brew a pot of tea and pour it into cups without scalding herself. But Carolyn mastered that feat and many others. She enrolled in high school, graduated, then signed up for community college.

Everyone on campus knew Carolyn as "the disabled person." They would see her sitting in a wheelchair, hunched over, painstakingly typing out notes on a device called a Canon Communicator. Few felt comfortable talking with her; they could not follow her jumbled sounds. But Carolyn persevered, stretching out a two-year Associate of Arts degree program over seven years. Next, she enrolled in a Lutheran college to study the Bible. After two years there, she was asked to speak to her fellow students in chapel.

Carolyn worked many hours on her address. She typed out the final draft—at her average speed of forty-five minutes a page—and asked her friend Josee to read it for her. Josee had a strong, clear voice.

On the day of the chapel service, Carolyn sat slumped in her wheelchair on the left side of the platform. At times her arms jerked uncontrollably, her head lolled to one side so that it almost touched her shoulder, and a stream of saliva sometimes ran down her blouse. Beside her stood Josee, who read the mature and graceful prose Carolyn had composed, centered around this Bible text: "But we have this treasure in jars of clay to show that this all-surpassing power is from God but not from us."

For the first time, some students saw Carolyn as a complete human being, like themselves. Before then her mind, a very good mind, had always been inhibited by a "disobedient" body, and difficulties with speech had masked her intelligence. But hearing her address read aloud as they looked at her onstage, the students could see past the body in a wheelchair and imagine a whole person.

Carolyn told me about that day in her halting speech, and I could only understand about half the words. But the scene she described became for me a parable of transposition: a perfect mind locked inside a spastic, uncontrolled body, and vocal cords that fail at every second syllable. The New Testament image of Christ as head of the body took on new meaning as I gained a sense of both the humiliation that Christ undergoes in his role as head, and also the exaltation that he allows us, the members of his body.

We, the church, are an example of transposition taken to extreme. Sadly, we do not give off indisputable proof of God's love and glory. Sometimes, like Carolyn's body, we obscure rather than convey the message. But the church is the reason behind the entire human experiment, the reason there are human beings in the first place: to let creatures other than God bear the image of God. He deemed it well worth the risk, and the humiliation.

He who descended is the very one who ascended higher than all the heavens, in order to fill the whole universe. It was he who gave some to be apostles, some to be prophets, some to be evangelists, and some to be pastors and teachers, to prepare God's people for works of service, so that the body of Christ may be built up until we all reach unity in the faith and in the knowledge of the Son of God and become mature, attaining to the whole measure of the fullness of Christ.

Then we will no longer be infants. . . . Instead . . . we will in all things grow up into him who is the Head, that is, Christ. From him the whole body, joined and held together by every supporting ligament, grows and builds itself up in love, as each part does its work.

[1]William James, *The Varieties of Religious Experience*, 233.
[2]C. S. Lewis, *The Weight of Glory*, 18, 19.
[3]C. S. Lewis, *God in the Dock*, 212.
[4]C. S. Lewis, *Christian Reflections* 37.
[5]Jürgen Moltmann, *God in Creation*, 244.

Bible references: Colossians 1; Matthew 25; Philippians 3; Matthew 10; Acts 9; 2 Corinthians 4; Ephesians 4.

Why do you hide your face
    and consider me your enemy?
Will you torment a windblown leaf?
Will you chase after dry chaff?
                —Job 13:24–25

Chapter 28

Is God Hidden?

T O GET the full emotional impact of Job's plight, I winnowed the book's speeches for Job's own words. I expected to find him complaining about his miserable health and lamenting the loss of his children and fortune; but to my surprise Job had relatively little to say about those matters. He focused instead on the single theme of God's absence. What hurt Job most was the sense of crying out in desperation and getting no response. I had heard that same feeling described by many suffering people, perhaps best by C. S. Lewis, who wrote these words in the midst of deep grief after his wife's death from cancer:

> Meanwhile, where is God? This is one of the most disquieting symptoms. When you are happy, so happy that you have no sense of needing Him . . . you will be—or so it feels—welcomed with open arms. But go to Him when your need is desperate, when all other help is vain, and what do you find? A door slammed in your face, and a sound of bolting and double bolting on the inside. After that, silence. You may as

well turn away. The longer you wait, the more emphatic the silence will become.[1]

Above all else, Job demanded a chance to plead his case before God. His friends' pieties he shook off like a dog shaking off fleas. He wanted the real thing, a personal appointment with God Almighty. Despite what had happened, Job could not bring himself to believe in a God of cruelty and injustice. Perhaps if they met together, at least he could hear God's side of things. But God was nowhere to be found. Job heard only the whining cant of his friends and then a dreadful, vacuous sound. The door slammed in his face.

A Fact of Faith

Oh sweet Lord, I really want to see you, I really want to be with you. . . .
                                          —George Harrison song

I know God is alive: I talked with him this morning!
                                          —bumper sticker

God loves you and has a wonderful plan for your life.
                                          —evangelism booklet

And he walks with me and he talks with me, and he tells me I am his own.
                                          —Christian hymn

Human longing for the actual presence of God may crop up almost anywhere. But we dare not make sweeping claims about the promise of God's intimate presence unless we take into account those times when God seems absent. C. S. Lewis encountered it, Job encountered it, Richard encountered it: at some point nearly everyone must face the fact of God's hidden-ness.

The cloud of unknowing can descend without warning, sometimes at the very moment we most urgently desire a sense of God's presence. A South African minister, the Reverend Allan Boesak, was thrown in jail for speaking against the government.

He spent three weeks in solitary confinement, almost constantly on his knees, praying for God to set him free. "I do not mind telling you," he later related to his congregation, "that this was the most difficult moment of my life. As I knelt there, the words couldn't come anymore and there were no more tears to cry."[2] His experience was one common to blacks in South Africa: they pray, they weep, they wait, and still they provoke no answer from God.

Some would argue that God does not hide. One religious bumper sticker reads, "If you feel far from God, guess who moved?" But the guilt implicit in the slogan may be false guilt: the Book of Job details a time when, apparently, it was God who moved. Even though Job had done nothing wrong and pled desperately for help, God still chose to stay hidden. (If you ever doubt that an encounter with God's hiddenness is a normal part of the pilgrimage of faith, simply browse in a theological library among the works of the Christian mystics, men and women who have spent their lives in personal communion with God. Search for one, just one, who does not describe a time of severe testing, "the dark night of the soul.")

For those who suffer, and those who stand beside them, Job offers up an important lesson. The doubts and complaints of Meg Woodson and of Allan Boesak, and of Job, are valid responses, not symptoms of weak faith—so valid, in fact, that God made sure the Bible included them all. One does not expect to find the arguments of God's adversaries—say, Mark Twain's *Letters from the Earth* or Bertrand Russell's *Why I Am Not a Christian*—bound into the Bible, but nearly all of them make an appearance, if not in Job, then in the Psalms or Prophets. The Bible seems to anticipate our disappointments, as if God grants us in advance the weapons to use against him, as if God himself understands the cost of sustaining faith.

And, because of Jesus, perhaps he does understand. At Gethsemane and Calvary in some inexpressible way God himself was forced to confront the hiddenness of God. "God striving with God" is how Martin Luther summarized the cosmic struggle played out on two crossbeams of wood. On that dark night, God learned for himself the full extent of what it means to feel God-forsaken.

Job's friends insisted that God was not hidden. They brought up reminders—dreams, visions, past blessings, the splendors of nature—of how God had proved himself to Job in the past. "Don't forget in the darkness what you learned in the light," they chided. And those of us who live after Job have even more light: the record of fulfilled prophecy, and the life of Jesus. But sometimes all insights or "proofs" will fail. Mere memory, no matter how pleasant, will not deaden pain or loneliness. Perhaps, for a time, all verses of Scripture and all inspirational slogans will likewise fail.

Three Responses

I know too well my own instinctive response to the hiddenness of God: I retaliate by ignoring him. Like a child who thinks he can hide from adults by holding a chubby hand over his eyes, I try to shut God out of my life. If he won't reveal himself to me, why should I acknowledge him?

The Book of Job gives two other responses to such disappointment with God. The first was shown by Job's friends, who were scandalized by his assaults on the most basic tenets of their faith. Job's profound disappointment with God did not match their theology. They saw a clear-cut choice between a man who claimed to be just and a God they knew to be just. The very idea of Job demanding an audience with God! Suppress your feelings, they told him. We know for a fact that God is not unjust. So stop thinking that! Shame on you for the outrageous things you're saying!

The second response, Job's, was a rambling mess, a jarring counterpoint to his friends' relentless logic. "Why then did you bring me out of the womb?" he demanded of God. "I wish I had died before any eye ever saw me." Job lashed out in a protest he knew to be futile, like a bird repeatedly hurling itself against a windowpane. He had few sound arguments, and even admitted that his friends' logic sounded right. He wavered, contradicted himself, backtracked, and sometimes collapsed in despair. This man renowned for his righteousness railed against God: "Turn away from me so I can have a moment's joy before I go to the place of no return, to the land of gloom and deep shadow."

And which of the two responses does the book endorse? Both parties needed some correction, but after all the windy words had been uttered, God ordered the pious friends to crawl repentantly to Job and ask him to pray on their behalf.

One bold message in the Book of Job is that you can say anything to God. Throw at him your grief, your anger, your doubt, your bitterness, your betrayal, your disappointment—he can absorb them all. As often as not, spiritual giants of the Bible are shown *contending* with God. They prefer to go away limping, like Jacob, rather than to shut God out. In this respect, the Bible prefigures a tenet of modern psychology: you can't really deny your feelings or make them disappear, so you might as well express them. God can deal with every human response save one. He cannot abide the response I fall back on instinctively: an attempt to ignore him or treat him as though he does not exist. That response never once occurred to Job.

The Big Picture

Freedom to express feelings is not the only lesson from Job, however. The "behind the curtain" view of proceedings in the unseen world shows that an encounter with the hiddenness of God may badly mislead. It may tempt us to see God as the enemy and to interpret his hiddenness as a lack of concern.

Job concluded just that: "God assails me and tears me in his anger." Those of us in the audience know that Job was mistaken. For one thing, the prologue makes the subtle but important distinction that God did not personally cause Job's problems. He permitted them, yes, but the account of The Wager presents Satan, not God, as the instigator of Job's suffering. In any event, God was surely not Job's enemy. Far from being abandoned by God, Job was getting direct, almost microscopic scrutiny from him. At the very moment Job was pleading for a courtroom trial to present his case, he was actually participating in a trial of cosmic significance—not as the prosecuting attorney jabbing his finger at God, but as the main witness in a test of faith.

By no means can we infer that our own trials are, like Job's, specially arranged by God to settle some decisive issue in the universe. But we can safely assume that our limited range of vision will in similar fashion distort reality. Pain narrows vision. The most private of sensations, it forces us to think of ourselves and little else.

From Job, we can learn that much more is going on out there than we may suspect. Job felt the weight of God's absence; but a look behind the curtain reveals that in one sense God had never been more present. In the natural world, human beings only receive about 30 percent of the light spectrum. (Honeybees and homing pigeons can, for example, detect ultraviolet light waves invisible to us.) In the supernatural realm, our vision is even more limited, and we get only occasional glimpses of that unseen world.

An incident in the life of another famous Bible character makes this same point in a very different way. The prophet Daniel had a mild—mild in comparison with Job's—encounter with the hiddenness of God. Daniel puzzled over an everyday problem of unanswered prayer: why was God ignoring his repeated requests? For twenty-one days Daniel devoted himself to prayer. He mourned. He gave up choice foods. He swore off meat and wine, and used no lotions on his body. All the while he called out to God, but received no answer.

Then one day Daniel got far more than he bargained for. A supernatural being, with eyes like flaming torches and a face like lightning, suddenly showed up on a riverbank beside him. Daniel's companions all fled in terror. As for Daniel, "I had no strength left. My face turned deathly pale and I was helpless." When he tried talking to the dazzling being, he could hardly breathe.

The visitor proceeded to explain the reason for the long delay. He had been dispatched to answer Daniel's very first prayer, but had run into strong resistance from "the prince of the Persian kingdom." Finally, after a three-week standoff, reinforcements arrived and Michael, one of the chief angels, helped him break through the opposition.

I will not attempt to interpret this amazing scene of the universe at war, except to point out a parallel to Job. Like Job, Daniel played a decisive role in the warfare between cosmic forces of good and evil, though much of the action took place beyond his range of vision. To him, prayer may have seemed futile, and God indifferent; but a glimpse "behind the curtain" reveals exactly the opposite. Daniel's limited perspective, like Job's, distorted reality.

What are we to make of Daniel's angelic being who needed reinforcements, not to mention the cosmic wager in Job? Simply this: the big picture, with the whole universe as a backdrop, includes much activity that we never see. When we stubbornly cling to God in a time of hardship, or when we simply pray, more— much more—may be involved than we ever dream. It requires faith to believe that, and faith to trust that we are never abandoned, no matter how distant God seems.

At the end, when he heard the Voice from the whirlwind, Job finally attained that faith. God reeled off natural phenomena—the solar system, constellations, thunderstorms, wild animals—that Job could not begin to explain. *If you can't comprehend the visible world you live in, how dare you expect to comprehend a world you cannot even see!* Conscious of the big picture at last, Job repented in dust and ashes.

God is like a person who clears his throat while hiding and so gives himself away.

—*Meister Eckhardt*

[1]C.S. Lewis, *A Grief Observed*, 9.
[2]Allan Boesak, "If You Believe," *Reformed Journal*, (November 1985), 11.

Bible references: Job 10, 16; Daniel 10.

I know that my Redeemer lives,
    and that in the end he will stand upon the earth.
And after my skin has been destroyed,
    yet in my flesh I will see God;
I myself will see him
    with my own eyes—I, and not another.
    How my heart yearns within me!
                —Job 19:25–27

Chapter 29

Why Job Died Happy

A FTER ITS ACCOUNT of tragedy and woe, of breast-beating and fierce debate, of a cosmic wager lost and won—after all that, the story of Job ends almost cozily, with Job entertaining his great-great-great-grandchildren in perfect serenity. The book gives a meticulous accounting of Job's restored fortunes: 14,000 sheep, 6000 camels, 1000 donkeys, and 10 new children.

That halcyon ending frustrates some readers, such as Elie Wiesel (Nobel Prize-winning author).[1] For him, Job had been a hero, a champion of dissent against God's injustices. Yet, says Wiesel, Job caved in. He shouldn't have let God off the hook. No amount of new prosperity could make up for the suffering Job had undergone. What of the ten children who died? No parent could believe for a moment that a bustling new brood of children would erase the sorrow of the ones Job lost.

But let Job speak for himself. This is what he said after God's majestic speech from the whirlwind:

239

> Surely I spoke of things I did not understand,
> things too wonderful for me to know. . . .
> My ears had heard of you
> but now my eyes have seen you.
> Therefore I despise myself
> and repent in dust and ashes.

Evidently, what I have called God's "non-answer" satisfied Job completely.

On the other hand, some readers point to the happy ending as the final answer to disappointment with God. See, they say, God delivers his people from adversity. He restored Job's health and riches, and he will do the same for all of us if we learn to trust him as Job did. These readers, however, overlook one important detail: Job spoke his contrite words before any of his losses had been restored. He was still sitting in a pile of rubble, naked, covered with sores, and it was in *those* circumstances that he learned to praise God. Only one thing had changed: God had given Job a glimpse of the big picture.

I have a hunch that God could have said anything—could, in fact, have read from the Yellow Pages—and produced the same stunning effect on Job. What he said was not nearly so important as the mere fact of his appearance. God spectacularly answered Job's biggest question: Is anybody out there? Once Job caught sight of the unseen world, all his urgent questions faded away.

From God's viewpoint, Job's comfort was—however harsh it may sound—insignificant *in comparison with* the cosmic issues at stake. The real battle ended when Job refused to give up on God, thus causing Satan to lose The Wager. After that tough victory, God hastened to shower good gifts on Job. *Pain? I can fix that easily. More children? Camels and oxen? No problem. Of course I want you happy and wealthy and full of life! But, Job, you must understand that something far more important than happiness was at stake here.*

Of Two Worlds

My friend Richard, who still looks to Job as the most honest part of the Bible, has yet another response to its conclusion. He finds it almost irrelevant. "Job got a personal appearance by God, and I'm happy for him. That's what I've been asking for all these years. But since God hasn't visited me, how does Job help with my struggles?"

I believe that Richard has put his finger on an important dividing line of faith. In a sense, our days on earth resemble Job's *before* God came to him in a whirlwind. We too live among clues and rumors, some of which argue against a powerful, loving God. We too must exercise faith, with no certainty.

Richard lay prone on the wooden floor of his apartment, pleading for God to "reveal" himself, gambling all his faith on God's willingness to step into the seen world as he had done for Job. And Richard lost that gamble. Frankly, I doubt whether God feels any "obligation" to prove himself in such a manner. He did so many times in the Old Testament, and with finality in the person of Jesus. What further incarnations do we require of him?

I say this with great care, but I wonder if a fierce, insistent desire for miracle—even a physical healing—sometimes betrays a *lack* of faith rather than an abundance of it. Such prayers may, like Richard's, set conditions for God. When yearning for a miraculous resolution to a problem, do we make our loyalty to God contingent on whether he reveals himself yet again in the seen world?*

If we insist on visible proofs from God, we may well prepare the way for a permanent state of disappointment. True faith does not so much attempt to manipulate God to do our will as it does to position us to do his will. As I searched through the Bible for models of great faith, I was struck by how few saints experienced anything like Job's dramatic encounter with God. The rest responded to God's hiddenness not by demanding that he show himself, but by going ahead and believing him though he stayed hidden. Hebrews 11 pointedly notes that the giants of faith "did

---

*In his mercy, God may answer a prayer of mixed motives—witness all the "Lord, if you only get me out of here. . ." foxhole conversions. But that is for him to decide, not us.

not receive the things promised; they only saw them and welcomed them from a distance."

We human beings instinctively regard the seen world as the "real" world and the unseen world as the "unreal" world, but the Bible calls for almost the opposite. Through faith, the unseen world increasingly takes shape as the real world and sets the course for how we live in the seen world. Live for God, who is invisible, and not for other people, said Jesus in his words about the unseen world, or "the kingdom of heaven."

Once the apostle Paul directly addressed the question of disappointment with God. He told the Corinthians that, in spite of incredible hardships, he did not "lose heart": "Though outwardly we are wasting away, yet inwardly we are being renewed day by day. For our light and momentary [!] troubles are achieving for us an eternal glory that far outweighs them all. So we fix our eyes not on what is seen, but on what is unseen. For what is seen is temporary, but what is unseen is eternal."

A Taste of the Future

Paul endured trials and died a martyr, still anticipating his reward. Job endured trials, but received a fine reward in this life. So what, exactly, can we expect from God? Perhaps the best way to view the ending in Job is to see it not as a blueprint for what will happen to us in this life, but rather as a *sign* of what is to come. It stands as a sweet, satisfying symbol, a solution to one man's disappointment that offers us all a foretaste of the future.

In one respect, Elie Wiesel is right: the pleasures of Job's old age did not make up for the losses that had gone before. Even Job, happy and full of days, died, passing on the cycle of grief and pain to his survivors. The worst mistake of all would be to conclude that God is somehow content to make a few minor adjustments to this tragic, unfair world.

Some people stake all their faith on a miracle, as if a miracle would eliminate all disappointment with God. It wouldn't. If I had filled this book with case studies of physical healings, rather than the stories of Richard and Meg Woodson and Douglas and

Job, that would not solve the problem of disappointment with God. Something is still badly wrong with this planet. For one thing, all of us die; the ultimate mortality rate is the same for atheists and saints alike.

Miracles serve as signs pointing on to the future. They are appetizers that awaken a longing for something more, something permanent. And the happiness of Job's old age was a mere sampling of what he would enjoy after death. The good news at the end of Job and the good news of Easter at the end of the Gospels are previews of the good news described at the end of Revelation. We dare not lose sight of the world God wants.

The promise of Job 42, then, is that God will finally right the wrongs that mark our days. Some sorrows—the deaths of Job's children, for example, or the deaths of Meg Woodson's children—never heal in this life. No words of solace can assuage the grief in Meg Woodson's heart, for that grief has a precise shape, the shape of her daughter Peggie and her son Joey. But at the end of time, that grief too will vanish. Meg will get her daughter back, and her son, remade. And if I did not believe that, did not believe that Peggie and Joey Woodson are right now breathing in great gulps, and dancing, and exploring new worlds, then I would not believe anything and would have abandoned the Christian faith long ago. "If only for this life we have hope in Christ, we are to be pitied more than all men."

The Bible stakes God's reputation on his ability to conquer evil and restore heaven and earth to their original perfection. Apart from that future state, God could be judged less-than-powerful, or less-than-loving.* So far the prophets' visions of peace and justice have not come true. Swords aren't being melted into plowshares. Death, with ugly new mutations of AIDS and environmental cancers, is still swallowing people up, not being swallowed. Evil, not good, appears to be winning. But the Bible

---

*Once the Spanish mystic Unamuno, conversing with a peasant, suggested that perhaps there was a God but no heaven. The peasant thought a minute and then replied, "So what is this God for?"

calls us to see beyond the grim reality of history to the view of all eternity, when God's reign will fill the earth with light and truth.

In any discussion of disappointment with God, heaven is the last word, the most important word of all. Only heaven will finally solve the problem of God's hiddenness. For the first time ever, human beings will be able to look upon God face to face. In the midst of his agony, Job somehow came up with the faith to believe that "in my flesh I will see God; I myself will see him with my own eyes." That prophecy will come true not just for Job but for all of us.

Homesick

Many people have trouble even imagining such a future state. As Charles Williams said, "Our experience on earth makes it difficult for us to apprehend a good without a catch in it somewhere."[2] Rather than try to project ourselves into a future we can never quite grasp, perhaps we would do better to look at the unfulfilled dreams—the disappointments—of the present.

To a refugee or peasant, heaven represents a dream of a new country, a place of safety, a family reunited, a home abundant with simple things like food and fresh drinking water. (Many of the prophets spoke to refugees, which may explain why they used such earthly images.)

At some level, we all share such longings. This world may be full of pollution, war, crime, and greed, but inside us—all of us—linger remnants that remind us of what the world could be like, of what *we* could be like. You can sense such longings in the environmental movement, whose leaders yearn for a world preserved in its pristine state; and in the peace movement that dreams of a world without war; and in therapy groups that try to reconnect broken strands of love and friendship. All the beauty and joy we meet on earth represent "only the scent of a flower we have not found, the echo of a tune we have not heard, news from a country we have never yet visited."[3]

The prophets proclaim that such sensations are not illusions or mere dreams, but advance echoes of what will come true. We are given few details about that future world, only a promise that God will prove himself trustworthy. When we awake in the new heaven and new earth, we will possess at last whatever we longed for. Somehow, from all the bad news, incredible Good News emerges—a good without a catch in it somewhere. Heaven and earth will again work the way God intended. There is a happy ending after all.

Fantasy writer J. R. R. Tolkien invented a new word for this good news: it will be a "eucatastrophe," he said. A scene from his trilogy, *The Lord of the Rings*, expresses it well:

> "Is everything sad going to come untrue? What's happened to the world?" [asked Sam].
>
> "A great Shadow has departed," said Gandalf, and then he laughed, and the sound was like music, or like water in a parched land; and as he listened the thought came to him that he had not heard laughter, the pure sound of merriment, for days upon days without count. It fell upon his ears like the echo of all the joys he had ever known. But he himself burst into tears. Then, as a sweet rain will pass down a wind of spring and the sun will shine out the clearer, his tears ceased, and his laughter welled up, and laughing he sprang from his bed.
>
> "How do I feel?" he cried. "Well, I don't know how to say it. I feel, I feel"—he waved his arms in the air—"I feel like spring after winter, and sun on the leaves; and like trumpets and harps and all the songs I have ever heard!"[3]

For people who are trapped in pain, or in a broken home, or in economic misery, or in fear—for all those people, for all of us, heaven promises a time, far longer and more substantial than the time we spent on earth, of health and wholeness and pleasure and peace. If we do not believe that, then, as Paul plainly stated, there's little reason to believe at all. Without that hope, there is no hope.

The Bible never belittles human disappointment (remember the proportion in Job—one chapter of restoration follows forty-one chapters of anguish), but it does add one key word: temporary. What we feel now, we will not always feel. Our disappointment is itself a sign, an aching, a hunger for something better. And faith is, in the end, a kind of homesickness—for a home we have never visited but have never once stopped longing for.

> And the end of all our exploring
> Will be to arrive where we started
> And know the place for the first time.
> —T. S. Eliot

> Then I saw a new heaven and a new earth, for the first heaven and the first earth had passed away, and there was no longer any sea. I saw the Holy City, the new Jerusalem, coming down out of heaven from God, prepared as a bride beautifully dressed for her husband. And I heard a loud voice from the throne saying, "Now the dwelling of God is with men, and he will live with them. They will be his people, and God himself will be with them and be their God. He will wipe every tear from their eyes. There will be no more death or mourning or crying or pain, for the old order of things has passed away.

[1] Elie Wiesel, *Messengers of God*, 233.
[2] Charles Williams, *The Image of the City*, 136.
[3] C. S. Lewis, *The Weight of Glory*, 5.
[4] J. R. R. Tolkien, *The Return of the King*, 283.

Bible references: Job 42; Hebrews 10; 2 Corinthians 4; 1 Corinthians 15; Job 19; Revelation 21.

Chapter 30

Two Wagers, Two Parables

*Is there then any terrestrial paradise where amidst the whispering of
the olive leaves people can be with whom they like and have what
they like and take their ease in shadows and in coolness, or are all
men's lives . . . broken, tumultuous, agonized and unromantic
lives, periods punctuated by screams, by imbecilities, by deaths, by
agonies?*

—Ford Madox Ford, The Good Soldier

I TALIAN AUTHOR Umberto Eco tells of a day when, at the
age of thirteen, he accompanied his father to a soccer
match. Umberto did not really enjoy sports, and as he sat in the
stadium observing the game his mind began to wander. "As I was
observing with detachment the senseless movements down there
on the field, I felt how the high noonday sun seemed to enfold
men and things in a chilling light, and how before my eyes a
cosmic, meaningless performance was proceeding. . . . For the first

time I doubted the existence of God and decided that the world was a pointless fiction."[1]

Perched high in the stadium, the adolescent Eco had imagined a viewpoint from above, like God's. But from that vantage the frantic scramblings of the human race seemed as senseless as the frantic scramblings of grown men chasing a leather ball across grass. It occurred to Eco that there must be no one "up there" watching what takes place on this planet. And if someone was there after all, he must care as little about life on earth as Umberto Eco cared about soccer.

Eco's image of the stadium raises the most basic question of faith, the question on which all else hinges: *Is anyone watching?* Are we dashing about in meaningless chaos, engulfed in "the benign indifference of the universe," or are we *performing* for Someone who cares? Job received his answer in a blinding revelation, but what about the rest of us? There is no more important question, and five years after the conversation that spawned this book I found myself discussing this question at length with my skeptical friend Richard.

When I had first met Richard, he was like an estranged lover in the early stages of separation and divorce—from God. Anger smoldered in his eyes. But when I saw him five years later, it was clear that the passage of time had mellowed him. His passion would still break out as we talked, but mingled with wistfulness, or nostalgia. He could not put God completely out of mind, and God's absence made itself felt, hauntingly, like pain from a phantom limb. Even if I didn't bring up matters of faith, Richard, still hurt, betrayed, would circle back to them.

Once he turned to me with a puzzled look. "I don't get it, Philip," he said. "We read many of the same books, and share many of the same values. You seem to understand my doubt and disappointment. And yet somehow you find it possible to believe, but I don't. What's the difference? Where did you get your faith?"

My mind sped through possible answers. I could have suggested all the evidences for God: design in creation, the story of Jesus, proofs of the Resurrection, examples of Christian saints.

But Richard knew those answers as well as I, and still did not believe. Besides, I did not get my faith from them. I got it in a dorm room in a Bible college, on a particular night in February, and so I proceeded to tell Richard about that night.

A Night of Faith

I have already mentioned that Bible college was for me, initially, a breeding ground of doubt and skepticism. I survived by learning to mimic "spiritual" behavior—a student had to, in fact, just to get good grades. There was the odious matter of "Christian service," for instance. The college required each student to participate in a regular service activity, such as street evangelism, prison ministry, or nursing home visitation. I signed up for "university work."

Every Saturday night I would visit a student center at the University of South Carolina and watch television. I was supposed to be "witnessing," of course, and the next week I would dutifully report on all the people I had approached about personal faith. My embellished stories must have sounded authentic, because no one ever questioned them.

I was also required to attend a weekly prayer meeting with four other students involved in university work. Those meetings followed a consistent pattern: Joe would pray, and then Craig, and Chris, and the other Joe, and then all four would pause politely for about ten seconds. I never prayed; and after the brief silence, we would open our eyes and return to our rooms.

But one February night to everyone's surprise, including my own, I did pray. I have no idea why. I had not planned to. But after Joe and Craig and Chris and Joe had finished, I found myself praying aloud. "God," I said, and I could sense the tension level in the room rise.

As I recall it, I said something like this: "God, here we are, supposed to be concerned about those ten thousand students at the University of South Carolina who are going to hell. Well, you know that I don't care if they all go to hell, if there is one. I don't even care if I go to there."

You would have to attend a Bible college to appreciate how these words must have sounded to the others in the room. I may as well have been invoking witchcraft or offering child sacrifices. But no one stirred or tried to stop me, and I continued praying.

For some reason, I started talking about the parable of the Good Samaritan. We Bible college types were supposed to feel the same concern for university students as the Samaritan felt for the bloodied Jew lying in the ditch. But I felt no such concern, I said. I felt nothing for them.

And then it happened. In the middle of my prayer, just as I was describing how little I cared for our assigned targets of compassion, I saw that story in a new light. I had been visualizing the scene as I spoke: an old-fashioned-looking Samaritan, dressed in robes and a turban, bending over a dirty, blood-crusted form in a ditch. But suddenly, in the internal screen of my brain, those two figures changed. The kindly Samaritan took on the face of Jesus. The Jew, pitiable victim of a highway robbery, took on another face too—a face I recognized with a start as my own.

In a flash I saw Jesus reaching down with a moistened rag to clean my wounds and stanch the flow of blood. And as he bent over, I saw myself, the wounded robbery victim, open my eyes and purse my lips. Then, as if watching in slow motion, I saw myself spit at him, full in the face. I saw all that—I, who did not believe in visions, or in biblical parables, or even in Jesus. It stunned me. Abruptly, I stopped praying, got up, and left the room.

All that evening I thought about what had happened. It wasn't exactly a vision—more like a daydreamed parable with a moral twist. Still, I couldn't put it behind me. What did it mean? Was it genuine? I wasn't sure, but I knew that my cockiness had been shattered. On that campus I had always found security in my agnosticism. No longer. I had caught a new glimpse of myself. Perhaps in all my self-assured and mocking skepticism I was the neediest one of all.

I wrote a brief note to my fiancée that night, saying

guardedly, "I want to wait a few days before talking about it, but I may have just had the first authentic religious experience of my life."

Two Wagers

I told that story to Richard, who listened with genuine interest. Everything in my life had changed from that moment on, I said. Before then, if anyone had suggested I would spend my life writing about the Christian faith, I would have thought him insane. But since that February night I have been on a slow, steady pilgrimage to reclaim what I had once rejected as religious nonsense. I received eyes of faith that opened up belief in the unseen world.

Richard was kind, but unconvinced. He pointed out gently that there were, after all, alternative explanations for what had happened. For several years I had been resisting a fundamentalist upbringing, and undoubtedly that repression had caused a deep "cognitive dissonance" within me. Since I had not prayed for so long, should it surprise me that my first prayer, no matter how tentative, would release a flood of emotions that might find an outlet in such form as the "revelation" of the Good Samaritan parable?

I had to smile as Richard talked, because I recognized myself in his words. I had used that same language to explain away the personal testimonies of scores of my fellow students. But ever since that night in February I have seen things differently.

Richard and I were describing the same phenomenon two different ways: he was looking "at the beam," while I was looking along it. He had certain evidence on his side. I had certain evidence on mine—mainly the profound and unexpected change in my outlook on life. But conversions only make sense from the inside out, to the fellow-converted. We were back where we had started in our conversation five years before: we had arrived at the mystery of *faith*, a word Richard detested.

I found myself wishing I could make faith crystal clear for him, but I felt powerless to do so. I sensed in Richard the same restlessness and alienation that I had lived with, and that God had gradually healed. But I could not transplant faith into Richard; he must exercise it for himself.

It was during this conversation that I realized there are actually two cosmic wagers transpiring. I have focused on The Wager from God's point of view, The Wager as pictured in the Book of Job, in which God "risks" the future of the human experiment on a person's response. I doubt anyone fully understands that wager, but Jesus taught that the end of human history will boil down to the one issue: "When the Son of Man comes, will he find faith on the earth?"

The second wager, reflecting the human viewpoint, is the one that Job himself engaged in: should he choose for God or against him? Job weighed the evidence, most of which did not suggest a trustworthy God. But he decided, kicking and screaming all the way, to place his faith in God.

Each one of us must choose whether to live as if God exists, or as if he does not exist. When Umberto Eco sat high in the stadium under a noonday sun and looked down on a field of soccer players, he seized upon the most important question of his life—of any life. Is anyone watching? And the answer to that question rests squarely upon faith—by that and only that the just shall live.

Two Parables

I end this book with two stories, both of them true, which for me stand as parables for the alternatives: the way of faith and the way of non-faith.

The first comes from a sermon by Frederick Buechner:

> It is a peculiarly twentieth-century story, and it is almost too awful to tell: about a boy of twelve or thirteen who, in a fit of crazy anger and depression, got hold of a gun somewhere and fired it at his father, who died not right away but soon afterward. When the authorities asked the boy why he had done it, he said that it was because he could not stand his father, because his father demanded too much of him, because he was always after him, because he hated his father. And

then later on, after he had been placed in a house of detention somewhere, a guard was walking down the corridor late one night when he heard sounds from the boy's room, and he stopped to listen. The words that he heard the boy sobbing out in the dark were, "I want my father, I want my father."[1]

Buechner says that this story is "a kind of parable of the lives of all of us." Modern society is like that boy in the house of detention. We have killed off our Father. Few thinkers or writers or moviemakers or television producers take God seriously anymore. He's an anachronism, something we've outgrown. The modern world has accepted The Wager and bet against God. There are too many unanswered questions. He has disappointed us once too often.*

It is a hard thing to live, uncertain of anything. And yet, sobs can still be heard, muffled cries of loss, such as those expressed in literature and film and almost all modern art. The alternative to disappointment with God seems to be disappointment without God. ("The center of me," said Bertrand Russell, "is always and eternally a terrible pain—a curious wild pain—a searching for something beyond what the world contains.")

I see that sense of loss in the eyes of my friend Richard, even now. He says he does not believe in God, but he keeps bringing up the subject, protesting too loudly. From where comes this wounded sense of betrayal if no one is there to do the betraying?

Frederick Buechner's parable concerns the loss of a father; the second concerns the discovery of a father. It too is a true story, my own story.

---

*"Have you not heard of the man who lit a lamp on a bright morning and went to the marketplace crying ceaselessly, 'I seek God. I seek God'. . . . They laughed, and . . . the man sprang into their midst and looked daggers at them. 'Where is God?' he cried. 'I will tell you. We have killed Him, you and I.' We are all His killers, but how can we have done that? How could we swallow up the sea? Who gave us the sponge to wipe away the horizon? What will we do as the earth is set loose from its sun?"—Friedrich Nietzsche, *The Gay Science*

One holiday I was visiting my mother, who lives seven hundred miles away. We reminisced about times long past, as mothers and sons tend to do. Inevitably, the large box of old photos came down from the closet shelf, spilling out a jumbled pile of thin rectangles that mark my progression through childhood and adolescence: the cowboy-and-Indian getups, the Peter Cottontail suit in the first grade play, my childhood pets, endless piano recitals, the graduations from grade school and high school and finally college.

Among those photos I found one of an infant, with my name written on the back. The portrait itself was not unusual. I looked like any baby: fat-cheeked, half-bald, with a wild, unfocused look to my eyes. But the photo was crumpled and mangled, as if one of those childhood pets had got hold of it. I asked my mother why she had hung onto such an abused photo when she had so many other undamaged ones.

There is something you should know about my family: when I was ten months old, my father contracted spinal bulbar polio. He died three months later, just after my birthday. My father was totally paralyzed at age twenty-four, his muscles so weakened that he had to live inside a large steel cylinder that did his breathing for him. He had few visitors—people had as much hysteria about polio in 1950 as they do about AIDS today. The one visitor who came faithfully, my mother, would sit in a certain place so that he could see her in a mirror bolted to the side of the iron lung.

My mother explained to me that she had kept the photo as a memento, because during my father's illness it had been fastened to his iron lung. He had asked for pictures of her and of his two sons, and my mother had had to jam the pictures in between some metal knobs. Thus, the crumpled condition of my baby photo.

I rarely saw my father after he entered the hospital, since children were not allowed in polio wards. Besides, I was so young that, even if I had been allowed in, I would not now retain those memories.

When my mother told me the story of the crumpled photo, I had a strange and powerful reaction. It seemed odd to imagine someone caring about me whom, in a sense, I had never met.

254

Two Wagers, Two Parables

During the last months of his life, my father had spent his waking hours staring at those three images of his family, my family. There was nothing else in his field of view. What did he do all day? Did he pray for us? Yes, surely. Did he love us? Yes. But how can a paralyzed person express his love, especially when his own children are banned from the room?

I have often thought of that crumpled photo, for it is one of the few links connecting me to the stranger who was my father, a stranger who died a decade younger than I am now. Someone I have no memory of, no sensory knowledge of, spent all day every day thinking of me, devoting himself to me, loving me as well as he could. Perhaps, in some mysterious way, he is doing so now in another dimension. Perhaps I will have time, much time, to renew a relationship that was cruelly ended just as it had begun.

I mention this story because the emotions I felt when my mother showed me the crumpled photo were the very same emotions I felt that February night in a college dorm room when I first believed in a God of love. *Someone is there,* I realized. Someone is watching life as it unfolds on this planet. More, Someone is there who loves me. It was a startling feeling of wild hope, a feeling so new and overwhelming that it seemed fully worth risking my life on.

[1]Umberto Eco, *Travels in Hyper Reality,* 167–168.
[2]Frederick Buechner, *The Magnificent Defeat,* 65.

Bible reference: Luke 18.

Thanks

SOMEDAY I may have to write a book on my own, but I hope that time doesn't come soon because I now rely very heavily on the editorial suggestions of other readers. I am hopelessly and gratefully dependent on my friend Tim Stafford, who read this manuscript in three successive drafts. That was a labor of love: before Tim's expert suggestions on needed cuts, the manuscript was fifty percent longer.

I also had the good fortune of participating in a manuscript evaluation session with four other writers—Steve Lawhead, Karen Mains, Luci Shaw, and Walter Wangerin, Jr.—who helped me set the tone for the final draft. Then in separate sessions Walter unveiled to me some of the mysteries of storytelling. And these others also read and critiqued the manuscript, giving me valuable advice: Elsie Baker, Dr. John Boyle, Dr. Paul Brand, Harold Fickett, Hal Knight, Lee Phillips, and Dr. Cornelius Plantinga.

After I had acted on all these folks' advice, Judith Markham, my editor on three previous books, edited the final result. Judith offers a rare combination of diplomacy, literary wisdom, kindness, and, above all, a pursuit of excellence. She is a good friend, and a fine editor.

Some names—Augustine, Buechner, Chesterton, Eliot, Lewis, Moltmann, MacDonald, Pascal, Sayers, Thielicke, and Williams—you have already met, for they appear throughout the book. In the truest sense, they are my "pastors." Because of them, in no small measure, I continue to believe.

A class I taught at LaSalle Street Church assured that for at least five years I would study the Old Testament in detail, and its members contributed many fine insights and daunting questions.

I referred several times to an inspiring visit to the Colorado mountains: I'm grateful to the Konemans and the Braytons, who made that time possible.

And I want to thank Richard. He has the courage to be honest; I have learned much from him. I hope that he never stops asking questions, that he never abandons his search.

Bibliography

Augustine, Saint. *The Confessions of Saint Augustine.* Translated by John K. Ryan. Garden City: Doubleday, 1960.

Brown, Colin. *Miracles and the Critical Mind.* Grand Rapids: Eerdmans, 1984.

Buechner, Frederick. *The Hungering Dark.* New York: Seabury, 1981.

———. *The Magnificent Defeat.* New York: Seabury, 1979.

———. *A Room Called Remember: Uncollected Pieces.* New York: Harper & Row, 1984.

———. *Wishful Thinking: A Theological ABC.* Harper & Row, 1973.

Dostoyevsky, Fyodor. *The Brothers Karamazov.* Garden City: Nelson Doubleday (no date).

Eco, Umberto. *Travels in Hyper Reality: Essays.* Edited by Helen & Kurt Wolff. Translated from the Italian by William Weaver. New York: Harcourt Brace Jovanovich, 1983.

Eiseley, Loren. *The Star Thrower.* Harcourt Brace Jovanovich, 1979.

Hall, Douglas John. *God and Human Suffering.* Minneapolis: Augsburg, 1986.

James, William. *The Varieties of Religious Experience.* New York: Modern Library, 1936.

Kierkegaard, Søren. *Philosophical Fragments.* Translated by David Swenson. Princeton: Princeton University Press, 1962.

Lewis, C. S. *Christian Reflections.* Grand Rapids: Eerdmans, 1974.

_____. *God in the Dock.* Edited by Walter Hooper. Grand Rapids: Eerdmans, 1970.

_____. *A Grief Observed.* New York: Seabury, 1961.

_____. *The Weight of Glory and Other Addresses.* Grand Rapids: Eerdmans, 1975.

_____. *The World's Last Night and Other Essays.* New York: Harcourt Brace Jovanovich, Inc., 1959.

MacDonald, George. *Life Essential: The Hope of the Gospel.* Edited by Rolland Hein. Wheaton, Ill.: Harold Shaw, 1978.

MacDonald, Greville. *George MacDonald and His Wife.* London: George Allen and Unwin, Ltd., 1924.

Moltmann, Jürgen. *God in Creation: A New Theology of Creation and the Spirit of God.* New York: Harper & Row, 1985.

Spark, Muriel. *The Only Problem.* New York: Putnam, 1984.

Thompson, William I. *The Time Falling Bodies Take to Light.* New York: St. Martin's Press, 1982.

Tolkien, J. R. R. *The Return of the King.* New York: Ballantine, 1976.

_____. *The Tolkien Reader.* New York: Ballantine Books, 1966.

Wiesel, Elie. *Messengers of God: Biblical Portraits and Legends.* New York: Summit Books, 1985.

Williams, Charles. *He Came Down from Heaven.* London: William Heinemann, Ltd., 1938.

_____. *The Image of the City.* London: Oxford University Press, 1958.

We want to hear from you. Please send your comments about this book
to us in care of the address below. Thank you.

ZondervanPublishingHouse
Grand Rapids, Michigan 49530
http://www.zondervan.com